D1378141

SECOND EDITION

PRACTICAL ASPECTS OF **RAPE**

INVESTIGATION

A MULTIDISCIPLINARY APPROACH

CRC SERIES IN
PRACTICAL ASPECTS OF CRIMINAL
AND FORENSIC INVESTIGATIONS

VERNON J. GEBERTH, BBA, MPS, FBINA *Series Editor*

SECOND EDITION

PRACTICAL ASPECTS OF **RAPE** **INVESTIGATION**

A MULTIDISCIPLINARY APPROACH

EDITED BY

Robert R. Hazelwood
Ann Wolbert Burgess

CRC Press

Boca Raton   New York   London   Tokyo

**W
795
P895
1999**

Library of Congress Cataloging-in-Publication Data

Practical aspects of rape investigation : a multidisciplinary approach / editors, Robert R. Hazelwood.
    Ann Wolbert Burgess. -- 2nd ed.
    p. cm. -- (Practical aspects of criminal and investigation series)
    Includes bibliographical references and index.
    ISBN 0-8493-8152-5
    1. Rape--Investigation. 2. Rape--United States--Investigation. I. Hazelwood, Robert R. II.
    Burgess, Ann Wolbert. III. Series.
    HV8079.R35P7   1995
    363.2'59532--dc20   95-4841
                                                              CIP

No claim to original U.S. Government works
International Standard Book Number 0-8493-8152-5
Library of Congress Card Number 95-4841
Printed in the United States of America 1 2 3 4 5 6 7 8 9 0
Printed on acid-free paper

Contents

Section I
ATTITUDES AND BELIEFS ABOUT RAPE

Section II
INVESTIGATION OF RAPE

8 The Behavioral-Oriented Interview of Rape Victims: The Key to Profiling 139
Robert R. Hazelwood and Ann Wolbert Burgess

9 Analyzing the Rape and Profiling the Offender 155
Robert R. Hazelwood

10 Collateral Materials and Sexual Crimes 183
Robert R. Hazelwood and Kenneth V. Lanning

11 Classifying Rape and Sexual Assault 193
Allen G. Burgess, Ann Wolbert Burgess, and
Robert R. Hazelwood

Section III
MEDICAL AND NURSING ASPECTS OF RAPE INVESTIGATION

15 Medical Exam of the Live Sexual Assault Victim 253
Joseph A. Zeccardi

16 Victim Care Services and the Comprehensive Sexual Assault Assessment Tool 263
Ann Wolbert Burgess, Jacqueline Fawcett
Robert R. Hazelwood, and Christine A. Grant

Section IV
PROSECUTION OF RAPE

17 Prosecuting Rape Cases: Trial Preparation and Trial Tactic Issues 285
William Heiman, Ann Ponterio, and Gail Fairman

18 Rape Trauma Syndrome: A Review of Case Law and Psychological Research 301
Patricia A. Frazier and Eugene Borgida

Section V
SPECIAL OFFENDER POPULATIONS

19 Child Molestation — Law Enforcement Typology 323
Kenneth V. Lanning

20 The Serial Rapist 337
Robert R. Hazelwood and Janet I. Warren

Preface

Sexual crimes have shown the highest increase of 21% nationally in the past decade. In terms of reported rape cases, the FBI Uniform Crime Reports cite an increase from over 37,000 in 1970 to 78,918 cases in 1983 to 112,080 cases in 1993. However, only slightly more than half (52%) of the reported rape cases in 1983 resulted in the arrest of a suspect — a percentage that has not changed into the 1990s. These figures become even more critical when realizing that less than half of all rapes believed to occur are reported to law enforcement, and of those assailants arrested even fewer are convicted of rape. Although it is impossible to determine whether the increase in rape is due to better reporting methods or to the sex offenders who are not arrested or convicted repeating their behavior, the problem is now being addressed by all professions whose work brings them into contact with the victim or the offender.

Concurrent with the increasing numbers of rape victims has been a burgeoning of research into a myriad of factors interwoven with sexual violence and its aftermath. Substantial contributions have been made to advancing the state of knowledge for law enforcement agents, health professionals, and criminal justice staff. Although most people working with the problem of sexual crimes see either the victim or offender, the investigator and prosecutor frequently encounter both the victim and the offender of sexual assaults. Thus, it becomes crucial that these two groups have the benefit of research results in the fields of victimology, criminology, behavioral sciences, forensic sciences, and criminal justice. Such information has the potential to impact substantially the effectiveness of the investigative interview, the collection of forensic evidence, and the prosecution of cases.

The aim of this second edition of *Practical Aspects of Rape Investigation* is to present the research findings on the FBI study of the serial rapist and new and challenging directions for the investigation and prosecution of rape cases. A unique feature of the book is the incorporation of traditional police procedures in rape investigation with new and contemporary techniques developed during the past decade, such as criminal investigative analysis as well as current classification of rape and sexual assault.

The book is divided into four sections. Part One includes three chapters that provide a basis for examining some of people's thoughts and reactions to the problem of rape. Myths and stereotypes surrounding rape are influential because they represent what people believe. In the first chapter on "Public Beliefs and Attitudes Toward Rape", Ann W. Burgess identifies the wide range of feelings and reactions that people experience when confronted with the topic of rape. These reactions are both immediate and subjective reactions having their origins in the past on the basis of personal experience or long-held societal beliefs and reactions to the subject of rape. The intent is for the reader to examine his or her own subjective responses as a way to increase sensitivity to the nuances of this social problem. Chapter 2 on "Police Attitudes and Beliefs", by John C. LeDoux and Robert R. Hazelwood, serves as a companion chapter to the first, and reports a national random sample survey conducted with over 2,100 police officers. The survey asked about police officers' attitudes toward rape and how their attitudes affect the effectiveness of their work with rape victims, the suspect and the criminal justice system in general. The third chapter on "The Victim's Perspective", by Ann W. Burgess and Robert R. Hazelwood, captures both the thoughts and reactions of the victim going through the assault and its distressing aftermath. Myths about the victim are interspersed in outlining the investigator's approach to interviewing the victim as a method to help the officer understand the wide range of behaviors that occur related to reporting a rape. Such understanding will benefit the victim and his or her recovery and the officer in his or her investigation.

The second section of the book is on the Investigation of Rape, and deals primarily with the investigative aspects of the crime. Updated Chapters 4 and 5, written by Dale M. Moreau and P. David Bigbee, discuss the collection and observation of physical and trace evidence of the victim, the offender and the scene of the crime itself. The chapters also discuss the presentation of this evidence in court.

Criminal profiling is one of the most promising investigative tools available to the investigator. It involves the gathering of information concerning offender behavior in an attempt to focus the investigation and to identify a subject quickly. Updated Chapter 6, "Criminal Investigative Analysis: An Overview", is written by Robert R. Hazelwood, Robert K. Ressler, Roger L. Depue, and John E. Douglas. It traces the history of criminal investigative analysis within the FBI Academy's Behavioral Science Unit, and presents the criteria necessary for preparing an investigative profile and the criteria necessary to begin a criminal investigative analysis. In new Chapter 7, "The Relevance of Fantasy in Serial Sexual Crime Investigation", Robert R. Hazelwood and Janet I. Warren propose that fantasy is the link between the underlying motivation for sexual assaults and the behavior exhibited during the crime. In Chapter 8, "The Behavioral-Oriented Interview of Rape Victims: The Key To Profiling", Robert R. Hazelwood and Ann W. Burgess describe interviewing the victim to determine the verbal, physical, and sexual behavior exhibited by the offender during the commission of the crime. The purpose of this interview is to elicit information from the victim, which will allow a person to prepare a profile on the unidentified offender. In Chapter 9, "Analyzing the Rape and Profiling the Offender", Robert R. Hazelwood presents an initial categorization of rapists from a profiling standpoint. It then sets forth a detailed case history followed by an analysis of that case history and the resultant profile derived from the analysis. New Chapter 10, "Collateral Materials and Sexual Crimes" by Robert R. Hazelwood and Kenneth V. Lanning, describes trial use of collateral evidence.

"Classifying Rape and Sexual Assault" is presented as a new Chapter 11 by Allen G. Burgess, Ann W. Burgess, and Robert R. Hazelwood. Updated Chapter

12, "Indirect Personality Assessment" written by Richard L. Ault, Jr. and Robert R. Hazelwood sets forth the value of assessing a person's strengths and weaknesses before interrogating that person as a rape suspect. A list of questions is presented to provide guidance in determining the site of the interview, the approach best used with this particular personality, the persons who should participate, and the attire that should be used during the interview.

One of the thorniest problems in rape investigation is that of false allegations. An inherent conflict arises between the investigator's obligation to accept the victim's complaint as legitimate and his duty to develop the facts of the case. Chapter 13, "False Rape Allegations", written by Margaret M. Aiken, Ann W. Burgess, and Robert R. Hazelwood reviews the literature on rape allegations, proposes a model for understanding the concept, and includes discussion on the motivation for rape allegations and red flags to suspect an allegation; some of which is reprinted from a chapter by Charles P. McDowell and Neil S. Hibler from the first edition. A new syndrome is discussed for investigators to consider in people who injure themselves and then report rape. Cases of false allegation fall on a long continuum from the extreme of obscene telephone calls to the other extreme of self-mutilation and/or amputation to substantiate a claim of rape. In Chapter 14, "The Rape Investigators: Vicarious Victims", James T. Reese places in perspective the stressful aspects of investigative work and recommends strategies for stress management as a means to cope with the work.

Section III is on Medical and Nursing Aspects of Rape Investigations. In an updated Chapter 15, "Medical Exam of the Live Sexual Assault Victim", physician Joseph A. Zeccardi orients the rape investigator to the conduct of a medical examination and the manner in which evidence should be collected. The rationale as well as the intricacies of the medical examination are presented. A new Chapter 16, "Victim Care Services and the Comprehensive Sexual Assault Assessment Tool" by Ann W. Burgess, Jacqueline Fawcett, Robert R. Hazelwood, and Christine A. Grant, discusses prototypes for victim care services and provide a data collection instrument for rape and sexual assault.

Section IV is on the prosecution of rape cases. In William Heiman's updated Chapter 17, "Prosecuting Rape Cases: Trial Preparation and Trial Tactic Issues", Ann Ponterio and Gail Fairman describe the standard processing of rape cases in the criminal justice system. Difficult cases discussed include identification issue cases, consent issue cases, and the imperfect victim. The use of expert testimony is also discussed. In Chapter 18, "Rape Trauma Syndrome: A Review of Case Law and Psychological Research", Patricia A. Frazier and Eugene Borgida, present judicial decisions that highlight key issues in the prosecution of sexual assault cases. They also discuss current rape trauma syndrome cases in terms of the arguments made for and against their admissibility and address some of the particular objections that have been raised, and suggest some responses to those objections.

A new fifth section on special offender populations completes the book. Chapter 19, "Child Molestation: A Law Enforcement Typology" by Kenneth V. Lanning, describes a typology of offenders who assault children that is designed for law enforcement investigators looking at child molesters. This typology includes both incest offenders and pedophiles, as well as psychopathic character-disordered offenders. This carefully designed typology is derived from cases investigated from the law enforcement perspective. Chapter 20, "The Serial Rapist" written by Robert R. Hazelwood and Janet I. Warren, includes findings from their study of 41 serial rapists. Major findings contradict popular stereotypes. For example, most serial rapists are not carefully stalking a particular woman; rather, their choice of victim is more dependent on general proximity, the victim's availability and access to her residence. Chapter 21, "The Criminal Sexual Sadist" by Robert R. Hazelwood, Park Elliot Dietz, and Janet I. Warren, contains findings from their study of men who sadistically raped and/or murdered their victims.

This book represents a major commitment by its authors to present the most current knowledge for the investigation and prosecution of rape cases. We wish to thank the many people who helped in both the first and second editions of this book.

Editorial Note

While it is recognized that males are also victims of rape, the gender descriptor "she" is primarily used in this text. The male pronouns are also used at times when the female gender would be equally applicable. This is done in the interest of sentence structure and readability.

Acknowledgments

The editors wish to acknowledge the following individuals without whose efforts this book would not have been possible.

For their encouragement and support: Peggy Driver-Hazelwood, Allen G. Burgess, Retired Assistant Director James D. McKenzie (FBI), Retired Deputy Assistant Director James A. O'Connor (FBI), and Retired Unit Chief Roger L. Depue (FBI).

Others deserving special thanks are E. Rene Smith, for her dedication and untiring editorial assistance; Mr. Charles Stanley, for his invaluable assistance in the preparation of Chapter 3; and Retired Supervisory Special Agent Howard D. Teten (FBI), for his insight and professional advice over the years.

A special word of thanks to Vernon Geberth and George Novotny, without whose assistance this book would not have been included in the CRC series.

About the Authors

Margaret M. Aiken, Ph.D. is an Associate Professor at the Loewenberg School of Nursing, University of Memphis, Memphis, Tennessee. Dr. Aiken's clinical background is in psychiatric nursing. She has been active at the University of Memphis on the University Ethics Committee and the General Education Committee. At the Loewenberg School of Nursing she currently chairs the Curriculum Committee and the Faculty Review Committee. Dr. Aiken has a clinical practice in forensic nursing at the Memphis Sexual Assault Resource Center (MSARC). At MSARC she serves as forensic nurse evaluator, expert witness, coordinator of research, ethics consultant, and forensic nursing consultant to the attorney general. Dr. Aiken has many publications on a variety of topics.

Richard L. Ault, Jr., Ph.D. served four years in the U.S. Marine Corps. He received his B.S. degree in psychology from Huntington College in Montgomery, Alabama; his M.A. in counseling psychology from the University of Alabama; and his Ph.D. in counseling and development from the American University, Washington, D.C. Dr. Ault has also studied at George Washington University, Washington, D.C., and Sophia University, Tokyo, Japan. Before joining the FBI, Dr. Ault worked briefly in the federal prison system as a test administrator for prisoner classification. He retired from the FBI Academy at Quantico, Virginia in 1994 and is a member of the Academy Group, Inc. in Manassas, Virginia.

P. David Bigbee has been an FBI Agent since August 20, 1980. He is currently the supervisor in charge of the Violent Crimes/Fugitive Task Force of South Florida and the Caribbean based in Miami. Prior to that, he served in the Albuquerque and Tampa Field Divisions, as an examiner in the Serology Unit of the FBI Laboratory, as an instructor in forensic science at the FBI Academy, and as Chief of the DNA Analysis Unit of the FBI Laboratory. Special Agent Bigbee was the recipient of the U.S. Attorney General's Award for Excellence in Law Enforcement in 1990, and the University of Virginia-FBI National Academy Thomas Jefferson Award for Excellence in Law Enforcement Education in 1989.

Eugene Borgida, Ph.D. is Professor of Psychology and Adjunct Professor of Law and Political Science at the University of Minnesota in Minneapolis. He recently completed his appointment as Associate Dean for Research and Planning in the University of Minnesota's College of Liberal Arts. He received his undergraduate degree from Wesleyan University and his Ph.D. in social psychology from the University of Michigan in 1976. Much of Dr. Borgida's research focus has concerned the psychology of legal evidence.

Allen G. Burgess is Adjunct Associate Professor in the College of Business, Northeastern University, Boston. He received his B.S.E.E. from Massachusetts Institute of Technology and his M.B.A. and D.B.A. from Boston University. Dr. Burgess's background has been in the computer industry for over 25 years. Through his faculty appointment, he teaches operations management and management in high tech industry, and he provides consulting services in a variety of areas. His most recent assignments have been technology assessment for commercial feasibility of a file-server system for personal computers, specific requirements for high-performance graphics boards for personal computers, evaluation of a new scanner technology, a perception study of the computer-aided engineering market, and development of a specialized data base system for work stations. His current research is management's role in the early detection and prevention of workplace crime.

Ann Wolbert Burgess, R.N., D.N.Sc., F.A.A.N., is the van Ameringen Professor of Psychiatric Mental Health Nursing at the University of Pennsylvania School of Nursing. She studied at Boston University and received the Doctor of Nursing Science in psychiatric-mental-health nursing at Boston University. Dr. Burgess has held faculty appointments at Boston College and Boston University. She has written textbooks in the field of nursing and crisis intervention; coauthored articles in the field of victimology; and coauthored *The Crime Classification Manual* with John Douglas, Allen Burgess and Robert Ressler. Her research has been funded by the National Institutes of Health, National Institute of Justice and the National Center on Child Abuse and Neglect. She was elected to membership in the National Academy of Sciences Institute of Medicine in 1994.

Park Elliot Dietz, M.D., M.P.H., Ph.D. is President of Threat Assessment Group, Inc., in Newport Beach, California, Clinical Professor Psychiatry and Biobehavioral Sciences at UCLA School of Medicine, the forensic psychiatry consultant to the FBI's National Center for the Analysis of Violent Crime, and President of the American Academy of Psychiatry and the Law. Educated at Cornell, Johns Hopkins, and the University of Pennsylvania, Dr. Dietz was previously a professor at Harvard and the University of Virginia. He served as the government's chief expert in the trials of John Hinckley, Jr. and Jeffrey Dahmer and has testified in hundreds of trials throughout the U.S.

Roger L. Depue, Ph.D., was appointed a Special Agent with the Federal Bureau of Investigation in 1968. He was assigned to the New Orleans, Louisiana, and the Washington, D.C., Field Offices. In 1974, he was assigned as a Supervisory Special Agent to the Behavioral Science Unit of the FBI Academy at Quantico, Virginia. In 1980, Dr. Depue served as Chief of Behavioral Sciences, and in 1984, he was appointed as the administrator of the FBI National Center for the Analysis of Violent Crime (NCAVC). Special Agent Depue holds a bachelor of science degree in psychology from Central Michigan University and a master of science degree in the administration of justice and a Ph.D. in counseling and development from

American University. Dr. Depue is an adjunct faculty member in psychology and sociology at the University of Virginia. Before entering on duty as a Special Agent with the FBI, Dr. Depue was employed on the local level of the criminal justice system as a county juvenile officer for the Clare County, Michigan, juvenile Court, and served as a police officer and as Chief of Police in the city of Clare, Michigan. Since retiring from the FBI, Dr. Depue serves as President of the Academy Group.

John E. Douglas entered the FBI in 1970 following four years service in the U.S. Air Force. He is a graduate of the University of Wisconsin where he earned his master's degree in educational psychology. He received a Ph.D. in adult education at Nova University. Mr. Douglas was a Supervisory Special Agent and Unit Chief of the FBI National Center for the Analysis of Violent Crime Unit. He managed the FBI Criminal Personality Profiling and Consultation Program until he retired in 1995. He has participated in the crime analysis of hundreds of rapes, homicides, kidnappings, arsons, and bombing matters. Currently he is with Mind Hunters, Inc. in Virginia.

Gail Fairman, is an Assistant District Attorney in the city of Philadelphia, Pennsylvania. Ms. Fairman received her AB degree from Franklin and Marshall College and her JD degree from the National Law Center of George Washington University. She was in private practice and a Deputy District Attorney in Bucks County, Pennsylvania before her assignment to the Rape Prosecution Unit in the Philadelphia District Attorney's Office. Currently she is assigned to the Homicide Unit.

Jacqueline A. Fawcett, Ph.D., R.N., FAAN received her Bachelor of Science degree from Boston University in 1964; her Master's in Parent Child Nursing from New York University in 1970; and her Ph.D. in Nursing, also from New York University, in 1976. Dr. Fawcett is a professor at the University of Pennsylvania School of Nursing and an adjunct professor at Vanderbilt University School of Nursing. She has conducted studies dealing with wives' and husbands' pregnancy-related experiences, and responses to cesarean birth and vaginal birth after cesarean, as well as a program of research dealing with functional status in normal life transitions and serious illness. In addition, Dr. Fawcett is internationally known for her meta-theoretical work, including four books: *Analysis and Evaluation of Conceptual Models of Nursing,* which has been translated into Finnish and Japanese, *Analysis and Evaluation of Nursing Theories, The Relationship of Theory and Research* (with Florence Downs), and *Family Theory Development in Nursing* (with Ann Whall).

Patricia Frazier, Ph.D., is an Associate Professor at the University of Minnesota in Minneapolis, Minnesota. Professor Frazier received her Ph.D. in Social Psychology and Counseling Psychology in 1988 from the University of Minnesota. Her research interests include sexual victimization and the interface between psychology and the law.

Christine A. Grant, R.N., Ph.D., is Associate Professor of Psychiatric Mental Health Nursing and Director of the Australian Centre for the Development of Psychiatric Nursing Excellence at the Royal Melbourne Institute of Technology in Melbourne, Australia. Dr. Grant received her doctorate in psychiatric nursing at the University of Pennsylvania. She has had faculty appointments at Widener University ant the University of Pennsylvania School of Nursing. She has published in the area of rape victimology and battered women who kill.

Robert R. Hazelwood is a retired Supervisory Special Agent of the Federal Bureau of Investigation, currently with the Academy Group, Inc. in Manassas, Virginia. He received his undergraduate degree from Sam Houston State College and earned his master's degree from Nova University. Mr. Hazelwood also attended a one-year fellowship in forensic medicine at the Armed Forces Institute of Pathology. Before joining the FBI in 1971, he served 11 years in the U.S. Army's Military Police Corps, attaining the rank of Major. His works have been published by *the Journal of Police Science and Administration, Social Science and Medicine, American Registry of Pathology, Journal of Forensic Sciences, FBI Law Enforcement Bulletin,* and other professional journals. He coauthored the book *Autoerotic Fatalities* and has lectured extensively on criminal sexuality throughout the United States, Europe, Canada, and the Caribbean. He has consulted law enforcement agencies throughout North America, Canada, Europe, and the Caribbean in the investigation of sexual assaults and homicides.

William Heiman, Esq., graduated from the Wharton School of the University of Pennsylvania in 1964 and Temple University School of Law in 1967. He was an assistant district attorney in the Philadelphia District Attorney's Office from 1972 to 1985. He served as Chief of Rape and Child Abuse Unit from 1978 to 1984. In 1981, he received the Program of Excellence Award from the National Organization of Victim Assistance, recognizing the Philadelphia District Attorney's Rape Unit as the most outstanding unit of its type in the country. Mr. Heiman is author of several articles on rape prosecution issues and is currently a member of the law firm of Sacks, Basch, Brodie and Sacks in Philadelphia.

Neil S. Hibler, Ph.D. is the Command Clinical Psychologist and Chief of the Behavioral Sciences Division, Directorate of Investigation Support, Headquarters, U.S. Air Force Office of Special Investigations, Washington, D.C. Before becoming the first mental health professional to work exclusively with a federal investigative agency, he was a Special Agent with the USAF Office of Special Investigations and later an instructor at the USAF Special Investigations Academy. His professional training includes two master's degrees and a doctorate in clinical and community psychology from the University of South Florida. Dr. Hibler is a Diplomate in Clinical Psychology, American Board of Professional Psychology.

Kenneth V. Lanning is a Supervisory Special Agent assigned to the Behavioral Science Unit at the FBI Academy in Quantico, Virginia. He has made presentations before the National Conference on Sexual Victimization of Children, the National Conference on Child Abuse and Neglect, and the American Orthopsychiatric Association. He has testified before the U.S. Attorney General's Task Force on Family Violence, the President's Task Force on Victims of Crime, and the U.S. Attorney General's Commission on Pornography. He has also testified before the U.S. Senate and the U.S. House of Representatives, and as an expert witness in state and federal courts. Mr. Lanning has lectured before and trained thousands of police officers and criminal justice professionals.

John C. LeDoux, Ph.D. was appointed a Special Agent of the Federal Bureau of Investigation in 1971. He is currently the Program Manager of Computer Based Training for the Training Division of the FBI. He has published research in the areas of higher education for law enforcement, police attitudes toward rape, and computer-based training. He holds a doctorate in adult and vocational education from Auburn University and has been selected for inclusion in the 1986 edition of the Marquis *Who's Who in the South and Southwest.*

Charles P. McDowell, Ph.D. has held a variety of academic positions. He received his M.P.A. degree from the City University of New York, his M.L.S. from the University of North Carolina at Greensboro, and his Ph.D. from North Texas State University. Dr. McDowell is the author of four books and numerous articles in the professional literature.

Dale M. Moreau, Supervisory Special Agent, entered the Federal Bureau of Investigation in 1971 and served as a Fingerprint Technician and as a Physical Science Technician in the Laboratory Division. He has also served as a field investigator in three FBI field offices. In 1975, he was transferred to the FBI Laboratory as an examiner in the Document Section. In 1979, he joined the Forensic Science Training Unit at the FBI Academy, Quantico, Virginia. Mr. Moreau has been providing technical assistance to the FBI and other law enforcement agencies regarding crime-scene searches and physical evidence recovery techniques. In 1985, he was designated to serve as a special advisor on a national advisory committee established to study protocols of investigation in sexual assault cases. Mr. Moreau has a B.A. degree from Louisiana State University, Baton Rouge, Louisiana, and a M.A. degree from George Washington University, Washington, D.C. He maintains membership in professional forensic science organizations and is an adjunct faculty member of the University of Virginia.

Ann Ponterio was appointed an Assistant District Attorney in the Philadelphia Distric Attorney's Office in 1984. She received her BA from St. Bonaventure University, her JD from New England School of Law and a Master of Government Administration from the University of Pennsylvania in 1994. Since her appointment in 1984, Ms. Ponterio has been assigned to the Rape Prosecution Unit, the Juvenile Unit where she prosecuted child physical and sexual abuse cases, the Major Trial Unit where she prosecuted robbery, aggravated assault, burglary and arson cases and the Municipal Court Unit where she prosecuted misdemeanor cases.

James T. Reese, Ph.D. has been a member of the Federal Bureau of Investigation since 1971, and is currently assigned as Supervisory Special Agent and faculty member of the FBI Academy's Behavioral Science Unit. He holds a B.A. and an M.S. and received his Ph.D. from American University, Washington, D.C. Dr. Reese managed the pilot program for psychological services within the FBI and is responsible for FBI research and training in law enforcement stress. As an adjunct faculty member of the University of Virginia, he teaches advanced and applied criminology, police psychology, and stress management courses. Dr. Reese was an exchange faculty member of the Police Staff College, Bramshill, England, and is on numerous editorial and advisory committees. He is co-editor of a book titled *Psychological Services for Law Enforcement* and is currently co-editing three other books on police psychology.

Robert K. Ressler, M.S., is a criminologist in private practice and the Director of Forensic Behavioral Services, a Virginia-based organization. He is a 20 year veteran of the Federal Bureau of Investigation, serving 16 years in the FBI's Behavioral Science Unit as a Supervisory Special Agent and Criminologist, retiring in 1990. Mr. Ressler served with the U.S. Army, 10 years of which was active duty during the Vietnam era. He recently retired at the rank of full Colonel with 35 years of total active duty and reserve service. He has lectured, published, consulted, and testified in the area of violent criminal offenders.

Janet I. Warren, DSW, LCSW, is an Associate Professor of Clinical Psychiatric Medicine at the University of Virginia. She is faculty at the Institute of Law, Psychiatry, and Public Policy where she evaluates criminal defendants and conducts research on serial and violent crime. Dr. Warren also serves as faculty for the diverse training offered through the Institute and maintains the Forensic Evaluation Information System, an information management system of all court-ordered forensic evaluations conducted in Virginia each year. Dr. Warren has published extensively in the areas of serial rape, sexual sadism, and serial murder and has been a research consultant to the FBI Behavioral Science Unit since 1986.

Joseph A. Zeccardi, M.D. earned his B.S. degree from Villanova University in 1961 and his M.D. degree from Temple Medical College in 1965. Following a rotating internship at Mount Zion Hospital in San Francisco, he completed pediatric residency training at St. Christopher's Hospital in Philadelphia in 1968. After two years as a Lieutenant Commander in the Navy assigned as a pediatrician in Morocco, he worked as a pediatrician with the Kaiser Permanente Group in Hayward, California. He also served as Director of the Children and Youth Program in Thomas Jefferson University's Pediatric Department and Director of the Emergency Department at Thomas Jefferson University Hospital. Since 1976, Dr. Zeccardi has been the Director of the Sexual Assault Unit at Thomas Jefferson.

I

ATTITUDES AND BELIEFS ABOUT RAPE

Public Beliefs and Attitudes Toward Rape

1

ANN WOLBERT BURGESS

> I prefer five clean murders to one rape case. The more you investigate and get into it, the stickier it gets... Murder I can understand, but I can't really understand rape.
>
> **Detective**

Relatively few problems are as emotionally entangling and as scientifically elusive as that of rape. Society's perception of rape is strongly influenced by a puzzling mixture of prejudice, credence, and voyeuristic curiosity. Perhaps reactions stem from acquired attitudes and perhaps reactions stir deep-lying aggressive or defensive impulses in people; perhaps the myths and stereotypes surrounding rape are influential because they represent what people believe.

It is the author's intent to show that there is a wide range of feelings and reactions that people experience when confronted with the subject of rape. Two types of reactions experienced by people are (1) the immediate, "gut" response to the distress of victims and (2) the subjective reactions. These subjective feelings are unique reactions having their origins in the past on the basis of personal experience or long-held societal beliefs and reactions to the subject of rape. For example, a police officer may suspect that every rape victim is making a false accusation because he was warned of such "women" early in his career or has experienced one or more false complaints. One officer reported that he had been very sensitive to the plight of rape victims and consequently was ridiculed by fellow officers and accused of being more of a counselor than a police officer. After accepting and actively pursuing a complaint of rape, he later determined it was false. He felt he had been "burned" and vowed it wouldn't happen again. The officer then responds to every victim as if she were falsely accusing a man, thus not relying on his immediate, nonbiased gut reaction. Or a hospital staff nurse may think the victim is not telling the truth because she once heard a supervisor state that "half of the rape victims make up their stories". Or a prosecutor may say, "This wasn't like some rapes where I grew up... with the women really upset afterwards".

Both the intuitive and subjective reactions have implications for the rape victim. She suffers not only from the incident itself — the painful, violent penetration of her body — but also from the reactions of people, especially the negative subjective reactions to the myths and stereotypes surrounding the subject.

0-8493-8152-1/95/$0.00+$.50

It is very important for the police officer working with rape victims to be aware of these two kinds of reactions. They are to be seen in the network of people who deal with the victim officially — police officers, detectives, nurses, physicians, lawyers, judges, counselors, and crisis workers. They are to be seen in the police officer who is beginning to investigate a rape case, the staff nurse who first talks with the victim in the emergency ward, the nurse-practitioner or physician who examines the victim, and the district attorney who prosecutes the case. All people who are involved in a rape investigation and want to help the rape victim must come to terms with these feelings in themselves in order to function effectively and to be of the most help to the victim.

This chapter will describe the themes that have been expressed again and again by police officers. The remarks were made spontaneously during the course of the Holmstrom and Burgess study (1983). They are presented here in order to help the police officer understand his or her own attitudes, or those of society which may be reflected in the victim. They may also serve as the basis for a discussion group where officers can share their feelings with colleagues in order that they may come to terms with their emotional and subjective reactions and thus be better able to provide emotional support to the victim.

Intuitive Reactions to Rape Victims

Feelings of Distress

Two professional groups who usually see the rape victim within hours of the attack are the police and the hospital emergency service staff. They routinely see all victims and often their immediate reactions are of distress. One detective said, "I have five daughters and I would want them to fight a rapist even if this provoked him to kill them. If you live you will look back on the rape as a bad memory. If you are dead you have nothing to worry about".

There are many unpleasant and difficult situations that police must face as part of their daily work. Although there are many reasons why a person might feel depressed when dealing with a rape victim, one of the most common is a feeling of helplessness, of not knowing what to do to relieve the victim's distress. As one becomes more aware of crisis intervention skills, this feeling diminishes considerably; or as noted in the quote, the officer believed that death was a better option than having to live with the memory of rape. The knowledge that the words said and approach taken to a victim can positively affect the recovery process gives officers and front-line crisis intervenors considerable influence with the psychological state of the victim.

Feelings of Involvement

A patrolman said, "I don't get involved in these cases. I just bring the girl to the hospital and that's it. You'd go soft if you really thought about the rape cases you see every night".

People who work with rape victims admit to having difficulties in thinking about the problem and thus imply that it is overwhelming; or the professional might say she is too busy to think about it or listen to the victim; or they may not know how to deal with the victim and they seek advice.

The more aware officers become of their own feelings, the better they are able to control the feelings. For example, if a victim frustrates the officer working with her, that is acceptable as long as the officer does not act on the feelings, terminate the meeting, or allow the victim to know his or her feelings and thus delay the interview, possibly losing valuable time and information. Being aware of one's own feelings and reading one's own reactions prevent the officer from overinvolvement, overreaction, and overcompensation.

Feelings of Avoidance and Silence

A patrolman said, "Rape cases are closed-mouth affairs. No one likes them. Police develop certain attitudes toward them".

Sexuality is not generally discussed openly in American society, and criminal sexuality is even less openly spoken about. It is apparent that by not addressing the topic, society, in general, and the criminal justice system, in particular, deny the extent of the problem and insulate themselves from the possibility of its happening to them. Indeed, those who force our attention to the subject are often deemed to be strange or involved in "kinky work".

Historically, rape has been treated with silence. People find it difficult to talk about and the police and legal system find it equally difficult to deal with. Professionals have avoided rape cases because of the inconvenience of the legal process.

Sympathy for the Victim

A gynecologist said to a police officer, "When you see a victim like that who has evidence of trauma and you know she has been emotionally raped and sexually assaulted and all, well, your heart just goes out to her".

The severely bruised, the elderly, and the young victims of rape receive considerable sympathy from professionals. Perhaps in such cases, the violence and nonsexual aspect of rape may be seen most clearly.

Feelings of Anger and Revenge

One patrolman was heard to say, "Only one thing to do with these guys — cut it off". The biblical solution of an "eye for an eye" is offered by some people as a method of compensation to the victim for the trauma she had to suffer. In fact, the earliest beginnings of social order were based on a primitive system of retaliatory force — *lex talionis.*

Other people feel anger or feel that such a crime should be dealt with by sending the assailant to jail or for psychiatric treatment or death. Still others state how they would deal with the assailant.

Anger at the System

The police, medical, and legal personnel are prime targets for many people to express angry feelings against. The frustration felt by people in effecting concern for the victim is displaced on those people they believe can influence the system.

Quite often the victim displaces her anger and frustration from the rapist, who is no longer there, to the responding police. We are in possession of a police tape recording of a rape in progress. After phoning the police to advise them that a man was attempting to enter her home, she kept her phone off the hook. Following the assault, she returned to the phone and hysterically berated the police officer on the line. Shortly thereafter, an officer arrived at the residence and the victim profanely attacked him for not getting there in time to protect her.

The police and hospital receive many unfavorable comments about the treatment others have received. Protection of the victim in court from added psychological insult is not a priority of the court and the news media very often present a biased opinion.

On the other hand, one part of the system, the police, expresses its frustration over another part of the system, the courts. As one officer noted, "We break our necks to get these guys to court and then the door just opens and they walk right back on the street".

Along with the immediate and intuitive reactions that people express in terms of positive feelings for the victim, there are many ambivalent and negative feelings and reactions that people express.

Feelings of Voyeurism

There is an aspect of rape that people find fascinating, and often they spontaneously express it. Perhaps the fact that this crime has thrived on prudery and silence attests to people's interest and curiosity about the circumstances of rape. On the other hand, some people feel it is not a subject to be discussed and feel it has an exhibitionistic quality to it.

When listening to police audiences, it is not uncommon for officers to advise that other officers who are not involved in sexual assault investigations are often voyeuristic about crimes of rape. While verbally expressing anger, rage, and desire for amputatory revenge, they pour over the victim's statement.

The Ideal Rape Victim

The police have in their minds an image of the ideal rape victim and the ideal rape case, often based on personal beliefs. By keeping track of all comments made by police it was possible to see what criteria they used in making this distinction. The criteria fall into four types.

First, police look at the quality and consistency of the information they can get. To be strong, the case cannot rest on the victim's statement alone; instead, there must be corroborating evidence. Further, there cannot be inconsistencies.

Describing a strong case, officers will say, "Everything fits together so well". Conversely, describing a weak case, officers say, "She used a fake name. She's a runaway... Everything she said was a bunch of lies". Police also like to have witnesses — especially police witnesses — to the crime. In one case, the officers arrived while the assailant was still at the scene and were so enthusiastic they said; "We'll testify even if the girl doesn't". Police hope the victim can provide a good description of the assailant or of his belongings, such as his car. Officers look for corroborating medical evidence such as clinical evidence of intercourse or physical injuries. Police are most impressed with a consistent and unchanging story.

Second, police officers look at the victim's characteristics — her behavior and her moral character. In a strong case, the victim was forced to accompany the assailant, and in a weak case, she accompanied him willingly or asked him to accompany her. As one officer said, "She won't have much of a chance in court. She invited him over".

Third, police look at the relationship between victim and offender. In a strong case, the assailant is a stranger. Ages of victim and offender are also important and they are more enthusiastic about pursuing the case if there is an age difference.

Fourth, police look at the offender's characteristics. Nothing makes them more enthusiastic about a case than to find out the assailant has other charges against him or a prison record.

Subjective Reactions Based on Myths and Stereotypes

Our society's belief system supports and promotes rape in many ways. Victims have difficulty convincing others — police, hospital personnel, prosecutors, judges, and jurors — that they were victimized. Some victims have difficulty convincing husbands, partners, associates, and friends. This problem exists because family, friends, authorities, and the general public often have in their minds an image of rape that does not allow rape scenarios outside the parameters of that image.

There are studies that indicate how the stereotypes and beliefs of people operate in the general society. Burt's (1980) work on "rape culture" is one such example. Burt is interested in whether people in the general population believe such myths as "only bad girls get raped", "any healthy woman can resist a rapist if she really wants to", and "rapists are sex-starved, insane, or both". Her data were obtained by interviews with a random sample of 598 adults in Minnesota. The results show that many people do believe the rape myths, and that their attitudes toward rape are strongly associated with other strongly held attitudes. Among these other attitudes, the person's acceptance of interpersonal violence is found to be the strongest attitudinal predictor of his/her acceptance of rape myths.

Another group studied was convicted rapists. Scully and Marolla (1982) divided their sample of convicted rapists into those who admitted the rape and those who denied their rape conviction. Deniers described the victim in a way that made their own behavior seem more justified or appropriate. For example, one denier said of his victim, "She semi-struggled but deep down inside I think she felt it was a fantasy come true". The important observation made by Scully and Marolla is that these rapists do not invent lies, but rather their vocabulary is drawn from the culture or society and reflect what they have reason to believe others will find acceptable.

It is no myth that in our society men have more power and status than women, both in the area of interpersonal relations and in our structural systems (i.e., law, politics, education). It has been suggested that men's possession of (and in some cases, desire for) greater power contributes to the rape of women.

Much attention has been given to the changing role of women in our society in areas such as equality in employment and in the family, but much less attention has been given to the fundamental way in which the rights of women are violated through sexual assault. Because of the prevailing attitudes regarding male-female relationships, and because of the position of women in our society, the following types of subjective reactions, based on myths and stereotypes, are to be expected from large numbers of people.

Struggle and Force as Elements of Rape

Although force and penetration of the body are key elements in the definition of rape, there is the myth that a woman cannot be raped against her will, or sometimes the comment is made that women provoke rape.

Rape is not perceived by the public to be the result of a society in which women are defined as the appropriate objects of male violence. Rather, our society is more likely to believe that the victim provoked the crime. As one police officer predicted as to emotional problems after rape, "This girl won't have any problems... It's not right for a girl to go into a stranger's apartment, drink beer, and then be upset when the guy makes advances".

In terms of the struggle and force element, most women are socialized against aggressiveness and do not know how to fight successfully against a male. They are also expected to be passive and submissive sexual partners. The irony is that when confronted with a rapist who is physically stronger and may be armed, a woman is suddenly expected to struggle, fight, and resist to a degree not otherwise expected.

Reporting the Rape

Societal expectations concerning the reporting of rape are in conflict. One is that if a woman is raped she should be too upset and ashamed to report it, and therefore this crime goes largely unreported. The other is that if a woman is raped she should be so upset that she *will* report it. Both expectations exist simultaneously; it is the latter one, however, that is written into law. This legal principle was researched and reported by Brownmiller (1975) to have been carried since the 13th century, when according to Henry of Bratton (Bracton) who lived and wrote in the 13th century and is considered an authority for the ancient Saxon times, the procedure a raped virgin was to follow went like this:

She must go at once and while the deed is newly done, with the hue and cry, to the neighboring townships and show the injury done to her to men of good repute, the blood and her clothing stained with blood and her torn garments.

The rule then continues that if the accused man protests his innocence, the raped virgin must then have her body examined by four law-abiding women sworn to tell the truth as to whether she was defiled or is still a virgin.

In more modern language, this is called "making a fresh complaint". The assumption is that if she really has been raped, she will make it known to others immediately. In modern procedure there is often the same interest in the state of the hymen, although the examination of the raped victim today is by a hospital staff.

Blame the Victim

While it is well known that the main strategy of defense lawyers is to blame the victim, this belief is equally evident when others comment on a rape victim. To again review Bracton's writings, the man accused of rape in the 13th century also had several possible defenses.

1. There was a prior sexual relationship. This defense states that the accused man had the woman as his concubine before the date of the accused rape. This defense is still viable in court today and is quickly used when such a relationship has been present.
2. It was consent and not against her will (i.e., "she was defiled with her consent"). Defense lawyers attempt to broach the issue of consent in a variety of ways. They use anything they can about the victim's behavior, emotional state, or character that increases the plausibility in the people's minds that the woman consented. Often, the defense trades on current normative expectations for sex roles. They know that anything the female does that deviates from the norm of "appropriate female behavior" can be used to attack her in court. As one police officer put it, "A lot of rape cases are for spite; the woman is just getting back at the guy". Or another, "After six years on the force, I don't believe any of them". And a third officer, "Just had a case of a girl hitchhiking and the guy raped her. Most officers aren't sympathetic. Many feel there is more behind the story than the woman tells". Suspicions about women — their motives and their truthfulness — are realities that the victim faces when telling her "story" to the officer or nurse.

Woman as Fickle and Full of Spite

Another stereotype is that the feminine character is especially filled with malice. Woman is seen as fickle and as seeking revenge on past lovers. This stereotype is also used against the rape victim, and is especially effective when she knew the assailant, as in a former boyfriend.

A Victorian belief is that good girls don't get raped and bad girls should not complain. As one detective said, "She is a known prostitute and junkie. She stated she took drugs with her consent prior to the experience. She didn't struggle. She knew the men and the women involved. Her facts kept on changing".

Sometimes people make statements that refer to the game of rape and who wins. Sometimes people infer prostitution rather than victimization and some statements refer to the myth that women secretly wish to be raped.

Sexual Reputation

Individual women are seldom thought of as having integrated personalities that encompass both maternal love and erotic desires. Instead, they are categorized into one-dimensional types: they are maternal or they are sexy; they are good or they are bad. They are Madonnas or they are whores. This split view of woman has been noted by many writers. The historian Bullough (1974), discussing the formation of Western attitudes, describes the "two faces of woman": the dutiful housewife and loving mother on one hand; the erotic lover and temptress of man on the other. Chafetz (1974), a sociologist, has reported on a study of the words people think most Americans use to describe masculinity and femininity. "A basic dualism is… displayed toward the female, who is simultaneously held to be 'sexually passive, uninterested' (the Virgin Mary image) and 'seductive, flirtatious' (the wicked Eve tempting poor innocent Adam). This theme runs through the history of Western civilization and our mores concerning 'good' and 'bad' females has no parallels for males".

The Female Under Surveillance

Females in our society are more tightly restricted in their sexual activities than are males. Their sexual behavior is more subject to surveillance. Before marriage, they are expected to abstain from sex. After marriage, they are to be the sexual property of their husbands. Even though in practice it is common for females to have premarital or extramarital sex, the norm still exists that they should not, and this norm is used against them in rape cases. It is assumed that the female's sexual behavior, depending on her age, is under the surveillance of her parents or her husband and, more generally, of the community. Thus, the argument may be made that if a woman was raped it must have been because she consented to sex that she was not supposed to have. She got caught and now she wants to get back in the good graces of whomever's surveillance she is under. A variation is to argue that she was out later than she was supposed to be, got caught, and needed an excuse for her tardiness.

Disputing that Sex Occurred

That females fantasize rape is another common stereotype. Females are to make up stories that sex occurred when, in fact, nothing happened. According to the stereotype, the sexual details of the report are imaginary, part of a fantasy world. Similarly, women are thought to fabricate the sexual activity, not as a part of a fantasy life, but out of spite. Thus, another way to blame the victim is to say that she invented the sexual activity.

Emotionality of Females

Females are assumed to be "more emotional" than males. The expectation is that if a woman is raped she will get hysterical during the event and she will be visibly upset afterward. If she is able to "keep her cool" then people assume that "nothing happened" — that she was not raped. In fact, data show that many victims, through a conscious act of will, retain control over their emotions in order to survive the assault, and that even afterward, they present themselves to others in a composed manner.

The normative about emotionality puts women in a double bind. If women live up to the expectation and become so upset during the rape that they cannot remember details, they are blamed for not being able to testify about the details, or some other reason is advanced for their being upset. If, however, they retain their cool and remember details, it is assumed that nothing happened.

Rape is a Way of Life

Some people feel that rape is different to some women, some ethnic groups, or some cultures. Consider the following statement: "There is the South Boston rape. That is where a young girl is a junkie who goes around to bars to gather contacts and then she gets her head beat in and she comes to the hospital and cries rape".

Insulting the Victim

As if the original rape were not distressing enough, in court the woman again must submit to direct and psychological insults to which she must remain silent. In the following statements, a defense lawyer presents his opinion of the victim and a judge explicitly states his opinion of the victim.

> Your honor, this young lady is obviously a woman of the world. The judge interrupted angrily and said, "I don't know what you mean by that phrase". The defense lawyer, grinning, said, "Well, your honor, I didn't mean it the way you probably thought I did". The judge replied, "What do you know about the way I think?" The defense lawyer said, "I apologize, your honor. Strike that from the record".

In some cases the judge takes a firm stand in that such statements are not to be allowed to be passed over. However, even if the words are stricken from the record, they have registered with the jury. In another case, the judge himself insulted the victim as he gave his succinct summary of the case: "She is an alcoholic. She is no good. But you have no right to rape a drunk either".

Summary

In summary, perhaps there is a continuum of relationship to male sexuality as is being proposed by some sociologists. Perhaps there is a relationship between rape and women's role in society. Perhaps research will provide some answers. But most importantly, perhaps the human dimension may be brought into sharper focus for rape victims and they will matter as human beings in the process by sensitizing police officers, hospital staff personnel, and court officials to victimology as they conduct their rape cases. In order to accomplish such a goal, police officers need to understand their intuitive and subjective responses to rape and to be aware of the influence strongly held beliefs and stereotypes have to one's response.

References

Brownmiller, B., *Against Our Will: Men, Women and Rape,* Simon & Schuster, New York, 1975.

Bullough, V.L., Formation of Western attitudes, in *The Subordinate Sex: A History of Attitudes toward Women,* Penguin Books, Baltimore, 1980, 49.

Burt, M.R., Cultural myths and supports for rape, *J. Pers. Soc. Psychol.,* 38, 217, 1980.

Chafetz, J.S., *Masculine/Feminine or Human? An Overview of the Sociology of Sex Roles,* F. E. Peacock, Itasca, IL, 1974, 39.

Holmstrom, L.L. and Burgess, A.W., *The Victim of Rape: Institutional Reactions,* Transaction Books, New Brunswick, NJ, 1983.

Scully, D. and Marolla, J., Convicted Rapists' Construction of Reality: The Denial of Rape, paper presented at the American Sociological Association meetings, San Francisco, September 1982, 13.

Police Attitudes and Beliefs Concerning Rape

2

JOHN C. LEDOUX
ROBERT R. HAZELWOOD

Unlike many other crimes, rape is seriously underreported (PCLEAJ, 1967). Victims of rape may decide not to report the crime because they fear police attitudes and beliefs concerning rape, the perpetrators of rape, and, above all, themselves, the victims of rape. Blumberg and Niederhoffer (1973), in fact, agree that "in practice, the average policeman exercises greater judicial discretion over cases than does a judge".

Because the public's perception of police beliefs and attitudes concerning various crimes can affect its willingness to report crime, help in identification, to convict an offender, and to support new legislation, law enforcement should study its own beliefs and attitudes — and reform, modify, or use them as indicated. The purpose of this chapter is, thus, to describe briefly the prevailing literature on police attitudes toward rape and to present the findings of a nationwide survey of county and municipal police officers conducted by the authors of this chapter.

Traditional Views of Police Attitudes

Historically, descriptions of police attitudes toward the crime of rape and its victims have come primarily from two sources. One source is anecdotal literature wherein popular writers examine and express opinions on the issue of rape. Another source, not necessarily mutually exclusive with the first, is empirical research wherein officers have been questioned about their opinions.

The anecdotal literature finds that rape victims are generally greeted with hostile, callous, and indifferent treatment by police officers. Brownmiller (1975) states that "despite their knowledge of the law they are supposed to enforce, the male police mentality is often identical to the stereotypic views of rape that are shared by the rest of the male culture. The tragedy for the rape victim is that the police officer is the person who validates her victimization. A police officer who does not believe there is such a crime as rape can arrive at only one destination". Brownmiller thus generalizes her opinion of the male police officer to include the entire male culture — and she implies that male and female police attitudes are different.

A similarly negative view is presented by Greer (1975) who writes that "bored policemen amusing themselves with girls who come to them to complain of rape often kick off the proceedings by asking if they have enjoyed it". Hurst (1977)

0-8493-8152-1/95/$0.00+$.50
© 1995 by CRC Press, Inc.

reserves most of her criticism for the male officers first dispatched to the crime scene. She states, "he (the police officer) is there because his was the patrol car nearest to the address given by the victim and speed in answering a rape call is important... it is at this point in the encounter with the police that the insensitivity usually occurs". Hurst, however, concludes that "some policewomen have as little compassion as policemen".

The empirical literature presents a more balanced view, although the data clearly suggest that some officers are influenced by the particular circumstances of the victim, the assailant, and the act itself. Feldman-Summers and Palmer (1980), after examining data from questionnaires provided by 54 criminal justice system (CJS) personnel in the Seattle area, suggest that the frequent complaints of unsympathetic treatment by rape victims can be linked to "beliefs held by the CJS members which tend to place blame and responsibility on the victim". The authors noted that the beliefs of police officers were similar to those of judges and prosecutors with regard to the causes of rape and ways to reduce its frequency. Social service personnel were found to have significantly different beliefs. However, there was no significant difference between the CJS members and the social service personnel in the section of the questionnaire examining what constituted a valid rape.

Gottesman (1977) examines the impact training may have on police attitudes about rape. The subjects were police officers from two departments in the Midwest. She reports that most (95%) of the officers responded positively to training and increased, for example, their understanding of the rape victim. She finds unchanged by training, however, a belief that victims are partly to blame for the assault due to their manner of dress or their behavior.

A study of police investigators in Texas by Galton (1975) examines the criteria by which rape complaints are evaluated. The findings are based on analysis of rape complaints during a 10-week period of time, interviews with investigators and complainants, and questionnaires completed by police officers. Galton concludes that investigators hold rape victims to a higher standard of behavior than the law requires.

Feild (1978) included 254 police officers from an unspecified number of departments in a study examining attitudes toward rape. Also included as subjects were citizens and rape counselors. Based on a principal component factor analysis with varimax rotation, eight factors were extracted. The factors were labeled: (1) Woman's Responsibility in Rape Prevention, (2) Sex as Motivation for Rape, (3) Severe Punishment for Rape, (4) Victim Precipitation of Rape, (5) Normality of Rapists, (6) Power as Motivation for Rape, (7) Favorable Perception of a Woman after Rape, and (8) Resistance as Woman's Role during Rape. Feild suggested that future research should seek to refine the content of his instrument and explore additional content areas.

The major difficulty with these studies is that they have generally been restricted to a single agency and are based on relatively small numbers of subjects who were not randomly selected. The Feldman-Summers and Palmer study, for example, was based on the responses of 15 police officers. This represented only

24% of those asked to participate in the study. Twenty-one people participated in the Gottesman study; ten in the Galton study. Consequently, their findings cannot be generalized to the law enforcement community.

The FBI Study

During the early months of 1983 the authors speculated on the effect a course taught by Hazelwood to officers attending the FBI National Academy would have on students' attitudes toward rape investigations. This discussion spurred a decision to conduct research on the impact of such training on police attitudes. LeDoux, however, held that the study would be invalid if restricted to students who were not representative of the law enforcement community in general. Thus, the authors decided to conduct a nationwide study on police attitudes toward rape. A review of the literature, as cited above, indicated that police officers were regarded as insensitive to the plight of rape victims. The authors questioned whether this was generally true, or whether only a small number of officers held unsympathetic attitudes.

Methodology

The study was limited to sworn officers of county and municipal law enforcement agencies because, statistically, they are most frequently involved in rape cases. Respondents were obtained through the Uniform Crime Report list of contributing law enforcement agencies. These agencies are grouped by geographical region and size of agency and are classified as either a county or municipal agency. The authors selected a desired total sample of 3000 participants and determined the percentage of officers in each region/size/type agency cell. Agencies were randomly selected from each cell, and a list of random numbers equal to approximately 10% of the size of the department was drawn until each cell had a sufficient number of potential respondents. They sent the selected agencies the quota for their organization, and the agencies determined the actual respondents. The respondents were given both questionnaires and envelopes in which to seal the questionnaires, to insure the complete anonymity of their responses. Usable returns were received from 2170 officers, or 72% of those queried. To the authors' knowledge, these returns represent the largest national survey of police attitudes toward rape.

The questionnaires contained demographic data such as age, sex, and number of rape cases investigated, and listed 39 statements on the subject of rape (e.g., "Most charges of rape are unfounded"). Each officer was asked to indicate (1) to what extent he/she agreed with a given statement by circling one of four numbers (1, strongly agree; 2, agree; 3, disagree; 4, strongly disagree), and (2) how this belief affected the amount of effort the officer would devote to a rape investigation (1, much more effort; 2, more effort; 3, same effort; 4, less effort). Many of the statements were adapted from the work of Feild (1978). The reliability and validity of the instrument were established prior to its administration. Reliability of the study data was tested and found to be acceptable.

Table 1 Description of Respondents

Mean age	36
Years of law enforcement experience	11.5
Race (%)[a]	
White	90.2
Black	5.6
Hispanic	2.9
Other	1.4
Marital status (%)[a]	
Single	9.4
Married	79.1
Other	11.6
Ever divorced	
No	69.9
Yes	30.1
Sex (%)	
Female	6.4
Male	93.6
Job category	
Traffic	8.2
Patrol	42.1
Rape investigator	1.3
Vice (including sexual assault)	0.3
Homicide	0.7
General criminal investigator	14.1
Supervisor	10.5
Staff/administrator	6.2
Other	15.4
Education (%)	
Less than high school	0.7
High school	32.2
Some college	41.7
Four-year college degree	15.6
Some graduate study	5.9
Master's degree or more	3.9

[a] Totals do not equal 100 because of rounding error.

Description of Respondents

A profile of the respondents is given in Table 1. The authors have determined that the respondents are typical of sworn county and municipal law enforcement officers because a comparison of their results with a recent nationwide study of similar law enforcement officers (Chronister et al., 1982) reveals that the demographics are practically identical. At the end of the analysis section, the authors will discuss specifics of the data as they relate to the respondents' experience in rape investigation and the amount and type of training they have received.*

* For details of the methodology, see LeDoux and Hazelwood (1985).

Table 2 Factors Listed by Factor Set

Victims
Women as victims
Legal responsibility of victim
Victims' innocence
Victim provocation of rape
Rapists
Sexual motivation for rape
Normality of rapists
Masculinity as a motivation for rape
Trial
Punishment
Victim's influence in trial
Prosecution

Analysis

A technique called factor analysis was employed to determine the underlying sets of attitude (factors) that made up the officers' overall attitude. The 39 statements were reduced mathematically to ten factors and reduced logically to three sets of factors — victims, rapists, and trials (see Table 2). Although the authors will not attempt in this brief chapter to describe factor analysis as a statistical technique, they used extensive analysis to show the relationship among the factors and the factor sets. Even so, they prefer to consider the factor sets as a logical framework rather than a precise statistical statement.

They will present the statements contained in the various factors, then indicate the average reality assessment (belief of the respondent) given by law enforcement officers. In the case of items 14, 28, 29, and 31 (which were associated with two factors), they will list the statements only under the factor with which the association was the greatest. Four items (1, 2, 9, 36) did not meet the criterion established for inclusion in a factor and were not used. Table 2 lists the factors by factor set.

Victims. The first factor set concerned how law enforcement officers view rape victims. The first factor in this set was entitled "women as victims". As may be seen in Table 3, law enforcement officers, contrary to popular belief, are not insensitive to the plight of rape victims. As a group they disagree vehemently with statements that suggest the raped woman is not truly a victim.

The second factor in the victim set was entitled "legal responsibility of victim". The items in this factor deal with the legal responsibilities of the victim in rape cases. As may be seen in Table 4, the officers tend to disagree with statements that suggest women should have to prove they did not precipitate or encourage rape.

The third factor of the victim set was entitled "victims' innocence". The statements in this factor examine the innocence of victims. As shown in Table 5, police officers did see women as innocent victims.

Table 3   Women as Victims

Statement	Average assessment[a]
10 A raped woman is a less desirable woman	3.3
11 If a woman is going to be raped she might as well relax and enjoy it	3.6
13 Most women secretly desire to be raped	3.4
14 Some women deserve to be raped	3.4
16 Nice women do not get raped	3.6
23 In most cases when a woman was raped she was asking for it	3.4

[a] 1 = agree strongly; 2 = agree; 3 = disagree; 4 = disagree strongly.

Table 4   Legal Responsibility of Victim

Statement	Average assessment[a]
6 A charge of rape made two days after the event is probably not a rape	3.1
7 A woman should be responsible for preventing her own rape	3.0
17 Most charges of rape are unfounded	3.0
18 In order to protect the male, it should be more difficult to prove rape than other crimes	3.2
25 Rape of a woman by a man she knows can be defined as a woman who changed her mind	3.0
28 The degree of a woman's resistance should be the major factor in determining if a rape occurred	3.3
38 Previous and willing sex with the accused reduces the seriousness of the offense	2.5

[a] 1 = agree strongly; 2 = agree; 3 = disagree; 4 = disagree strongly.

Table 5   Victims' Innocence

Statement	Average assessment[a]
27 A woman should feel guilty following a rape	3.5
29 A raped woman is a guilty victim, not an innocent one	3.5
31 Rape serves as a way to keep women in their place	3.7

[a] 1 = agree strongly; 2 = agree; 3 = disagree; 4 = disagree strongly.

The final factor dealing with attitudes toward the victim was entitled "victim provocation of rape". This factor is similar to the factor dealing with the victim's legal responsibility to prove rape. The data in Table 6 reveal divided opinions on whether or not women cause or provoke rape. No clear consensus was reached on "victim never causes the crime" and "women provoke rape".

Rapists.   The second factor set dealt with law enforcement officers' perception of the rapist. Each of its three factors was related to motivations for rape, but none

Table 6 Victim Provocation of Rape

Statement	Average assessment[a]
4 In forcible rape, the victim never causes the crime	2.4
15 Women provoke rape by their appearance or behavior	2.7

[a] 1 = agree strongly; 2 = agree; 3 = disagree; 4 = disagree strongly.

Table 7 Sexual Motivation for Rape

Statement	Average assessment[a]
19 Rape is the expression of an uncontrollable desire for sex	2.9
20 Rape is a sex crime	2.2
22 Rapists are sexually frustrated	2.4
24 The reason most rapists commit rape is for sex	3.0

[a] 1 = agree strongly; 2 = agree; 3 = disagree; 4 = disagree strongly.

Table 8 Normality of Rapists

Statement	Average assessment[a]
3 Rapists are "normal" men	3.2
5 All rapists are mentally sick	2.5

[a] 1 = agree strongly; 2 = agree; 3 = disagree; 4 = disagree strongly.

of the statements was associated with more than one factor. As seen in Table 7, the first factor in this set, "sexual motivation for rape", clearly relates to sex as the primary motivation for rape. The responses indicate confusion over the sexual aspect of rape. Many do not agree that rape is an "uncontrollable desire for sex" and that "most rapists commit rape for sex", yet most agree that rape is a "sex crime" and that "rapists are sexually frustrated". The second factor in this set, "normality of rapists", determines the reason for rape in terms of the underlying mental state of the rapists. Table 8 reveals that while the officers do not believe that rapists are "normal", they also do not presume rapists are mentally ill.

The final factor in this set, "masculinity as a motivation for rape," reveals that officers do not consider rape as an opportunity for rapists to show their manhood, although they do believe rape is an exercise in power over women. The two items for this factor are listed in Table 9.

Overall, the rapist factor set, which especially examines beliefs about the rapist's motivations for the crime, reveals that officers do not believe rapists are mentally ill, i.e., not legally responsible for their acts. However, they don't believe them to be "normal" either. The respondents may be saying that they believe rape is outside the normal behavior of men — but, importantly, does not usually tip into the realm of mental illness.

The other two factors in the set ("masculinity" and "sexual motivation") indicate ambivalence on the part of the officers. On the "masculinity" factor,

Table 9   Masculinity as a Motivation for Rape

Statement	Average assessment[a]
12 Rape provides the opportunity for many rapists to show their manhood	2.8
21 Rape is a male exercise in power over women	2.2

[a] 1 = agree strongly; 2 = agree; 3 = disagree; 4 = disagree strongly.

Table 10   Punishment

Statement	Average assessment[a]
8 A man who has committed rape should be given at least 30 years in prison	2.3
26 A convicted rapist should be castrated	2.5
30 Judges are too lenient on convicted rapists	1.8
39 The laws concerning rape are too lenient	2.0

[a] 1 = agree strongly; 2 = agree; 3 = disagree; 4 = disagree strongly.

respondents indicated that rape is an exercise in power over women, but rejected the contention that it is an opportunity for the rapist to show his manhood. Perhaps the male respondents were unable to correlate rape with the assertion of manhood because such an action would be foreign to them personally.

In the "sexual motivation" factor, respondents were in doubt as to whether or not rape is a sexual crime. Their confusion is not surprising since experts in sexual assault have only within the recent past recognized the nonsexual motivational factors underlying rape. The authors are of the opinion that respondents' confusion in this area is caused by the fact that sexual assault typically uses sexual parts of the body to express nonsexual motivation.

Trial. The final factor set deals with the judicial process. The three factors in this set are "punishment", "victim's influence in trial", and "prosecution". No item is associated with more than one factor.

The first factor, "punishment", examines the degree of retribution that should be dealt a convicted rapist. Table 10 indicates that officers believe a rapist should be treated with severity. Such a response is hardly surprising. Past studies have long confirmed that law enforcement officers adhere rather closely to traditional values and desire punishment for those who violate these values (see, for example, Balch, 1972). The respondents' evaluation of judicial sentencing (item 30) parallels their belief that punishment should be severe.

The second factor in the prosecution set, "victims' influence in trial", consists of two items. Both, as may be seen in Table 11, examine beliefs about how the victim personally may influence a trial. Officers believe the victim's history, age, and appearance influence the outcome of the trial.

Table 11 Victim's Influence in Trial

Statement	Average assessment[a]
35 The victim's history often affects the case	2.1
37 The victim's age or appearance influences the jury	1.9

[a] 1 = agree strongly; 2 = agree; 3 = disagree; 4 = disagree strongly.

Table 12 Prosecution

Statement	Average assessment[a]
32 Prosecutors are not properly prepared for court	2.3
33 The public is uneducated concerning rape	1.9
34 The victim often fails to testify	2.1

[a] 1 = agree strongly; 2 = agree; 3 = disagree; 4 = disagree strongly.

The final factor in this set is somewhat difficult to label. Recognizing the trial experience of their respondents, the authors entitled this factor "prosecution". As seen in Table 12, the officers believe that in practice neither prosecutors, the public (potential jurors), nor the victims are prepared for the rape trial. "Prosecution", as a label for this factor, would not be as appropriate for persons outside of law enforcement because the public would believe the items in this factor describe a "normal" or "fair" trial, whereas experienced officers realize this is not necessarily true.

The trial factor set demonstrates that officers agree rape is a serious crime that deserves severe punishment. The strong influence of the victim at a court hearing is clearly seen in this factor set. More importantly, the officers believe that the public, who will ultimately make up the jury at a rape trial, and the prosecutors who will try the case are not adequately prepared to play their roles in court. Finally, the respondents believe when a conviction is obtained, judges are too lenient in the sentences they give to rapists.

Rape Investigators. The authors thought it important to single out and examine specifically the responses of those officers who are currently investigating rape cases. Approximately 31% of the total respondents stated that they investigate rape cases; only 3.8%, however, said they were assigned to a specialized squad in rape investigations. The data in Table 13 describe the responses of the 31% currently involved in rape investigations.

Descriptive Data. The "typical" rape investigator is a married, 34-year-old, white, male patrol officer who has attended college, been in law enforcement for 5 years, and has investigated fewer than ten rape cases. Of course, this description is based on the appropriate average responses and is not meant to be taken as a literal description. See Table 13 for a complete breakdown by age, sex, race, law enforcement experience, rank, number of cases investigated, marital status, and education.

Table 13   Descriptive Data — Rape Investigators

	Percentage[a]
Age	
21–30	32.9
31–40	47.0
41–50	15.7
51 or more	4.4
Sex	
Female	8.4
Male	91.6
Race	
American Indian	0.9
Black	3.5
Hispanic	3.5
Oriental	0.2
White	91.9
Other	0.2
Law enforcement experience (years)	
Less than 2	17.1
2–5	35.8
6–10	27.3
11–15	2.8
More than 15	7.2
Rank	
Deputy sheriff	10.1
Patrol officer	46.1
Corporal/sergeant	12.9
Lieutenant	2.9
Detective	21.6
Captain or above	4.2
Other	2.1
Number of cases investigated	
10 or fewer	54.1
11–50	33.0
51–100	7.2
More than 100	5.7
Marital status	
Single	10.2
Married	77.6
Separated	1.8
Divorced	9.8
Spouse deceased	0.6
Education	
High school or less	30.9
1 Year of college or less	10.9
More than 1 year of college but no bachelor's degree	32.4
Bachelor's degree	16.9
Graduate work or degree	9.0

[a] All totals do not equal 100% because of rounding error.

Table 14   Type and Amount of Training

	Percentage[a]
Sexual assault training (h)	
None	4.5
1 to <10	36.7
10 to <20	27.5
20 to <40	12.9
40 or more	18.3
Rape victimology training (h)	
None	22.0
1 to <10	56.3
10 to <20	12.7
20 to <40	5.3
40 or more	3.8

[a] Totals do not equal 100% because of rounding error.

Training.   One of the primary goals of the study was to examine the type and amount of training rape investigators had received. The authors were looking particularly for two major types of training: sexual assault training and rape victimology training. One could justifiably argue that other types of training could be important to rape investigators (e.g., human sexuality), but to restrict the length of the questionnaire, the authors focused only on the two areas. They asked about the recency and amount of training the officer had received prior to working on a rape case.

Table 14 shows that the overwhelming majority (95.5%) of rape investigators had received at least a few hours of training in sexual assault. A smaller but healthy percentage (88%) had received some training in rape victimology. The question- naire was worded in such a way that rape victimology training could have been concurrent with sexual assault training. Though the vast majority of the officers had received training, relatively few had 40 or more hours of training in sexual assault (18.3%) or rape victimology (3.8%). Only 4.5% had received absolutely no training on sexual assault. This statistic is gratifying and confirms that law enforce- ment recognizes the importance of such investigations. On the other hand, 22% had received no victimology training, a statistic that suggests a need for further educational efforts since the emotional trauma suffered by the victim can affect her ability to relate facts about the assault and to assist in the prosecution of the offender.

Table 15 sets forth the length of time since the officers last received training in the specified areas. Of those trained, approximately one half (52.1%) had attended courses within the past 2 years. The table also contains data on the amount of training the officers had received prior to first investigating a rape case. One fifth of the officers (20.4%) had received no training prior to their first rape investigation. Few (5.6%) had received more than 20 hr of training; most (63.8%) had received less than 20 hr of training.

Table 15   Time Factor of Investigative Training

	Percentage
Sexual assault training received	
Less than 2 years ago	50.0
2 to <6 years ago	36.6
6 to < 10 years ago	9.9
10 or more years ago	3.5
Rape victimology training received	
Less than 2 years ago	52.1
2 to <6 years ago	37.6
6 to <10 years ago	8.0
10 or more years ago	2.3
Prior training received	
None	20.4
1 to <6 h	41.8
6 to <11 h	22.1
11 to <20 h	10.1
20 or more hours	5.6

Summary

Ever since rape became an issue in this country, the public has believed that law enforcement officers deal with victims in a hostile and suspicious manner. Several studies have, in fact, suggested that officers do have unsympathetic attitudes. These studies, however, used such extremely small population samples that their conclusions could in no way be extrapolated to include law enforcement generally.

The authors of this chapter, therefore, conducted a national study of 2170 county and municipal law enforcement officers to examine their attitudes concerning rape. Using logic and statistical techniques, the authors divided the responses of the officers into categories dealing with the victim, the rapist, and the trial.

Analysis of the resulting data revealed that officers are not typically insensitive to the plight of rape victims. They are, however, suspicious of victims who meet certain criteria, such as previous and willing sex with the assailant, or who "provoke" rape through their appearance or behavior. Further, there is a small subset of officers who agree strongly with inappropriate statements such as "nice women do not get raped" or "most charges of rape are unfounded". These officers clearly have a prejudiced attitude toward the rape victim. To involve such officers in rape investigations would be a disservice to the victim and, ultimately, to the agency and the public. Responsibility rests with the supervisor to ensure that professional officers are assigned to sexual assault cases.

The respondents' attitudes toward the rapist were ambivalent. While the officers saw rape as an exercise in power, they did not see rape as an opportunity to demonstrate manhood. Also, the officers as a group were confused as to whether or not rape is a sex crime. These attitudes, when linked with their attitudes toward the victim, indicate a need for increased training of officers in the area of rape investigation and victimology.

Although some of the early studies held that police did not view rape as a "real" crime, the results of this study show that most officers view rape as a serious crime that deserves severe punishment. The study also reveals that law enforcement officers believe prosecutors, victims, and potential jurors are not properly prepared to play their assigned roles in a jury trial.

One of the most encouraging aspects of the study concerned the impact of training. The overwhelming majority of rape investigators had received sexual assault and/or victimology training. The fact that most training occurred relatively recently might explain the difference between the historical picture of police attitudes toward rape and the attitudes expressed in this study. Most importantly, however, the law enforcement community continues to provide education and training in matters pertaining to sexual assault. As a consequence, the authors expect that investigative capabilities will continue to improve, and that a more educated public will increasingly assist the law enforcement community.

References

Balch, R. W., The police personality: fact or fiction?, *J. Crim. Law Criminol. Police Sci.*, 63, 106, 1972.

Blumberg, A. S. and Niederhoffer, A., Eds., The police in social and historical perspective, in *The Ambivalent Force: Perspectives on the Police*, Rinehart Press, San Francisco, 1973.

Brownmiller, S., *Against Our Will*, Simon & Schuster, New York, 1975, 352.

Chronister, J. L., Gansneder, B. M., LeDoux, J. C., and Tully, E. J., A Study of Factors Influencing the Continuing Education of Law Enforcement Officers, U.S. Department of Justice, Washington, D.C., 1982.

Feild, H. S., Attitudes toward rape: a comparative analysis of police, rapists, crisis counselors, and citizens, *J. Pers. Soc. Psychol.*, 36, 156, 1978.

Feldman-Summers, S. and Palmer, G. C., Rape as viewed by judges, prosecutors, and police officers, *Crim. Justice Behav.*, 7, 19, 1980.

Galton, E. R., Police processing of rape complaints: a case history, *Am. J. Crim. Law*, 4, 15, 1975.

Gottesman, S. T., Police attitudes towards rape before and after a training program, *J. Psychiatr. Nursing Ment. Health Serv.*, 15, 1977.

Greer, G., Seduction is a four-letter word, in *Rape Victimology*, Schultz, L. G., Ed., Charles C. Thomas, Springfield, IL, 1975, 382.

Hurst C. L., *The Trouble with Rape*, Nelson-Hall, Chicago, 1977, 116.

LeDoux, J. C. and Hazelwood, R. R., Police attitudes toward rape, *J. Police Sci. Adm.*, 1985.

President's Commission on Law Enforcement and Administration of Justice (PCLEAJ), U.S. Government Printing Office, Washington, D.C., 1967, 23.

The Victim's Perspective

3

ANN WOLBERT BURGESS
ROBERT R. HAZELWOOD

Victims confront endless new situations as they wind their way through the criminal justice system. The police are often the first on the scene; it is to them, the first course of protection, that the victim first turns. They should be mindful that, in fulfilling their obligations to solve the crime and apprehend the criminal, they must also treat victims with the attention due them. The manner in which police officers treat a victim affects not only an immediate and long-term ability to deal with the event, but also willingness to assist in a prosecution. This chapter describes the emotional aftermath of rape and is intended to describe the stress response of rape trauma syndrome in order that the police officer and prosecutor are aware of the basic response pattern many victims experience and to which is added the effects of trial preparation.

Rape Trauma Syndrome

> It's been three years and I still won't get in an elevator alone or go out alone unless it is very necessary. When I enter my apartment I don't dead bolt it till I get my knife out and check everywhere — under the bed, in the shower, in the closets. Then I deadbolt the door. I do this two or three times a night. I don't enjoy walking anymore. I never had these problems before I was raped... I'm scared I will be like this forever.
>
> Rape Victim

In 1974 Burgess and Holmstrom published a study of reported cases of rape and sexual assault in which 146 victims were interviewed at the emergency ward of a hospital and followed up 4 to 6 years later in regard to the problems they experienced as a result of being attacked. The term *rape trauma syndrome* was used to describe an acute phase and long-term reorganization process that occurred as a result of forcible rape or attempted forcible rape. The syndrome of behavioral, somatic, and psychological reactions was deemed an acute stress reaction to a life-threatening situation.

The above quote by a rape victim captures some of the distressing and repetitive symptoms that a victim continues to experience long after the rape. The symptoms of this victim highlight the fears and phobias that have developed and the terror that she may not recover.

The Acute Phase: Disorganization

Immediate Impact Reaction

A prevailing myth about rape victims is that they are hysterical and tearful follow-ing a rape. On the contrary, victims in the Boston study described and indicated an extremely wide range of emotions in the hours immediately following the rape. The physical and emotional impact of the incident may be so intense that the victim feels shock and disbelief. As one victim said, "I did some strange things after he left such as biting my arm... to prove I could feel... that I was real".

The emotional demeanor of the victim noted during the initial interview may be one of two types: *expressive* or *guarded*.

In the expressive style, the interviewer will be able to observe either on the face or through the body language the feelings the victim is experiencing. Fear, anger, and anxiety can be visually noted by the expression of the victim. Victims will express these feelings during the interview by becoming tense when certain ques-tions are asked, or crying or sobbing when describing specific acts of the assailant. Interviewers should be aware that some victims may smile when certain state-ments are made. Such a reaction is not uncommon and denotes anxiety, not amusement, on the victim's part. Practically everyone associated with the identi-fication, arrest, and prosecution of the rapist is reassured if the victim exhibits the "expressed" demeanor initially. However, this is not always the case and should not be expected.

In the guarded style, the victim's feelings will not be observed directly. The victim may appear very composed and able to calmly discuss the rape. The feelings are controlled, masked, or hidden. The composed victim is not lying, but rather is able to control her true feelings, is in a state of shock, or is physically exhausted. Silence does not usually mean the victim is hiding facts, but rather that she is having trouble talking and thinking about the assault. This victim typically talks in a calm or subdued manner.

The interviewer may note a change between the expressed and guarded style and it may be related to time, place, and length of interview. For example, one victim who was expressive during the initial interview which took place at the hospital was very guarded the next day when the police officer came to talk to her at work. In her employment as office manager, the victim was aware that her employees noted the policeman's presence and the fact that she did not wish to tell them of the rape. Thus, her demeanor was significantly different. The police officer had not telephoned before coming and later the victim refused to proceed with charges. In another case, a victim who was guarded during an initial interview later became less anxious when talked to in her home and was able to offer additional information to the police. It is clear that interviewers can influence the amount of cooperation provided by the victim in proportion to the respect that is shown the victim for privacy and communication.

Physical Reactions to Rape Trauma

Rape is forced sexual violence against a person. Therefore, it is not surprising that victims describe a wide gamut of physical reactions in the days following the assault. Many will describe a general feeling of soreness all over their bodies. Others will specify the body area that has been the focus of the assailant's force such as the face, jaw, throat, chest, arms, or legs. In the case of a 29-year-old woman who was attacked in bed by a 16-year-old male who hit her on the hand and head with a heavy lamp before the rape, the victim later reported the following:

> At the hospital I had 19 stitches in the back of my head and my hand was so swollen I couldn't move it for a week. I had bad eye problems — lines zagging in my vision. For months I had headaches and even now, when I'm under stress, a headache starts and I think back to the rape.

Sleep pattern disturbances. Victims have difficulty sleeping in the months following the rape. They complain that they cannot fall asleep or, if they do, they wake up during the night and cannot go back to sleep. Victims who have been attacked while sleeping in their own beds may awake each evening at that time again. It is not uncommon for victims to cry or scream out in their sleep, with or without nightmares.

Eating pattern disturbances. The victim's eating pattern may be affected. Some victims report a marked decrease in appetite and complain of stomach pains or nausea. Some victims will report an increase in eating and weight gain; however, the eating is often a coping response to stress rather than a genuine appetite increase.

Physical Symptoms

Victims also report physical symptoms specific to the area of the body which was a focus of attack. Throat and neck symptoms may be reported by victims who have been strangled or forced to have oral sex. Victims forced to have vaginal sex may complain of vaginal discharge, a burning sensation on urination, and generalized pain. Those forced to have anal sex may report rectal bleeding and pain in the days immediately following the rape.

Emotional Reactions

Prevailing stereotypes of rape are that the main reactions of victims are to feel ashamed and guilty after being raped. To the contrary, one of the primary feelings reported by victims is that of fear — fear of physical injury, mutilation, and death. It is this main feeling of fear that explains why victims develop the range of symptoms called the rape trauma syndrome. Their symptoms are an acute stress reaction to the threat of being killed. Most victims feel they had a close encounter with death and are lucky to be alive.

Victims express other feelings in conjunction with the feeling of fear of dying. These feelings range from humiliation, degradation, guilt, shame, and embarrassment to self-blame, anger, and revenge. Because of the wide range of feelings experienced during the immediate phase, victims are prone to experience mood swings. The following quote is from a 31-year-old singer who was attacked shortly after entering her apartment by an intruder.

> I moved immediately from the apartment. I was unable to return to work. I felt I was being watched and followed. My panic was unbelievable. I could not sleep at night and had to catnap during the day. I hugged the walls walking down the street. I could not concentrate, would break out crying for no reason. I threw out every reminder of the rape — my bed, mattress, sheets, pillows, and clothes. I became a hermit and stayed in and stared at the television set for months.

Many victims will realize their feelings are out of proportion to the situation they are in. They will report feeling angry with someone and later realize the anger was unfounded in the situation. Women become quite upset over their behavior which, in turn, produces more stress for them.

One young woman reported feeling constantly on the verge of tears. In a situation involving her child, one mother reported her distress over noting that she was disciplining her children more severely than before the rape.

Victims also report feeling irritated with people during the first few weeks when their symptoms are acute. Victims are very sensitive to the reactions of people when they learn of the rape. Perceived lack of concern as well as insensitive remarks will devastate a victim who already feels on an emotional roller coaster. As one professional woman said, "My supervisor told me to take time off but not to come back till I had my feelings about this under control".

Thoughts

The continual stream of thoughts relating to the rape haunt many victims. Victims usually try to block the thoughts of the assault from their mind. However the thoughts — called intrusive imagery — continue to break through into consciousness ("It's the first thing I think of when I wake in the morning"). Day images are common ("Something will trigger in my head and it all comes back"). The victim may feel as though the traumatic event was recurring ("I panicked at work when two people came into the store and acted suspicious").

There is a strong desire for victims to try and think of how they might have escaped from the assailant or how the situation might have been handled differently. Generally, the outcome of such thinking is that they would have been beaten or killed if they had not complied with the assailant's demands.

Victims vary as to the amount of time they remain in the acute phase. The immediate symptoms may last a few days to a few weeks, and more often than not, overlap with the symptoms of the long-term recovery process.

The Long Term Process: Reorganization

> I feel embarrassed that I have not gotten over the rape... it has been 3 years and my self-confidence is still shattered. I find it unacceptable in me that an event of 10 minutes could so interfere with my entire life
>
> **48-year-old rape victim**

A rape represents a disruption of the victim's lifestyle, not only during the immediate days and weeks following the incident, but well beyond that to many weeks,
months, and years. On the surface the victim will often appear to function well,
resuming work and family/social activities. The well-hidden psychological scars
may be undetected except when someone takes the time to really listen to the path
of reorganization.

Various factors seem to influence how the victims reorganize their lives such
as personality style, people available for support, and the way they are treated by
people who learn of the rape. This section identifies four lifestyle areas most
vulnerable to disruption following rape: physical, psychological, social, and sexual.

Physical Lifestyle

As previously discussed, immediately following rape, victims report many physical
symptoms related to musculoskeletal pain, genitourinary difficulties, gastrointes-
tinal upset, general distress, as well as eating and sleeping pattern disruption. The
health areas victims have most difficulty with over a long period include (1) body
areas where injury caused interference to functioning, i.e., broken bones, lacerations, or organ trauma; and (2) gynecological and menstrual functioning. Victims
with the latter problems report chronic vaginal problems and changes in menstrual cycle functioning.

Psychological Lifestyle

Dreams and nightmares are major symptoms with the rape victim and occur
during both the acute phase and long-term process. The 48-year-old victim quoted
earlier reported three dreams that recurred frequently during the third year of the
reorganization process. First, she reported waking up suddenly and feeling that
someone is in the room. Her fear, in response to such a dream, is that the assailant
will come back to kill her. Second, in a dream she is walking down a hallway and
a stranger grabs her. She wakes up with the same feeling she experienced when the
assailant grabbed her while she was jogging. Third, she dreams that she is being
drowned in a boat. This dream triggers her memory of the location where the rape
occurred — along a jogging path by a river.

Dreams may be of three types: (1) replication of the state of victimization and
helplessness ("I use my mace and it turns to water"); (2) symbolic dreams which
include a theme from the rape ("I am grabbed from behind and raped"); and (3)
mastery dreams in which the victim is powerful in assuming control ("I took the
knife and stabbed him over and over"). Nonmastery dreams dominate until the
victim has recovered.

Phobias. A common psychological defense seen in rape victims is the development of fears and phobias. Fears are a normal and a protective device used by
people to warn them of danger. A phobia may become maladaptive if it prevents
a person from acting in a situation. Victims described fears and phobias to a wide
variety of circumstances: fear of indoors if the rape occurred indoors; fear of

outdoors if the rape occurred outside the home; fear of being alone ("I just can't stand it if no one else is home"); fear of elevators or stairs or people behind them ("I won't go in some buildings because I am terrified of elevators and stairwells"). There are a wide variety of activities that can trigger a flashback ("Violence on television really upsets me").

The victim may develop specific fears related to characteristics noted in the assailant such as the odor of beer on the assailant's breath. A facial feature, such as a moustache, may trigger a reaction in a victim raped by a man with a moustache. Some victims describe a very suspicious, paranoid feeling ("I felt everyone on the bus knew I was a victim").

The occurrence of a second upsetting victimizing situation following a rape can produce additional fearful feelings. One victim was involved in a car accident the day following the rape and re-experienced the fright and fear of dying.

Social Lifestyle

The rape has the potential to disrupt the victim's normal social routine. In some cases, several areas of social functioning are disrupted.

Many victims are able to resume only a minimal level of functioning even after the acute phase ends. These women go to work or school but are unable to be involved in other than business-type activities. Other victims respond to the rape by staying home, by only venturing out of the house with a friend, or by being absent from or stopping work or school.

A common response is to turn for support to family members not normally seen on a daily basis. Often this meant a trip to some other city and a brief stay with parents in their home. In most cases, the victim told the parents what had happened. Occasionally the parents were contacted for support, although the victim did not tell why she was visiting. The decision to tell or not to tell seemed to be based on how the victim predicted the parent would respond to the news ("I didn't tell mother because I knew she would be very upset and worry about me that I might be raped again").

There is often a strong need to get away ("I thought I'd go stir crazy if I didn't get out of the city"). Victims who are able to will move, sometimes to another city. Another change victims make in their lifestyle is to change their telephone number; many request an unlisted number. The victim may do this as a precautionary measure or after receiving threatening calls. Victims fear that the assailant may gain access to them by telephone. They are also hypersensitive to obscene telephone calls which may or may not be from the assailant.

The need of victims to become anonymous and to move around serves a protective purpose; it is their way of trying to gain control over a terrorizing experience. Sometimes police officers incorrectly interpret the victim's behavior as emanating from a desire not to prosecute. For victims with this need for protection, the officer should talk with the victim about ways to improve her safety environment as a strategy to ensure the victim keeps contact with the office.

Sexual Lifestyle

Many female victims report a fear of sex after the rape. The normal sexual style of the victim becomes disrupted following a rape. The rape is especially upsetting if the victim has never had any sexual experience before, in that there is no experience with which to compare it. For victims who have been sexually active, the fear increases when the boyfriend or husband confronts the woman with resuming their sexual pattern.

Partner Reactions

Rape can precipitate a crisis not only for the victim, but for family, friends, and others in her network of social relationships. Police officers and attorneys very likely will have to deal with these family members and some understanding of the impact the rape has on their lives may help to create a more cooperative victim and partner.

One crucial dimension to observe is whether male partners see the victim as a victim. In other words, who do they perceive to be the victim of the rape — the woman herself, her parents, her husband/boyfriend? Do they see her as a person in her own right who has been hurt by the assault, or do they view her more as their possession whose value has diminished? Do they see the rape as an unfortunate incident that was externally inflicted upon her, or do they see it as evidence of her bad character? Who do they blame — the assailant, the woman, or themselves? Perhaps the most crucial and typically unstated underlying issue is whether the family member sees the rape primarily as sex or primarily as violence.

The rape of a wife or girlfriend has an enormous psychological impact on her male partner. News of the violation brings forth a great surge of emotion on his part and he often experiences many conflicting feelings. The process of sorting out what the rape means to him has two major components. The first component is dealing with his feelings. In his reactions, three issues predominate: (1) perceptions and feelings about who is hurt, (2) the desire to get the guy, and (3) the "if-only" reaction. The second component is having to cope with his wife/girlfriend — a woman who now is very upset and in a state of crisis — and to cope with the impact that the event has had on their relationship. The second component also involves dealing with three main issues: (1) their discussions of the rape, (2) the woman's new phobias, and (3) the resumption of sexual relations. In addition, for those cases that go to court, the man must deal with the court process and with a wife/girlfriend who is as upset by going to court as she was by the rape itself (Holmstrom and Burgess, 1983).

Partner's Own Reactions

The first issue is who is the victim. The view that rape is an act with a victim seems to be widely accepted. Where there is a difference of opinion, however, is in regard to *who* is hurt by the rape. A traditional view would be that the woman's husband is injured because the wife's value is diminished by the rape. The violation makes her worthless or it reflects badly on him that he should have such a wife. She is stigmatized and can be blamed as well. One such husband clearly was wrestling with the issue of whether or not his wife had betrayed him by having sex with another man. Although she was quite bruised, he implied she should have resisted the assailant more:

> I can't understand her reaction at the time. I can't understand why she did what she did… I don't think the whole truth will come out even in court. But I haven't had any trouble with her with other men in 15 years of marriage, so I'll stick by her now.

Another husband said he was ashamed and blamed his wife for the incident. She was a cocktail waitress who was raped as she went to her car after work and described his response:

> I am having problems with my husband. He doesn't want me around his family. He told his mother on Sunday he was ashamed of me. He said I shouldn't have been working there, that it was my fault that I had been working there.

In still another case, the boyfriend was worried whether he would be sexually repulsed by the woman now that she had been raped. The girlfriend's account follows:

> That night as soon as we got back to the apartment he wanted to make love… He admitted he wanted to know if he could make love to me or if he would be repulsed by it and unable to.

A more modern view would be that the woman has been hurt as a human being, but that this in no way diminishes her value as a wife or reflects badly on her character or her husband. In one such case, the woman spoke as follows:

> My boyfriend has been so wonderful about it. He is the reason I got through it. His concern was for me. He was just glad to have me alive and well.

Getting the Guy

Strong feelings of wanting to "get the guy" are common among male partners. This desire to get the guy means the husband/boyfriend wants to go after the assailant himself and/or that he wants very much to pursue the assailant legally through the police and courts. Sometimes police note that the male partner urges the victim not to press charges, or harasses the officer during the investigation. In such cases, it might be helpful for the officer to talk with the man about his own feelings about the rape. Such a response may represent a more traditional view of rape where the partner feels "victimized" and wants to deny what has happened.

Because victims experience a great deal of ambivalence over reporting a rape, it is not uncommon to see the male partner take the initiative. Sometimes this unilateral decision then becomes an issue between the partners. One woman described such a situation as follows:

> As soon as we got to the hospital, he marched up to the police car that was sitting in the emergency yard and said, "Sir, my girlfriend has just been raped". (How do you feel about that?) I was furious. I didn't want to report it and to have him do it really made me mad.

Having the "if only" reaction, very often husbands and boyfriends indicate they wish they had done something differently and thus perhaps the incident would not have turned out the way it did. As one husband said, "If only I hadn't been working that night... maybe it wouldn't have happened".

Dealing with the Raped Woman

While dealing with his own emotions, the male partner must also interact with the wife or girlfriend who is herself in a state of psychological crisis. Often the partner will say, "She is different since the rape". The woman clearly needs some psychological support during this time of crisis, and most often looks to family members.

One important issue is whether the couple feels able to talk about the rape openly. The rational view is that if they can express their feelings, they will be able to identify the issues upsetting them and gain more control over these feelings. Thus, the memory of the event will not evoke the painful reaction that it once did. However, more often than not, the topic is avoided.

The second important issue is dealing with the new phobias triggered by the rape. Often this area is where the partner is most helpful; he is able to provide for her protection and safety and is willing to be more available to her.

The third major issue is resuming sexual relations. Since sex is the means that the rapist used to attack the woman, it is not surprising that she develops a phobia to resuming sex; and because of societal views regarding sex, it is not surprising that males have difficulty in resuming sexual relations with the raped partner. There can be two interpretations regarding this issue. The first interpretation concerns the maintenance of a double standard of behavior. For example, one husband who reported that although he himself had "not been an angel" all his married life, he still felt betrayed when his wife was raped (i.e., "had sex with another man").

A second interpretation focuses on mutual sexual exclusiveness expectations that couples may have — expectations that apply to both partners. One example of this involves a homosexual couple. The woman was raped by a man, and her homosexual partner with whom she had lived for three years was very upset. For this couple, each partner was very jealous over any outside relationships that the other partner might have. Further support for this interpretation is found in the case of a *male* victim in which the husband was raped homosexually, and the wife's reaction was to blame him. She questioned why he was out, why a big man like himself could not fend off an assailant. His "unfaithfulness" during the rape was an issue for her.

Many couples have difficulty resuming normal sexual relations. The main problems from the woman's point of view are her (1) temporary aversion to physical contact, (2) experience of flashbacks of the rape, (3) physical discomfort during sex, (4) changes in physical response to sexual stimulation, and (5) worry over her partner's reaction.

Dealing with Court

Court is as upsetting to the woman as the original rape. While testifying in court the victim mentally relives the rape. Also, court has its own set of pressures; there is the embarrassing public setting, the confrontation with the offender, and the difficult cross-examination by the defense lawyer. The victim generally finds the courtroom to be very stressful, and psychologically it often returns her to a state of crisis. The husband/boyfriend has this added stressful event in which to support his partner.

Counseling Implications

Law enforcement officers are often the first professionals with whom the victim interacts after the crime. It is critical to both the well-being of the victim and to the criminal investigation that she be able to successfully resolve the emotional turmoil being experienced.

An emotionally healthy victim will be better able to help the police in investigating the crime; for that reason, officers should be aware of the value of counseling in such matters.

An understanding of the disruptive capacities of a rape attack requires a brief discussion of the concept of homeostatic balance and the relationship of coping behaviors to stable psychological functioning. The principle of homeostasis is that there needs to be a stable balance within the body in order to manage effectively in the world. When these psychological balances are upset, self-regulatory mechanisms (i.e., coping behaviors) are triggered to help to return these balances to healthy levels for the individual. Crisis theory is based on this principle applied to psychological functioning.

For each person there exists a reasonably consistent balance between the way we think and the way we feel. Although this homeostatic balance varies from person to person, the primary characteristic of this balance is its stability for that individual, a stability that is "normal". However, everyday experiences disrupt this balance, and negative and uncomfortable feelings can arise. These experiences may be termed emotionally hazardous situations. Such events give rise to stress and motivate the person to bring into play coping behaviors that help to re-establish the balance. When the person experiences an emotionally hazardous situation and is unable to effectively use previously learned coping behaviors, an emotional crisis may ensue. In rape, a crisis usually develops because the event is so traumatic, unexpected, and uncontrolled and the person is unable to cope effectively.

Rape, a criminal victimization, poses a situational crisis. The victim was unprepared for the hazardous event, feels out of control, and is unable to cope.

Crisis intervention is clearly the treatment of choice when a rape is disclosed immediately after it has occurred. The rationale for this type of treatment includes: (1) the rape represents a crisis in that the victim's style of life is disrupted; (2) the victim is regarded as "normal" or functioning adequately prior to the external stressor; (3) crisis intervention aims to return the victim to his or her previous level of functioning as quickly as possible. The crisis intervention strategy is to provide or mobilize support for the victim during the acute phase of disruption. The speed of intervention is crucial. Other crisis services to offer the victim include advocacy services, especially regarding legal matters, work with victim's support system, and victim mutual support groups.

Compounded Reaction to Rape

Victims of rape may describe a past or current difficulty with a psychiatric condition, a physical condition, or behavior pattern which creates difficulty for them living in society. These victims are often known to other therapists, physicians, or agencies. These victims need more than crisis counseling, because under the stress of the rape the victim becomes vulnerable to earlier difficulties. For example, the victim may develop increased physical problems or increased drinking or drug use, become suicidal, or exhibit psychotic behavior. A careful study of the victim's background will help determine if the previous therapist or physician needs to be identified for referral; the referral suggestion is made to the victim.

Silent Reaction to Rape

It seems to be a fairly well-accepted statement made by police and law officials that there are many victims of rape who do not report the assault; this information alerted clinicians to a syndrome called *silent reaction to rape*. This syndrome occurs in the victim who has not reported the rape to anyone, who has not dealt with feelings and reactions to the incident, and who, because of this silence, has further burdened her- or himself psychologically. When this situation is defined, the referral should be for victim therapy.

Police Response to the Rape Victim

Victims of rape are often first seen by a police officer who responds to a call for help. The treatment that a victim receives at this point will influence his or her recovery process. Except for homicide, rape is the most serious violation of a person's body; it deprives the victim of both physical and emotional privacy and autonomy. The victim's response to rape primarily reflects her reaction to violation of self; it is an emotional as well as a physical assault. The officer must remember that the victim is being asked to discuss with a stranger the details of probably the most traumatic and personal experience of her life.

Police officers generally see victims and their families immediately after the crime, when they are most in need of help. The officer's response to these persons often has a major effect on how swiftly and how well the victim recovers.

Police officers who respond quickly after a report is made, who listen attentively, and who show concern for the victim's plight will greatly reassure the victim and help him or her overcome a sense of fear and helplessness. Rape victims who comment favorably on their initial contact with a police officer seem to feel more comfortable with police officers who project both personal concern and professional objectivity. Steps in the initial phase of the police interview include the following.

Introduction

The initial interaction with the victim, the introduction, is the most critical phase of the interview process. Depending on the victim's perception of the interview, she will or will not feel comfortable and confident in the ability of the police to help her. The officer should introduce him/herself in a professional, confident, and sincere manner using the victim's last name preceded by Ms., Miss, Mrs., or Mr. The interviewer(s) should accomplish three important tasks during this phase: express regrets that the victim was assaulted (do not use the term "rape") and assure her that she is the *victim* of a crime that was not her fault; assure her of her safety and that everything possible and reasonable will be done to maintain that safety; and convince her of the competence and experience of the interviewers.

An example scenario might proceed as follows:

> Good evening, Ms. Roberts. I am Bob Jackson of the Sexual Assault Unit and I would like to discuss the crime which occurred, if you are feeling up to it at this time. I want you to know how deeply I regret your being the victim of such an assault, and that I and the other members of the department will do our best on your behalf. Other officers have completely checked your residence (where the assault occurred) and have secured it. I've arranged for our patrols to increase their travel through your neighborhood and I will also give you an emergency police number before I leave. I've been an investigating officer for nine years and am experienced in these matters, so please don't hesitate to ask questions during our time together.

The officer(s) should explain that the interview will be as brief as possible and that while the questions will necessarily be personal, their importance cannot be overemphasized and will aid greatly in identifying the offender.

The Interview

The officer(s) would be well advised to remember that the process involved is an interview and not an interrogation. The victim has agreed to be interviewed and this strongly suggests that she wants to cooperate and has faith in the abilities of law enforcement. Consequently, it is recommended that the following guidelines be followed during the interview phase:

1. Involve the victim in the interview process. Explain the procedures which have taken place and which will occur. Give her a phone number which she can call to get information about the investigation's progress, or advise her that you will periodically call to keep her informed. Ask for her opinions throughout the interview.

2. Allow the victim as much control as possible. Ask how she would like to be addressed, e.g., Ms. Jones. Do not use her first name without her permission; do not presume that right. Ask if the interview environment is agreeable to her or if she would be more comfortable elsewhere. Ask if she would prefer to describe the crime in her own words or if she would rather have you ask questions. Determine if she wants anyone else to be called.

3. Listen and respond to her wishes and requests if at all possible.

4. Pay attention to what she is saying and be alert to expressions of (1) guilt ("I shouldn't have gone to the market so late"), (2) fear ("He said he would know if I called the police"), (3) humiliation ("I didn't want to do that"), and (4) unnecessary attempts to convince ("I know this sounds strange, but it really did happen" or "I tried/wanted to stop him"). Upon hearing such phrases, the officer(s) should reassure the victim: (1) "You have a right to travel as you wish without becoming a victim", (2) "You're safe now inside your home", (3) "You had no choice in the matter", (4) "It doesn't sound strange and I'm sure it happened" or "You're not expected or required to become injured or killed".

5. Balance questions having to do with humiliating acts or sexual aspects with ones relating to the victim's feelings. For example, if the victim had been asked about the occurrence of ejaculation (never ask if she "climaxed"), it should be balanced by a question such as "Do you feel safe now?" or "May I get you something to drink?" or "Would you like to stop for a while?".

6. Begin by using professional terminology. One can always lower the level of terms, but it is very difficult, if not impossible, to raise the level of terminology. An example would be questions pertaining to forced oral sexual acts. The professional interviewer will begin by using the term "fellatio". It is quite possible that the victim may not be familiar with the term and the officer would then use "oral sex". Should the victim fail to understand at this level, the officer could ask, "Did he make you put your mouth on his penis?" To appreciate the value of such an approach, simply reverse the sequence.

7. Use language which is not judgmental or threatening to the victim. Instead of "Tell me about your rape", use "Please describe the assault". Instead of stating a bias ("What were you doing out so late?"), give the victim an opportunity to tell what happened ("Please describe what lead up to the assault"). Rather than saying, "Why didn't you fight him?", ask "Was there

any opportunity to resist?". The phrasing of the question reveals to the victim the interviewer's personal biases and feelings, and may impede the investigation.

8. Throughout the interview, it should become clear to the victim that the issues of power, control, anger, and aggression, and not sexuality, are central to the crime. Sexuality is not the salient feature of the assault. A crime of violence has occurred and the victim should understand that it is this aspect (violence) that the investigation will focus on.

9. Obtain the facts of the crime in as factual a manner as possible. The interviewer should take precautions to ensure the victim does not perceive the process as being voyeuristic in nature. It must be remembered that the victim is most likely the only witness to the crime and should she perceive the officer as being invasive, she may withhold vital information. The victim is in a stressful situation. The officer must try to decrease stress, not increase it. Dwelling on sexual activities, or rushing through them, may precipitate flashbacks to the rape experience. In other words, a very narrow area exists for the interviewer to operate within, and common sense must prevail. In general, the best information is gathered by allowing the victim to tell the story in her own words. This method will help relieve some of her emotional tension as well as allow the officer to listen carefully to what she is saying and to evaluate her mood, general reactions, and choice of words. When asking direct questions, the officer should be sure the victim understands what is being asked. It is important to talk on her level. Always give the reason for asking the question.

Concluding the Interview

Following the interview, the investigator should continue to include the victim in the process of the investigation. This approach is used to prevent the victim from feeling "used" by the system. The rapist has already conveyed such a feeling and it must not be perceived that she will be victimized by the system designed to prosecute her attacker. Therefore, it is suggested that the following information be provided to the victim:

1. Advise her of the next step in the investigative process. At this point, the victim needs to have stability in her life and to be reassured that she will not become just a statistic in some file. She is important and should be made to feel that this is recognized and that everything possible will be done to ensure justice is served.

2. As previously mentioned, she should be given a number to call or be told that she will be kept appraised of investigative progress.

3. The victim should be referred to, or preferably introduced to, supportive services which have advocacy systems designed to assist her through this emotionally traumatic time.

4. Ask whether the victim has any questions, and ensure that she fully understands what will happen in the future and her role in those events.
5. Thank the victim! Express your appreciation for the time she has taken to help in the investigation. The victim should leave feeling safe, guiltless, and confident about what will be accomplished as a result of her cooperation.

In conclusion, the investigator should be aware that initial descriptions and interviews are likely to be colored by the trauma and crisis nature of the assault. Follow-up interviews with the victim are likely to reveal more details as the victim calms down and tries to resume her life. The investigator should be aware that the victim, in trying to return to a normal life, may want to forget the assault ever occurred, and subsequently forget who the investigator is or refuse to talk to him or her. The victim should be alerted to the fact that she may want to forget the assault ever happened, but that submerging the memory will not make it go away. Instead, it will reappear in nightmares, phobias, and other symptoms. She needs somebody to talk with until the memory can finally fade naturally.

Special Issue — Fresh Complaint

The issue of "fresh complaint" is a legitimate concern of the criminal justice system and arises quite often in matters involving sexual assault. It has been well noted that the victim may choose not to divulge the crime to anyone, including law enforcement; or, in other situations, she delays reporting it for hours, days, or even longer.

The issue really involves looking at the process of reporting a rape, and to understand such a process means looking not only at the victim herself, but at her social network and at the community. A striking finding in the sociological study of rape victims by Holmstrom and Burgess was the degree to which people other than the victim were involved in the chain of events leading her to the police. In more than half of the 92 adult rape victims, someone other than the victim was involved in reporting the rape to the police; someone other than the victim made the decision to contact the police, acted as intermediary at the request of the victim, or persuaded the victim herself to call.

The hesitation of many victims and the tendency for family and friends to discuss whether to report the rape can be discouraging and sometimes bewildering to police. In many ways there is a similar feeling among health professionals as to why patients do not report their symptoms earlier and seek medical attention. However, police cannot do their work unless the rape is reported. They also know that any delay "looks bad" in court. Some members of the criminal justice system even label victims "collaborators" when they do not immediately report the crime.

Socially and psychologically, however, the need of many victims to seek out others for support or for advice makes sense. Rape victims typically experience rape as an attack that threatens their very lives, and as a result, they are in a state of psychological crisis. They have experienced an overwhelming danger that they could neither escape nor solve with their customary psychological resources. People in crisis typically have difficulty making any decisions at all. It is thus understandable that victims should turn to others. It may be added that some victims of rape also are physically incapable of making any decision at all. The assailant may have beaten them so badly or so terrified them regarding reporting that their faculties are not completely available to them — a fact not always appreciated by professionals.

The officer needs to understand the wide range of behaviors that can occur related to reporting a rape. Rather than project a reason onto the victim for why she delayed, it is a better strategy to ask the victim to describe how she was finally able to make the decision to report, implying that the decision must have been a difficult one for her and to acknowledge this process rather than judging it.

Summary

This chapter outlines the rape trauma syndrome as a two-phased process of physical, psychological, and social symptoms experienced by individuals following attempted or completed forcible rape. There are immediate impact reactions as well as acute and long-term symptoms. Partner reactions include his own reactions, getting the assailant, dealing with his raped partner, and court. Counseling implications are discussed as well as the police officer's response to the rape victim.

References

Burgess, A. W. and Holstrom, L. L., Rape trauma syndrome, *J. Am. Psychiatry*, 131, 981-986, 1974.

Holstrom, L. L. and Burgess, A. W., *The Victim of Rape: Institutional Reactions,* Transaction Books, New Brunswick, NJ, 1983.

II

INVESTIGATION OF RAPE

Concepts of Physical Evidence in Sexual Assault Investigations

4

DALE M. MOREAU
P. DAVID BIGBEE

This and the next chapter focus on various aspects of physical evidence in sexual assault cases. The prominent forms of evidence that have established reliability in science and the courtroom are usually available in these investigations. In the past few years new techniques, such as DNA analysis, have increased the arsenal of scientific evidence used in court, particularly in sexual assault cases. Once the possible evidence is recovered, a lengthy and complicated process is set in motion. The "silent witness" potential of physical evidence can be affected by many persons, including the responding officers, investigators, crime scene search technicians, prosecutors, medical personnel, and forensic laboratory examiners. Evidence integrity is the responsibility of all those coming in contact with the physical evidence at each progressive stage of the investigation.

This chapter and the next do not discuss physical evidence from the viewpoint of the forensic laboratory analyst; instead, attention is given to the philosophy of evidence utilization, as well as the effective recognition, collection, packaging, and preservation of the types of evidence normally of value in sexual assault cases. The information and recommendations in these chapters are confined to the more salient aspects of the crime scene, suspect, and living victim.

The two chapters on physical evidence should be read in sequence because, for example, the discussion of sexual assault evidence collection kits in Chapter 4 sets forth the types of evidence collection choices often included in them, while Chapter 5 covers specific details and mechanics associated with the actual recovery of the evidence.

Introduction

The very mention of the words "forensic science" conjures up images of scientific instruments, exotic techniques, and sophisticated crime laboratories. Most often, physical evidence located at a crime scene is thought to depend on analysis in a laboratory for it to be useful in court. The scientific examination of evidence in a laboratory setting, however, is but one of a series of interrelated tasks that make it possible to use physical evidence toward legal proof of a crime in the courtroom. The admissibility and relevance of tangible evidence can be affected by persons

0-8493-8152-1/95/$0.00+$.50
© 1995 by CRC Press, Inc.

who may know very little about conducting a forensic examination. Consider, for example, the role of the first responding officer to a crime. This person may lack the training or knowledge required to deal properly with physical evidence. Evidence can be unnecessarily moved, touched, contaminated, or destroyed by improper actions by the first respondent or any subsequent person who comes on the scene.

All facets of physical evidence must be given appropriate attention to ensure effective courtroom use. This evidence is often called a "silent witness", offering objective facts regarding the crime. This statement presupposes the organized and detailed handling of evidence materials from the start of the crime scene search to the presentation of the evidence in the courtroom. Unless this entire process is efficient and uncontaminated, the weight of the evidence material is, and should be, subject to serious question.

The contemporary view of forensic science must be expanded to encompass a broad range of functions, disciplines, and techniques. If investigators feel uncomfortable with the intricate nature of dealing with the various forms of physical evidence, they may be reluctant even to collect and submit certain kinds of physical evidence to a crime laboratory. Often the investigators tend to rely solely on nonforensic information derived from participants or witnesses. Forensic laboratory examinations may not be used to their fullest potential because the investigators do not understand the value of certain types of scientific evidence and how that evidence can support or contradict the testimony of participants or witnesses.

Often, the location of such evidence as latent prints is emphasized to the exclusion of other items, such as small or minute samples of hairs, blood, saliva, fibers, and soil. In many instances, the officer on the scene may have little or no knowledge of the correct methods of locating, recovering, packaging, and preserving evidence specimens. The problem is compounded when the investigator is not adequately supported by funding and does not have access to a crime laboratory.

Certain areas of forensic disciplines, such as DNA profiling, are in their infancy, and yet DNA has had a major impact on the conduct of criminal investigations and litigations. It is an established fact that evidence is often present after contact between a victim and a suspect. Accordingly, there is an increasing awareness of its prominence in the legal determination of guilt or innocence. Court decisions regarding the rights of defendants have made it incumbent on the law enforcement community to constantly improve its ability to make use of physical evidence in court.

Many significant questions raised in the courtroom due to conflicting or confusing statements by witnesses are answered by the use of tangible items collected as possible evidence. As evidence admissibility is established in prominent trials where physical evidence is the key, the tendency for attorneys virtually to insist on its use will increase. Attorneys are certain to become more knowledgeable about potential challenges to the integrity of items of evidence. Skillful legal challenges to the admissibility of evidence will likely focus to a greater extent on chain of custody considerations. Seemingly fundamental evidence procedures are often neglected or carried out incorrectly, and these problems can surface during the trial. Especially when extremely powerful new forensic techniques such as DNA profiling are used, attorneys will attack the chain of custody, quality control of the laboratory, and just about every other aspect of the physical evidence to prevent a jury from hearing and seeing the results.

It is figuratively, and sometimes literally, a long way from the actual scene of a crime to a modern crime laboratory. There is often a marked tendency to evaluate physical evidence only from the standpoint of technologically advanced forensic tests. One must remember that a crime laboratory cannot properly examine items that were improperly handled, nor can a forensic scientist examine evidence that was not recognized and collected during an investigation.

The Nature of Physical Evidence

Although physical evidence can represent an impartial source of facts, these facts do not appear mystically; information derived from evidence is the result of laborious work beginning at the crime scene. Articles gathered at the scene will be of no value unless efforts are made to interpret them. Many kinds of physical evidence are subject to collection and laboratory analysis, and it can be an overwhelming task to study the appropriate procedures for each. Therefore, it is advantageous to establish basic points that permit the investigators, attorneys, and other involved persons to categorize evidence and the factors that have a bearing on its value in court. This categorization can also enable a jury to systematically organize, understand, and interpret the evidence introduced during a trial.

The techniques of forensic science and laboratory examinations are becoming more complex. On one hand, science is able to give greater forensic insight. On the other hand, the increasingly complex nature of scientific techniques makes it more difficult for the lay person to understand the facts. The attorney must not only present physical evidence in the trial, but make its pertinence in the case clear and unmistakable. Much greater attention should be given to courtroom presentation of information designed to familiarize a jury with the basic nature of physical evidence. This educational approach can help the jury understand the central issues addressed by evidence. Incriminating evidence may be presented in a trial, but if the presentation is confusing or unconvincing to the jury, it fails to accomplish the attorney's objective.

The major concepts usually applicable to evidence in sexual assault cases are

1. Evidence identification
2. Class characteristic evidence
3. Individual characteristic evidence
4. Evidence transfer
5. Evidence environment
6. Evidence contamination

Evidence Identification

The term "identification" as related to the scientific meaning of the many forms of physical evidence is routinely used in forensic science. There are various levels of what actually constitutes forensic identification. Each discipline of forensic science attaches a distinct meaning to this concept, depending on the type, amount, condition, and source of the evidence in question.

One type of identification is of a single object or substance. In these cases laboratory results identify the evidence based on its physical and/or chemical properties. For example, a forensic chemist can state that a suspected drug substance has been identified as heroin because it conforms to scientifically established and reliable data related to heroin.

In some identifications, it can be determined that two or more separate articles were once joined together to form a single object. These identifications, called fracture matches, are positive and unequivocal from the forensic standpoint. Illustrations of this category would be physically matching the edges of pieces of torn paper or the broken ends of two pieces of wood.

Many identifications are based on the premise that certain objects leave unique imprints or markings when in contact with other objects. A prime example would be latent fingerprints on glass which can be positively identified with the dermal ridges of a suspect. Another classic illustration would be a shoe print at a crime scene that can be identified by unique wear characteristics on the sole of a suspect's shoe.

Many identifications involve the comparison of two or more items of evidence to establish that these items may come from the same source. Even though they may constitute a strong association scientifically, however, a conclusive statement of unequivocal identification cannot be made. A comparison of hair discovered on the victim's clothing with known hair samples obtained from the suspect is an example.

Official reports of crime laboratory analyses are often written in the form of a summary. Words such as *association, correspondence, consistent with,* and *clarification,* which appear in these reports, may not be fully understood by the investigator or attorney. Such wording is usually a product of the synthesis of all raw data developed in the course of the laboratory examination. For this reason, the laboratory examiner should be contacted for a precise explanation of the full ramifications of forensic analyses whenever questions arise as to the interpretation of a report.

On occasion, physical evidence may fall into a category of identification which is not readily understood, or is debatable among the scientific and legal communities. An example of this is DNA analysis. "DNA fingerprinting" is a term erroneously used in the U.S. judicial system. First, it implies that the DNA is a fingerprint, which it is not, and second, it implies that it is, in fact, positive identification. The debate with new technology centers on the fact that no two people on earth have exactly the same DNA except for identical twins. However, when a laboratory examiner reports or testifies to the results of DNA analysis, he or she will give only the probability of finding two individuals with the same DNA pattern in the population at random. This probability can be very high, such as 1 in 7, or extremely low, such as 1 in 10 billion. These numbers come from how frequently the patterns are seen in the data bases compiled by laboratories around the world. Most research and forensic scientists believe that when enough data are collected worldwide to unequivocally show that, indeed, no two people have the same DNA, the courts will recognize that fact and give the weight of the DNA match the same credence as that of a true fingerprint match. Until that time, the results of DNA analysis will continue to be considered consistent with a subject or to absolutely eliminate one.

A well-recognized approach to distinguishing among varieties of physical evidence is to separate it into two categories: class characteristic evidence and individual characteristic evidence. This scheme is relatively simple and applies to virtually any type of physical evidence.

Class Characteristic Evidence

Class characteristic evidence is that which cannot be forensically identified with a specific source to the exclusion of all others. Examples include hairs, fibers, blood, saliva, semen, soil, glass, and minute wood particles. Forensic science has no current methods to positively associate such items with a single or unique source. Here, forensic examination of evidence is directed at giving as much information as possible about each feature exhibited by each item, and about many different types of this evidence in combination. The more material of different types can be associated with a suspect, and because these are considered independent events, the stronger the association becomes in the minds of the jurors. Class evidence can be presented in such a manner that there is almost a direct inference of positive, or negative, association of the suspect with the victim, particularly when a preponderance of evidence exists. For example, as mentioned previously, an expert witness may testify that the DNA profile from semen found in the vaginal vault of the victim matches a blood sample from the suspect and the chances of finding someone in the population at random with the same DNA profile is 1 in 300 million. Another expert witness may testify that a pubic hair from the suspect matches in all characteristics one taken from the victim. These two together are very damaging testimony to the defendant, even though they are both class characteristic evidence.

There are inherent problems with the effective use of class characteristic evidence. The major difficulties appear to be caused by the following incorrect notions:

1. The types of evidence in this category do not provide positive identification of a person, in contrast to an identification provided by latent prints, and are, therefore, not worth collecting. Many persons involved in crime scene searches believe the time spent looking for class evidence could be better directed at searching for latent prints.
2. Collection and handling of very small evidence are too difficult to accomplish at a crime scene or too awkward to carry out with a victim or suspect. Some persons feel that because they cannot see certain evidence with the naked eye, it cannot be present.
3. Typical class evidence (especially hairs and fibers) is so common that, even with the best forensic techniques, it is of limited value in the courtroom.

4. The courtroom introduction of only class evidence may actually have a negative impact. For the most part, this is a result of the belief that any detailed scientific testimony will very likely confuse a lay-person jury.
5. There are many forensic laboratories that do not routinely provide examinations of certain forms of class characteristic evidence.

These and other misconceptions should not be used as reasons simply to ignore the presence, or use, of class characteristic evidence. Many recent advances in forensic science have been made regarding this kind of evidence. Perhaps the best reason to pursue class evidence is that it is often the only pertinent physical evidence found at a crime scene. Many sexual assault cases are totally devoid of individual evidence such as latent fingerprints, but almost always semen, hairs, fibers, and other class characteristic evidence are found. To not pursue it would be gross injustice to the victim(s).

Individual Characteristic Evidence

The other category of physical evidence has individualizing characteristics. This category covers any evidence that can be positively identified with a specific source to the exclusion of all others. Of all possibilities in this category, latent prints of dermal ridge skin are probably the most frequently sought after in evidence recovery.

Individual characteristic evidence is usually less common than the class type. The investigator or attorney who relies solely on evidence that has the potential to be definitely associated with a singular source is hindered from the outset.

Often an item of evidence collected in an investigation has the potential to furnish information on both class and individual levels. An illustration of this possibility would be a section of cloth ripped from the suspect's shirt by the victim during a rape. Because of the transitory nature of debris-type evidence that may be on the cloth and shirt, the laboratory would first remove any debris present. A subsequent laboratory comparison of the shirt with the torn cloth could result in positive determination that the cloth was once part of the shirt. However, if the torn edges of the cloth were frayed or worn, the laboratory might not be able to positively match the cloth with the shirt.

The next step would be to compare the composition, color, design, and construction of the torn section of cloth. Such a comparison might result in a determination that the torn cloth corresponded in these features with the shirt and, therefore, could have originated from it.

A further examination of individual characteristic evidence reveals two basic subdivisions:

1. Associations that identify a specific "person" as a source
2. Associations that identify a specific "thing" as a source

Identification of a person as the immediate source of a piece of evidence is usually the most desirable situation. Placing a suspect at a crime scene by means of a latent print recovered as evidence allows for an unequivocal statement that the person was at the scene at some time. Naturally, this evidence is diminished if the suspect had frequent and normal access to the scene of the crime. Conversely, the weight of the evidence is enhanced if it can be shown that the suspect had no reason or occasion to enter the scene area before the crime, or has denied ever being at the scene. Any type of positive association of evidence should be supported by corroborating investigation, whenever possible, no matter how straightforward the forensic aspects of the evidence appear to be.

The next chapter will discuss specific kinds of physical evidence. Here it is noted only that there are three primary methods routinely used in forensic science to establish beyond doubt that a particular person is the only source of evidence: latent prints, bite marks (forensic odontology comparisons), and handwriting/hand printing. Considering the multitude of specimens that conceivably could be recovered in a case, it is apparent that the avenues for conclusively identifying a person as a source of individual characteristic evidence are relatively few.

Evidence Transfer

The basic premise behind the use of most evidence as an element of proof is that a person often leaves something at a crime scene and takes something from it. This arose from a basic principle of forensic science known as the "transfer theory of Locard". In violent crimes, this leads to the intensive search for very small pieces of evidence, generically referred to as "trace evidence". This term covers almost every possibility from fibers to small deposits of blood and semen and saliva. The very fact that this evidence is so varied and so often difficult to see with the naked eye should be considered an asset. The person committing a crime of violence may think to wipe away latent prints or completely destroy a weapon; it is unlikely, however, that this person would even consider the minute trace evidence substances that could be transferred to the victim, his/her clothing, or surroundings.

A reasonable idea of the actions and events of a crime can be revealed by the transfer of evidence from one person or place to another. This is best seen by considering the kinds of evidence found in transfer situations. Two such situations are significant: direct and indirect transfer (also commonly referred to as primary and secondary transfer).

When a transfer of trace evidence is considered, an investigator's initial thought is usually of direct transfer. Physical evidence in this instance is a direct result of the contact between suspect, victim, and the crime scene area. Fibers from the victim's clothes may readily transfer to the suspect's clothing, and vice versa, depending on the type of clothing. The suspect may be cut and leave a small bloodstain on the carpet in the scene. In these examples, the transfer of evidence is an immediate result of the contact between the participants and/or the crime scene.

The evaluation for transfer items should not stop at this point. One should consider that evidence can be carried away from the scene of victim/suspect confrontation to other locations. Among other kinds of physical evidence, fibers, hairs, and soil from a scene can be transferred to the suspect's person or clothing and then deposited in a vehicle; the vehicle will then have received the resulting evidence indirectly from the scene and/or victim. This process is referred to as indirect transfer. The distinction between modes of transfer is important due to the necessity of expanding the search for small physical evidence away from the immediate crime scene. The collection of such indirectly transferred evidence will help in gaining insight as to the movement and actions of the persons involved in a crime. It should be noted, however, that indirect transfer of evidence is much less likely to happen than the direct transfer of evidence.

Evidence transferred in the course of a crime is ultimately deposited in a specific location, depending on the physical actions of persons before, during, and after the crime. Whether transfer takes place between persons, between objects, or between persons and things, trace evidence can serve to corroborate other information in a case. The interrelationship between evidence recovery procedures and forensic examination in placing items of evidence in a specific place is a critical one. For example, if a suspect was kneeling on a carpet while vigorously assaulting the victim, it would be logical to assume that the majority of transfer evidence (carpet fibers) would be on the knees and lower legs of his trousers and shoes. The trousers and shoes would have to be handled, from time of recovery to the conducting of a crime laboratory examination, in a manner that would protect the fibers and leave them in place. This may seem a minor point, but it can become a major issue in a trial when an attorney attempts to use such physical evidence to support the victim's testimony regarding the suspect's presence and actions.

Evidence Environment

The concept of evidence environment can be useful in increasing the preponderance of trace evidence. The term "environment" is used here to mean that any given area has a combination of different types and kinds of materials. The mingling of these materials can result in identifiable combinations, which can represent a relatively unique condition. When a person enters a particular environment, there can be a transfer of combinations of many separate materials, which together could serve as evidence. The amount and variety of items transferred from the environment to the person depend primarily on the number and types of materials present, the person's actions and movements, and the time span of contact.

The practical value of this approach can be seen in the following hypothetical situation. Fabric articles in a bedroom, such as bedding, throw rugs, curtains, or chair coverings, may be composed of many different fiber types and colors. Furthermore, different types and colors of fibers may appear in each article, such as a blanket having a cotton, polyester, and acetate fiber composition. A suspect entering the room to commit a rape may pick up these fiber variations on his person or clothing. Through forensic examinations, foreign fibers discovered on the suspect's clothing can be shown to correspond to the varied nature of the scene environment. Thus, a strong association can be made connecting the suspect with the bedroom.

To use the environment concept effectively, a structured foundation must be established to depict the meaning of the evidence in a given investigation. Major points that should be incorporated in order to reach this goal are

1. Due to the transitory nature of the kinds of physical evidence usually involved, the transferred evidence tends to reflect the nature of the last environment contacted by a person or object.
2. The meaning of the evidence is greatly enhanced by the presence of any materials that can be shown to be peculiar or relatively unique. Conversely, if the evidence is extremely common, less weight, if any, may be attached to it. For example, fibers from a shirt manufactured in limited quantity and using a unique one-time dye will mean more than a cotton fiber from a commonly manufactured pair of underwear.
3. It is advantageous to demonstrate that multiple types of evidence have been associated between an environment and the object or person in question. Also, it should be emphasized that the places from which these materials were recovered as evidence coincide with the known actions and movement of persons or objects associated with the crime.
4. The greater the number of transfers of trace evidence, the more strongly the association is inferred between an environment and person or object. This point is of special importance when the types of evidence are limited. For example, it would be more meaningful to find numerous hairs on the victim's clothing from more than one body area that correspond to those of the suspect than it would be to locate one such hair from only one body area. The sheer quantity of transferred evidence is suggestive of the nature of the struggle that took place.

Effective use of the environment concept is often limited or even nonexistent. There are many possible reasons for this. Two that predominate are

1. Crime scenes are often searched primarily for evidence that appears to be foreign to the scene itself. "Known" articles that existed in an area prior to and during the time of the crime are not sampled. In terms of the previous bedroom example, this would mean that known fiber samples were not taken from the carpet, bedspread, chairs, and other appropriate items. The fiber evidence from the room on the suspect's clothing would have no probative value without a direct forensic comparison with the fiber content of the scene environment.
2. Transfer evidence is often introduced in the courtroom in a disjointed and piecemeal fashion without any planned and organized attempt to demonstrate interrelationships. This circumstance can result in an inability to portray the evidence in a way that would lead to the conclusion that the victim and the suspect once shared a common environment.

Evidence Contamination

The two most important aspects of a crime scene are to protect and preserve the crime scene. In view of this, one of the prime responsibilities in processing evidence, whether in the field or in the crime laboratory, is to avoid contaminating it. Physical evidence is frequently subjected to various contaminating influences from environmental or natural sources long before it is discovered in an investigation. When the evidence is discovered, attention should be given to halting or limiting further contamination. Another major area of concern is inadvertent contamination as a direct result of improper handling or packing of the evidence. The four main categories of inadvertent contamination are

1. Nature of the evidence environment
2. Field personnel
3. Packaging materials
4. Laboratory environment

Physical evidence may exist in any environment, from a crime scene in an apartment to the physical person of a victim or suspect. Some environments have so much inherent potential to contaminate evidence that personnel have to be exceedingly cautious in the most routine collection and movement of the evidence. For example, when a suspect and a victim both have bled in the immediate area of a crime scene, it would be easy to contaminate an item bearing the victim's blood with some of the suspect's blood. Also, an environment containing numerous fabric items may make it difficult to keep extraneous fibers from contaminating items that did not actually come into contact as a result of the crime. Personnel should be fully aware of the potential of a given evidence environment to provide contamination of this sort. The best way to control such contamination is to conduct a preliminary survey of the environment for the purpose of identifying potential contamination hazards. A thorough evaluation of the evidence-gathering conditions peculiar to the given case will help devise a strategy to avoid difficulties.

The very presence of law enforcement personnel in an evidence environment tends to promote the possibility of contamination. On a practical level, someone has to be present to assess and collect the evidence. The number of people having these duties should be kept to a minimum so that organization will be maintained and contamination minimized. Further, field personnel who collect physical evidence should be cognizant of the fact that they can increase the potential for contamination through excessive handling of the evidence.

When an item is to be recovered, it should be marked for identification and placed in an appropriate labeled container. The container should be sealed at the scene and not opened until the evidence is subjected to analysis in the crime laboratory.

The evidence should not be placed in one package or container, transported, and then removed for separate packaging and marking in a different location. Not only would this procedure increase chances of contamination, but it would also make it virtually impossible to state with certainty that trace evidence came from a particular item to the exclusion of all others in that package. This often becomes a major point at trial.

There is little in forensic literature regarding the clothing worn by law enforcement personnel in evidence recovery circumstances, but the type of their clothing and its fiber composition can influence or contribute to the level of contamination. Clothes not only can add extraneous materials to the evidence environment, but may also collect foreign materials.

Even the specific fiber composition of garments worn by search personnel is important for consideration. Suppose, for example, that blue polyester fibers are found on the skin of a victim during an evidence examination and, subsequently, the clothing of a suspect, including a blue shirt, is obtained via a search warrant. Forensic laboratory comparison then determines that the shirt could have been the source of the blue fibers recovered from the victim's body. A logical question that could be asked of persons who were near the victim at the scene might be, "What were you wearing at the time of the crime scene investigation?". This question suggests that fibers on the victim may have originated from the clothing of police. This simple argument could be expanded to include other very transitory forms of evidence materials such as hairs. Also, it could be quite persuasive to a jury, whose members may not understand the realities that make evidence searches and recoveries difficult.

Personnel can take steps to avoid this problem by wearing clothing that does not easily shed or collect foreign materials. They might also wear the same type of clothing, thereby limiting the types of fibers that might be transferred. Jumpsuits or similar coverall garments having a tight weave pattern are some of the choices to be considered. The emphasis here is that the fiber content of the clothing worn by evidence recovery personnel would be known in case it became a point of contention. An ancillary advantage is that such detailed thinking about potential contamination promotes an awareness of personal responsibility for its control.

Evidence containers are key items in the recovery process and should be viewed as tools designed to protect the evidence in its original and uncontaminated form. Many packaging materials can be used for the different types of physical evidence. Whatever the choice, packaging materials should be treated in the same manner as the evidence itself. Packaging can be contaminated with foreign debris before it is used to store the evidence. Thus, it would be incomplete to discuss extreme care in the collection of physical evidence without considering contamination due to packaging.

There are several potential sources of contamination with regard to containers and packaging which can be divided into the following major categories:

1. The packaging medium creates an unfavorable environment for preservation. Airtight containers commonly used to pack biological fluids (e.g., blood, saliva, semen) often foster the growth of microorganisms that can degrade the specimens. The evidence may be drastically affected before forensic tests are even started in the crime laboratory.

2. The packaging medium itself contains substances that can act as contaminants. For example, if empty, open containers or bags are kept in the trunk of a vehicle, debris may accumulate on them. This can be avoided if any items used to package the evidence are kept clean and stored in a sealed and uncontaminated manner. Another potential source of contamination has to do with the manufacturing of the packing material. Of particular concern is the use of paper bags or wrapping paper for evidence collection. Many previously unused paper bags and rolls of wrapping paper contain small pieces of paper, fibrous debris, and other possible contaminants.

Physical evidence can also be contaminated in the crime laboratory, although the controlled environment usually greatly minimizes or eliminates this. Attempts of the crime laboratory personnel to keep evidence uncontaminated can be supported if the evidence is packaged correctly by field personnel. Proper packaging will allow laboratory personnel to keep evidence separated for storage and examination.

Field personnel who routinely forward evidence to the crime laboratory should discuss the aspects of recovery, preservation, packaging, documentation, and transmittal with appropriate laboratory examiners. Laboratories have varying requirements and suggestions which can help the field investigator avoid contamination and realize the potential offered by the evidence. Laboratory examiners and field investigators who fail to communicate with each other are making their work more difficult and less effective.

In summary, there are three significant and unfortunate consequences of contamination:

1. Evidence contamination is misleading to an investigation. Foreign materials not actually associated with the crime under investigation can lead personnel on wild chases for information. This results in wasted manpower and time.
2. Evidence contamination results in an inability on the part of the crime laboratory to evaluate the true meaning of forensic results. The crime laboratory may get misleading results and make confusing associations.
3. The confusion created by contamination offers an opportunity for the real evidence issues to become obscured in the courtroom. The credibility of evidence-handling personnel and procedures can then be seriously challenged, making the task of using the evidence effectively much more difficult.

General Considerations Relating to the Victim, Suspect, and Crime Scene

The recovery of physical evidence in a sexual assault investigation is only the initial stage of the overall evidence collection process. In order to analyze the complex nature of this task, it is relevant to keep in mind four points during the discussions which follow:

1. Major sources that provide evidence
2. Kinds of evidence that one can expect to recover
3. Routine procedures necessary to obtain evidence and ensure its integrity and chain of custody
4. Specialized techniques that can enhance the chance of discovering evidence that is present in small amounts or is difficult to detect

The victim, suspect, and crime scene — primary sources of evidence in sexual assault cases — normally come to the attention of law enforcement at varying points in time after the crime. These three sources require that systematically planned guidelines and methods for evidence recovery be established and followed.

The Victim

The protection of possible evidence should be initiated as soon as the victim contacts medical or law enforcement personnel. Frequently, the first such contact is by telephone. The victim should be counseled, whenever possible, to make no attempts to clean, bathe, change clothing, or take other action that may destroy or contaminate any evidence present. If the immediate crime scene is in the control of the victim, suggestions should be offered to protect that location. All medical, counseling, and law enforcement personnel must be made aware of this responsibility. These preliminary steps in evidence protection may make the difference between success and failure in bringing a case to a logical conclusion. Additionally, certain forms of evidence present immediately after the assault, such as semen and pubic hair, tend to corroborate the sexual contact indicative of the crime. Such evidence can often be lost to the investigator through actions of the victim.

A patrol officer often has the first personal contact with a victim after the crime. The actions required of the officer to preserve the area and the evidence present in it make this person a major participant in the evidence process. Because caring for the well-being of the victim is the initial and dominant concern, the officer sometimes tends to neglect the need to secure the crime scene and preserve the integrity of the evidence. Evidence potential of the crime scene can be deemphasized during the rapidly occurring events at the outset of the investigation.

The authors have personally discussed these problems with police officers from throughout the U.S. who attend classes at the FBI Academy in Quantico, VA, and these discussions revealed difficulties in the evidence collection process when the victim is first contacted. The ones that are indicated most often and appear to cross agency boundaries are

1. Most patrol officers have inadequate training in the areas of evidence handling and dealing with the psychology of a person who has been mentally and physically abused in an assault.
2. Rarely does a patrol officer ask the victim for information regarding possible items of physical evidence and their location at the scene.

3. It is common for patrol officers to be sympathetic to the victim who is obviously traumatized by the rape. They sometimes permit such victims to wash or change clothes before being taken to a medical facility for examination. In several cases discussed, condoms worn by the suspect were thrown into the toilet which was subsequently flushed after the victim was allowed to use it. These condoms, which were lost, often held the only seminal fluids present at the scene.

4. Some patrol officers do not regard physical evidence handling as within their sphere of responsibility. As a matter of formal or informal policy, many agencies discourage these officers from becoming involved in the evidence process.

It is not appropriate to regard the patrol officer as an uninvolved party in relationship to physical evidence. Certainly, it is not recommended that the officer embark on a major search for evidence, but the first officer does have an opportunity to take basic steps to protect the scene and the evidence it contains.

The initial contact with the victim often requires that a decision be made about the victim's clothing. In some agencies, the victim is requested to undress before being transported for the medical examination. If this is done, the victim must undress over a clean, previously unused, section of white cloth or piece of wrapping paper supplied by the officer. Otherwise, evidence may become dislodged from the clothing as garments are removed. The cloth or paper is then marked to identify which side faced the victim, and then folded to retain any evidence. The proper containers for each article should be readily available when the victim undresses. The ideal field investigation setting in which to use this approach would be when the victim is in no need of immediate medical attention and is in a controlled environment, such as a home.

Sometimes during field investigation, items of potential value as evidence might be seen on the clothing of the victim before this person undresses. If the items are barely clinging to the clothing or person of the victim, they may be dislodged and lost when the clothing is removed. Therefore, when evidence such as hairs, tufts of fibers, yarns, etc. is seen, a recovery effort should be made. Photographs may be taken and a rough sketch made to document the relative positioning of the items on the victim. The materials should be removed, immediately packaged, and the appropriate chain-of-custody data recorded. The person who takes the evidence from the victim should wear surgical gloves so that any contaminating substance on his or her hands or fingers will not come into contact with the evidence. This is particularly important when a type of DNA analysis called PCR is to be used. The DNA from the skin of the person collecting the evidence (e.g., saliva or semen stains) will contaminate the DNA from the suspect.

Careful consideration should also be given to the handling of the victim's clothing when the victim is at the hospital or other medical examination facility. Photographs should be taken of the victim before the removal of clothing, if possible. These pictures can be used to supplement later photographs that will depict specific injuries and possible evidence observed during the examination.

Again, it is advisable to have the victim undress over a section of cloth or wrapping paper so that evidence that falls away as the clothes are removed is not lost. Each item of clothing removed from the victim should be placed immediately in a separate evidence container which is then securely sealed.

The victim's clothing is sometimes cut away in the hospital due to the life-endangering nature of wounds sustained during the crime. These items normally end up in a disheveled pile as they are discarded from the treatment area. The realities involved in caring for the victim give hospital personnel or law enforcement officers no ideal alternatives here. Steps should be taken in such situations to recover, package, and seal the evidence as soon as practical. Whenever possible, the table on which the victim was treated as well as the area immediately underneath the pile of garments should be studied for dislodged items. The fact that the clothing was cut from the victim by hospital personnel must be documented. Assailants in sexual assaults sometimes remove the clothing of the victim by cutting it off; the damage to the clothing by each party may become an important issue during trial.

The field or hospital recovery of materials directly from the clothing should be confined to situations in which evidence would otherwise be lost. An unsystematic examination of the clothing accomplished on a routine basis will probably destroy, lose, or contaminate more evidence than it obtains. It is better for the evidence to be acquired directly from the clothing during a complete forensic laboratory examination.

At some point toward the beginning of the investigation, the victim is examined in a medical facility. Medical personnel who come into contact with this victim are trained primarily in evaluating his/her physical health and emotional needs. However, there is a need to expand this education into the evidentiary realm. Many law enforcement agencies have established liaison and training programs regarding physical evidence collection for hospital personnel. As a direct result of these programs, the use of preassembled sexual assault evidence collection kits has increased. Such kits are designed to collect certain forms of physical evidence directly from the body of the victim. These types of evidence are those that can corroborate sexual activity itself (e.g., semen present in the vaginal area) as well as serve to associate a suspect with the victim. The makeup of the kits and the philosophy behind their use will be discussed later in this chapter.

The victim of a sexual assault is usually released from the hospital when his/her physical and emotional condition permits. In cases where the crime was committed in the victim's home, he/she must be reminded to leave the scene of the assault intact, should he/she return there before the evidence technicians arrive.

The physical evidence recovered from victims in sexual assault cases is of paramount importance. The ideal or perfect evidence-gathering situation is very difficult to attain. Nonetheless, all activity should be directed at coming as close as possible to the ideal in recovery of physical evidence. The victim should be considered the focal point of the crime. This frame of mind will automatically lead to effective handling of the evidence, because the search of the victim is then considered, in essence, as a detailed crime scene search.

The above discussion has focused on a living victim. In the event of a sexual assault/homicide, different methods of collection and preservation of evidence are obviously used; however, the evidence is essentially the same. Loose hairs, fibers, etc. must still be recovered before the body is moved, and care taken to preserve any that may fall away. Body bags should always be treated as evidence and sent to the forensic laboratory for processing.

The Suspect

One of the primary goals of physical evidence collection is to link the suspect and the victim to each other, and the suspect and/or victim to the crime scene. There can be a number of problems inherent in actually doing so. While the victim is normally examined for possible evidence as soon as practical, the suspect may not be identified for some time. This time span permits the suspect to destroy clothing, shower or bathe, or thoroughly clean out a vehicle used in the crime. The longer it takes for a suspect to be developed, the greater the potential for evidence loss. Once again, attention is directed to the fact that minute evidence of the type commonly encountered in sexual assault cases tends to be advantageous to law enforcement. Very large items, like clothing and bedding, may be thrown away or totally destroyed, but it is very likely that some of the small debris may still remain in the general area where the larger articles were handled by the suspect. Although it is somewhat unlikely, hairs, fibers, and other small evidence also can be dislodged and transferred to the new clothing of the suspect. This possibility of indirect transfer should not be excluded when one deals with a suspect.

The approach to the acquisition of evidence involving the suspect will be directly influenced by the time span problem already mentioned. There are three main situations which are normally encountered:

1. The suspect is developed immediately following the commission of the crime.
2. The suspect is developed as a direct result of having sustained injuries which warrant medical treatment.
3. The suspect is developed a lengthy time after the assault.

The ideal situation, of course, is for the suspect to be identified immediately after the crime. The evidence on the clothing of the suspect most closely resembles the evidence represented by the victim, the victim's clothing, and the crime scene at this point. Often, the clothing worn during the assault can be obtained without any destruction of evidence. Also, the suspect's body should be scrutinized for possible evidence materials that might be indicative of contact with the victim. The chance of discovering significant evidence items is at its highest level; it is at this stage that the evidence acquired can be so overwhelming that the guilty party eventually confesses to the crime.

Sometimes, a suspect is physically injured during the assault and may need medical attention, which leads to identification of the suspect by authorities. Records of the pretreatment extent of injuries and the nature of treatment undertaken, and acquisition of clothing and biological samples (e.g., blood, hairs, saliva), are necessary from the physical evidence viewpoint. Photographs should be taken whenever possible while the suspect is in the medical setting, as an integral part of the documentation procedure. These photographs can be vivid representations of the truth, which will assist the jury in overcoming possibly conflicting data during a trial. Photographs are the investigator's best opportunity to corroborate the victim's statement about the nature of injury to the suspect.

Often, the suspect is not developed until long after the crime is committed. Many evidence materials on the suspect or in the immediate environment have been completely eliminated by deliberate cleaning or as a result of the time span involved. Even so, very small pieces of physical evidence may linger on clothing or in vehicles for a lengthy period of time, and a diligent search may locate significant evidence. The investigator commits an error when the assumption is made that evidence could not be present, or would have no meaning in court, due to the time lapse since the crime occurred. At the very least, appropriate known samples should be obtained from the suspect and a search conducted for clothing matching that described by the victim.

Another factor often overlooked by investigators is the presence of disease states in the suspect. If a sexual assault victim with no previous history of disease is infected by the subject, this can be incriminating evidence at the time of trial. Attempts should be made to determine the disease state of all subjects in sexual assault cases. This may not be such an easy task. Depending on state or local medical confidentiality laws, the suspect may or may not be required to reveal this information.

No matter which of these time spans is involved, physical evidence should be collected from a suspect. Investigators sometimes fail to institute necessary steps to seek out physical evidence when the suspect "confesses" to the crime. This is based on the premise that the confession alone is enough to result in a guilty plea or courtroom conviction. This is a high-risk assumption, considering the manner in which the courts have dealt with the legal admissibility of confessions. If the suspect retracts the statement of guilt and no physical evidence has been collected, serious tactical problems will be encountered by the prosecution from the preliminary hearing to the actual trial. Physical evidence is needed to corroborate or dispute verbal statements by the parties involved. In today's courtroom arguments, actions not taken by investigators regarding physical evidence can be of greater discussion and pertinence than those that were taken.

Sexual Assault Evidence Collection Kits

The role of physical evidence in sexual assault crimes is not only to associate the victim and suspect with one another, but also to establish that sexual contact has in fact occurred. The search for physical evidence in this regard is extended from the crime scene itself to the medical examination of the victim and/or suspect. The necessity of establishing a connection between victim and suspect, and the sexual aspects of the criminal act, require that the victim, and suspect whenever possible, be suitably examined for the presence of physical evidence. It should be kept in mind that virtually *all* forensic examinations of evidence are accomplished by comparisons. For example, in many sexual assault cases, before a suspect is located, the investigating agency sends a known blood sample from the victim along with seminal stains to the crime laboratory for DNA analysis. The purpose of the victim's blood sample is to eliminate his/her DNA type from being the same as the suspect. The DNA analysis of the seminal stain from the suspect is absolutely meaningless to the investigator unless a blood sample from the suspect is provided for comparison purposes. The same comparison principle applies to hair samples.

In some instances, the victim first becomes known to law enforcement authorities as a result of hospital treatment for injuries suffered in the assault. It is at this point that the benefits of planning and liaison between law enforcement and the medical community can be realized.

If medical personnel have been properly advised and educated in the evidentiary aspects and medical features of treating a victim, the task of using evidence in the courtroom will be greatly facilitated. On the other hand, improperly trained medical personnel can so impair the physical evidence that the suspect cannot be brought to trial. Successfully recovering physical evidence in sexual assault cases must be a combined effort of law enforcement and medical personnel. Medical personnel include emergency responders such as medical technicians and paramedics who may transport the victim to the hospital.

The direct involvement of police officers in the evidence recovery process in the medical environment differs considerably depending on such factors as locale, funding, personnel availability, and training. In some areas, a law enforcement representative will be present for the entire course of the examination or at least during the collection of evidence. This situation facilitates maintenance of chain of custody and can decrease the number of witnesses necessary to introduce the evidence in the courtroom. There is the added advantage that any questions about the evidence from the medical personnel can be answered immediately.

In many jurisdictions, however, law enforcement personnel have virtually no direct involvement with the medical examination of the victim. Any evidence materials obtained by medical personnel are packaged and then provided to a law enforcement representative later. The burden of providing critical testimony in court relating to the recovery of this evidence is sometimes then placed on the medical professionals. This testimony can often go beyond the realm of normal medical procedures to the establishment of chain of custody and evidence integrity.

Considering the vital role physical evidence plays in sexual assault cases, it is preferable on occasion to have a trained law enforcement officer present during the medical examination of a victim. This can be of special importance when medical personnel have not been trained and are unfamiliar with evidence recovery procedures. The officer's presence should be professional, unobtrusive, and consistent with concern for the mental and physical condition of the victim.

The presence of a law enforcement officer during the examination is an extremely controversial issue. Some law enforcement, medical, legal, and counseling personnel feel this presence is abhorrent and unnecessary. Others feel the evidentiary concerns are so important that a reasonable method of having a trained officer present is sometimes desirable. Decisions must be made about this issue before cooperative protocols are established about dealing with the victim.

Cooperation between law enforcement agencies and the medical profession concerning controlled evidence-gathering procedures is improving. One of the components of ongoing cooperative education and training programs is the preassembled evidence collection kit. The major goal of using these kits is recovery of certain physical evidence materials in strict keeping with proper medical, forensic, and legal requirements. Medical facilities having contact with a sexual assault victim are usually supplied with kits for use on short notice.

The contents of these items often are assembled by trained persons, such as crime laboratory employees. The materials supplied in the package are organized so that they are relatively easy to use in a systematic fashion, and designed to recover physical evidence substances associated with sexual assaults.

Even though the kits are designed with ease of use in mind, medical personnel involved in the contact with assault victims should be trained in their use. Their actions will often determine whether highly transitory evidence is recovered or whether it will be lost or contaminated. Therefore, law enforcement officials knowledgeable about the kits and their use should educate appropriate medical personnel in the forensic and legal procedures involved. This is the first step in building a responsible and successful evidence collection program that will survive the rigors of courtroom challenge.

Before discussing the items that can be used as components of sexual assault evidence collection kits, it is necessary to review the role of these kits in the framework of the medical examination of a victim. This examination normally involves several major areas, each having a potential impact on evidence recovery and the investigation as a whole. These areas are

1. Acquisition of a medical history of the person examined, as well as documented legal and competent permission for the examination. Discretion should be used in obtaining his or her history, and it must include information concerning the last time the victim had consensual sexual relations. It may be necessary to obtain a blood sample from his/her sexual partner for elimination as the suspect.
2. Inquiry regarding the nature of the assault itself
3. Physical examination, including identification of trauma or injury attributable to the assault
4. Evidence recovery procedures
5. Detailed chain of custody records concerning physical evidence

Preassembled evidence collection kits can be found in a variety of designs. Directions on proper use are typically included. Also, often included are forms covering (1) medical examination and interview of the victim, (2) consent/release regarding evidence obtained from the victim, (3) consent/release concerning authority to disseminate victim-related information, and (4) chain-of-custody documentation. Such documents are best formulated by joint discussion and agreement between law enforcement and medical representatives who treat rape victims.

Many physical evidence recovery methods and procedures can be incorporated into a sexual assault evidence collection kit. These methods and procedures usually depend on the age and sex of the person on whom they are used, as well as whether this person is a victim or a suspect. The following is a general description.

The reader should refer to the next chapter for the actual mechanics and precautions of evidence recovery.

Clothing — All clothing worn by the victim should be obtained and packaged in a sealed, secure condition. Each item must be packaged separately to avoid transfer of evidence from one item to another. Sections of manila-type wrapping paper or sturdy paper bags can be supplied for packaging.

Head hair combing/brushing — The head hair region of the victim is combed or brushed for evidence substances. This needs an uncontaminated comb or brush specifically for the head area only. The comb or brush and adhering materials are packaged and sealed. The combings should be done before known head hairs are obtained.

Known head hairs — An appropriate amount of hair, at least 25 full length hairs, to represent color, length, and area variation is obtained. Hairs should be pulled rather than cut whenever possible. Known hairs should be acquired after the head hair combing/brushing is completed. These hairs are packaged and sealed.

Pubic hair combing/brushing — The pubic region of the victim is combed or brushed for evidence materials. This requires an uncontaminated comb or brush specifically for the pubic area only. The comb or brush and adhering materials are packaged and sealed. The combings should be accomplished before known pubic hairs are obtained.

Known pubic hairs — An appropriate amount of hair, at least 25 full length hairs, to represent color, length, and area variation is obtained. Hairs should be pulled whenever possible. These hairs are packaged and sealed. Known hairs should be acquired after the pubic hair combing/brushing procedure is completed.

Combing/brushing of body hair regions other than head and pubic — In the event an individual is observed to have excessive body hair, a separate uncontaminated comb or brush and appropriate packaging material can be used to collect trace evidence that may be present.

Vaginal swabbings — The vaginal cavity is swabbed to detect the presence of spermatozoa and/or seminal fluid. An unstained control sample of the gathering medium is retained and packaged separately.

Oral swabbings — The oral cavity is swabbed to detect the presence of spermatozoa and/or seminal fluid. An unstained control sample of the gathering medium is retained and packaged separately.

Anal swabbings — The anal cavity is swabbed to detect the presence of spermatozoa and/or seminal fluid. An unstained control sample of the gathering medium is retained and packaged separately.

Microscope slides of smears made from vaginal, oral, and anal swabbings — Any such slides prepared for the examination of spermatozoa should be retained along with the swabs used to prepare them.

Penile swabbings — The penis is swabbed to detect the presence of blood or other evidence. An unstained control sample of the gathering medium is retained and packaged separately.

Vaginal aspirate — In addition to vaginal swabbing, aspiration of the vaginal region is accomplished by irrigation with saline solution. Spermatozoa not located through the swabbing procedure may be recovered in this manner. A separate tube or small vial into which the solution is placed should be supplied. A control sample of the irrigation fluid is retained and packaged separately.

Oral rinse — The mouth of the person examined can be rinsed in order to remove spermatozoa not collected by the swabbing procedure. The rinse is expectorated into a tube or vial. A control sample of the rinse is retained and packaged separately.

Nasal mucus sample — This type of sample is obtained by having the person being examined blow his/her nose on cloth. The mucus may contain spermatozoa that were deposited in the mouth or facial area or in the sinuses by a gagging reflex. An unstained portion of the cloth can function as a control sample.

Fingernail scrapings — Using appropriate materials, the areas underneath the fingernails are scraped for significant debris such as hairs, fibers, blood, or tissue. The gathering implement is kept. It is suggested that each hand be scraped individually and the resulting debris packaged separately.

Miscellaneous debris collection — Evidence substances not included in the previous techniques can often be observed during the examination of a person. At least two individually packaged swabs or sections of cotton cloth should be available to collect such items as blood or semen found on the skin. Several separate containers should be included to collect debris taken from the clothing or body of the individual.

Known blood — Blood is drawn into a sterile test tube for blood grouping and DNA analysis purposes. A minimum of 5 milliliters is recommended. Samples should include one tube containing no chemical preservatives or anticoagulants (red top tube) and another containing "EDTA" (purple top tube) for DNA analysis.

Known saliva — Saliva is sampled from the person to assist in the determination of secretor status if DNA analysis is not to be performed. An unstained control sample of the gathering medium is retained and packaged separately.

"Catch" paper/cloth — A section of paper or cloth on which the person can stand while undressing can be supplied. A separate piece of paper or cloth can be used to cover the examining table to collect any evidence that is dislodged during the examination.

Sheets/body bags — If the victim is transported by ambulance to the hospital, or is a homicide victim, the sheet in the ambulance or the body bag should be retained by law enforcement for trace evidence.

The foregoing general information on the possible evidence collection methods that can be included in a preassembled kit is set forth in terms of possibilities, not as an unalterable formula. The exigencies of each case, as well as the personnel and agencies involved, will dictate the contents of a potentially successful kit. There are some additional points, however, which are important regarding what is and is not assembled or used in this kit.

1. Head hair combings are sometimes not provided as components of sexual assault evidence collection kits. A great deal of minute evidence could be present in head hair, including such substances as foreign hairs, fibers, and plant material. Hairs from the suspect bearing root tissue can also be used for DNA analysis in certain circumstances. Also, only one comb is often contained in a kit for combing all body hair areas. A separate comb should be used for each area.

2. The use of oral and anal swabs is recommended on a case-by-case basis in many kits. Since some victims are extremely reluctant to report the facts in cases where oral or anal contact took place, it may be best to perform these procedures simply as a precaution.

3. The inclusion of a section of paper or cloth on which the person can stand while undressing is a critical item that is often overlooked. Evidence can be lost simply by excessive movement and handling of clothing on its removal. The examinee's physical condition following the assault may not permit this action to be taken.

4. The acquisition of questioned liquid or wet body fluids should take into account that these specimens are extremely vulnerable to bacterial attack. Such samples should be air dried, out of direct sunlight, with no heat source used, and frozen to retard deterioration. A sample of the known blood sample(s) should be removed from the tube and dried, preferably on washed cotton swatches or sterile gauze, and frozen.

5. Different procedures for collection of evidence have varying degrees of success in forensic examinations. For example, one of the authors, formerly a serology examiner in the FBI laboratory, has noted that fingernail scrapings, penile swabbings, nasal mucus samples, vaginal aspirate, and oral rinse do not usually yield pertinent evidence. This statement is not meant to imply that such procedures should not be used; it is included to emphasize that some techniques may be more routinely productive than others.

6. The sequence in which the components of a kit are used is significant. Most preassembled kits include recommendations on the order of using these components. No particular order is set forth in this discussion, because the complexities of each case will often dictate the appropriate sequence of action. The user of a kit should consider that the collection of evidence usually follows a most-transitory to least-transitory progression.

7. The medical examination of the victim or suspect often involves the recovery of specimens used to test for sexually transmitted diseases. These specimens are usually taken during the evidence collection procedures, but

will normally not be submitted to the crime laboratory. The testing of specimens for disease is conducted by an appropriate medical lab. As an additional health and safety precaution, the crime laboratory should be notified immediately if disease is detected or suspected.

Sexual assault evidence collection kits are primarily designed for evidence recovery from a female victim who has been raped by a male assailant. Nonetheless, the typical kit contains sufficient collection materials to cover an adult male, an adult female, or even a child victim. The type of victim and the acts committed would determine the techniques that would be used. The forms of physical evidence normally of importance in cases of sexual assault generally differ very little depending on the sex of the victim. Saliva, blood, hairs, and fibers, for example, are at issue in almost any sexual assault matter.

Consideration should be given to extending the use of evidence kits to suspects in sexual assault investigations. The types of evidence materials that may be located on the clothing or person of the suspect are similar to those found on the victim. The acquisition of known biological samples is basically the same for both victim and suspect. Trace evidence existing on the suspect can be collected in the same manner as that on the victim. In fact, the applicable components of a victim-oriented sexual assault evidence collection kit serve as a good guide for kits used on a suspect.

The primary benefit of the sexual assault evidence collection kit is that it emphasizes the inherent significance of the victim or suspect as a source of physical evidence, and what types of potential evidence to pursue. The focus is on treating the victim or suspect as, in fact, a crime scene. This statement is not intended as a crude or insensitive reference to a victim who has suffered through the tragic and brutal events of a sexual assault. It is a fact that must be recognized in the collection of physical evidence pertaining to sexual assault. The rules that necessarily govern proper evidence recognition, collection, and preservation are as applicable in a hospital examination of a sex crime victim as they are at a crime scene.

The Crime Scene

The phrase "crime scene investigation" is in common use in law enforcement. However, there can be an erroneous assumption that conducting a crime scene search involves no more than picking up articles and placing them into evidence containers. Anyone familiar with this topic realizes that what might appear to be an elementary exercise can become a very complicated task.

Crime scene searches generally are conceived only as efforts to methodically locate and gather physical evidence. However, the evidence recovered will be only as effective, under normal circumstances, as the administration, management, documentation, and collection techniques allow. It is simply not enough to collect the evidence; precise documentation of the scene and the evidence recovered must meet chain-of-custody and procedural challenges in the courtroom. There can be cases in which incriminating physical evidence is discovered but is poorly used in court or deemed altogether inadmissible because of poor documentation and cohesion at the crime scene. When this happens, all previous efforts are wasted and become moot when the suspect who indeed committed the crime walks away from the trial a free person.

Searches of scenes involving sexual assaults sometimes are not viewed from the same perspective as searches of areas where a homicide has occurred. When a murder is investigated, the victim's body frequently is in place and, therefore, is a major concern for those gathering physical evidence at the scene, and subsequently at the autopsy. In contrast, the victim in a rape case often survives the attack and is not physically at the scene itself. Thus, the attention given to the victim occurs primarily at the medical examination of this person.

There can be a tendency to concentrate on this facet of evidence collection, without serious effort to conduct an intensive search of the scene itself. Such a condition can result in the loss of pertinent evidence.

At this point, it is useful to discuss the fundamental steps through which a crime scene search normally progresses. The following material is not a complete study of crime scene searches, but a concise summary on the essential progression of events.

General Stages of the Search

It is of utmost importance that a proper framework of administration and procedures be used on a consistent basis in crime scene searches. Despite different administrative procedures developed by various agencies, there remains a series of events that should be followed in any search in order to realize the full potential of evidence from the scene. The following sets forth a suggested pattern of crime scene search steps, without advocating the imposition of an inflexible system in conducting crime scene investigations. The person who tries to operate in an identical manner on each search will soon discover that there is always some eventuality that does not fall into a preplanned scheme. These basic steps are

1. Approach scene
2. Secure and protect
3. Preliminary survey eventuality that does not fall into a preplanned sequence
4. Narrative description
5. Photograph scene
6. Sketch scene
7. Evaluation of latent fingerprint evidence and other evidence
8. Detailed search for evidence collection, preservation, and documentation of evidence
9. Final survey
10. Release of scene

The following discussion summarizes these critical stages of a search and includes some important practical suggestions to assist in conducting an efficient search.

Approach Scene. Law enforcement personnel responding to a crime scene should be alert to a variety of items or events that ultimately may be connected with the investigation. People, vehicles, and objects observed by officers may provide details concerning the crime and the person(s) responsible for it. For example, evidence may have been discarded along a route used by a subject, or potential witnesses may be seen along the roadside as officers proceed to the scene. Further, evidence of possible getaway vehicles may be discovered. All personnel in the area of a crime scene should be alert for information sources that may provide a necessary "link" in the successful investigation of the case.

Secure and Protect. To avoid contamination and prevent unnecessary disturbances of the crime scene, all personnel must strive to secure and protect the scene. Such an effort requires continuous attention and cannot be successful with a haphazard approach. "Securing the scene" and "protecting the scene" should be thought of as two separate but interrelated duties. Before a complete crime scene area can be realistically protected, it must first be adequately secured. Securing the scene will necessitate the establishment of its perimeter as soon as possible. After the perimeter has been established, all reasonable efforts can be made to prevent any disturbance of the original conditions. Thorough control over all persons entering the immediate crime scene area is of extreme importance. Many major courtroom difficulties that can surface regarding contamination of evidence and of the scene revolve around the lack of initial steps taken by law enforcement officers to ensure that the scene was adequately protected.

Preliminary Survey. During the preliminary survey of a crime scene, the foundation for management, organization, and logistics should be developed to suit the needs of the particular crime scene. Examples of the purposes of the survey are

1. To establish administrative and emotional control
2. To delineate the extent of the search area
3. To organize the methods and procedures needed
4. To determine manpower and equipment needs
5. To develop a general theory of the scene
6. To identify and protect transitory evidence

The preliminary survey begins after the crime scene has been thoroughly secured and protected. An initial walk-through of the scene is undertaken so that the officer in charge has a solid understanding of the scene as a whole, including the existence and location of observable items with possible evidence value. The initial walk-through should be done by as few persons as feasible to ensure that no one is operating in an uncoordinated and unrecorded manner. The preliminary survey may be the most important stage of administration, because it promotes an organized plan of action and prevents uncontrolled physical activity that could destroy pertinent evidence.

Narrative Description.   The narrative description is one of the primary means of documenting the original conditions of the scene as found by law enforcement personnel. It can best be described as a general view of the scene, without undue attention to extraneous detail. The narrative description should not be confused with the use of sketches, close-up photographs, and finely detailed evidence notes that later are part of the search. The narrative description usually will not have the preciseness of the specialized evidence search of the crime scene. Instead, it is normally limited to a general view of the scene as first observed by law enforcement officers. The ultimate value of this description is to show a jury how the crime scene initially would have appeared to them if they had been present at the scene in the role of the law enforcement officer. Also, the narrative description provides a documented means of determining whether any evidence or scene conditions were inadvertently disturbed as a result of a later detailed search.

The three common modes of preparing a narrative are handwritten notes, audiotape recorder, and videotape with sight/sound or sight-only capability. Each of these methods has inherent capabilities and limitations that should be considered. For example, videotape equipment can record both the sights and sounds at the scene. The system sometimes also will record irrelevant or off-the-cuff statements on the part of personnel at the scene. Such advantages and disadvantages should be explored before the mode of preparing the narrative description is selected.

Photograph Scene.   The courtroom role of photography in portraying a crime scene cannot be overestimated. Photography is such a common medium that its use in the adjudication of criminal cases should be expected. Photographing a crime scene is a continuous process and must include long-range, mid-range, and close-up photographs. These will show the immediate focal point of the crime as well as the entire location. Photographs must be prepared so that the pictures can portray all pertinent segments of the scene. Long-range photographs are often neglected during crime scene searches. If blood spattering is present, sufficient quality photographs should be taken so that the entire scene, including ceilings and floors, can be depicted in a panorama by overlapping photographs.

Photographic views of the crime scene can usually be categorized as those (1) focusing on the location of the crime, (2) concentrating on the nature of the crime, (3) centering on the results of the crime, (4) featuring the physical evidence at the scene, and (5) illustrating follow-up activity not directly occurring at the immediate scene.

The location photographs should depict the various places that are part of the crime scene. Aerial photographs are an example of this. The nature and results of the crime should be depicted by the photographs so as to assist the investigation in determining the type of crime and actions of the persons involved. For instance, a rape incident may have begun with a house break-in through a kitchen door, continued with vandalism, and culminated with the rape of the victim who confronted the intruder. Therefore, the results of each portion of the crime should be depicted in a sequence that reproduces the events.

Photographs of physical evidence are of great relevance, including the use of measurement scales when appropriate. The representation of observable evidence in relation to the entire scene will ultimately enable the evidence to be connected in the courtroom with the crime scene, the victim, and the suspect. Also, photographs of physical evidence can be a major component in establishing the chain of custody of items from the scene introduced in the courtroom.

The follow-up photographs are an outgrowth of the crime scene investigation. Photographs of a victim or suspect showing bruises, wounds, or bite marks are examples of this category. Integration of the information recorded photographically at both the actual scene and during follow-up activities will produce a greater depth of understanding of the realities of the crime scene itself.

Sketch Scene. A sketch or diagram is a commonly neglected method that can be used to document certain important conditions at a crime scene. Many persons mistakenly consider the use of sketches to be outmoded by photographs. A photograph reduces to two dimensions a scene that actually contains three dimensions. Distance relationships can be distorted and incorrectly interpreted from a photograph. A sketch gives true distance relationships that will complement and supplement photographic representations of the crime scene. The locations of all pertinent evidence can be set forth in a sketch for display in court. A sketch can also be made of locations or items that are very difficult to photograph in a manner that shows desired conditions and detail. Some law enforcement agencies are now using lap top computers with programs that create excellent sketches directly in the field.

Evaluation of Latent Fingerprint Evidence and Other Forms of Evidence. The crime scene search is concentrated on the discovery and collection of physical evidence that can be used in the investigation. There is a series of organizational and planning requirements involved in bringing the crime scene investigation to the point at which a systematic search can be undertaken. The same type of planning applies to the evaluation of the evidence before it is collected. Both latent fingerprints and other forms of physical evidence present at a crime scene must be studied before attempts are made to collect evidence. For example, a careless dusting procedure for possible latent fingerprints may contaminate, or result in complete loss of, transitory evidence such as hairs or fibers. Likewise, in a poorly executed attempt to collect hairs or fibers, valuable latent fingerprints may be destroyed. Each case will dictate the sequence in which evidence is collected. However, in all cases, the possibilities of the types of physical evidence must be explored and the detailed search should proceed accordingly.

Detailed Search for Evidence: Collection, Preservation, and Documentation of Evidence. Once a systematic evaluation of the evidence has been accomplished at the crime scene, a detailed search can proceed. This stage of the crime scene search will produce the bulk of the potential evidence at the scene. However, the success or failure of the efforts during this portion of the investigation depends on planning and organization done earlier. If an organized and methodical approach has been fostered, the search of the scene will have the greatest potential for success.

Specialized methods needed to recover different forms of evidence come into play at this time. These procedures should be designed to preserve the recovered physical evidence in its original form to the greatest extent possible. Photographic and written documentation should record the locations of items of evidence within the scene. Also necessary chain-of-custody data must be recorded as the evidence recovery operation proceeds. The possible evidence articles and information acquired during this time are, in essence, the real goals of the search.

Final Survey. Following the complete documentation of the crime scene and the collection of physical evidence, a final survey should be conducted. The purpose of this survey is to review the crime scene investigation process from the beginning. All elements must be weighed against one central idea: has the crime scene investigation effort considered all possibilities for telling the events of the crime? This introspective approach may prevent such oversights as important evidence being missed, critical photographs being neglected, or obvious facts being overlooked. Especially in view of the stress and confusion often accompanying a crime scene search, time should be taken to review all observations made and actions taken.

Release of Scene. Upon completion of the final survey a decision must be made to relinquish control of the scene. This decision should be formal and official and leave no room for misinterpretation. The authority for this decision should rest with the person who is in charge of the crime scene investigation. If it is common knowledge that a formal declaration of release must be made, then those persons involved will realize that the job remains unfinished until they are otherwise informed. When considering this decision, the officer in charge should accept input from selected persons involved in the crime scene search effort. In this way, formal release of the scene becomes a joint effort to decide whether or not all reasonable actions have been taken.

In some investigations, there are situations in which forensic specialists examine the crime scene. For example, the patterns of blood present at the scene can offer valuable information about what took place. This can require the presence of specialists during and/or after the initial search. Once a scene is released, legal complexities can be involved in regaining access. Also, the scene may be cleaned or otherwise disturbed after it is released. The crime scene should be protected and not released until any specialists required can observe its conditions and perform their examinations.

A completed crime scene investigation does not end the evidence process. The forensic evidence must still be examined by the crime laboratory. When all forensic analyses are completed and results reported for use in the investigation, the crime scene once again must be reviewed. The physical evidence from the scene should not simply be stored away in packages. A thorough evaluation of the total information picture offered by the crime scene, laboratory results, and other investigative work is a necessity. Doing so in a diligent manner is the primary difference between "searching" a crime scene and "reconstructing" a crime scene. The search is the evidence documentation and recovery process. The reconstruction is the interpretation of the facts observed and retrieved in that process. It is entirely possible that a search accomplished in the most competent manner would be of no use if no attempt was made at reconstruction. From the viewpoint of the courtroom, crime scene search and crime scene reconstruction are tools to one end: logical portrayal of the facts.

Bloodborne Pathogens

On March 6, 1992, the federal Occupational Safety and Health Administration (OSHA) of the U.S. Department of Labor released requirements for the handling of bloodborne pathogens by public service agencies including law enforcement agencies. The "Bloodborne Pathogens Act" included in their requirements that all law enforcement officers who might be handling blood and other body fluids be offered the vaccination against hepatitis B on a voluntary basis at no charge to the officer. Further, the act requires training and safety equipment to be provided to the officers.

Blood, semen, saliva, and other body fluids from either victims or suspects in sexual assault cases could be contaminated with infectious microorganisms capable of causing sickness or death. For those reasons, law enforcement officers should follow the so-called "universal precautions" when handling any body fluid from any source: assume it is infectious. The purpose of this chapter is not to go into detail regarding this act, but to remind law enforcement that these requirements exist.

Summary

This chapter has dealt with general concepts of physical evidence relevant to sexual assault investigations. Also, it has provided information pertaining to the primary sources of evidence: the victim, the suspect, and the crime scene. The physical evidence associated with the crime of sexual assault is not unlike that associated with other types of crime. Nonetheless, the direct sexual contact between suspect and victim tends to leave different and predictable kinds of evidence. Generally, the evidence in sexual assault cases is of the class characteristic kind. This sometimes makes it more difficult to establish, beyond reasonable doubt, that the suspect was or was not involved in the crime. For this reason hairs, semen, and other class evidence must be used in combination to show whether there are strong or weak evidence associations between suspect and victim, which may or may not corroborate the victim's statements. The investigator and attorney must be prepared for a range of arguments designed to destabilize the weight of the physical evidence either for or against the suspect. One aspect of this preparation is the laying of a reasonable and convincing evidentiary foundation for the jury. It is hoped that the discussion of the elements of such a foundation set forth in this chapter assists in that effort.

Major Physical Evidence in Sexual Assault Investigations

5

DALE M. MOREAU
P. DAVID BIGBEE

Virtually any form of physical evidence can figure in the successful identification or elimination of a suspect in the crime of sexual assault. Latent fingerprints, shoe print and tire tread impressions, body fluids, bite marks, fabric impressions, tool marks, paints, cosmetics, glass, soil, tape, cordage, and documents often play major roles in these cases. *All* evidence possibilities should be considered before evidence collection is undertaken. Important items can be overlooked if searches are conducted for only the expected evidence.

The types of evidence discussed in this chapter are limited to those crucial in the majority of sexual assault investigations. They are hairs, fibers, blood, semen, and saliva. These materials were selected because they (1) appear frequently in sexual assault cases, (2) are primary targets of sexual assault evidence collection kits and crime scene searches in sex crime instances, (3) are used in the courtroom to corroborate the victim's testimony, (4) are illustrative of the close contact and sexual nature of the crimes committed, (5) are often overlooked because they can be difficult to locate and collect at crime scenes, and (6) are within the forensic examination capability of the modern crime laboratory.

The distinction between "questioned" evidence and "known" evidence is used in this chapter. Questioned evidence is physical evidence that typically is of unknown origin when it is found. It is collected to compare with a potential source at some later time. Known evidence are those materials that must be collected as comparison standards against the questioned evidence. For example, questioned hairs found on the floor of an apartment during a crime scene search have extremely limited value until they are compared with known hair samples taken from the suspect and the victim. A deoxyribonucleic acid (DNA) profile from semen taken from the victim is useless unless there is a known blood sample with which to compare it.

There are also limited instances in which the comparison of questioned evidence with other questioned evidence may be pertinent. For instance, questioned debris on a victim's clothing might be compared with the questioned debris recovered from the carpet of a vehicle in which the victim is suspected of having been assaulted.

Law enforcement today has many technological resources available for evidence location and collection. These tools, when used with adequate training, experience, and discretion, can be effective in determining whether or not possible evidence is present. Some devices or methods, however, may destroy or contaminate evidence if used incorrectly or unsystematically. All too often, devices or methods are used in an effort to save time, when the best way is normally the most difficult and time-consuming alternative.

The distinction is made here between the discovery and the collection of evidence materials. For some forms of evidence, special techniques can be applied to help in *locating* the evidence before attempts are made to collect it. This situation usually applies to items that are difficult to see but can become visible using various methods. Then there are techniques that are used to *collect* the evidence without really knowing if it is present. Such would be the case with minute particles or debris that are virtually impossible to see with the naked eye under most evidentiary search conditions.

Many systems of evidence discovery and collection available in the controlled conditions of a forensic laboratory may not be readily applicable to field work. Generally, it is more advantageous for the crime laboratory actually to remove the pertinent evidence (e.g., hairs, fibers, blood) from items recovered during field investigations. The techniques used in the laboratory permit the collection of evidence materials that are very difficult to see and/or recover at a crime scene.

Some crime laboratories give the field investigator a wide range of options for evidence handling. Other laboratories feel that giving the investigator too many options will result in decisions being made by this person without the proper forensic considerations. In this chapter, the advantages and disadvantages of various techniques are enumerated. The reader must study the issues raised and seek counseling from the crime laboratory to which physical evidence is to be submitted.

Discussions with laboratory personnel should include safety issues and procedures pertaining to the collection of physical evidence. For example, certain diseases can be transmitted through the handling of materials often collected as evidence, such as clothing and body fluids. Surgical-type disposable gloves should be worn routinely. Disposable clothing and protection for the eyes, nose, and mouth may also be warranted. Cutting implements (e.g., razor blades, scalpels) should be used with care so as not to damage protective gloves or clothes or to cut the skin. Needlestick injuries, in particular, must be avoided during searches.

The evidence discussions that follow assume that, when appropriate, before evidence is moved or recovered, (1) it will be photographed, using a scale when necessary, and (2) documentation such as sketches and evidence logs will be used to record chain-of-custody data.

Recovery of Questioned Evidence

Hairs and Fibers

Hairs can be identified in the crime laboratory as being animal or human. In most cases, the type of animal from which hairs originated may be established. A human hair may be classified as to its racial origin (Mongoloid, Caucasoid, Negroid), color, method of removal from the body, artificial treatment, body area origin, damage, diseases, and presence of foreign substances.

It is not currently possible forensically to positively identify a questioned human or animal hair as having originated from a particular person or animal source to the exclusion of all others, but DNA profiles from the sheath cells on hairs can now be obtained and may ultimately lead to a positive identification of an individual. Research is currently being conducted in several laboratories toward this goal. Nonetheless, forensic analysis can determine that the questioned and known hairs could have originated from the same source, which is of great value in indicating an association in the courtroom.

Textile fibers are classified in the crime laboratory, on a basic level, as being of natural or synthetic (man-made) origin. The specific kind of natural or synthetic fiber can be readily determined and the color and other information pertaining to the microscopic and optical properties of fibers can be established. Foreign substances appearing on fibers also may be of significance. Such features can be used to compare questioned fibers with fibers from a known source to show a high probability of association. It is not possible to state, on the basis of forensic comparisons, that a questioned fiber definitely came from a specific known garment or other fibrous object to the exclusion of all similar ones.

In terms of actually finding and recovering hair and fiber evidence, hairs are normally more visible to the naked eye than minute fibers; the possible exception would be fibers found together in the form of a yarn or tuft. Hairs and fibers are often difficult to find and collect, and such efforts can be somewhat frustrating, especially when a large crime scene area is involved. The scene may have so many possible sources of evidence that it is difficult to choose the best course of action. The scene should be evaluated to pinpoint those evidence sources that are likely to be most valuable.

When hairs and fibers are found, it is necessary either to remove this evidence or to collect the item on which the samples are observed. It is preferable to collect the items that would retain hairs and fibers, rather than to attempt to remove each minute piece of debris. Removal of such evidence in the field is exceedingly cumbersome and can result in its loss and contamination.

Different methods of locating and recovering hairs and fibers have varying levels of success. The major techniques are

1. General unassisted visual search (naked eye)
2. Oblique light
3. Ultraviolet (UV) light
4. Vacuuming
5. Adhesive lifts
6. Combing/brushing
7. Fingernail scrapings and clippings
8. Lasers and alternate light sources

Naked Eye.   It is feasible to find hairs and fibers through a visual search. However, especially with textile fibers, this is a limited approach. The many colors and backgrounds on which the evidence can be located may make it difficult to see. For example, fine human hairs or fibers resting on a carpet can easily go unnoticed. Unfortunately, there are instances in which this is the sole technique used in the search of a person or crime scene.

Oblique Light.   In this method, light is shined across a surface to highlight small debris that is present, and this is a good technique for discovering fibers and hairs. It can be accomplished with a flashlight or other light source that has a directed and narrow beam. Floors, walls, windows, furniture, etc. can be searched at crime scenes in this fashion. This procedure can also be effective in finding small items on the clothing or body of a person involved in the crime.

Ultraviolet Light.   Although it can definitely be of value, UV light is an instrument not often readily considered as a tool for hair and fiber evidence. This device produces light in the UV portion of the light spectrum. This area of the spectrum generally is divided into short-wavelength and long-wavelength designations. The term nanometer is used to measure wavelengths of light in the entire spectrum, with short-wavelength UV light generally measured at 200 to 300 nm and long-wavelength UV light at 300 to 400 nm. To use the UV light technique effectively, a device having both capabilities is recommended. Short UV irradiation is dangerous to the human eye and therefore may not be included in some of the commercially available lights. This point is significant because many materials react differently to long or short UV irradiation. (Care should be taken to avoid exposure of the eyes to the light. Safety glasses are available for eye protection and should be used.) When UV light strikes certain materials, these items have a fluorescent (glowing) appearance, highlighting the specimen against its background.

Many UV lights have poor-quality filters, which permit a visible purple/violet light to emanate from the device. This emission can further mask out the visible fluorescence of certain materials. Thus, a filter that would permit no visible light to emerge from the UV light source is recommended.

Fibers may react to UV light due to the chemical additives which are used in the manufacturing process or, for example, as a result of the addition of optical whiteners and brighteners in detergent used to wash clothing. Hairs normally do not react to UV irradiation unless they are contaminated with substances that fluoresce, such as some cosmetics.

A major problem with the UV light method is that the visibility of hairs or fibers also directly depends on the substrate that contains the evidence. The substrate may itself fluoresce to the point where one would be unable to separate that effect from the fluorescence of the evidence. For this reason, it is recommended that items such as bedding and clothing be collected intact and submitted to the crime laboratory.

Vacuuming.   Sometimes it is impractical to submit extremely large items (e.g., carpets, furniture) to a crime laboratory. Here, vacuum cleaner devices can be effective aids in collecting hair and fiber evidence. However, the area in question should be first visually examined for all forms of evidence materials, so that important items are not destroyed or contaminated. For example, small bloodstains in dried, crusted form can be contaminated by intermingling with the debris that is vacuumed. More importantly, the crusted blood could be lost, or the amount present reduced, by vigorous vacuuming.

Special vacuum kits are made specifically for gathering hair and fiber evidence. Typically, a filter attachment at the nozzle end serves to collect the vacuumed material. Special porous filters are used for debris collection and should be collected intact with the evidence material on them. The filter is small, so it is not feasible to vacuum more than a small area at a time. The entire area to be vacuumed should be divided into segments, and a separate filter used for each segment. The vacuum filter housing and adjacent area of the vacuum should be cleaned thoroughly before a new segment is vacuumed.

Major disadvantages to be considered before a vacuum device is used for evidence recovery include:

1. Contamination could be a problem if the vacuum is not cleaned thoroughly. The collection area of the nozzle can retain debris from one area that could contaminate potential evidence taken from another site.
2. Investigators sometimes gather so much possible evidence by vacuuming at a crime scene that it is difficult for crime laboratory personnel to locate and extract the pertinent materials. This can be caused, for example, by vacuuming too large an area without changing filters.
3. Fibers in tufts or clusters can become separated, possibly losing some of their forensic significance.
4. It is often very important to demonstrate that particular hairs or fibers were collected from a specific location. If relatively large areas are vacuumed per sample, it is difficult, if not impossible, to be certain of the exact recovery location of such evidence. This may reduce or dilute its significance in court.

Adhesive Lifts.   There are occasions in general evidence recovery when the use of various adhesive lift techniques may be practical. As an example, a suspect has been arrested a short time after a rape. It is learned by interviewing the victim that the assailant wore a mask, probably of the ski-mask type. The mask was discarded by the suspect in the yard of the victim's residence during his departure from the scene. Minute fibers like those in the mask may be contained in the suspect's head hair and could be recovered by combing or brushing. There may also be fibers adhering to the beard stubble on the suspect's face, even if he appears to be clean shaven. The application of an adhesive lift could remove those valuable materials. Tape lifts can also collect hairs and fibers from a variety of crime scene sources such as vinyl upholstery, tile floors, smooth countertops, and sinks. However, it normally would not be reasonable to completely "tape" every item in a large crime scene. A methodical approach of carefully surveying the scene before acting, therefore, is recommended.

The tape used for lifting purposes should be clear and have an adhesive that is strong enough to retain trace evidence. Any such tape must be cautiously protected from contamination before use, as adhesive tends to attract and pick up small debris. Once a lift is made, it is essential that the tape not be folded over on itself. It can be mounted on Plexiglass, a plastic sheeting, or a similar transparent and resilient material. Glass is suitable for this purpose, but is subject to breakage, and appropriate measures should be taken. Paper, cardboard, card stock, or similar items should be avoided as mounting substrates; these materials create difficulty in laboratory viewing and removal of the evidence for examination purposes.

The tape used for lifting can be difficult for the laboratory to deal with. The investigator should discuss the use of taping with the crime laboratory to determine its recommendations and precautions.

Combing/Brushing. Questioned hairs and fibers, as well as other small materials, may be transferred to body hair as a result of physical contact. A technique commonly termed "combing" or "brushing" is most often used to extract these materials from the head and pubic regions of a person. The combing/brushing procedure need not be limited to the head and pubic regions, but may include other locations where body hair is heavily concentrated.

Two variations of this procedure are the following.

The use of a fine-tooth comb or multibristle brush to collect the transferred evidence — This technique involves the relatively simple procedure of combing or brushing through the hair and retaining whatever debris is removed. This is a reasonably reliable method if accomplished thoroughly.

The use of a fine-tooth comb and white cotton batting to collect the transferred evidence — This involves pushing the teeth of the comb through the cotton, using the cotton as a handle, and then combing so that the cotton is a backing to assist in the collection of hairs and other evidence. Because the white cotton backing increases the probability of picking up debris and the visibility of the hairs and fibers by way of contrast, many people consider this method superior to the use of a comb and brush alone. The use of the cotton batting, however, may be a disadvantage, because some debris, such as fibers, can be lost in the cotton.

Each body hair region of concern must be combed and brushed with a previously unused and clean implement, preferably one with fine teeth or bristles. The comb or brush and the evidence adhering to it are packaged intact as recovered. It is critical that combings/brushings obtained from different body regions be collected and packaged separately. Also, since the combing/brushing method is normally accomplished when known hair samples are taken from an individual, it is recommended that the combing/brushing process be completed before the known sampling is begun. This will ensure that all foreign hairs are removed from the person, so that they will not be intermingled in the known sample.

If the person being examined has long head hairs, the combing/brushing procedure can be difficult, especially if the person is standing. The person can lie down with a section of clean, white cloth or sturdy paper under his or her head. The hair is gently spread over the section and the combing or brushing taken. The light-colored background helps make foreign debris visible and serves to collect any that may be dislodged from the hair and not retained on the comb or brush. A similar procedure can be used in combing/brushing pubic hair.

Although somewhat unorthodox, the following two other methods of removing foreign hairs and fibers from body hair locations have been brought to the author's attention; they are not recommended as substitutes for the standard combing/brushing procedure.

The application of a tape-style lift to the body hair region in question — This technique has many negative aspects, three of which are possible physical discomfort to the person; the gathering of only loose, surface hairs; and the retention of numerous hairs forcibly removed from the person. A further disadvantage from the laboratory viewpoint is that there can be difficulty in removing the hairs intact from the lift without using a solvent.

The use of a small vacuum cleaner device to remove the foreign hairs and fibers from a person — This method has most of the decidedly negative features mentioned regarding the tape-style lift.

Fingernail Scrapings and Clippings.   Almost any form of transfer evidence can be recovered from under fingernails. Minute fragments or quantities of hairs, fibers, blood, semen, etc. can be removed with any clean, suitable tool that will not cause discomfort to the person. Clean knife blades, toothpicks, thin wood depressor sticks, and other devices can be useful in this regard. Questioned material from each hand should be removed and packaged separately. The implements used to acquire the specimens also should be sent to the crime laboratory. The end portions of the nails can be removed with a clean fingernail clipper. Some dried materials will not be removed easily by the scraping method and may be detected on the nail.

Lasers and Alternate Light Sources.   The use of laser technology in forensic science is expanding very rapidly. Lasers have been used primarily in the crime laboratory for the development of latent prints on porous and nonporous articles, but it has been found that many additional types of evidentiary materials can be detected by laser instruments. Fibers, threads, semen, urine, and saliva potentially can be observed.

The laser produces a very concentrated and coherent light, which can cause certain materials to luminesce. The specimens must be viewed through special filters that permit the luminescent effect to be seen. Photography to record the evidence involves the same types of filters.

Various laser instruments are available, usually at fairly substantial price. Several "alternate light sources" are also available, which are generally less expensive and for the most part can obtain similar results. Generally these light sources have a differing range of light wavelengths and are more portable than lasers. Due to the size and operating requirements of most lasers used for forensic analysis (such as the argon-ion and copper vapor types), evidence can only be examined in the laboratory. Smaller lasers, designed to be portable, are available and can be used in field evidence searches. Laser instruments are gaining in popularity, but are often too expensive to suit the budgets of many agencies.

A detailed discussion of laser technology is beyond the scope of this chapter. However, lasers are brought to the reader's attention because they will become more easily available as research and technology progress. Although the lasers are exotic tools to witness in operation in the laboratory or field, they are simply additional tools to increase visibility and detection of potential evidence. They assuredly will not solve all evidence collection problems faced in day-to-day operations. As long as this fact is kept in perspective, lasers are and will continue to be extremely valuable in the discovery of certain physical evidence.

Blood

Depending on the facts of a given case, blood can become a major evidence substance in sexual assault investigation. Some crime laboratories conduct what is traditionally called "conventional blood groupings" and do not have the capability for DNA analysis. The conventional analysis of blood will first be discussed, followed by DNA analysis.

All laboratories must establish that an unknown substance is definitely blood, and differentiate between animal and human blood. The family of animal can often be identified when animal blood is encountered. Human blood can be further characterized by many genetically controlled grouping systems. This capability is based on the forensic identification of many complex chemical substances that exist in the cells and serum of blood. These substances include various protein and other genetic marker systems, divided into a limited number of types within each system. For example, in one enzyme system called *esterase D*, the population can be divided into six categories, and each member of the population will fall into one of these categories. Known blood samples can be compared with questioned blood based on these markers.

A great deal of research is being devoted to enhancing the ability of a crime laboratory to detect and interpret the complex substances contained in the blood in order to increase its weight as class evidence. Although blood cannot be identified at this time as having come from one specific person, its components can establish a high degree of probability for the association of a person with a questioned blood sample, depending on the array of types it has.

DNA Analysis.   For more than two decades, the ability to resolve and detect polymorphic markers has made possible the genetic characterization of body fluid stains for forensic scientists. Although the polymorphic protein and genetic markers used by many laboratories provide the potential for a high degree of discrimination among different individuals, this upper limit is rarely attained because of the instability of some of these markers in dried stains. Moreover, of the markers that retain their structure and activity in the dried state, the number of expressed or observed forms is limited. Thus, in practice, the individualization of many evidentiary stains cannot be carried out to any great extent given the present array of polymorphic markers.

Advances in recombinant DNA technology have provided the molecular tools that enable scientists to detect the extraordinary variability that exists among individuals at the level of their DNA. This technology holds promise of affording the forensic serologist the ultimate in discrimination power, the ability to identify a body fluid/tissue donor to the exclusion of all other individuals.

In all life forms, from viruses to humans, the basis for variation lies in the genetic material called DNA. Every living organism, with the exception of some viruses which possess ribonucleic acid (RNA), has this chemical as its genetic "blueprint". In every cell of the same person which contains DNA, the blueprint is identical, whether it is a white blood cell, a piece of skin, spermatozoa, or a hair root cell. This extremely complex chemical is made of five simple elements: carbon, hydrogen, oxygen, nitrogen, and phosphorus. The five elements then combine to form sugar, phosphate, and nitrogenous base molecules to constitute what is called a "nucleotide". The language of DNA consists of an alphabet comprised of only four letters. These letters stand for the four nitrogenous bases found in DNA: thymine, cytosine, adenine, and guanine abbreviated T, C, A, and G. Even though this alphabet is very short, an enormous array of different sequences of nucleotides can exist in a single strand of DNA that is hundreds of thousands to millions of nucleotides long. The chromosomes found in one human cell are composed of 6 billion nucleotides. For example, if we consider only ten positions in the chain, each of which could be occupied by any one of the four nucleotides, the number of combinations would be 1,048,576. Hundreds of thousands of nucleotides are linked together in a long chain of DNA in a specific sequence of the nitrogenous bases which then combines with protein to become a chromosome.

Humans have 23 pairs of these chromosomes. One chromosome of each pair originates from the mother and the other from the father. Because the many genes found on the chromosomes for each trait in humans are a combination of the maternal and paternal genes, variation is generated in the offspring. No two people, except for identical twins, even though born from the same parents, will be exactly alike. Two brothers, though they may be similar, are not physically or genetically identical; their DNA is different.

DNA is actually made up of two strands forming a double helix (similar to a spiral staircase in structure). The bases pair with each other in a specific way; A always pairs with T and G always pairs with C on opposite strands of the DNA molecule. This is called complementary base pairing. Thus, if the sequence of one strand is known, then the sequence of the other strand can be determined. This is the basis of all DNA tests.

When evidence bearing DNA source material is received in the laboratory, such as bloodstains or seminal stains, the process of DNA typing begins. There are several methods for performing DNA analysis, but the two most common are designated restriction fragment length polymorphisms (RFLP) and polymerase chain reaction (PCR). We will discuss RFLP first. The intact DNA is chemically extracted from the sample and then enzymes called "restriction endonucleases" are added which act like molecular scissors and cut the DNA into fragments. The double-stranded DNA is then chemically divided so that single strands are now found. These DNA fragments are placed in a sieving gel and separated by electrophoresis according to size. The separated DNA fragments are blotted from the gel onto a nylon membrane in a process called "Southern Blotting".

At this point "DNA probes" are prepared and applied. These probes are single-stranded pieces of DNA which can bind via complementary base pairing with the target DNA. A single locus probe "looks" for only one area of the DNA molecule, whereas a multilocus probe "looks" for several areas at once. Before the probes are applied to the DNA they are made radioactive by using an isotope of phosphorus. The radioactive DNA probe then combines with the specific DNA sequences found on the fragments in the membrane. Subsequently, X-ray film is placed in contact with the membrane to detect the radioactive probe pattern. This image, which may develop in several hours to several days, resembles the optically read "bar codes" seen on products in supermarkets. These images are evaluated by an examiner visually and with computer-assisted image analysis to "size" them, which means to measure their length. The evidence stains are then compared to the known samples and a determination of either a match or a no-match is made. The suspect is then either absolutely excluded as the stain donor or a match is made. When a match is made, the frequency of the profile is determined by consulting the human data bases, and the probability of finding the same match at random is then calculated. Depending on how rare or common the DNA fragments found are in the population, the probability of a random match can range from very high, such as 1 in 10, to extremely low, such as 1 in 10 billion. Until there are enough people in the DNA data bases worldwide to positively prove that no two people have the same DNA, courts will only allow expert testimony concerning the probability of a random match. Ultimately, this technology will be able to absolutely identify a suspect from a body fluid left at the scene of a crime.

DNA typing procedures are especially useful in sexual assault cases. As will be discussed later, conventional analysis cannot differentiate between blood groups substances found in mixed seminal/vaginal secretion stains. Therefore, if the rapist and the victim have the same blood type, the scientist could not determine from whom the blood group substance was derived. DNA analysis eliminates this problem. The technology can separate the DNA from the victim's vaginal tract and the semen from the rapist. Because semen normally contains a large number of spermatozoa, there is a correspondingly large quantity of DNA available for typing. Seminal fluid does not contain DNA; however, in seminal stains lacking spermatozoa, it may still be possible to obtain a DNA type from epithelial tissue or white blood cells present in the stain. For example, a rapist with a vasectomy would not deposit spermatozoa but might deposit epithelial cells in his semen.

Like seminal fluid, saliva does not contain DNA; but, again, generally there will be epithelial tissue or white blood cells present which can be typed for DNA. Even though a bloodstain may appear to be large enough for RFLP analysis, it should be kept in mind that red blood cells do not contain DNA. The DNA from bloodstains is contained in the white blood cells, which are much fewer than the red cells. Urine and perspiration do not contain DNA.

PCR technology is now being used in many laboratories in conjunction with, or as an alternative to, RFLP. This technology is capable of using minute amounts of DNA that are too small for RFLP analysis, and chemically "amplifies" the DNA sequences until enough is obtained for analysis. Some laboratories use only one

PCR marker and others use an array of markers. This technology is particularly useful for DNA typing of saliva stains, small amounts of tissue, and the root cells from hairs. As previously mentioned, saliva does not contain DNA but does contain epithelial tissue and may contain white blood cells. An example where this technology is particularly useful is the DNA typing of saliva stains left on stamps, envelopes, cigarette butts, and chewing gum. In one case in the FBI Laboratory, PCR technology was used to determine a DNA profile from the sweatband of a hat dropped at the scene of a homicide. Perspiration does not contain DNA but the skin cells from the suspect had sloughed off onto the sweat band. PCR technology is also very useful when body fluid samples are degraded.

Two other DNA technologies which are currently being researched are the literal nucleotide sequencing of the DNA to produce a "map", and studies on mitochondrial DNA in hairs. Mitochondria are small organelles found in cells which contain their own nonnuclear DNA. This DNA is highly variable from person to person and is maternally inherited. This offers a chance for the forensic scientist to obtain a DNA profile from hairs that are devoid of root cells, such as cut hairs.

The collection of body fluids for DNA analysis is virtually the same as for conventional analysis, with a few exceptions which will be covered later in this chapter.

Two main dilemmas face forensic laboratories in dealing with blood evidence as well as other body fluid evidence, such as semen and saliva:

1. Blood is often mixed with contaminants and other body fluids, making forensic interpretations difficult and limited. In sexual assault cases, serologists often receive test results indicating that, in fact, genetic markers apparently have been contributed by both victim and suspect. The forensic interpretation of this mixture can be confusing, especially when the laboratory results appear to be inconsistent with the facts of the crime. It is essential that any recent sexual activity of the victim be noted by the investigator and made known to the crime laboratory. Body fluids on clothing items (especially undergarments) can be transferred and mixed with other body fluids. Therefore, it is important not only to know the date of last sexual contact, but also to know whether the clothes worn by the victim after that contact were the same clothes worn after the sexual assault. Investigators often neglect to obtain this type of information, thus possibly hampering the serologist's work.
2. Most blood evidence received by a laboratory is in a dried form that is subject to degradation. More potentially probative data can be obtained from fresh, dried blood than from dried blood aged for long periods. In time, genetic information imparted by the proteins and other markers contained within the blood is lost.

The recovery of questioned blood evidence usually involves dealing with various sizes and conditions of stains. Additionally, these stains will be found on items of different colors, textures, and composition. The person collecting the stains has to use good judgment in establishing the most appropriate manner in which to recover the evidence. Collection of questioned wet and dry blood samples is usually done by (1) recovering the entire item bearing the blood, or (2) separate removal of all, or a portion, of the blood exhibited on an object.

Wet blood samples should be recovered only when the evidence can be immediately transmitted to a crime laboratory or frozen under uncontaminated conditions for a short time before being taken to the laboratory. It is usually difficult in the field to collect bulky evidence (e.g., clothing, bedding, carpet, tile, drywall) bearing wet blood. Small items exhibiting this form of blood generally are more suitable. The personnel involved in field recovery of wet blood should determine whether or not the crime laboratory to which evidence will be sent can accommodate wet evidence. Some forensic laboratories need blood specimens in an air-dried condition because of the problems of properly storing massive amounts of damp evidence. Wet blood samples can also be hazardous to crime scene personnel, in that they can be more likely to transmit contagious diseases, such as hepatitis B or AIDS.

Eye droppers and syringes are convenient tools for removing wet blood, but the sample must be frozen or shipped to the laboratory immediately. It is almost impossible to air-dry blood in such devices, and separate eye droppers or syringes must be used for each sample collection so as to prevent cross-contamination. Because of these and other difficulties, it is best to avoid collecting wet blood in eye droppers, syringes, or similar articles.

Another technique is the use of swabs, cotton cloth, cotton threads, or filter paper to absorb the wet stain. As much blood as possible should be concentrated on the gathering medium so that a dense stain results. Simply obtaining smears or small deposits of blood can hinder detailed forensic testing. Many times most of the blood is left on the source object, and the absorbent material permits only a limited blood examination, or possibly one of no evidentiary value at all. Most absorbent methods often collect surface dirt and other extraneous debris in addition to the blood.

When absorbent cloth is used to collect blood or any other body fluid, residues of detergent and chemical additives (e.g., optical whiteners) should be rinsed from the cloth before it is used. These materials can detrimentally affect serological testing of biological fluids. Some laboratories boil a new sheet (already washed several times) for several hours before drying and cutting it into appropriate sizes to use for collection of stains. Individual threads removed from this cloth can be used when extremely small stains must be absorbed. The thread can be gently maneuvered to concentrate the blood in a dense manner.

In summary, the recovery of wet blood evidence during field investigations has numerous disadvantages. Because of significant time-span and evidence-storage problems, it is recommended that wet bloodstains be collected, air-dried, and forwarded to the laboratory as soon as possible, or frozen until submitted. Drying allows the fixing of stains in a specific location, reduces the opportunity for intragarment and intergarment transfer, and reduces decay and disease possibilities.

Dried bloodstains are often encountered as physical evidence in sexual assault investigations. It is advisable to submit the entire item that bears the stain for forensic analysis. Blood in a dried state should be protected from heat, moisture, direct sunlight, and possible contaminants. Airtight containers are not recommended because they tend to retain moisture.

Dried blood samples can be removed from articles when it is impractical to submit the entire article to the laboratory or when the stained area is large. Methods most frequently used for removing such blood are

1. Removing the desired sample completely intact
2. Scraping
3. Reconstitution of the stain

Intact Samples. The removal of an intact stain from an object (when the entire object cannot be collected itself as evidence) is the best alternative. Cutting out the stained area with an appropriate tool is in many ways easier than undertaking other methods, especially when articles are large. The concentrated stained area acquired by this technique can also result in enhanced forensic examination of the blood. Removing various items such as concrete, drywall, and wood can require saws or similar tools, which produce dust and other particulate matter that can contaminate the blood evidence. In such cases, the stained area should be covered with paper, sections of plastic, or other suitable items before removal.

Scraping. Scraping is not the best way to retrieve dried blood from an object. This procedure often results in obtaining dust-like small particles and can also lead to the loss of the sample. The blood becomes separated to a great extent, making it difficult for the laboratory to evaluate. Furthermore, many possible contaminant substances on the surface from which the blood is scraped can be mixed with the stain. When it is absolutely necessary to use the scraping technique, the stain should be disturbed to the least possible extent. It is suggested that a clean razor blade be used and submitted to the laboratory as a control specimen accompanying the removed stain.

Reconstitution. The method of applying absorbent materials (swabs, cotton cloth, etc.) to a dried bloodstain sometimes does not remove enough of the sample. Therefore, it becomes necessary to reconstitute the dried stain so it can be retained on the material. A common medium used to perform this task is distilled water. The absorbent material is wetted slightly in this liquid and applied to the questioned stain area. The questioned stain is then concentrated on the material to the greatest extent feasible. Probably the most important drawback to this procedure is the dilution of the sample, which will almost always result in loss of probative genetic information. Further, a reconstituted bloodstain that is not analyzed promptly is fertile ground for bacterial growth, which can harm the sample. Also, as with the scraping technique, surface contaminants are obtained and intermingled with the blood. The reconstitution of bloodstains is best avoided except as a last resort.

There will be instances, however, when it is impractical to remove dried blood without using the reconstitution method. For example, in cases of sexual assault involving bleeding of the victim, it may be appropriate to swab the penis of the suspect for blood or other evidence. Dried blood can be sampled by using a swab moistened slightly with distilled water. The swabbing procedure should avoid the penile opening, unless blood is obviously present there. It is recommended that penile swabbing not be used routinely; instead, it should be limited to those instances in which blood is very likely to be present.

A major disadvantage of both the scraping and absorbent-material proce-dures of recovery is the difficulty of dealing with the porous media. Blood depos-ited on such articles as concrete, unfinished wood, cardboard, and drywall can be absorbed and much of the stain can collect below the surface. Scraping a porous object normally will remove only surface-level substances. Swabs, cotton cloth, etc., moistened with distilled water, can cause the stain, when reconstituted, to be further absorbed into the porous object. It is best to simply cut out the bloodstains and send them intact to the laboratory.

The subject of "control" samples is relevant to any situation in which blood is removed from an article. Blood is chemically complex, as are the forensic tests applicable to this type of evidence. Many substances common to everyday life (e.g., detergents, deodorants, fruit juices, plant materials) are capable of interfering with certain blood examination tests. It is a great advantage for the laboratory to know whether or not such substances are present in the area where a bloodstain has been deposited. Whenever a stain is recovered from an object or area that will not be sent intact to the laboratory, an unstained control sample adjacent to the ques-tioned stain should be obtained. A prime example would be the removal of a stain from a wall-to-wall carpet. If the stain is approximately the size of a quarter, it would be satisfactory to cut out a 4-in. square section of carpet bearing the stain. The unstained area surrounding the suspected blood could be tested by the laboratory to determine whether substances that could hinder examination are present. Also, instances where swabs, cotton cloth, or filter paper are applied to the collection of bloodstains, control samples of these gathering agents from the same source as those used for actual collection should be retained and submitted to the crime laboratory.

One of the problems in the effective recovery of blood evidence is deciding what amount of blood to remove when a large amount is actually present. Bloodstains that appear to be probative in the investigation should be secured as evidence. However, it is impractical to remove all the blood that is present under some circumstances. Violent physical contact may result in both suspect and victim bleeding in the same general area. Bloodstains in the crime scene, for example, may have come from the victim or the suspect, or be a mixture of blood from both persons. It is not possible to distinguish between different blood types simply by looking at stained areas. However, it is possible to see that blood has been deposited at several different points. Each area where the stains appear to be separated should be sampled.

The apparent path of blood as it moved through the air and struck an object can provide valuable clues in reconstructing a crime. In some instances, a determination can be made as to the position of the person who was bleeding. This determination can assist in identifying possible areas from which samples are to be taken. However, the interpretation of bloodstain patterns involves a detailed examination of the configuration of individual stain areas. Care should be taken not to disturb the stains by sampling until documentation and analysis appropriate for this interpretation have been completed.

The application of good judgment based on training and experience will almost always be the final determinant regarding collecting questioned blood samples under such situations. Still, one must avoid the tendency to take random samples without any attention to the amount of blood present or indications that the blood deposits are from more than one person. It is important to note that the terminology in forensic science for properly recovering these specimens is "representative", as opposed to "random".

Representative sampling involves collection of the blood evidence that is felt to be probative, based on the facts and circumstances of the case. Samples are taken by evaluating the size and location of stains. In some instances, the location of a stain may be of more significance than its size. Also, consideration should be given to determining how much blood should be taken per sample and how many samples should be recovered.

In contrast, random sampling involves the recovery of blood evidence in an unorganized fashion. Here, there is no attempt to evaluate the relevant sampling areas before collection is accomplished.

Forensic laboratories have long made use of so-called preliminary tests for the presence of blood. These chemical tests react with the hemoglobin present in the blood of animals and humans and are used to determine whether a stain could be blood. Various substances, such as certain plant materials, have the potential to cause false-positive reactions to these tests. Therefore, these procedures do not establish that blood is unequivocally present, only that it may be. In the crime laboratory environment, preliminary (also sometimes referred to as "screening" or "presumptive") blood tests are under controlled conditions and are supplemented with a variety of other procedures to identify a stain as containing blood and to classify it further.

There has been a marked increase in interest in the potential use of preliminary tests for blood at the field investigative level, primarily due to circumstances in which it would be advantageous to distinguish blood from other substances. Dried blood exposed to numerous environmental conditions can take on a variety of shapes and colors and be difficult to recognize. Similarly, minute spots of blood and diluted blood can escape detection if an individual collects only what can be seen by the unaided eye.

There are a number of commercially available test kits that claim to be ultimate solutions to these problems. However, it is probably better to have the chemical testing agents prepared by the crime laboratory for field analysis. This procedure will better ensure the quality and reliability of results. It is incumbent on an individual who is not a serologist to seek training and guidance in effective use of the tests from experienced personnel in a crime laboratory.

Like any other procedure, preliminary blood tests are to be used with care. This is because

1. It is possible to destroy or contaminate minute samples by overzealous and uneducated administering of a test.
2. When the suspected blood can be seen by the investigator, generally it should not be tested in the field. Instead, it should be protected and submitted to the laboratory for analysis.
3. In instances when the blood cannot be seen but is believed to be present, field testing is appropriate. This situation is common when an area that at one time contained blood has been washed or cleaned. However, if the investigator cannot visually observe the suspected blood, it is very unlikely that the laboratory will be able to do a great deal with the evidence from the forensic standpoint.
4. Chemical components of the preliminary tests are subject to deterioration as a result of storage time and conditions. When deterioration has occurred, the tests will not be functional even when blood is present. Quality control of test materials must be maintained.
5. Many tests are suited for application in small areas at a time, making it time consuming and difficult to cover large areas or surfaces.
6. The tests can differ in their susceptibility to false-positive reactions. The investigator must consult a knowledgeable serologist as to the potential for these reactions.

Chemical agents of various types are used for preliminary blood analysis. Some of those encountered are

1. Ortho-tolidine
2. Phenolphthalein
3. Luminol
4. Tetramethylbenzidine
5. Leuko malachite green
6. Benzidine

The ortho-tolidine, phenolphthalein, and other tests (except luminol) work fundamentally in the same manner. The area of the suspected stain is swabbed and treated with the test chemical, and the user visually examines the treated swabs for the appearance of a color. The color reaction (bluish green for ortho-tolidine and reddish pink for phenolphthalein) is indicative of the probable existence of blood in the location swabbed.

Luminol is a chemical test that operates somewhat differently. When luminol comes into contact with blood, it has the capacity to undergo chemiluminescence. This means a positive result would cause the stain to give off visible light that can be seen in a darkened setting with the naked eye. The user then recovers the items that so respond for examination in the forensic laboratory. Luminol testing usually involves spraying of large areas suspected of containing blood. It is not recommended, however, that someone enter a crime scene and completely spray the whole location as a routine procedure. Because of the potentially destructive effect on substances in blood that are characterized during serological examination, the application of luminol to suspected blood evidence normally is undertaken with caution. Usually, this method is used when bloodstains are so minute or washed out (previously cleaned up with a mop, for example) as to be virtually impossible to see with the naked eye. Luminol can also be used in identifying a specific unknown crime scene when there are a number of possible areas in question.

Anyone applying the tests should know that some of them contain harmful chemical substances. For example, benzidine, which was once used widely (but is now used only by a few individuals), is known to be carcinogenic. This fact reinforces the point that the choice of a preliminary test should be made on an educated basis.

When used properly, preliminary blood tests can be effective, especially in locating blood that might otherwise go undetected. However, preliminary tests should not be viewed as shortcuts to substitute for proven evidence collection procedures. These tests can become misused tools for those persons who are not willing to spend the time and energy required to conduct a search in a methodical and quality manner.

Extreme care should be used when trying to develop fingerprints in blood. Protein-based stains (i.e., comasse blue), while enhancing the visibility of these prints, can destroy the blood proteins and make further blood testing impossible.

One final difficulty with blood evidence regards handling or touching of stains, or even unstained areas, with bare hands. Aside from health and safety considerations, evidence can be inadvertently contaminated by the presence of biological residues (e.g., saliva, perspiration, body oils exuded from the skin) on the hands of the person recovering it. The person collecting the evidence can protect it by wearing gloves. Surgical-type gloves can be suitable for this purpose, but latent or visible prints can be deposited by someone who is wearing this kind of glove. The gloves can conform so tightly to the skin that dermal ridge detail in the form of a print may be left on an area that has been touched. This possibility, although usually very slight, should be taken into consideration to avoid leaving confusing prints.

Semen

The type of physical evidence probably most frequently associated with sexual assault investigations is semen. The very presence of this male reproductive fluid indicates the occurrence of sexual activity and can assist in corroborating the victim's contention of rape.

The forensic laboratory can determine that an unidentified substance recovered as evidence is semen if male reproductive cells (spermatozoa) are present.

Depending on the time that has passed since the crime, these cells may be alive and motile (free moving) or dead. The motile cells indicate relatively recent sexual contact.

A major distinction must be made between the microscope examination for motile cells, typically conducted immediately following the medical examination of a victim, and the normal analysis for spermatozoa in the crime laboratory. The crime laboratory does not usually encounter motile spermatozoa in its serological analyses. The serologist almost exclusively deals with dried stains and nonmotile cells, if present. Microscopic examination for motile spermatozoa is best accomplished by a physician or medical technician, as soon as possible after evidence recovery is accomplished. Spermatozoa have the capability to remain motile for a few hours or several days depending on the nature of their environment. It is reasonable to expect that spermatozoa can normally be present within the vaginal areas for no more than 72 hr. There are numerous variables that can affect whether or not these cells are present, including normal drainage, action of the vaginal environment, and cleansing actions taken by the person involved. Also, the fact that spermatozoa are present does not necessarily mean they are motile or even intact.

There are times when the collected evidence consists of seminal fluid that is devoid of these reproductive cells. This can occur for a variety of reasons, including a vasectomized suspect, low spermatozoa count, and the difficulty of recovering spermatozoa in the laboratory.

Seminal fluid has various chemical constituents, some of which also appear in other fluids. However, it is scientifically recognized that a protein referred to as prostate-specific antigen (p30) can be identified and used to conclusively determine that a substance is semen.

Once semen has been identified, it can be analyzed by DNA or for chemical substances that will indicate the ABO blood type of the donor. Approximately 80% of the population are *secretors* who have detectable amounts of blood group substances present in body fluids other than blood, such as semen and saliva. Known blood samples and known saliva samples from an individual in question normally are required by the forensic laboratory for the purpose of determining secretor status.

Certain enzymes, or genetic markers, that exist in blood can also be identified in semen. The particular type located in an individual's blood will be consistent with that identified in the other body fluids. The types found in the enzyme systems are independent of the donor's ABO type.

Techniques to remove evidence of semen are most commonly directed at collecting spermatozoa, or chemicals known to exist in seminal fluid, in the vaginal or cervical region of a victim. Even when penetration of the vagina by the penis did not occur, there is still the possibility that semen will be present. Furthermore, even when the victim states that only vaginal contact took place with the suspect, consideration should be given to her potential reluctance to admit that oral or anal contact did, in fact, also occur. This situation is often the case due to embarrassment and revulsion at the notion of such sexual violation. Based on the circumstances of an incident, it may be advisable to take oral and anal swabbings along with vaginal samples, to cover just such a possibility. Each area should be swabbed separately. The resulting swabs should be packaged individually and labeled as to their origin. At least two swabs, but no more than four, should be used for each area. Unstained control swabs should be furnished to the laboratory.

If the swabs used for evidence collection are subsequently used to make smears on microscope slides (to facilitate a microscopic examination for spermatozoa), both swabs and slides should be furnished to the crime laboratory. Additionally, when the slides are examined by the physician or technician, they should not be treated with a fixative if a serological examination is anticipated, because the fixative may interfere with subsequent laboratory testing.

A somewhat unusual and often unproductive method of evidence recovery is to have a victim who has had oral/nasal contact with semen actually blow his/her nose on a clean section of cotton cloth. It is possible that spermatozoa and/or seminal fluid have entered the nasal passages after first entering the mouth or facial region. This method of evidence recovery is easily accomplished and normally would not be as traumatic to the victim as others used to recover evidentiary materials during a clinical examination. A section of cloth approximately 6 in. square can be sufficient to both gather the evidence and serve as a control specimen. As is the case when dealing with any form of body fluid evidence, efforts should be made to ensure that the bare hands of evidence technician, physician, nurse, etc. do not touch the cloth prior to the necessary forensic analyses. This recommendation obviously also applies to the swabs, already mentioned, for the collection of semen.

Swabbing of the oral region may not extract spermatozoa that is located in places that are difficult to reach, such as between the teeth and under the tongue. Therefore, another possible way to obtain semen evidence is to have the victim's mouth rinsed with distilled water. The solution can be expectorated by this person into a sterile container for submission to the laboratory. It is possible, but unlikely, that motile spermatozoa could be discovered if a microscopic analysis is performed soon after the rinse is taken. After this analysis is accomplished, such a liquid sample should be frozen and sent to the laboratory. The retention of a control sample of the fluid rinse is advisable, should it be needed later in forensic analyses. Semen has a relatively short survival rate in the oral cavity. This means that sampling in the oral cavity should be done as soon as possible after the sexual assault. The examination for motile spermatozoa requires microscopic observation to detect these cells. The analysis of "wet" samples immediately following the medical examination of the victim usually is necessary in this situation. If circumstances do not permit such rapid examination, the obtained specimens of swabs, microscope slide smears, or cloth should not be packaged in a wet condition. To do so can result in deterioration of the evidence from the serological perspective. It is proper to air-dry these materials and then package them in paper or cardboard containers for immediate shipment to the crime laboratory. Once the evidence reaches the crime laboratory, it should be frozen until the time of examination.

There is a tendency to concentrate on the presence of semen on the person of a victim because it is indicative of evidence transfer through sexual contact. Semen is also often found on clothing, bedding, carpets, and car seats, but can be located on almost any other article, depending on the movements of the victim and the suspect. Reasonable efforts should be undertaken to recover the entire item containing a suspected semen stain. With large items (e.g., wall-to-wall carpets), regions on which semen is believed to have been deposited should be cut out. An uncontaminated and unstained area surrounding the semen deposit, large enough to function as a control sample for forensic testing, should be included. Before it is cut, the area in question should be scrutinized for other forms of evidence, such as hairs and fibers, that may inadvertently be lost during the removal process. Also, the area should be covered during removal if a considerable amount of extraneous debris is expected to be generated. No matter whether the entire item or a portion of it is to be retained as evidence, any wet item that cannot be immediately examined in a forensic setting must be air-dried, packaged in a paper or cardboard container, kept free of moisture, and frozen whenever possible.

Despite the best attempts to recover semen evidence in the previously discussed manner, there will be situations in which it is necessary to remove wet or dried semen from a particular kind of surface. Recovery of dry specimens can be accomplished by cutting, chipping, or scraping; and of wet samples, via swabs, sections of cloth, or filter paper. Of particular concern is the collection of dried semen from such materials as glass and painted substrates when entire items cannot be recovered. Semen can be removed from glass by gently scraping it into a paper or cardboard container. As much of the sample as possible should be scraped. As such scrapings are often of small quantity, small containers should be used. A painted surface bearing dried semen should be sampled, if possible, by cutting or chipping out the entire section of paint exhibiting the evidence. In this way, the stain will be preserved in its original state.

One suggestion for the recovery of dried semen is the use of distilled water to reconstitute the stain onto a swab or similar gathering medium. The reconstitution of any dried body fluid is to be regarded as a technique of last resort. The difficulties and disadvantages of this method, previously referred to in the discussion of blood evidence, pertain to semen collection and preservation as well.

Wet stains can be recovered through the use of swabs, sections of cotton cloth, or filter paper. The correct procedure would then be to air-dry the swab, cloth, or filter paper. This wet stain then ends up being handled generally in the same manner as a dry stain.

One of the salient points regarding field recognition of semen evidence is the utilization of lighting techniques and preliminary chemical testing when investigators are attempting to identify the crime scene itself. Often, the exact location of the scene is not known, due to circumstances in the case. As with blood evidence, reliance on lighting techniques or chemicals has the potential of becoming a means to avoid the more detailed and tedious work needed to locate potential evidence.

The UV light or alternate light sources are commonly utilized as a major tool in the location of semen in crime scene investigation. These instruments certainly can function as an aid, but cannot discriminate between stains that are exclusively seminal in origin and those that are not. Semen stains may fluoresce when exposed to UV light. However, the level of fluorescence visible to the unaided human eye is minimal in many instances. Fluorescence of a stain is sometimes difficult to see, even when semen is located on a nonfluorescent background. If the substrate is highly fluorescent under UV light, the semen often will appear darker than the surrounding unstained area. If an individual is looking only for the florescent effect associated with semen, this darker spot could be overlooked as evidence.

A field technician is likely to discover numerous items that exhibit a high level of visible fluorescence and are not semen. Clothing, bedding, cosmetics, deodorants, laundry detergents, and other common articles can exhibit a high level of visible fluorescence under UV light, which may obscure the low visible fluorescence normally exhibited by semen. When used without knowledge of this limitation, the UV light procedure could be extremely misleading and even cause pertinent evidence to be overlooked or disregarded.

Presumptive chemical testing for the presence of semen is in general use in crime laboratories. This analysis is utilized in the attempt to determine whether a specimen could be semen. The application of chemical testing procedures has also been expanded to field investigation. Kits are available in the law enforcement supply market that are designed for field testing of suspected semen stains. The most common type of such kits is directed at detection of acid phosphatase, a chemical present in relatively high levels in semen.

There are a variety of difficulties inherent in the indiscriminate use of any preliminary chemical tests for semen at the field investigative level. One major difference between field situations necessitating preliminary analysis of blood and of semen is that semen deposits are more likely to be found only in the immediate area of the assault. This circumstance is due simply to the amount of semen usually ejaculated and the time span in which ejaculation takes place. Blood, on the other hand, may appear in areas that are completely separated due to the size of a wound, blood velocity, movement of the person who is bleeding, and other related variables.

Therefore, the items that have a high probability of containing semen (e.g., bedding, clothing, upholstery) can be logically identified in many instances. This is not to imply that the semen will be easily visible to the unaided eye in all cases, but that the articles that could hold it can be discovered with reasonable effort. Correspondingly, the emphasis should be on collection of the items that may contain semen, rather than selective recovery of only the articles that react positively to a chemical field examination. Selective recovery could result in loss of many other forms of physical evidence. For example, a pillowcase exhibiting no positive reaction to the acid phosphatase preliminary analysis may contain hairs, fibers, cosmetics, etc. that are trace in nature and could serve to furnish valuable forensic information.

To realize the worst implication of chemical field testing, imagine an investigator who feels that the discovery of semen must occur for prosecution of a sexual assault suspect to be successful in a given case. This person could quickly test the areas where semen should, using common sense, be detected at the crime scene. If no positive results are observed, the collection of evidence might stop at that point. This unfortunate situation has on too many occasions been related to the author by individuals involved in day-to-day field investigations.

The discussion thus far has centered primarily on semen evidence when it is recovered as an intact, uncontaminated substance. In realistic terms, there are numerous cases in which semen will be mixed with urine, blood, vaginal fluid, saliva, and other materials. Analytical difficulties can arise in the laboratory when there is a mixture of body fluids from two or more persons by conventional analysis. Blood groupings, for example, can be dramatically affected. However, as previously stated, newer DNA techniques have successfully separated and detected semen, even when it is mixed with other body fluids.

Every attempt should be made to ensure that suspected semen deposits do not come into contact with other possible body fluid stains as field technicians or laboratory personnel handle articles of evidence. For instance, a blouse worn by a victim of a sexual assault may bear semen from the suspect on the lower portion and blood from the victim's head wound on the upper area. Folding the blouse, causing direct contact between the semen and blood, could contaminate both evidence substances. Furthermore, an item exhibiting wet stains should be dealt with in a manner designed to eliminate inadvertent transfer of this evidence to a location that was previously unstained. This is of significance regarding semen evidence because the location in which the stain appears can be of great relevance. A wet stain mistakenly transferred by improper handling or packaging may subsequently be placed in an area that is inconsistent with a statement, for example, of a victim.

Saliva

The conventional forensic analysis of saliva involves the detection of its suggested presence and a determination of the possible ABO blood group of the depositor, if that individual is a secretor.

Compared to blood and semen, saliva evidence is encountered less frequently in the field and the crime laboratory. Blood and semen have an obvious physical appearance, including their color and texture, unlike saliva. Stains of blood and semen, having a crustlike appearance and recognizable color, can be distinguished in both wet and dry forms. Saliva, on the other hand, tends to defy detection by the naked eye once the initial "wet" appearance of the stained area has disappeared. To further complicate matters, saliva evidence tends to be located in places and under conditions which promote contamination. A typical example is cigarette butts in an ashtray filled with debris. Furthermore, the presence of saliva in a given area is sometimes easier to explain than blood or semen. Saliva is readily emitted from the mouth, whereas blood and semen are internal body fluids that appear externally only under certain physiological conditions.

Saliva can be located on both porous and nonporous articles. As with other biological fluids discussed, each situation will dictate the proper method of retrieval and preservation. Bare wood, wallboard, paper, and like porous items bearing possible saliva deposits should be removed intact without adding contamination to the area of concern. The evidence material should be permitted to air-dry, packaged in a paper, cardboard, or another container that will allow the movement of air, and submitted to the crime laboratory as soon as possible. A control sample of the area surrounding the potential saliva stain should be acquired for forensic analysis.

The utilization of swabs, cotton cloth, or filter paper with distilled water as a mechanism to reconstitute dried saliva is definitely not recommended on porous substrates. Such techniques can serve to dissipate the evidence even further by causing it to migrate deeper into the porous material. It is reiterated that stain reconstitution is to be regarded as a last resort in almost any situation relative to body fluids.

Cigarette butts represent examples of porous articles that are often collected for saliva evidence. The environment of ashtrays and similar trash disposal receptacles can be disastrous to the forensic potential of saliva. One of the erroneous recommendations about handling evidence in these cases is to package all of the debris, including the cigarette butts, into one container for preservation as evidence. Doing so only serves to further contaminate the cigarette butts, as cigarette ashes are highly alkaline and can have a harmful effect on any saliva that is present. The cigarettes should be placed in a separate container to minimize contact with potential contaminants.

Cigarette butts, aside from furnishing saliva evidence, can be sources for the recovery of latent prints, but recovering both types of evidence can be a problem. Laboratory methods used for chemical processing of latent prints are detrimental to serological analyses for saliva, and vice versa. Because of this laboratory problem, a choice normally has to be made as to whether the item is to be examined for saliva or prints. Sometimes, it is opted to pursue both, despite the fact that saliva is class evidence and latent prints have the potential of furnishing a positive identification of a specific person.

The decision to recover both types of evidence is dependent on the size and condition of the cigarette butt(s) in question. Saliva is most likely to be present in the end of the butt having direct contact with the mouth. Latent prints are many times located on the portion of the butt nearest the burning segment of the cigarette. It is possible, then, to examine these two areas separately by cutting the butt and conducting appropriate analyses of each section. There are too many variables to preclude the presence of saliva or prints on any given portion of a cigarette butt. The salient consideration is to collect as many intact cigarette butts as reasonable, while limiting contamination to them. The greater the size of the intact cigarette butt, the more specimen the laboratory has with which to make decisions regarding the most advantageous examinations to conduct.

Other items on which saliva may be found can be recovered in the same disposal areas as cigarettes. Chewing gum, small bits of food, toothpicks, paper matches that may have functioned as toothpicks, etc. should also be regarded as possibly containing saliva, but are often realistically of limited value. When such items are observed, they should be segregated from ashes and other particulate debris, which have a tendency to contaminate. Any of these evidence materials discovered in a wet condition should be air-dried and packaged in containers that have the capacity for air movement and will not retain extraneous moisture.

Saliva on occasion will appear on nonporous items, such as painted surfaces, plastics, glass, and metal cans. The high possibility of contamination or inadvertent destruction of the saliva due to its low visibility and ready solubility in water can create inherent difficulties. Dried saliva is extremely difficult to see with the naked eye and can be wiped away with the slightest touch. Also, there is often a minimal amount of saliva on nonporous surfaces because they tend not to collect saliva. The field investigator should be cognizant of the need to avoid abrasion of nonporous items that may bear saliva. This should extend to the handling of these items with unprotected bare hands. There is the slight possibility that residues that could interfere with crime laboratory examinations would be transferred from the hands to the saliva.

As with blood, it is feasible to remove a section of nonporous area bearing the suspected saliva stain. Large and bulky articles or things that cannot be moved for practical reasons can be handled in this manner, if care is taken to protect the area in question from debris generated by the removal process. In sexual assault cases, such instances will usually not be encountered with great frequency. A further point for the field investigator is the need to cover an area exhibiting saliva on a nonporous surface. A section of cardboard or other pliable material can be configured to act as a protective cover over this region to prevent rubbing or abrasion from destroying the evidence. The article can be packaged and subsequently furnished to the forensic laboratory.

Saliva can be removed from a nonporous surface with swabs and distilled water. This technique can serve as a last option when the entire item, or an appropriate portion of it, cannot be removed from the scene and submitted to the laboratory. The same cautions already set forth for other biological fluid evidence apply here regarding the reconstitution of a questioned specimen. Control specimens of swabs and control sampling of the region surrounding the area in consideration are also necessary.

Although a somewhat infrequent occurrence, a wet saliva deposit could be located in the course of field investigation. Swabs, sections of absorbent cotton cloth, or filter paper could be used to effect recovery. This is especially useful when the intact item on which the saliva is located cannot be removed from the scene for some reason.

A great deal of attention has been directed both in crime scene investigations and in forensic pathology to the role and nature of bite mark evidence in sexual assaults. Direct contact between the suspect's mouth and the skin of the victim often results not only in a bite mark, but also in the presence of saliva in the immediate region of the mark. The recovery and forensic analysis of this saliva evidence are of extreme importance, especially in cases where the bite mark itself does not exhibit sufficient clarity of detail for positive identification with the dental configuration of the suspect.

The first stage of utilizing saliva in bite mark cases is the recognition of the mark and immediate protection of that location from contaminating or destructive activity. Care should be given to ensure the area of concern is not touched with the bare hands. After documenting the initial condition and location of the mark photographically, a protective cover (e.g., cardboard) should be placed over the region to prevent abrasion or contamination while the person bitten, if deceased, is removed from the scene. When possible, this should also be done with a living person. This task normally involves advising the individual to refrain from washing or touching the area, as well as taking steps to protect it with a small cover. Liaison between hospital personnel and law enforcement is critical, due to the medical treatment necessitated for victims or suspects. It is possible that hospital officials may have the first contact with a victim or suspect and would be in a position to protect the saliva from contamination or loss. Medical personnel should be made aware of the need to refrain from washing a bite mark unless this is necessary during treatment.

Saliva can be removed from a bite mark by using swabs and/or cotton thread wetted with distilled water. The area adjacent to, but not part of, the bite mark should be sampled as a control. The bite mark itself is sampled separately. Special attention should be given to ensuring that the mark is not altered by the saliva collection procedure. Additionally, sampling from bloody areas of the mark should be avoided. The collection media used to acquire the control samples should not be packaged with the samples recovered from the bite mark. Unstained swabs and/ or cotton threads used for evidence collection should be retained as additional control samples.

Saliva can be deposited on the skin in areas other than bite marks. Sometimes a suspect has licked, sucked, or lightly bitten the victim's skin without leaving a recognizable mark. The statements of the victim concerning the actions of the suspect should be considered as indicating locations from which questioned saliva may be recovered.

In some instances of sexual assault, efforts by the suspect to bite the victim (or vice versa) may not necessarily result in a bite mark directly on the skin, due to intervening articles such as clothing, bed sheets, and pillowcases. Therefore, biting through a fabric article may result in the creation of a mark on the skin and the deposition of saliva on the intervening article. Attention for saliva evidence should be given to an area on a fabric item, particularly clothing, which corresponds to the locations of a bite mark on the skin. This potentially valuable source for saliva could be missed as a result of not considering that a bite may have occurred through fabric. This circumstance may occur, for example, when an unconscious victim is found nude with her clothing nearby. An assumption that the bite mark was administered to the naked skin may be incorrect and result in pertinent evidence being overlooked.

Recovery of Known Evidence

The recovery of questioned physical evidence will only have real meaning when comparisons with the known evidence sources are conducted. Crime laboratories continually face the inadequacy or lack of known standards required for comparison purposes. Also, forensic examinations frequently are hindered by the use of poor methods to acquire these standards. The recommended techniques for collection of known samples of appropriate quality, which follow, are set forth with the intent of providing the laboratory with the best chance of reaching optimum results from the evidence.

Known Hair Samples

The quality of known hair samples removed from a victim and suspect will directly affect the quality of forensic results coming from the crime laboratory. For a meaningful comparison to be accomplished between questioned and known hairs, the known hairs must be from the same body area as the questioned hairs and represent the variation range of hairs present in that body area. The crime laboratory examiner can categorize hairs as having originated from various areas, which generally are head, pubic, limb, beard or mustache, chest, axillary (under arm), and eye area. However, there can be situations in which hairs may lack certain features necessary for forensic categorization and/or comparison. Head and pubic hairs are the types most often of intrinsic value in sexual assault cases. The reason is that head and pubic hair characteristics vary more from one person to another within the same racial group and possess a greater number of identifiable characteristics. There are circumstances, however, in which hairs from other parts of the body, such as beard hairs, may be pertinent physical evidence.

There are basically five major regions on the head from which samples usually are taken: front, top, back, left side, and right side. Proper sampling of these areas is adequate. In the pubic region, the hairs on the pubic bone area can differ from hairs in the area of the vagina or testicles. Therefore, whenever possible, both these areas should be sampled as comparison standards.

A question frequently asked by investigators regarding the acquisition of known hair evidence is, "How many should be taken?". One or two hairs will be adequate for reliable comparisons to be conducted. Nonetheless, there are differing opinions among laboratory examiners about the exact number to acquire. For example, 100 head hairs (20 from each of the five regions previously mentioned) and 30 pubic hairs (from varying locations) have been suggested as ideal amounts for laboratory comparisons with questioned hairs. However, these numbers are much higher than the amounts of known samples often submitted for comparison purposes. Twenty-five full-length hairs taken from various areas of the head or pubic area generally are considered adequate to represent an individual's hair characteristics. The investigator should discuss this issue with the laboratory that will be responsible for hair comparisons *before* known hairs are acquired in an investigation.

Known hairs are usually taken by pulling out hairs from the area of concern. Removing hairs by this method ensures that the laboratory examiner has the opportunity to study features along the entire length of each hair.

Circumstances sometimes will not permit hairs to be forcibly pulled from the body. The known hairs should then be cut as close to the skin as possible, preferably at skin level with a razor or scalpel. The forensic laboratory which receives these hairs should be advised that the hairs were cut as close to the body as possible and, thereby, full-length hairs have been submitted. Many known hair samples sent to crime laboratories resemble sweepings from the floor of a barber shop because they have been snipped from near the end of the hair shafts. This method can be detrimental, especially if the hairs have been artificially colored or treated. The sampling would represent only the treated ends of the hairs and not the growing areas near the skin, which would have natural color. Transferred hairs in this instance will have treated and natural regions and will be difficult to compare with the inadequately cut known specimens. This could result in a false exclusion of a suspect or victim.

It is also advisable to obtain known hair samples via a "combing" procedure to serve as a supplement to the pulled specimens. Although this procedure is normally associated with the recovery of questioned hairs, fibers, and debris, it also serves as a source for collection of other types of hairs of importance. Human hairs go through a growth process having three stages: anagen (actively growing), catagen (resting), and telogen (dormant and ready to be shed from the body). In fact, there are subtle morphological differences which can be detected by a trained microscopist as the stages progress. Those hairs normally transferred from suspect to victim, and vice versa, during an assault tend to be those that are ready to be shed from the body, hence telogen. The hairs present on the victim that are in the growth cycle stage are those most likely transferred to the suspect and represent the best possible known comparison standards. There are the kinds of hairs frequently obtained via the "combing" procedure, although a certain number of those hairs obtained by pulling or cutting will be in this stage. There can be times when a hair examiner is forced to use these "combings" to supplement the known hair sample when the known hair sample is inadequate or no longer available.

It is evident from the preceding discussion of hair evidence that a multitude of factors influence its forensic interpretation and use in the courtroom. One difficulty relates to the time span between the assault and the collection of known specimens. If a suspect and victim come to the attention of authorities shortly after an assault has occurred, their hair features probably have not been altered by natural growing or intentional alterations on the part of either person. Many suspects take steps to bleach or dye hair, shave it off completely, or otherwise hinder the acquisition of reliable known standards for comparison. Therefore, known hairs should be taken from a suspect and victim as soon as their identities become known.

Sometimes it is necessary to acquire known "elimination" hair specimens from persons not involved in the sexual assault. For instance, the victim of a sexual assault may have had consenting intimate contact or sexual relations with someone shortly before the crime was committed. Some of the hairs obtained as evidence, especially those secured by the combing procedures, may have come from that contact, and known hair standards should be obtained from that person. This will assist the crime laboratory in eliminating hairs which would be of no real value as pertinent physical evidence.

On occasion, it becomes necessary to collect hair specimens from animals. A dog or cat, for example, can potentially represent a known source of animal hairs located on clothing or other items recovered in an investigation. There are two primary types of hairs on animals, guard hairs and fur hairs. Guard hairs are long and coarse when compared with the fur hairs, which are typically short and very fine. Both forms of hair should be obtained as known samples by removing them from representative areas. Effort must be made to collect numerous hairs in these locations that exhibit the color and length variations appearing on the subject animal.

Known Fiber Samples

The first known source of fibers that becomes apparent is clothing worn by persons involved in a crime. Although the clothing of victim and suspect is always considered as potentially containing questioned evidence, the fibers that compose the clothing are also utilized in a forensic laboratory as known comparison standards. The recommendation has been made consistently thus far that clothing and other items be recovered intact, whenever feasible. It is not advisable, in the field, for known samples to be removed from clothing by cutting small swatches of fabric. There are instances in which a tremendous amount of clothing is discovered as evidence. In these situations, it may be beyond reasonable practicality to package all the garments for laboratory submission. Still, there is a serious drawback to cutting off portions of the known materials. If clothing fibers were transferred directly to a suspect or victim, then there was some extent of physical contact between garments and person. Therefore, the person may have transferred hairs, blood, etc. to the garment, and they would be missed by only removing a portion of fabric sample and not examining the entire piece of clothing. The investigator faced with this situation may request the assistance of the laboratory in making the best determination when such known sampling in the field is being considered.

Aside from clothing, any other fibrous item recovered as evidence can be used as a source of known fibers. Bedding, small rugs, pillows, and similar articles can be excellent sources of fiber transfer and often become important as reliable evidence sources.

The types of fiber sources mentioned thus far are usually collected simply because field personnel are aware that questioned evidence can be contained on them. Many times these ordinary, expected items represent the only known sources secured from a crime scene. However, all of the fibrous materials at a given place represent the complete environment, not just those limited items often taken to the forensic laboratory. One of the methods of ensuring that adequate fiber standards are removed is to survey a scene, as a separate task, for the collection of realistic known fiber sources. This task can focus the attention of personnel on the known fiber acquisition problem.

The actual recovery of the fiber sample is not a matter of randomly cutting pieces of fabric from various items and pulling a cluster of fibers from others. The following questions should be considered before recovery is initiated:

1. How many fibrous objects are present?
2. What colors are these objects?
3. What are the physical conditions of the objects?
4. What is the best way to remove the samples?

Each fibrous article should be sampled if the known fiber environment is to be correctly represented. The samples should be individually packaged and each container labeled as to its item of origin. All the various colors of fibers are to be obtained from each article sampled. For example, a fabric chair having three separate colors would require sampling of fibers exhibiting all of these colors.

Fibrous articles are subject to wear and tear, as well as the deposition of stains from liquids, soil, and other foreign debris. Simple everyday activity on a carpet, for example, will result in varying degrees of wear in different areas, and stains will give more uniqueness to these areas. Known samples should be obtained to represent fibers from each that would exhibit these physical wear features and foreign substances.

It is advisable to remove intact sections of fabric to be utilized as comparison standards. The collector should ensure that these sections include a sample of yarn of each color present in the article. Any material to which the fibers adhere, such as the backing of a carpet, should also be included for forensic examination. Any sharp instrument will suffice for sample removal, provided it is clean and does not transmit debris or contaminants to the sample.

Known Blood Samples

Obtaining known comparison specimens of blood is a prime consideration in order that characterization of stains may be attained. There can be the assumption that taking known blood involves simply having a physician, or other medically qualified individual, draw the blood into a test tube, whereupon the resulting specimen is transmitted to the crime laboratory for analysis and comparison. However, there are important variables in terms of materials and handling that should be explored because they have a definite bearing on the quality and reliability of the sample.

Known blood samples must be obtained from suspect and victim and, on many occasions, from persons who could be considered as reasonable sources for elimination. The reasons for acquiring the specimens from suspect and victim are obvious because they are directly associated with the crime. However, collection of known specimens should also include those from recent sexual partners of the victim. Known blood samples should be taken from any other person who could have logically deposited a blood or other body fluid stain in the location in question. For example, the child of a rape victim may have bled on a bed sheet prior to the assault that occurred directly on this bedding article. Known blood should be collected to eliminate or include this person as a possible source.

The materials utilized for known blood sampling typically originate from three major sources:

1. Those prepackaged in a commercially available sexual assault evidence collection kit
2. Those prepared and prepackaged in a sexual assault evidence collection kit formed by a crime laboratory or police agency for use by law enforcement and medical personnel
3. Those not part of any prepackaged kit and normally consisting of materials available at the hospital or medical institution at the time samples are taken from the individual

For conventional serological analyses in sexual assault cases, a liquid whole blood sample usually is necessary and superior to a dried sample on, for example, a piece of cloth or filter paper. The determination of secretor status can be accomplished from whole blood through laboratory testing. Such analysis is not functional and reliable when dry blood is examined. Whole blood samples should be refrigerated as soon as possible after they are taken, but must not be frozen. Freezing whole blood will cause the cells to lyse (cellular rupture), which is not beneficial for serologist analysis. Refrigeration retards bacterial activity and growth and serves to protect the genetic factors sought by the serologist.

Many of the commercially available test tubes produced specifically for the collection of blood from a person contain chemical additives designed to either preserve blood or prevent its coagulation. These additives are normally placed in the tubes by the manufacturers before they are sealed and distributed for use in the medical community. A variety of different substrates are used, such as heparin, sodium fluoride, sodium oxalate, ethylenediamine tetraacetic acid (EDTA), and acid citrate dextrose (ACD).

There has been some concern as to whether or not these preservatives or anticoagulants affect forensic analyses. Sodium fluoride has been thought possibly to be detrimental to serological testing methods employing electrophoresis. This point is important, since electrophoresis furnishes much of the advanced blood grouping information at this time in forensic science. The majority opinion was that current methods of analysis make the preservation of anticoagulant almost an irrelevant factor in genetic analysis of whole blood samples. Nonetheless, the crime laboratory that is to be involved in a case should be contacted for its experience and/or requirements. Different laboratories can have varied require-ments, depending on the methods of analysis used for serology examinations. (Some serologists recommend the use of ACD as an anticoagulant, if one is to be used.)

Although anticoagulants or preservatives are often necessary in whole blood samples, forensic analysis of blood is more easily accommodated when no chemi-cal additive is present. Therefore, the acquisition of whole blood samples without any additive is recommended. It is common for the crime laboratory to receive one tube with and one tube without anticoagulant or preservative.

The foregoing statements in reference to utilization of anticoagulants or preservatives are directed primarily at blood grouping. Sometimes the facts of a case will dictate that forensic analysis of blood also encompasses drug and alcohol questions. The guidelines concerning chemical additives are then subject to change.

In addition to a test tube for blood grouping, one test tube each should be taken for alcohol and drug analyses. No preservative or anticoagulant should be incorporated in the sample to be used for drugs, and sodium fluoride can be included in the one to be used for alcohol testing. Thus, three separate known samplings may be submitted to the laboratory, each for a different purpose. Five milliliters of blood in a sterile test tube is a minimum recommended satisfactory amount to facilitate crime laboratory analysis for each of these types of examinations.

In those cases where DNA analysis is to be performed, it is recommended that one tube of blood be drawn with no preservative or anticoagulants present (red-top tube) and another drawn which contains a substance called "EDTA" (purple-top tube). DNA is extremely stable; however, if the liquid samples are to be retained refrigerated for more than 1 week, it is recommended that a portion of the blood (about the diameter of a 50-cent piece) be placed on clean cotton cloth, air dried, and frozen until submitted to the laboratory.

Known Saliva Samples

Known saliva samples used for ABO secretor status determinations can be collected through a variety of procedures. In general, collection methods can involve obtaining liquid or, preferably, air-dried samples.

Known saliva samples should not be routinely taken in liquid form due to chemical decay and the harmful activity of bacteria. Storage of liquid saliva, even for hours, is extremely detrimental.

The collection of saliva can be better accomplished by having an individual expectorate on cloth or a section of filter paper. The collecting substrate must be clean and free of detergents and chemicals to prevent interference with forensic testing. The sample should be acquired only after the individual has not smoked or had anything to eat or drink for at least 30 min. The saliva stain should be no smaller than the size of a quarter. The entire collection surface should not be treated with saliva; the unstained area can then function as a control sample. It can be of value to obtain another complete and unstained collection substrate as an additional control specimen. The saliva should be allowed to air-dry completely and then be packaged in a paper or cardboard container that allows the exchange of air and will not retain moisture.

The use of gauze pads is to be avoided for saliva sampling. Saliva taken in this manner can be too greatly dispersed and difficult to analyze in the laboratory.

The use of filter paper does have advantages that bear mentioning. When the saliva is acquired on this medium, a circle should be drawn around the perimeter of the stain to isolate it for crime laboratory analysis. This outline should be done with a pencil, as certain inks may diffuse and migrate in the paper through time and subsequently come into contact with the saliva. Additionally, steps should be taken to prevent the pencil marks from being smudged over the saliva deposit. Chain-of-custody data can be placed on the filter paper completely away from the saliva.

Another method of obtaining known saliva is to recover it directly from the mouth in the area between the molar teeth and cheek. One suitable technique is to use a piece of cotton or cotton swab, placing it in the mouth for deposition of saliva and removing it for air-drying. Clean forceps can be utilized to place and remove the cloth for sampling, in order to avoid contamination by the hands of the person responsible for taking it. As with other biological fluid evidence, control samples of the substrate used to gather the evidence are to be packaged separately and submitted to the crime laboratory. If DNA analysis is to be performed, no saliva sample is required by most laboratories. Those submitting samples should consult with their respective laboratories concerning this practice.

Marking of Evidence for Identification

The admission of evidence in the courtroom is dependent on adherence to guidelines of chain of custody. Essentially, physical evidence is subjected to challenges as to proper collection, storage, transportation, delivery, and documentation of that material. Incriminating evidence that cannot be introduced in a trial is realistically of no practical value. The generally accepted considerations for admittance of items as evidence in a trial are

1. The item of evidence must be authenticated by a knowledgeable person. This person is typically the one who personally recovered the evidence, or one who actually observed it at the scene and saw it being collected.
2. The item of evidence has not been altered to any appreciable degree. This guideline does take into account the need to alter the evidence in reasonable ways, such as marking an item for identification, or consumption of portions of it during a forensic analysis.
3. The item of evidence must be accounted for at all times, from its collection to its introduction as evidence in a trial. This process is designed to ensure that a similar item has not been substituted, either inadvertently or intentionally.

Physical evidence should be marked for identification whenever feasible. Some forms of evidence, such as debris, cannot be marked, but it is possible to do so with larger items. Two marking methods are commonly used: direct and indirect marking. Direct marking refers to the placement of identification marks on the item of evidence itself. Indirect marking involves placing notations of identification on a container in which the evidence is placed.

It is obvious that the most advantageous method is direct identification. The appearance of markings on the evidence itself leaves no doubt as to its authenticity, and chain of custody is more easily maintained for courtroom purposes. It is recommended that when the evidence is marked, the container into which it is placed also be labeled appropriately. The marks used must be suitable to refresh the memory of the person who collected it or examined it in the laboratory. Depending on the size of the evidence, the date of recovery and initials of the recovering person are adequate for authentication. There is no need to place extensive names, dates, times, and case notations on a piece of evidence. Such data may drastically alter its original condition. These items of information are better documented on an evidence log or similar document.

In contrast, the container housing the evidence normally should be labeled more extensively than the evidence itself. The minimum data recorded should be location and description of the recovered evidence, a specific number or similar designation, person who recovered the evidence, and date of recovery. This information is essential to conform to the fundamental guidelines in a court of law for the gathering of evidence. Agency experience and administrative criteria may dictate that additional data be recorded.

Field personnel in some agencies use tags to mark evidence or its container. These tags normally are attached to the evidence after appropriate notations are written on them. Many individuals feel that this system is convenient and makes it unnecessary to directly mark the evidence. On the contrary, the excessive use of these tags tends to make evidence handling more cumbersome and difficult. A tag can be accidentally torn off or intentionally removed as the evidence is handled or examined forensically. Worse yet would be a situation in which it is lost completely. This has been known to occur and not be noticed until trial, to the detriment of the entire case. The tagging method, thus, has drawbacks, and it does not alleviate the responsibility of the collector to mark the evidence itself whenever possible.

Experience has revealed that it is advantageous to have at least two people observe evidence in place before recovery. One person can actually recover it, mark it directly, and package it. The second party can witness this process and then initial the container bearing the evidence material. This procedure will ensure there is a second person who can authenticate the evidence in the event the person who recovered it is unavailable for court purposes. This may be somewhat impractical for some agencies, but it is mentioned as one additional mechanism that can be used when deemed feasible.

The marking of physical evidence at the time of its collection should be supplemented with an evidence log. This log serves to document the administrative and substantive information concerning evidence recovery. It should record the sequence in which the evidence is recovered, as well as the standard chain-of-custody information mentioned previously. The log should be prepared entirely at the scene. This is because more complete observations are made when personnel are actually in the process of gathering the evidence. The logging technique is especially valuable in cases where a vast amount of evidence is involved. When a question arises, it is more convenient to review a succinct, organized log for evidence information than it is to sort through many individual evidence containers.

The concept of maintaining chain of custody should extend beyond the field collection stage of the investigation. Transmittal of items of evidence from person to person must be documented in writing so that responsibility will be fixed for preservation and courtroom demonstrations of chain of custody. Records are necessary to document times, dates, identities of personnel with access, and other pertinent information regarding any evidence transactions. Recording such information takes only a small amount of time and effort and frequently counters potential challenges to important pieces of evidence. The lack of proper documentation is a hindrance to effective use of the evidence during field investigation, pretrial conferences, and, ultimately, courtroom proceedings.

Materials Used to Package Physical Evidence

The fragile and transitory nature of some types of evidence in sexual assaults makes packaging methods and procedures of utmost significance. Use of incorrect packaging materials can have a disastrous effect on the ability of the crime laboratory to obtain the maximum information afforded by each piece of evidence.

Packaging problems that most often confront field personnel involve either small/minute evidence or large/bulky evidence. A great variety of packaging containers are available, many offered by commercial suppliers. Each agency should study its own needs and make educated decisions. It is relatively simple to accumulate the necessary materials for most packaging situations without resorting to expensive commercially available evidence collection kits.

Sexual assault evidence often comes in the form of small/minute substances, such as tufts of fibers or several strands of hair. Some practical considerations regarding the preservation of such evidence are

1. Cardboard "pillbox" type containers are useful. These containers can be taped securely, are sturdy, and have surfaces that facilitate the writing of identification notations. Additionally, these items allow the exchange of air and tend not to retain moisture.

2. Envelopes having glued flaps are not recommended for prolonged storage. There is a chance the glued areas will come apart and result in the loss of some or all of the enclosed evidence. Also, it can be difficult for laboratory examiners to locate the evidence in the envelopes.

3. The druggist (pharmacist) fold is a useful technique. Bond paper cut in 3×5, 5×7, and $8\frac{1}{2} \times 11$-in. sizes will accommodate most small items. Bond paper is recommended because it is resilient and can be taped securely. It also supplies a good medium for evidence identification notations. The druggist fold is probably the best method for collecting scrapings and suspected blood.

4. Plastic zip-lock bags are not considered best for evidence storage. There is too much chance of accidental opening of the bags, resulting in loss of evidence. Locating a small fiber that is "somewhere" in one of these bags can be difficult for the crime laboratory. To increase the problems, static electricity can attract a considerable amount of foreign material on the exterior and interior of the bags. Moisture retention is difficult to eliminate in these conditions.

5. Film containers (35 mm) can be of value for small/minute evidence. These items are very sturdy and readily available. The containers should be cleaned thoroughly to ensure no contaminants are present before use. Tape can be applied to seal the lid in place as an additional precaution.

Chain-of-custody markings should be place on the selected container before the evidence is placed inside. This point is especially important when the druggist fold is used. Writing with a ballpoint pen or other instrument having a hard, resilient tip can damage the small evidence housed in the package.

The collection and packaging of large/bulky evidence materials typically present greater difficulty than dealing with the small/minute items. In sexual assault cases, field investigators are faced with the recovery of bedding, furniture upholstery, car seats, carpets, and other large objects. More often than not, the tendency is to cut out the stained regions or other areas containing possible evidence. Throughout the discussions it has been recommended that the entire item bearing the evidence be collected and submitted for laboratory analysis. This point is appropriate; however, it must be tempered with the exercise of good judgment by both crime scene investigators and laboratory personnel. The best approach in these situations is first to look over the bulky evidence for any evidentiary items that may be easily lost due to their transitory nature (e.g., hairs, fibers, threads). Much evidence can be lost in the attempt to collect and package large items at the crime scene.

The authors have frequently heard the comment from crime laboratory examiners that investigators often send in virtually all items found at a scene without determining if this is reasonable and, more importantly, worthwhile. On the other hand, the authors have dealt with many investigators who feel it is the responsibility of the crime laboratory to search for evidence on these terms that is beyond the vision or skill of the field investigator. Lack of communication and education many times is the real source of such conflicts. It is usually unnecessary to submit all items collected at a scene to the laboratory. Careful evaluation of the evidence will dictate which articles are ultimately submitted.

There are significant recommendations pertaining to the packaging of large/bulky evidence materials. The information that follows constitutes an effort to deal with common errors in handling this kind of physical evidence.

1. Any material that is damp or wet is to be air-dried, preferably away from direct sunlight. Storing moist evidence in an airtight environment promotes bacterial growth and putrefaction of most biological substances. Prolonged exposure of blood, semen, and other biological materials to sunlight will be harmful due to the negative effects of continued exposure to UV light.

2. Drying of large evidence presents a somewhat burdensome problem. A room or other secure location in which to allow moist evidence to dry should be available. Particular attention must be given to the selection of

a location that minimizes the chance for contamination and takes the health and safety of personnel into account. Appropriate steps are to be taken so that it also is secure and has a system of accountability to document chain of custody.

3. Plastic bags or other plastic-type containers are not advisable for the packaging and storage of large/bulky evidence often encountered in sexual assault investigations. Even when the evidence has been air-dried, sealed plastic bags may promote the accumulation of condensation. There are instances, however, in which plastic packaging materials will make it easier to transport evidence to the laboratory for forensic examination. Most often, this circumstance occurs when it is virtually impossible to air-dry numerous items of evidence at a crime scene. Because moist blood and other wet substances on evidence articles would soak through and destroy paper wrappings, sections of plastic wrap or plastic bags can be used here to advantage. The wrap or plastic bags should be retained when the evidence articles are removed later for the purpose of air-drying, as trace evidence may have been dislodged from the articles while they were housed temporarily. This situation is not to be confused with the requirements for extended storage of physical evidence. In fact, the destructive effect of tightly sealed plastic containers on evidence collected during investigation of violent crimes can be a major difficulty for the forensic laboratory.

4. Sturdy paper of the type commonly used for wrapping packages for mailing is easy to obtain and can accommodate a wide variety of evidence sizes and shapes. Identification notations relating to the evidence can be written on the outside of the paper before the evidence is wrapped and secured with tape. Paper bags also can be utilized, with double-ply bags being the most resilient to tearing and the demands of constant handling. As mentioned previously, these paper materials are to be checked for possible contamination produced as a result of the manufacturing process.

5. Steps should be taken to avoid excessive handling of the evidence that is gathered. Each handling of the evidence increases the opportunity of contamination and loss of transitory materials. Once the package containing the evidence is sealed, every effort is to be made not to open it prior to submission to the crime laboratory. This action assists an attorney in courtroom arguments as to the positive and detailed methods used to preserve evidence integrity.

6. Ideally, every item of evidence should be packaged separately and not intermingled with other evidence. This approach is recommended as the first choice for collection and preservation. There will be conditions, nonetheless, that make doing so somewhat impractical. It is not uncommon to recover voluminous amounts of clothing and similar materials that are found together and, therefore, can be conveniently packaged together. One important example in this regard involves the handling of bulky bedding items (sheets, blankets, bedspreads, etc.) appearing on a bed in which the victim was attacked. Rather than remove each pertinent bedding

article and package it separately, it can be advantageous to collect those bedding materials that logically could be valued together in the same order in which they were found on the bed. Doing so could prevent the possible loss of trace evidence. The sequence of bedding items can be appropriately marked for reconstruction should the sequence become an issue at a later date. These circumstances are to be regarded as exceptions rather than standard operations. In general, separate packaging is most conducive to laboratory analysis and can also provide a higher degree of credibility to the evidence in the courtroom.

7. Clothing and other articles of evidence from the victim, suspect, and crime scene must not be allowed to intermingle. Contamination can easily occur if contact takes place to even a small extent. The victim's and suspect's evidence should not be handled in the same area because of the extremely transitory quality of trace evidence materials. As an added precaution, the packages of evidence are to be well sealed. This approach can overcome evidence integrity challenges on the basis that storing these materials together in a box, even though separately wrapped, could result in contamination by the movement of extremely small debris.

The time to accumulate the necessary materials for evidence storage is before, not after, a crime of similar crisis occurs. The human tendency is to use whatever is at hand in times of stress or crisis-level circumstances. Every effort should be made to have the proper evidence packaging materials available to meet the needs, within reason, of almost any situation that could happen on a moment's notice. Neglecting to accomplish this seemingly basic task probably is responsible for many of the common difficulties in crime scene investigation and other evidence collection situations.

Summary

As reflected in this chapter, handling different types of physical evidence can represent a complex task. Specialized techniques that apply to the five major kinds of evidence covered here have been set forth as suggestions and recommendations. The vast possibilities that cannot adequately be anticipated make it incumbent on the crime scene investigator or other evidence-recovery party to evaluate each problem before action is instituted. The number of available personnel, evidence storage facilities, access to a crime laboratory, and requirements established by the laboratory for receipt of evidence from the field are aspects to be considered. Most of all, planning and cooperation will be the prime elements of success. These words are used routinely to the point that they may seem overly emphasized. Nonetheless, as with all areas of human endeavor, these two factors can make the difference between poor, mediocre, and exceptional performance. Physical evidence utilization is no different.

The information provided in this chapter and the preceding one indicate the methodology that law enforcement and the criminal justice community can apply to utilization and interpretation of physical evidence. Many elements must move cohesively toward the central goal of making correct sense of the evidence in the court. One element has been mentioned only in passing, but may actually be the one that truly makes the difference between success or failure. Training, experience, and techniques of evidence work progressing from the victim, suspect, and crime scene to the courtroom can be completely overshadowed by the attitudes of all persons involved. Attention to detail and care is the key element relating to the successful use of evidence. The ultimate in funding, technique, administration, and organization cannot outweigh the detrimental effects of poor attitude.

Conscious and subconscious psychological reactions are the most difficult aspects of people to predict and control. Law enforcement personnel are no different in this regard from persons in other professions. Thoughts brought about by witnessing the tragic results of the brutality and violence so characteristic of sexual assault crimes can affect a person to the point that good judgment is transformed into frustration and confusion. If responses to evidence collection situations or legal challenges to evidence are reactive and governed by personal feelings, the resulting turmoil can be reflected in a disorganized evidence effort during the investigation and subsequent trial.

The human side of evidence collection and utilization should be recognized and controlled with the intent of anticipating these kinds of problems. The one issue can transcend all the myriad components of forensic science. It must be given appropriate attention when physical evidence is used to assist in the determination of guilt or innocence in sexual assault cases.

Acknowledgments

The author would like to express sincere appreciation to the following personnel of the FBI Laboratory for their time and assistance concerning Chapters 4 and 5: Dr. F. Samuel Baechtel, Dr. Bruce Budowle, Supervisory Special Agent Harold A. Deadman, Jr., Assistant Section Chief James J. Kearney, Supervisory Special Agent Randall S. Murch, Supervisory Special Agent Wayne W. Oakes, Supervisory Special Agent Robert P. Spalding.

References

For the purpose of these two chapters and in consideration of the target population, the books that follow will provide relevant information to supplement and expand on the discussions. Additionally, the reader should refer to the suggested references, in particular, for coverage of evidence types beyond the intended scope of the chapters set forth here. The reader must also not neglect to obtain handbooks or similar published guidelines disseminated by the crime laboratory in the jurisdiction to which evidence is usually submitted for analysis. This effort is regarded as imperative by the author because of the varying requirements of evidence procedure from one crime laboratory to another.

Buckwalter, A., *The Search for Evidence*, Butterworth Publishers, Stoneham, MA, 1984.

Cunningham, C. L. and Fox, R. H., Crime Scene and Physical Evidence Handbook, U.S. Government Printing Office, Washington, D.C., 1973.

Deforest, P. R., Gaensslen, R.E., and Lee, H. C., *Forensic Science — An Introduction to Criminalistics*, McGraw-Hill, New York, 1983.

Eckert, W. G., *Introduction to Forensic Sciences*, C.V. Mosby, St. Louis, 1980.

Gaensslen, R.E., Sourcebook in Forensic Science Serology, Immunology and Biochemistry, U.S. Government Printing Office, Washington, D.C., 1983.

Inbau, F. E. and Moenssens, A. A., *Scientific Evidence in Criminal Cases*, Foundation Press, Mineola, NY, 1978.

Osterburg, J. W., *The Crime Laboratory — Case Studies of Scientific Criminal Investigations*, Clark Boardman, New York, 1982.

Saferstien, R., *Forensic Science Handbook*, Prentice-Hall, Englewood Cliffs, NJ, 1982.

The Science of Fingerprints — Classification and Uses, U.S. Government Printing Office, Washington, D.C., 1984.

Svensson, A., Wendel, O., and Fisher, B. A. J., *Techniques of Crime Scene Investigation*, 3rd ed., Elsevier, New York, 1981.

Wecht, C. H., *Forensic Sciences — Law/Science/Civil/Criminal*, Vol. 1–3, Matthew Bender, New York, 1983.

Criminal Investigative Analysis: An Overview

ROBERT R. HAZELWOOD
ROBERT K. RESSLER
ROGER L. DEPUE
JOHN C. DOUGLAS

> What is to be expected... is an understanding not merely of the deeds, but also the doers.
>
> Zilboorg, 1980

Analyzing a violent crime to determine identifiable characteristics of the unknown offender is not a new technique. However, the work being done by the FBI's National Center for the Analysis of Violent Crime (NCAVC), retired FBI agents, and selected law enforcement officers who have studied with the NCAVC represents law enforcement's continuing efforts to enhance their investigative methods and abilities. Until the recent past, this has been practiced primarily by clinical psychologists or psychiatrists who, while trained in matters of the mind, lacked experience in conducting investigations of violent crime. As a result, their "profiles" were couched in terminology largely alien to the intended audience: the criminal investigator and others in the criminal justice system.

A criminal investigative analysis (CIA) of an illegal and violent act may give the client agency a variety of useful information depending on the service requested. Previously termed "psychological profiling" and "criminal personality profiling", the term "criminal investigative analysis" was coined to differentiate the procedure from that used by mental health professionals.

CIA is an umbrella term incorporating several services performed by forensic behavioral specialists. While this chapter will focus on the most commonly requested service, the "profile" (characteristics and traits of an unidentified offender), the following is a brief description of the services incorporated in CIA:

Indirect personality assessment: an evaluation of behavioral information about a particular person in an attempt to determine areas of personality that are susceptible to investigative techniques, trial strategy, interview, and cross-examination. For a detailed discussion of this technique, see Chapter 12 of this book.

Equivocal death analysis: an opinion as to the manner of death (homicide, suicide, accident) based on a careful post-mortem evaluation of the victim and characteristics of the death.

Trial strategy: analyzing a case to provide attorneys with recommendations as to the strengths and weaknesses of the opposition's case, cross-examination techniques, and expert witnesses.

Profile: providing the client agency with the characteristics and traits of an unidentified offender that differentiate him from the general population. These characteristics are set forth in such a manner as to allow those who know and/or associate with the offender to readily recognize him.

Information Provided in a Criminal Investigative Analysis Profile

While the format of a CIA profile may vary with the person preparing it, the information is essentially the same. Some prefer an outline format that allows the reader to identify a specific characteristic quickly without having to read through the entire report; others prepare the profile in narrative style. The narrative style gives more detail and allows the reader to follow the process by which the analyst arrived at conclusions. Chapter 9 gives an example of the narrative style of profile. Regardless of the format, a profile should include most, if not all, of the following information: approximate age, sex, race, marital status, occupational pastimes or hobbies, approximate year and style of vehicle owned or operated, arrest history, appearance and grooming habits, residential information, and victim-offender relationship, as well as certain personality characteristics such as temperament, intelligence, emotional adjustment, pathological behavioral characteristics, and ability to interact socially and sexually.

Profiling and the NCAVC

Criminal investigative analysis was initiated by the Behavioral Science Unit* on an informal basis at the FBI Academy in 1972. Faculty members would encourage their students to discuss solved and unsolved cases with which they were familiar, and as a result of such discussions the instructors would note that in similar crimes, the offenders were a great deal alike. In subsequent classes, when a student presented an unsolved crime similar to ones previously discussed, instructors would give verbal profiles for the student. The students used the information on returning to their agencies and reported that the profiles saved many investigative man-hours by properly focusing the investigation. In a few instances, a profile was credited with being directly responsible for solving the crime.

As other investigative agencies learned of this assistance, the number of cases received for profiling rapidly rose. In that the faculty had a primary responsibility of teaching, the cases were analyzed on a time-available basis. The volume of requests grew to unanticipated proportions, and in 1978 the program was formalized and submitted cases were assigned to specific individuals for profiling.

---

* In 1984, President Reagan authorized the formation of the National Center for the Analysis of Violent Crime (NCAVC) which replaced the Behavioral Science Unit at the FBI Academy.

In 1981, 55 special agents were selected from various offices of the FBI and given 100 hours of instruction to train them as "profile coordinators"* in their respective geographic regions. Since then, agencies desiring this service from the FBI send their cases to the nearest NCAVC coordinator, who ensures that the materials necessary to prepare a profile have been included and that the case lends itself to profiling. If all requisites are met, the case is sent to the NCAVC and assigned to an analyst. When the profile is completed, it is returned to the responsible coordinator for delivery to the requesting agency. All submitted materials are kept by the NCAVC for future reference.

Eventually, the caseload became overwhelming for the available staff and additional analysts dedicated to crime analysis were needed. In 1983, four special agents (criminal investigative analysts) were chosen to understudy the NCAVC faculty and to assume responsibility for crime analysis. In 1984, four additional special agents were assigned as criminal investigative analysts. To make this service even more available to local law enforcement, a 1-year fellowship in CIA for police officers was in place from 1984 to 1991 (Hazelwood, 1986) and 36 investigators from the U.S., Canada, Australia, and Holland were trained in the technique. Regrettably, this training was terminated in 1991 due to budgetary and staff constraints.

The services of the NCAVC are provided at no cost to legitimate governmental criminal justice agencies. Due to the retirement of several of the original NCAVC staff members, this and other forensic behavioral science services are now available to non-governmental agencies on a fee basis.**

Procedure for Submission of Cases

Governmental agencies desiring a criminal investigative analysis (profile) submit the necessary documentation (see below) to the NCAVC coordinator in the FBI office nearest them.*** The NCAVC coordinator reviews the material to ensure that all necessary documentation has been given and forwards the case to the NCAVC where it is assigned to a criminal investigative analyst. The completed analysis is returned to the submitting agency through the coordinator.

Case Criteria

The criteria for a case to be analyzed are minimal. The case must involve a crime or series of crimes of violence or potential violence, the offender must be unknown, and all major investigative leads must have been exhausted. While virtually any crime showing mental, emotional, or personality aberration can be analyzed for profiling purposes, certain crimes are particularly appropriate for the

*   This designation has since been changed to NCAVC coordinators.
**   The Academy Group Inc. and the Forensic Behavioral Sciences Inc. are two such groups providing the CIA services.
***   Nongovernmental agencies or agencies desiring to pay a fee for such service may correspond directly with The Academy Group Inc. or the Forensic Behavioral Sciences Inc.

process; these crimes include a series of rapes, lust murder (mutilation or displacement of the sexual areas of the body) (Hazelwood and Douglas, 1980), serial murders, child molesting, ritualistic crimes, threat communications, violence in the workplace, and serial arson.

Case Materials Map

A commercially produced map is preferred to a hand-drawn one, as it gives vital information about the locales involved — deserted, industrial or residential, schools, hospitals, etc. If a commercial map is not available, a hand-drawn map will do if accompanied by a description of the areas involved. The map should be annotated to indicate all significant locations — where the victims were approached, where the assault occurred, where the victim was left, etc. If these locations are different, the distances between them should be given. Any other significant locations and distances should also be marked. For example, if the offender entered the victim's vehicle at point A, forced her to drive to point B where the assault occurred, left her there, and took her car to point C where he abandoned it, all three locations and the distances between them should appear on the map.

Victim Statement

The interview of the rape victim and its documentation are the most important factors in rape profiling. Unfortunately, the person preparing the profile seldom has the opportunity to speak with the victim and obtain the facts crucial to analyzing the behavioral aspects of the rape, and consequently depends on a third party, the investigator, to do so. For this reason, one of the authors (Hazelwood) developed a set of questions designed to help the investigator accomplish this task. The detailed interview of the rape victim is discussed in Chapter 8 and will not be addressed here, except to stress its importance.

Victimology. The final documentation needed is a summary of facts known about the victim to help the analyst determine why the rapist behaved verbally, physically, and sexually as he did. Ideally, information about the victim would include age, race, whether she was with anyone at the time of, or just before, the attack, her educational level, whether she appears to be passive or aggressive in nature (did she say or do something which may have caused the offender to become more violent?), type of employment, and a description of the socioeconomic characteristics of the area in which she lives. Any other facts the investigator deems important should be included.

Suspects. Organizations submitting cases should not include information that identifies suspects in the matter. If an analyst is reviewing a case and it becomes clear that seasoned investigators strongly believe a particular person committed the crime, it is almost certain to bias objectivity and may result in a profile that strongly resembles the suspect.

Nonprofilable Cases.   Not all violent crimes lend themselves to the profiling process; there are situations or circumstances that preclude the preparation of a valid profile. Of importance is the fact that the process depends not only on the crime and its documentation, but also on the analyst assigned the case. In other words, what may be a difficult case or set of circumstances for one normally proficient analyst, may be quite simple for another. As an example, one analyst may find it extremely difficult to profile a rape in which the offender is believed to be under the influence of drugs, while this poses no problem for another analyst. A case in which the rapist did not speak, used minimal force, and did not engage in atypical sexual activity is extremely difficult for most analysts; such a case would not give the reviewer sufficient behavior to evaluate. Rapes in which the victim was rendered unconscious or, for other reasons, cannot recall details are also very difficult, if not impossible, to profile. A good rule of thumb seems to be that if factors are missing (excluding offender identification) that the officer normally needs to investigate the case, it is not suitable for profiling. It should be noted that, after conversation with the investigating officers and acquisition of additional facts, cases that were originally thought to be inappropriate for profiling have been, in fact, deemed appropriate. Before a case is returned as nonprofilable, it will be studied for a considerable period of time, investigating officers will be consulted, and the matter will be discussed in detail with other investigative analysts. It should be noted that while a case may be determined to be nonprofilable, other services may be provided (i.e., interview/interrogation techniques and/or proactive/investigative strategies). However, the fact remains that there are cases that do not lend themselves to the process.

The Analysts

When discussing criminal investigative analysis, the authors are invariably asked what special attributes or education the analyst must have. Their answer, quite simply, is that the successful analysts with whom they have worked had no particular educational degree, although a background in the behavioral sciences is helpful. The qualities and attributes they have consistently noted in successful analysts include investigative and research experience, common sense, intuitiveness, the ability to isolate emotions, the ability to analyze a situation and arrive at logical conclusions, and the ability to reconstruct the crime using the criminal's reasoning process.

Experience

No amount of education can replace the experience of having investigated crimes. As an investigator, one begins to mentally and physically collect and store data that are automatically retrieved when a new case is opened. Experienced investigators accept nothing at face value, but question what is observed and go beyond what appears to be obvious. They do not depend on what others tell them about the crime, but check and verify each piece of information. This is the most significant factor differentiating the investigative analyst from the clinical psychologist or psychiatrist who prepares profiles.

During a conference on treatment of sexual offenders, a rapist in the treatment program was presented to the audience. After he had left, the treating mental health professional was asked about the rapist's criminal history. He had not previously inquired into this area, but promised to do so. Obviously he had not considered such information significant to the offender's treatment. A few minutes later, he told the audience that the rapist had no history of arrest other than a speeding violation. When asked about the source of this information, he said that it was the rapist himself!

Over a period of time, an investigator develops an ability to rise above the shock of violence and to move systematically through the often gruesome, but always necessary procedures. The authors know people who refuse to examine photographs depicting homicide victims, yet prepare profiles for law enforcement agencies. It is our opinion that this is akin to performing surgery without reviewing the patient's X-rays.

Common Sense

It has been the author's experience that a surprisingly large number of people do not have the quality of common sense. There are persons who, when confronted with a novel situation, find it impossible to plan a strategy unless that situation is precisely like one they previously experienced or learned. In law enforcement circles, such a person is often referred to as "one who goes by the book". For example, an overriding fear the authors have is that, regardless of their best efforts, some people will treat this text as a "cookbook" and, if faced with a situation not specifically addressed in these pages, will consider the entire process to be of no value. It must be remembered that no two crimes or criminals are identical. When dealing with human behavior, it is impossible to give examples dealing with every situation that may be encountered. The person who has "common sense" will recognize this and will be able to project techniques from the written page or spoken word onto generally similar situations.

Intuition

Webster defines intuition as "the direct knowing or learning something without the conscious use of reasoning — the ability to perceive or know things without conscious reasoning" (Webster, 1972). Police officers refer to it as a "gut feeling". Like common sense, it is not something that can be learned in a classroom or from a book. Realistically, it is probably not a trait that someone is born with either, but rather an ability born from similar but forgotten experiences, and from education and/or research. Regardless of its origins, it is a fact that some people have an intuitive ability that is extremely valuable in the analysis and profiling process.

> In the 1980s, an FBI stenographer was found dead in her apartment. She had been raped and murdered. One of the authors (Hazelwood) and James Wright, another crime analyst assigned to the NCAVC, were sent to view the scene, analyze the case materials, and prepare a profile for the investigators. The victim, a 22-year-old white woman, lived in an apartment complex with a racially mixed group of tenants (70% Hispanic, 20% black, and 10% white). Typically such crimes are interracial in nature and, based on that fact, the offender should have been categorized as white. However, the majority of tenants were Hispanic and, based on statistics, the offender was more likely to be Hispanic. On entering the death scene, Hazelwood said, "Jim, the guy who did this was black". Of course, Wright appropriately responded, "You can't say that, we just got here". The killer, a 22-year-old black male, was arrested 2 weeks later and subsequently convicted and sentenced to death.

Isolation of Affect

The successful analyst is one who is able to isolate his personal feelings about the crime, the criminal, and the victim.

> A 16-year-old girl was abducted by a 19-year-old male acquaintance. She was beaten and raped vaginally, anally, and orally. She had been stabbed 37 times and her upper torso was slashed repeatedly. Her killer threw her body into a ditch and left. He later assisted in the search for her and eventually participated as a pallbearer at her funeral.

As presented above, the case is somewhat clinical; however, the materials submitted consisted of graphic medical records and crime scene photographs. As parents, law enforcement officers, and members of society, we are outraged at the injustice of such an attack on a young person. As crime analysts, however, we cannot allow our feelings to interfere with the task at hand.

Personal feelings about the criminal must also be isolated. For instance, in crimes such as the one described above, one not knowledgeable about such matters might assume that the person responsible is insane, has an extensive arrest history, and is unable to function in society. In fact, the killer was not psychotic and led a normal life (stable employment, steady girl friend, attended church). He had been arrested for exposing himself to two college women and had been identified in a series of obscene and threatening phone calls. When analyzing a violent crime for the purpose of preparing a profile, one should try to describe the offender as those who know the person would describe him. The reader would do well to remember the infamous serial murderers who were outwardly rational and fully functional individuals: Kenneth Bianchi (Hillside Strangler), John Wayne Gacy, Theodore Bundy, and Wayne Williams (Atlanta child murders), to mention just a few.

Finally, the analyst must isolate his feelings about the victim. In many instances, the victims of sexual assault and/or homicide are what we refer to as *high-risk* victims. That is to say, the victims may have been particularly vulnerable because they were prostitutes, involved in drug-related activities, hitchhiking, or runaways. If the analyst allows personal feelings about the victim to enter the evaluation, this will seriously impair the process.

> A 15-year-old prostitute reported that she had been hired to perform sexual acts for a well-known citizen. He had beaten her and kept her in chains for 2 days. He then flew her to a desolate island where he forced her to undress and then told her she had 20 min to run after which he would stalk and kill her with a high-powered rifle. She refused to run and he allowed her to redress and flew her back to the mainland where he released her. The police reluctantly accepted her complaint but failed to aggressively investigate. Two years later, the man confessed to the murder of 17 women.

Analytical Logic

The ability to study a situation and arrive at logical conclusions is not one that all people have. In analyzing a crime and preparing a profile, one must make conclusions based on what has been observed, heard, or read. A great deal of the mystique surrounding the art of profiling disappears when one realizes that a large amount of the information provided in a profile is arrived at analytically and logically. For example, let's assume that the analyst believes that the offender is psychotic. It is then quite reasonable to assume that the offender will not be employed in a white-collar profession. Another example of the application of logic might involve a rapist who is believed, for one reason or another, to be employed in a white-collar job. It is then logical to assume that he will live in a middle- or upper-class residential area.

Analyze the Crime from the Criminal's Perspective

> In a large metropolitan area, a series of rapes had plagued the police over a period of months. In each instance, the rapist controlled his victim through threats and intimidation. One evening a hospital orderly went off duty at midnight and happened on a male beating a nurse in an attempt to rape her. The orderly went to her rescue and subdued the attacker until the police arrived. Predictably, he received much attention from the news media and was given a citation for bravery from the city. Shortly thereafter, the orderly was arrested for the series of rapes mentioned earlier. During interrogation, he was asked why he had rescued the nurse when he, in fact, was guilty of similar offenses. He became indignant and advised the police officers that they were wrong. He would never "hurt" a woman (Hazelwood, 1983, p. 9).

This offender equated "hurt" with physical trauma. The point is that intent becomes clear only if we try to view the crime from the motivational standpoint of the criminal (Hazelwood, 1983). The ability to observe a crime from the perspective of the criminal is the result of having dealt with violent crime and criminals over a number of years; it is not learned in a classroom. The analyst must forget that he is a parent, a spouse, or a law enforcement officer, and temporarily assume the role of the criminal. Then he must begin to ask questions about the crime: "Why would I continue to beat the victim after all resistance had ended?" "Why wouldn't I react more violently after the victim bit me?". To assume this role is not an easy task in that violence is what we, as law enforcement officers, are charged with preventing and/or investigating.

Two of the authors (Hazelwood and Douglas) provided on-site consultation on a murder case. It involved the kidnap and murder of a 12-year-old girl who was found 5 days after the crime. After the profile had been prepared and presented to the officers investigating the matter, a clinical psychologist stated that the authors were, in effect, describing a paranoid schizophrenic. When Douglas and Hazelwood concurred with that assessment, the psychologist asked how they could be so confident of that evaluation after simply studying the crime scene data. It was explained that profilers try to reenact the crime, to view it as the murderer did, and to reason as he did. When identified, the subject was diagnosed by psychiatrists as being a paranoid schizophrenic.

The Profiling Process

A profile (characteristics and traits of an unidentified person) is a series of subjective opinions about the unknown person(s) responsible for a crime or series of crimes. The process of arriving at these opinions is quite difficult to articulate in that the final product largely depends on common sense, intuition, and the analyst's experience. In that this topic is dealt with at length in Chapter 9, the authors will merely acquaint the reader with the process used when preparing a profile.

The preparation of a rapist profile consists of three basic steps: (1) to determine from the victim what behavior was exhibited by the rapist, (2) to analyze that behavior in an attempt to determine the motivation underlying the assault, and (3) to set forth the characteristics and traits of the person who would commit the crime in a manner that explains the motivational factor indicated by that behavior (Hazelwood, 1983).

In the authors' experience, similar crimes committed for similar reasons generally are perpetrated by similar offenders. Given a rape that occurred in Houston, TX, they can quote a rape that occurred in Arlington, VA that is so similar in nature one might assume the same person was responsible for both. The explanation for this is really quite simple: crimes are similar because the underlying motivation is basically the same; therefore, it is logical to assume that the offenders will be as similar as their crimes.

Determine Offender Behavior

It is the offender's behavior during the commission of a crime that is studied by the analyst. In sexual assaults, the victim may be able to provide information on three forms of offender behavior: verbal, sexual, and physical (force). She can advise the investigator as to what the offender said or demanded that she say, the type and sequence of sexual acts that were performed, and the amount of physical force used by the offender. Provided with this information, it is probable that the analyst can determine the underlying motivation for the assault. This step is discussed in detail in Chapter 8.

Analyze the Behavior

At this step, one studies and evaluates the verbal, sexual, and physical behavior of the rapist, with the purpose of determining the true motivation for the sexual assault. As Groth (1979, p. 88) points out, "rape is, in fact, serving primarily nonsexual needs". One should examine verbal behavior for indications of hostility, anger, a need for affection, concern, or politeness, among other things. The type and sequence of sexual behavior should be analyzed to determine whether the offender intended to degrade, involve, or punish the victim. Finally, the amount of physical force used should be studied. At what point did the rapist apply force? Was it to intimidate or punish? Did he continue to use force when resistance had ceased? One must be alert to the fact that the motivation for the crime is exhibited through the rapist's behavior.

Prepare the Profile

Once a determination has been made as to what motivated the crime, the characteristics and traits of the rapist can then be set forth. "The manner in which an individual behaves within his various environments portrays the type of person he or she is. Opinions are formed about a person's self-esteem, educational level, ability to negotiate interpersonal relationships, and goals in life by the manner in which the individual behaves" (Hazelwood, 1983).

A Word of Caution about Profiling

Experienced and knowledgeable people who lecture on this subject often begin by advising students that profiling, a subsection of criminal investigative analysis, is an art and not a science. It is simply another investigative tool to assist in the investigation of violent crime. It is not intended to supplant any other investigative step, and, in fact, we prefer not to prepare a profile until all conventional investigative procedures have been done and the case remains unsolved. If an investigator depends solely on a profile to solve a case, he will have acted irresponsibly and counterproductively.

Profiles have led directly to the solution of a case, but this is the exception rather than the rule. The primary purpose of a profile is to help the investigators narrow the focus of their investigation. In an evaluation of the profiling process, the Institutional Research and Development Unit (IRDU) of the FBI Academy surveyed user agencies as to the investigative value of profiles prepared in 192 cases (1981). In its report the IRDU stated: "In the 192 cases examined,... profiling helped focus the investigation in 77% of those cases where the perpetrator was identified and actually identified the subject in 15 instances. Even in cases where the suspect has not been identified... profiling was helpful... in that it insured a complete investigation was conducted... Profiling saved an estimated 594 investigative man days and all users overwhelmingly agreed that the service should be continued".

It should be made clear that the profile is not intended to identify a particular person, but rather a personality type. Consequently, a profile may describe more than one person who has come to the attention of the police. In one case of rape/murder, a profile was prepared and the investigators reported that the listed characteristics and traits were consistent with three different men who lived in close proximity to the victim. When the investigators informed one of the authors (Hazelwood) about this problem, they were advised that the killer was either one of the three or someone like them. They were not particularly pleased with that information, but understood the limitations of the technique.

Criminal investigative analysts are not blessed with a sixth sense, nor do they have a crystal ball that gives them mystical powers; they are encumbered with the same human frailties as anyone else. They have simply had the opportunity to observe a very large number of violent crimes and to assimilate that experience into their work. No one is more enthusiastic about the technique than the current and former members of the NCAVC. However, they are the first to acknowledge that proven investigative procedures, not profiling, solve crimes.

Summary

CIA and profiling were initiated in the FBI Academy's Behavioral Science Unit on an informal basis in 1972. The program was formalized in 1978, and in 1983, FBI analysts were specifically assigned the task of assisting law enforcement agencies in nonfederal investigations involving crimes of violence.

The criteria for cases submitted for criminal investigative analysis are that they involve a crime or series of crimes involving violence, or potential violence, and that remain unsolved after all investigative leads have been exhausted.

Successful analysts are experienced in criminal investigations and research and possess common sense, intuition, and the ability to isolate their feelings about the crime, the criminal, and the victim. They have the ability to evaluate analytically the behavior exhibited in a crime and to think very much like the criminal responsible.

When analyzing a crime, it is necessary to evaluate what happened in order to determine the underlying motivation for the crime. One can then construct a profile of the type of person who would have committed such a crime for such a reason. In sexual assaults, the verbal, sexual, and physical behavior of the offender are evaluated.

CIA and profiling should be used to augment proven investigative techniques and must not be allowed to replace those methods; to do so would be counterproductive to the goal of identifying the unknown offender.

References

Groth, A. N., *Men Who Rape,* Plenum Press, New York, 1979, 88.

Hazelwood, R. R., Behavior-oriented interview of rape victims: the key to profiling, *FBI Law Enforcement Bull.,* September 1983.

Hazelwood, R. R., NCAVC training program: a commitment to law enforcement, *FBI Law Enforcement Bull.,* December 1986.

Hazelwood, R. R. and Douglas, J. E., The lust murderer, *FBI Law Enforcement Bull.,* April 1980.

Institutional Research and Development Unit, FBI Academy, Memorandum, Evaluation of the Psychological Profiling Program, December 1981.

Porter, B., Mind hunters, *Psychol. Today,* April 1983.

Webster's New World Dictionary of the American Language, 2nd college ed., World Publishing, New York, 1972.

Zilboorg, G., *The Psychology of the Criminal Act and Punishment,* Greenwood Press, New York, 1968, 24.

The Relevance of Fantasy in Serial Sexual Crime Investigations

7

ROBERT R. HAZELWOOD
JANET I. WARREN

In 1990, a 24-year-old housewife was kidnapped from her home and murdered. At the time of her death, she was 4 months pregnant. A search of her home revealed that all of her panties and the bottom half of her bathing suit had been taken. Her badly decomposed body was discovered 2 days later. She died from paper towels being lodged in her throat. There were no other signs of physical trauma.

Four months later, a woman was abducted and raped. During the assault, the offender forced her to "model" several sets of teddies. He forced her to ask him to "make love" to her and, prior to releasing her, he requested a "date". Two days later, he was observed leaving a Christmas tree on her porch. He was arrested and convicted for the abduction-murder and the abduction-rape.

A search of his home uncovered several hundred pieces of lingerie, over 2000 3 × 5 cards containing information on women whose photographs and personal information appeared in soft pornographic magazines, a spiral notebook with cross-indexed information from the 3 × 5 cards, newspaper articles about women, lingerie catalogs, and the bottom half of the murder victim's bathing suit. His wife said that the man used the materials for masturbatory acts. The subject manifested several paraphilias during this and other crimes. They included fetishism, voyeurism, exhibitionism, and telephone scatology.

Sexuality is one of the more complex aspects of human experience. It integrates the cognitive, emotional, sensual, and behavioral elements of the individual into a uniquely personal pattern of experience that derives from both internal fantasy and external behavior. While usually a "private" aspect of a person's life, it becomes relevant to law enforcement once the element of coercion or exploitation is introduced into it.

Researchers Prentky et al. (1988) classify the underlying motivation for sexual assault into three main categories: aggression, sex, and power. These primary motivations are expressed in complex sexual fantasies that often begin to develop shortly after puberty. Through a gradual process of enactment, they also become the "template" for many offenders' patterns of serial, sexual offending. They serve a complex organizing function in the offender's behavior and frequently determine the choice of his verbal interactions with his victim, his preferred sexual acts, and his overall "ritualistic" patterns of behavior.

0-8493-8152-1/95/$0.00+$.50
© 1995 by CRC Press, Inc.

The criminal investigator and others involved in the identification, prosecution, and treatment of the offender can learn to make use of these fantasy-driven behaviors within a sexual offense. Through a detailed review of the verbal, sexual, and physical behavior of the offender, the underlying fantasy behavior can be deduced and the motivational themes formulated. This information can then be used to identify sexual assaults perpetrated by the same offender, determine future patterns of victim selection, and help predict the scenario of future crimes.

The Human Sex Drive

There are three principal components of the human sexual drive: (1) the biological, (2) the physiological, and (3) the psychosexual. Humans share the biological component with other forms of mammalian life; it constitutes the natural or instinctual urge to engage in sexual activities with others. This instinctual component influences the basic orientation of the sexual impulse, but has little influence on the individual form through which it is expressed. As such, it has limited relevance to sexual crime investigations. The physiological component is activated when the body begins to respond to stimuli in a sexual manner. This response pattern may vary in intensity and be interrupted by a variety of sexual dysfunctions that are physiological in nature. Such information may provide rudimentary information about an offender in unique cases. The psychosexual element constitutes the most variable and individualistic aspect of the human sexual experience. It integrates the highly specific cognitive, sensory, and behavioral stimuli that are arousing to an individual and reflects his/her unique pattern of experience and development. This psychosexual aspect of the sexual experience, in its almost unending variability, provides the criminal investigator and others with the richest source of information about an offender and provides him with the "flavor" of the specific individual he is seeking.

Sex is a Sensory Act

All human beings use their available senses to enhance their sexual arousal. A thorough review of the ways that the various senses are manipulated in a sexual assault will ensure that a comprehensive assessment of the psychosexual component of the offender's sexual arousal pattern has been captured from the victim.

Sight has been identified as the primary component of the human male's sexual response. As indicated in the case study presented at the beginning of the chapter, the offender forced his victim to model lingerie which he had bought as props to his fantasy. Without this visual stimulus, he tended to have difficulty becoming sexually aroused. Touch, another important sense related to sexual arousal, similarly showed itself in the offender's fondling of his victim and in his autoerotic, masturbatory activities with several hundred pieces of lingerie. The offender's request that the victim verbalize a desire to "make love" to him reflects a use of auditory stimuli to enhance arousal, while his postoffense delivery of a Christmas tree behaviorally demonstrates the reciprocity that lies at the core of his sexual fantasy. These fantasy-derived behaviors were consistent across the sexual assault and murder perpetrated by this particular offender and, as indicated, were instrumental in the linking of the two offenses to him.

The Paraphilias

Paraphilia is a term used by mental health to describe what is more commonly called "sexual deviation". The essential feature of a sexual deviation is that it includes "… intense sexual urges and sexually arousing fantasies generally involving either: (1) nonhuman objects, (2) suffering or humiliation of one's self or one's partner, or (3) children or other nonconsenting partners" (DSM IV, 1994).

Paraphilic behavior is fantasy driven and is commonly exhibited during sexual crimes. The sexual deviations recognized by the *Diagnostic and Statistical Manual, 4th edition (DSM-IV)*, include exhibitionism, fetishism, frotteurism, pedophilia, sexual masochism, sexual sadism, transvestitic fetishism, voyeurism, and "paraphilias not otherwise specified" including telephone scatology, necrophilia, zoophilia, coprophilia, klismiphilia, and urophilia. Abel et al. (1988) have documented that people tend to suffer from multiple paraphilias and that individuals identified as having one paraphilia generally suffered from at least two or three additional forms of sexual deviation. As indicated in the case presentation, the offender demonstrated multiple paraphilias including exhibitionism, fetishism, telephone scatology, and voyeuristic behavior. It is important for investigators to remain aware of this "clustering" of paraphilic behavior as it argues against one-dimensional descriptions of particular offenders (e.g., "he's just an exhibitionist") and helps to avoid the premature exclusion of offenders from other types of unsolved sexual crimes.

Paraphilic patterns of behavior have been found to remain highly consistent over time. Research suggests that some types of paraphilic behavior can be altered through comprehensive treatment (for example, exhibitionism), while the more aggressive forms of sexual offending (i.e., sexual sadism) are unlikely to be changed regardless of the types and length of treatment offered. This stability is demonstrated repeatedly in cases involving the release of a sexual offender from prison who, within months of his release, perpetrates another paraphilia-motivated crime. In such cases, it is assumed that the deviant sexual fantasy has been maintained through masturbatory reinforcement and motivates behavior as soon as external constraints are removed.

The dynamics of these sexual fantasies, their possible paraphilic underpinnings, and their behavioral enactments provide the criminal investigator and others with information that can be used to direct the investigation, prosecution, and treatment of a sexual offender. Contrary to popular belief, there are no obvious demographic characteristics that identify an individual as a sexual criminal. Indeed, the serial sexual criminal is most often found to be like the "guy next door" (Hazelwood and Warren, 1989). Understanding the role of motivationally driven fantasy and its interaction with the human sexual drive will give the investigator better insight into the criminal sexual behavior with which he is confronted.

Fantasy in Sexual Crimes

In analyzing serial sexual crimes, the investigator will find that the offender seldom acts out a fantasy with only one component; most often, the crime will exhibit multiple elements of fantasy. For example, a rape may have a relational component (i.e., date, sexual slave), a paraphilic component (bondage, sadism, fetishism), a situational component (war, arrest), a self-perceptional component (powerful, God-like), and a demographic component (victim characteristics). While it is not expected that the investigator will be able to determine all the components of the offender's fantasy from his criminal behavior, he should, at a minimum, be able to discern its relational and/or paraphilic elements.

It is important to note that for most people fantasy is sufficient to satisfy psychosexual desires and, regardless of its nature, there is no impulse to act it out in reality. For others, fantasy is not satisfactory and there appears to be a progressive desire to transform the fantasy into actual behavior. McCullough et al. (1983) studied 16 sexually sadistic offenders and found that their core sexual fantasy made its appearance around the age of 16 years but took a number of years to be encapsulated into the criminal behavior that lead to arrest. They found that in the interval between the appearance and enactment of the fantasy the offender engaged in gradual and partial reenactments of the fantasy (i.e., buying rope, following a woman home) and used these "behavioral tryouts" as stimuli to enhance his masturbatory activity.

Inanimate Objects

The use of nonliving objects for sexual fantasy play acting is not uncommon. Such items are passive, nonthreatening, and pose the least likelihood of criminal actions against the individual. In the experience of the authors, dolls, photographs, and clothing are the most common inanimate materials used by sexual criminals in lending a sense of reality to their fantasies.

Dolls.   People assigned to the FBI's National Center for the Analysis of Violent Crime (NCAVC) have seen many violent crimes in which female dolls are, in some way, involved. While such cases are often the subject of ridicule, it is to be remembered that such behavior is a reflection of the offender's motivationally driven fantasies. In cases observed by the authors, dolls have been subjected to burning, slashing, stabbing, binding, amputation, piercing, and a variety of other equally bizarre acts.

Case No. 2

A series of dolls, sent to a mental institution, had been subjected to a variety of violent activities including cutting, burning, penetration, and detonated explosive devices. The person responsible was identified and, after arrest, told the police that he had planned to kill his parents, shoot a police officer, and be killed by law enforcement.

Photographs/Magazine Pictures. Another common means of acting out fantasies is to alter photographs or pictures taken from pornographic and nonpornographic magazines. Such alterations include drawings (sexual bondage, mutilation, knives, guns, wounds, blood), cut and paste (replace faces, sexual parts), or the placement of "favorite" pictures in photo albums.

Case No. 3

A professionally employed individual died during dangerous autoerotic activities. A search of his office filing cabinets revealed over 100 bondage magazines. Without exception, each page had been altered by drawings or cut-and-pasting. He had taken such care that the alterations were all but imperceptible to the naked eye. The modification of such a large amount of material required an inordinate amount of time and effort and was significant in determining the importance he attached to such activity.

Clothing. Female clothing, particularly lingerie, is a favorite object for acting out a variety of fantasies. One of the most common activities is the slashing or removal of those portions of clothing which normally cover the sexual parts of the body. Such activities are typically classified as "nuisance" sexual offenses and officers have repeatedly advised the authors that teenagers are most frequently responsible for such acts. However, age does not excuse such behavior and recognizing that sexual behavior is predicated on fantasy should alert authorities to the need for expeditious identification and mental health intervention.

Consenting Partners

Prostitutes. Any experienced sexual crime investigator can testify to the value of speaking with prostitutes when investigating a series of violent crimes. Prostitutes earn money by being available for a variety of sexual behaviors. With them, men can act out their sexual fantasies without fear of rejection or ridicule.

Case No. 4

A professionally employed white male was convicted for the murder of a prostitute. He had bound her wrists behind her back and placed her in a bathtub full of water where he had intercourse with her. At the moment of ejaculation, he held her head under the water and she drowned. Investigation revealed that he had previously hired several other women for the same activity.

Girlfriends or Spouses as Partners. Stereotypically, it has been assumed that perpetrators of sexual crimes either did not have consensual sexual relationships or, if they did, that the more destructive aspects of their sexuality were kept divorced from it. Recent research by Hazelwood et al. (1993), however, has determined that many sexual offenders are, in fact, involved in ongoing sexual relationships and that they often act out their fantasies within this context.

Self Composition

Some people choreograph their fantasies using themselves as both the subject and object of the behavior. One offender, who tortured and murdered a number of women, audio-taped in detail his descriptions of what he would do to his victims and what he would have them say and do to him. At the end of the tape, he verbalized in a falsetto voice the script he was planning to have his victims repeat to him. His remarks involved statements such as "bite my titties… " and "fuck me in the ass", verbal behavior he subsequently forced each of his victims to repeat. Dangerous autoerotic activities also often contain a ritualized enactment of fantasy.

Case No. 5

A white male was found dead, hanging from a beam in the basement of his house. He was wearing his wife's sweater turned inside out, his wife's shorts turned inside out, and had placed her panties over his head and face. The belt from her bathrobe was wrapped tightly around his testicles. A video camera had been positioned to record his activities, and the videotape showed him accidentally dying of asphyxiation. A search of the area around the body turned up a number of sketches that portrayed sadomasochistic scenes, the hangings of a male and a female, and the written script of a woman undergoing a military execution by hanging.

Investigation of autoerotic fatalities has frequently revealed transvestitic behavior associated with ritualized hanging. The process of the man presenting himself dressed as a woman so as to elicit arousal from himself (he undoubtedly planned on later watching the video) seems to represent the inversion that lies at the core of this complex form of enactment.

Investigative Significance of Fantasy

Over the years, the authors have consulted and conducted research on violent sexual crimes and have testified as expert witnesses in such crimes. This experience has led to a great appreciation of the value of understanding the significant role that fantasy plays in sexual crimes. The rest of this chapter will focus on the practical investigative value such an understanding can provide.

Fantasy and Intelligence

Fantasy is essentially a play acted out in the mind of a person. This "play" requires a set, script, actors, a director, and, in some cases, a recording device. Occasionally, costumes and/or other props may also be involved (see Case No. 4). This ability to fantasize depends on the person's intelligence. Continuity of thought is needed when developing a fantasy involving multiple partners or a complex scenario, and continuity of thought requires a degree of intelligence. A person of less-than-average intelligence has a less complicated internal world and less ability to carry out complex criminal scenarios. Based on this association, the investigator can assume that the more complex the crime, the more intelligent the offender.

Case No. 6

A female realtor was found hanging by her neck in the attic of a recently built home valued at more than $200,000. She had been stabbed twice in the chest. Investigation determined that she had received a call from a man claiming to be a physician who was interested in purchasing an existing home located on 5 to 10 acres of land. He said that he was relocating his family and practice to the area and was on a house-hunting trip. The realtor, thinking of a substantial fee, told him that she would be happy to show the house. He told her that he had just arrived in town and was staying at an expensive hotel, and requested that she pick him up in front of the hotel. Investigation showed that he had not checked into the hotel.

This offender was later arrested and found to have committed a series of violent sexual crimes throughout the eastern U.S. An examination of the crime reveals a complex scenario designed to entice a selected victim to a remote location for torture and murder. Although his formal education was halted after 1 year of college, it became obvious that the perpetrator was well above average in intelligence.

Fantasy Is Always Perfect

A person's sexual fantasies are always perfect: every actor in the mental image plays his/her role to perfection. Reality, however, is never perfect and, for that reason, never lives up to the sexual offender's expectations.

Case No. 7

Police recovered an audio tape belonging to a professionally employed man who had died while on a business trip. On the tape, the man described the murder of a teenage couple. He recorded that he had killed the woman and then dwelt, at some length, on the rape and murder of the man. He expressed disappointment over the fact that the young man's blood had saturated the bed clothes and mentioned that he should have placed a plastic sheet beneath the victim's body. He also expressed regret at having cut the man's throat and opined that he should have stabbed him in the kidney as he would have lived longer.

The investigator requested one of the authors (Hazelwood) to listen to the tape and provide an opinion as to whether it was fact or fantasy. The opinion was that the tape was depicting an actual crime. As previously mentioned, fantasy is always perfect and, in this instance, the man was expressing disappointment and regret over things he had done or failed to do in reality.

It has long been recognized that certain sexual offenders record their sexual fantasies and/or their crimes. This is particularly true of the sexual sadist (Dietz et al., 1990) and the pedophile (Lanning, 1991). There are two widely accepted reasons for this: (1) to enable the offender to relive the crime for masturbatory acts and (2) to allow him to retain "souvenirs" or "trophies" of his crimes. The authors concur in both of these reasons, but suggest a third motivation: (3) to use the recordings of past crimes to more perfectly transform fantasy into reality. By recording the crime, the person can critique his own and his victim's performance, thereby allowing him to correct the imperfections that are invariably present in reality.

Case No. 8

A sexually sadistic killer kidnapped a series of young women and, after photo-graphing them during sexual acts, murdered them. In one series of photographs recovered by the police, a young woman is kneeling on a bed while performing fellatio on the man. At his feet are several photographs of another victim seem-ingly performing the same act on the same bed while in the same position.

It was the authors' impression that the offender was using the photographs to more carefully model and inform his preferred fantasy material.

Fantasy Enactment With Wives and/or Girlfriends

Research (Hazelwood et al., 1993) by the authors has focused on the wives and girlfriends of 15 sexual sadists. Through analysis of the sadists' recordings and exhaustive interviews with their former wives and/or girlfriends, it was found that, without exception, they acted out their cruel and sadistic fantasies on the women.

Case No. 9

A sexual sadist, known to have kidnapped and murdered one victim and kept a second victim in captivity for an extended period of time, acted out his cruel fantasies on each of the victims and simultaneously acted out those same fantasies on his wife. These acts included sexual bondage, hanging, whipping, and burning.

Investigators should ensure that efforts are made to find these women and to interview them to determine whether there is a consistent pattern to the offender's criminal and consensual sexual behavior.

Fantasy and the Linking of Cases

Douglas and Munn (1990) describe the difference between the "modus operandi" (MO) and "signature" (ritualistic) aspects of a sexual crime. Historically, law enforcement has used the MO to link a series of crimes. The crime analysts assigned to the FBI's NCAVC consider the MO, but rely on the "signature" or ritual to link a series of cases together. For the purpose of this chapter, the MO has three *practical* purposes: (1) to protect identity, (2) to ensure success, and (3) to facilitate escape. It has been the authors' experience that the MO is only valid in sexual crimes for a period of 3 to 4 months before it begins to change or evolve.

This change occurs as a result of the offender's experience gained through the experience of committing a series of crimes and/or education obtained from incarceration, media coverage of similar crimes, publications, or other public means of discussion.

The "signature" or ritualistic aspect of the crime, however, does not change dramatically; it is designed to meet the offender's motivationally driven fantasy and, therefore, remains psychosexually arousing to him over time.

Case No. 10

An 18-year-old man was tried and convicted of the rape-murder of a 17-year-old woman. She had been stabbed more than 30 times, her abdomen was slashed, and her throat cut. She was left in a ditch after having been vaginally, anally, and orally raped. The man had previously been found guilty of exposing himself to college coeds, and was known to have made over 100 obscene and threatening phone calls to two women when he was 15 years old. During that series of calls he threatened to cut the women's throats, slash and stab them, rape and anally assault them, and remove their breasts.

The link between the verbalization of the offender's violent sexual fantasies, via the phone calls, 3 years before the murder was obvious and one of the authors testified to that effect. Unfortunately, the responsible social agency took no action on the phone calls when the then 15 year old was referred to them. One of the women who had received the phone calls said that she had personally advised the mother of the young boy that he was "going to rape and kill someone if something isn't done".

Fantasy and Search Warrants

In criminally acting out sexual fantasies, offenders often use materials or props to create more psychosexually stimulating scenarios for themselves. By observing the physical, verbal, and sexual behavior acted out during a sexual crime, the investigator can determine the type of sexual fantasy being carried out. It is then a simple step to determine what type of materials, if any, the person would have accumulated to complement his fantasies. Upon identification of a person suspected, or known, to have committed the crime(s), the affidavit supporting any search warrant should list the materials that this type of assessment suggests. For example, in the case presented at the beginning of this chapter, the offender obviously had a fetish for teddies. It is quite reasonable, therefore, to suspect that he will have a collection of similar materials (lingerie) for his masturbatory fantasies.

Case No. 11

A young woman was kidnapped and kept in captivity for an extended period of time. She was physically, emotionally, and sexually tortured during her captivity. Her statement led the police to believe that they were dealing with a sexual sadist and, based on research conducted by Dietz et al. (1990), a search warrant was prepared. It listed bondage materials, recording devices, burning and pinching devices, violent pornography, and numerous other materials as items to be prioritized in the search. Items in each of these categories were recovered during the search.

A person's accumulation of materials and involvement with activities designed to enhance his sexual fantasies can contribute to a better understanding, by judge and jury, of the importance to the offender of such activities. Again, in the case presented at the beginning of this chapter, police investigation determined that the man had invested over $3000 and inestimable time in collecting, cataloging, and preserving lingerie. In case no. 3, the offender had "recreated" thousands of pictures in over 100 magazines to enhance his deviant fantasies.

Fantasy and Prosecutive Strategy

As noted above, the authors have testified as expert witnesses in trials of sexual offenders. One of the main functions of such testimony is to educate the jury not only about the offense, but also about the role that fantasy and fantasy materials play in violent sexual crimes. It should be noted that it is not unusual to find it necessary to also educate the prosecutive team in matters involving violent sexuality. They, like many investigators and the lay public, are often naive about the complexity of such crimes and the seeming normality of the offenders.

Case No. 12

A 36-year-old woman disappeared after a date with her fiance. Two years later, an ex-girlfriend said that she had helped him bury the victim's body. The body was recovered and the man was tried and acquitted. During the trial, the former girlfriend testified that he had brought the victim to the girlfriend's home, forced her to disrobe, and then raped her vaginally, anally, and orally. He also used a dildo on the victim anally and bound her in a variety of positions, using precut lengths of rope. The former girlfriend testified that he had taken over 100 photographs during the crime. Over 1 year later, the Federal Government indicted him on three counts of lying to federal agents about his role in the crime. Interviews of the former girlfriend and a former wife of the subject (15 years divorced) revealed that the man had subjected them to similar activities. Five days before the trial, the aforementioned photographs were found; he pleaded guilty and was sentenced to 8 years in prison.

The obvious problem, had the federal case gone to trial, was having to prove that the man killed the victim. This would have been necessary in order to prove that he had lied (perjured himself) about his involvement in the crime. A prosecutive strategy, suggested by one of the authors and another FBI agent, was to call the former wife and girlfriend to testify about the consistency of the man's sexual behavior over a 15-year period. In legal terms, this would be described as "a pattern of continuing behavior". Had it been necessary, the testimony of one of the authors, the women, and others would have educated the jury about the man's long-standing fantasy involving degradation and punishment, motivated by a deep-seated hatred of women.

Similar education and testimony were necessary in other cases set forth in this chapter. For example, in case no. 10, testimony was given about the number of obscene and threatening phone calls made by the man when he was 15, and the obvious importance of such activities to him.

Summary

The person involved in investigating sexual crimes should be aware of the value of understanding the role of fantasy in such crimes. Fantasy is the link between the underlying motivations for sexual assaults and the behavior exhibited during the crime. Such an understanding can help determine linkages between offenses perpetrated by one offender, identify materials to be sought through search warrants, and provide informed prosecutorial strategies.

References

Abel, G., Becker, J., Cunningham-Rathner, J., Mittleman, M., and Rouleau., J., Multiple paraphilic diagnoses among sex offenders, *Bull. Am. Acad. Psychiatry Law,* 16, 153, 1988.

American Psychiatric Association, *Diagnostic and Statistical Manual of Mental Disorders,* Am. Psychiatric Press, Washington, D.C., 1994.

Dietz, P., Hazelwood, R., and Warren, J., The sexually sadistic criminal and his offenses, *Bull. Am. Acad. Psychiatry Law,* 18, 163, 1990.

Douglas, J. and Munn, C., Violent crime scene analysis: modus operandi, signature and staging, *FBI Law Enforcement Bull.,* 61, 1, 1990.

Hazelwood, R., Warren, J., and Dietz, P. E., Compliant victims of the sexual sadist, *Aust. J. Med.,* 22, 474, 1993.

Hazelwood, R., Reboussin, R., and Warren, J., Serial rape: correlates of increased aggression and the relationship of offender pleasure to victim resistance, *J. Interpersonal Violence,* 4, 65, 1989.

Hazelwood, R. and Warren, J., The serial rapist: his characteristics and victims. I, *FBI Law Enforcement Bull.,* 11, January 1989a.

Hazelwood, R. and Warren, J., The serial rapist: his characteristics and victims. II, *FBI Law Enforcement Bull.,* 19, February 1989b.

Lanning, K. V., Child molesters, a typology for law enforcement, in *Criminal and Sexual Deviance,* U.S. Department of Justice, Washington, D.C., 1991.

McCullough, M., Snowden, P., Wood, J., and Mills, H., Sadistic fantasy, sadistic behavior and offending, *Br. J. Psychiatry,* 143, 20, 1983.

Prentky, R., Knight, R., and Rosenberg, R., Validation analysis on a taxonomic system for rapists: disconfirmation and reconceptualization, in *Human Sexual Aggression: Current Perspectives,* Prentky, R. and Quinsey, V., Eds., New York Academy of Sciences Annals, New York, 1988, 21.

Warren J., Reboussin, R., Hazelwood, R., and Wright, J., Prediction of rape type and violence from verbal, physical and sexual scales, *J. Interpersonal Violence,* 6, 55, 1991.

Warren, J., Hazelwood, R., and Reboussin, R., Serial rape: the offender and his rape career, in *Rape and Sexual Assault,* Vol. 3, Burgess, A. W., Ed., Garland Publishing, New York, 1991.

The Behavioral-Oriented Interview of Rape Victims: The Key to Profiling

8

ROBERT R. HAZELWOOD
ANN WOLBERT BURGESS

In October 1981, a police department submitted an investigative report of a rape to one of the authors (Hazelwood) and requested that a criminal personality profile of the unidentified offender be prepared. A synopsis of that report follows:

> On October 5, 1981, Alicia B., a 21-year-old Caucasian who lived alone, was asleep in her apartment. At approximately 2:30 a.m., she was awakened by a male who placed his hand over her mouth and held a knife to her throat. The intruder warned her not to scream or resist and told her that if she complied with his demands, she would not be harmed. He then forced her to remove her nightgown, kissed and fondled her, and then raped her. After warning the victim not to call the police, he left. Ignoring the rapist's warning, she notified the police. The victim said that nothing had been stolen and that she could not give a description of her assailant because he had placed a pillowcase over her head. The rapist had spent about 1 hr with the victim.

Before preparing a profile, Hazelwood provided the requesting agency with a set of questions designed to elicit specific information from the victim as to the rapist's behavior during the assault. Using the questions as a guide, the police reinterviewed the victim and were able to obtain a nine-page typewritten statement. Based on the new statement, a profile was prepared. Subsequently, the rapist was arrested and confessed to a series of rapes. The profile was compared with the offender, and only the marital status was found to be incorrect.

Since 1972, members of the FBI Academy's NCAVC have been helping city, county, state, and federal law enforcement agencies in their investigations of violent crimes by analyzing crime or crime scene data. Chapter 6 and previous publications by members of the BSU have addressed the development and use of profiling and related topics (Reese, 1979; Ault and Reese, 1980; Hazelwood and Douglas, 1980; Rider, 1980; Ressler et al., 1980; Hazelwood et al., 1982). This chapter will deal with questioning the rape victim specifically for the purpose of determining the behavior exhibited by the offender.

0-8493-8152-1/95/$0.00+$.50
© 1995 by CRC Press, Inc.

Motivation

During the past 20 years, the authors have reviewed thousands of rape victims' statements submitted by police agencies. The statements contained details of the crimes as well as a great deal of information about the offenders' physical characteristics, but there was a marked absence of clues as to the offender's motivation (through his behavior) in carrying out the assaults. Over a period of time, one of the authors (Hazelwood) developed a set of questions designed to elicit the behavioral aspects of the crime that may assist in identifying the motivation for the crime. These questions are set forth below.

1. Describe the manner in which the offender approached and gained control over you.
2. How did he maintain control of you and the situation?
3. Specifically describe the physical force he used and when during the attack it occurred.
4. Did you resist either physically, verbally, or passively? If so, describe each instance you can recall.
5. What was his reaction to your resistance?
6. Did he at any time experience a sexual dysfunction? If so, describe what type, whether he was later able to function sexually, and any particular act or behavior he performed or demanded that you perform to overcome the dysfunction.
7. Describe all sexual acts forced upon you or performed by the offender on himself and the sequence in which they occurred, including repetitions.
8. As precisely as possible, try to remember what he said to you, his tone of voice, and his attitude at the time he spoke.
9. Did he demand that you answer questions, repeat phrases, or respond verbally in any manner whatsoever? Try to recall specifically what he demanded you to say.
10. When, if ever, did his attitude appear to change? In what manner did it change, and what occurred immediately before the change?
11. What actions did he take to ensure that you would not be able to identify him? Did he take any precautions to ensure the police would not be able to associate him with the crime?
12. Did he take anything when he left? Have you carefully inventoried your personal belongings (undergarments, photographs, etc.) since the assault?
13. Did you receive any calls or notes from unidentified people before or since the assault? Have you had any experience to indicate that he specifically targeted you for the assault?
14. How do you believe people who associate with the rapist on a daily basis would describe him as a person?

The authors recognize the need for obtaining the offender's physical description, direction and mode of travel, etc., and would not suggest that any less effort be given to these important details. However, additional attention must be devoted to the behavior exhibited by the offender. In so doing, the underlying purpose of the assault becomes clearer, thereby allowing the officer better insight into the type of person he is seeking.

As addressed in Chapter 6, the profiling process in rape cases involves three basic steps:

1. Determine from the victim what behavior was exhibited by the rapist.
2. Analyze that behavior in an attempt to ascertain the motivation underlying the assault.
3. Set forth the characteristics of a person who would commit the crime, given the motivational factor indicated by behavior.

Steps 2 and 3 are accomplished by logic and common sense derived from the experience of having reviewed hundreds of rape cases. The first step, interviewing the victim, is the most crucial one. It is only through the victim that we can elicit the information necessary to complete an analysis of the crime. Therefore, it is essential for the investigator to establish rapport with the victim through a professional and empathetic approach to overcome her feelings of fear, guilt, and anger. The interviewer must also isolate his/her emotions and not allow them to interfere with objectivity. During the interview, the investigator will be dealing with three personalities: the victim's, the criminal's, and the interviewer's. Personal feelings about the offense, the victim, and the criminal must be put aside to allow unbiased opinions about the offender to develop. The investigator who is able to accomplish this will find that a much clearer impression of the offender begins to form.

The point is that intent becomes clear only if we attempt to view the crime from the criminal's motivational standpoint. Once a reasonably safe assumption is made as to why the rape occurred, it is probable that the rapist can be profiled. The basis for this hypothesis lies in the axiom that behavior reflects personality. The manner in which a person behaves within his various environments portrays the type of person he or she is. Opinions are formed about a person's self-esteem, educational level, ability to negotiate interpersonal relationships, and goals in life by the manner in which the person behaves. In rape cases, the victim's description of the offender's behavior enables the investigator to form an opinion as to the type of person responsible.

Questioning for Behavior

In developing the questions set forth earlier, the authors noted that three forms of behavior were exhibited by most rapists: physical (force), verbal, and sexual. A much clearer and less biased view of the offender emerged when his behavior was categorized into these areas.

Needless to say, the interview must be conducted in a tactful, professional, yet probative manner. It is imperative that the investigator impress upon the victim that he is concerned not only with the arrest and conviction of the offender, but also with the victim's welfare. She has been in a life-threatening situation, and the importance of recognizing this cannot be overemphasized. The investigator should inform the victim that the identification of the offender may be expedited through a behavioral analysis of the crime. Her contribution of detailed and personal information regarding the assault is necessary for this analysis to be completed.

Case No. 1

An elderly woman was raped by an unknown man. The victim's statement, submitted to the FBI for analysis, was found to be substantially lacking in detail and was returned to the requesting agency along with a reprint of an article dealing with rape victim interviewing. The police gave the victim a copy of the article, and after reading it, she expressed her understanding of the necessity for complete disclosure. She then gave the police a detailed description of the assault.

Each of the questions set forth earlier is fully discussed in the remainder of this chapter. Note that an analysis is not based on any single response, but rather upon all responses. An abbreviated format of the questions is found in Section 1 of the CSAAT in Chapter 16.

What Method of Approach Was Used by the Offender?

When a person decides to accomplish something, it is human nature to choose a method or course of action with which he or she feels most comfortable and capable. Therefore, it is logical to assume that the rapist, in choosing a method of approaching and subduing his intended victim, would do likewise. Because each aspect of a sexual assault has the potential for yielding information about the person responsible, it is necessary to categorize the styles of approach used by the offender toward his victim. These approaches will be referred to as Con, Blitz, and Surprise.

Con. In the Con style, the offender approaches the victim openly with a subterfuge or a ploy. Frequently, he offers some sort of assistance or requests directions. He is initially pleasant and friendly and may even be charming. His goal is to gain the victim's confidence until he is in a position to overcome any resistance she might offer. Quite often, and for different reasons, he exhibits a sudden change in attitude toward the victim once she is in his control. In some instances, the rapist alters his behavior to convince the victim he is serious. In other instances, the change is merely a reflection of inner hostility toward the female gender. This style of approach suggests a man who has confidence in his ability to interact with women.

Blitz. A person using the Blitz approach uses direct and immediate physical assault (physical injury) in subduing his victim. It is important to note that the term "blitz" refers to physical trauma associated with the approach and not the suddeness of the approach. He allows her no opportunity to cope physically or verbally and often will gag, blindfold, or bind his victim. His attack may occur frontally or from the rear, and he may use disabling gases or chemicals. Such an approach suggests hostility toward women, an attitude which may also be reflected in his relationships with women outside the rape environment. The offender's interactions with women in nonrape relationships are likely to be selfish and one-sided, resulting in numerous but relatively short involvements.

Surprise.   In the Surprise approach, the rapist may either lie in wait for the victim (back seat of a car, behind a wall, in the woods) or wait until she is sleeping. There is no physical trauma associated with this approach. Typically, this man uses threats and/or the presence of a weapon to subdue the victim. While certainly not conclusive, this style suggests two possibilities to the authors:

1.   The victim has been targeted or preselected.
2.   The offender does not feel confident enough to approach the victim either physically or through subterfuge tactics.

How Did the Offender Maintain Control of the Victim?

The manner in which the offender maintains control of his victim depends primarily on the offender's motivation for committing the assault. The authors have commonly observed four control methods: mere presence, verbal threats, display of a weapon, and use of physical force.

Mere Presence.   Depending on the passivity and fear of the victim, it is very possible that the offender's mere presence would be enough to control the victim. This is very difficult for a person removed from the actual situation and/or having a personality different from the victim's to accept. Quite often the investigator judges a victim's reaction on the basis of what he/she would do (or believes he/she would do), rather than taking into account the victim's personality, the circumstances surrounding the assault, and the fear factor involved. The following case is an example of this attitude.

Case No. 2

A woman left her town house at 10 a.m. and walked 10 ft to her car. As she was about to enter the car, a man across the street called her name and said, "I want to see you over here now!" Even though she was only 10 ft from her home, she walked to the location pointed out by the subject. At that point she was placed in a car, driven to another location, and raped. Following the assault, she was returned to within two blocks of her home and released.

Initially, the investigators did not believe the victim. They reasoned that if this happened, all she had to do was run to her home for safety. They failed to consider the victim's personality and instead judged her report based upon "common sense" and what they would have done.

Threats.   Many victims are intimidated by threatening remarks promising physical violence if compliance is not forthcoming. Clues to the motivation for the assault often lie in these verbal threats. Investigators should elicit the verbatim (if possible) context of the threats and whether or not they were carried out.

Weapon.   Many rapists display a weapon to obtain or maintain control of their victims. It is important to ascertain not only whether the rapist had a weapon, but also at what point he displayed it or indicated that he had one. Did the victim see it? Was it seemingly a weapon of choice (brought to the scene) or of opportunity (obtained at the scene)? Did he relinquish control of it (give it to the victim, put it down, or put it away)? Did he inflict any physical injury with the weapon?

Force.   The use and amount of physical force in a rapeare key determinants of offender motivation. The interviewer should determine the amount of force, when it was used, and the rapist's attitude before, during, and after its use.

What Amount of Physical Force Was Used by the Attacker?

The amount of force used by a rapist will give valuable insight into his motivation for the crime. The interviewer should elicit from the victim a precise description of the physical force involved. The victim may exaggerate when describing the level of force, either because she wants to be believed or because she has never been struck or physically attacked before. For example, a victim who was never slapped or spanked as a child or adult may report her attacker as brutal, when she was slapped twice during the rape. Another victim may not be able to distinguish between the sexual assault and the physical assault. For these reasons, the authors have developed descriptions of four levels of physical assault to help arrive at an opinion as to the amounts of force used.

Minimal Force.   At this level, there is little or no physical force used. While mild slapping may occur, the force is used more to intimidate than to punish, and the rapist is typically nonprofane.

Moderate Force.   When the rapist uses moderate force, he will repeatedly slap or hit the victim painfully, even in the absence of resistance. He typically uses profanity throughout the attack and is very abusive.

Excessive Force.   When excessive force is used, the victim is beaten, possibly on all parts of her body. She will have bruises and lacerations and may require hospitalization. Again, the rapist is very profane and directs personal and derogatory remarks toward the victim.

Brutal Force.   At the fourth level of physical assault, brutal force, the victim is subjected to intentional infliction of extremely violent physical abuse. He is extremely profane, abusive, and aggressive. Frequently, the victim dies or requires extensive hospitalization after the attack.

Did the Victim Resist the Attacker and, If So, How?

The victim, when ordered to act, may either comply or resist. Resistance can be defined as anything the victim did, or did not do, that precluded, delayed, or reduced the effect of the attack. While most interviewers are alert to physical or verbal resistance by victims, they often tend to overlook or disregard passive resistance.

Passive. Passive resistance is evidenced when the victim does not resist physically or verbally but does not comply with the rapist's demands. An example would be a victim who is ordered to disrobe, but simply, and without verbal or physical accompaniment, does nothing. Passive resistance is also overlooked quite often during the trial process. Prosecutors would do well to educate judges and juries in this regard and to emphasize that the victim, simply by not obeying the rapist's commands, did resist the attacker.

Verbal. Verbal resistance is offered when the victim screams, pleads, refuses, or tries to reason or negotiate with her attacker. While crying is a verbal act, it is not considered to be resistance in this context.

Physical. Hitting, kicking, scratching, gouging, and running are examples of this form of resistance. When considering the victim's resistance or lack thereof, the investigator should evaluate the victim's personality. He or she should attempt to determine whether the victim is a passive individual who is easily intimidated and controlled or one who is assertive and confident. Is the victim a person who has been protected and cared for during her adult life, or has she been self-sufficient? Factors such as these will have a great deal of bearing on the amount and type of resistance she offers.

If Resistance Occurred, What Was the Offender's Reaction?

People react to stressful situations in various ways. While rape is certainly stressful to the victim, it also creates stressors for the attacker: fear of being identified or arrested, fear of being injured or ridiculed, and fear of being successfully rebuffed. Therefore, it becomes crucial for the investigator to learn how the rapist reacted to any resistance (passive, verbal, or physical) offered by the victim. The authors have observed five rapist reactions: cessation of the demand, compromise, flight, threats, and force.

Cease Demand. In some instances, a rapist who encounters resistance will not insist or attempt to force compliance, but instead will cease his demand and move to another phase of the attack.

Compromise/Negotiate.   In other cases, the rapist will compromise or negotiate by suggesting, or allowing the victim to suggest, alternatives. For instance, the rapist may demand or attempt anal sex and, upon encountering resistance, instead demand vaginal sex with no further attempt to assault the victim anally.

Flee.   The authors have occasionally examined cases in which the rapist left the scene of the assault when resisted. This fleeing reaction is interesting in that it suggests the offender had no desire to "force" the victim against her will or was unprepared for the victim's reaction and/or the attention it might bring.

Threats.   Another reaction of the offender may be to resort to verbal or physical threats in an attempt to gain compliance. If the victim continued to resist, it is important to learn whether the offender followed through on his threatened action or not.

Force.   A final reaction of certain rapists is to resort to force if they encounter victim resistance. Again, if such is the case, the interviewer should determine the degree of force used and its duration.

Did the Rapist Experience a Sexual Dysfunction?

Coleman defines the term "sexual dysfunction" as an "impairment either in the desire for sexual gratification or in the ability to achieve it" (Coleman et al., 1980, p. 531). In a study of 170 rapists, Groth and Burgess (1977) determined that 34% of the offenders suffered a sexual dysfunction during the assault. The authors frequently encounter cases in which either the victim was not asked whether a dysfunction had occurred or the matter was simply noted without further inquiry.

The occurrence of offender sexual dysfunction and an investigative understanding of the dysfunction may provide valuable information about the rapist. The investigator should be alert to the possibility that a rape victim may not volunteer such information during the interview because she does not consider it significant, she is embarrassed about the sexual acts demanded to correct the dysfunction, and/or she is ignorant of such facts and did not recognize it as a dysfunction. It behooves the investigator to explain the various sexual dysfunctions affecting males and their meanings and to ask as to the occurrence of each type.

Erectile Insufficiency.   Formally termed impotence, this type of dysfunction affects the male's ability to obtain or maintain an erection for sexual intercourse. Masters and Johnson (1970) describe two types of erectile insufficiency as primary and secondary. Males suffering from primary insufficiency have never been able to maintain an erection sufficient for intravaginal ejaculation. While this type is relatively rare and not generally of concern to the investigator, it is listed here in the interest of completeness. In secondary insufficiency, the male is currently unable to obtain or maintain an erection.

Groth and Burgess (1977) identified a third form of insufficiency in their study, which they termed conditional. In such cases, the rapist is initially unable to become erect, but does so as a result of forced oral and manual stimulation by the victim. The authors would suggest that the methods of gaining an erection not be limited to the ones aforementioned, but include any act demanded by the offender. The act may be sexual (anal sex, analingus, etc.) or may consist of having the victim verbalize certain words or phrases or dress in certain clothing.

Groth and Burgess (1977) compared erectile insufficiency among rapists with a group of 448 nonrapist patients studied by Masters and Johnson. They found that in both instances it was the most commonly experienced dysfunction.

Premature Ejaculation. "Ejaculation which occurs immediately before or immediately after penetration is termed premature ejaculation" (Groth and Burgess, 1977, p. 164). In their study, Groth and Burgess found that this dysfunction affected 3% of the rapists.

Retarded Ejaculation. This dysfunction is the opposite of premature ejaculation in that the affected rapist experiences difficulty or fails to ejaculate. Contrary to popular belief, the individual experiencing retarded ejaculation is not controlling seminal discharge and prolonging enjoyment, but is unable to ejaculate and is, therefore, denied sexual gratification.

Groth and Burgess (1977) reported that 15% of the rapist population suffered retarded ejaculation. Masters and Johnson (1970) found it to be so rare among their patients that they did not rank it with a percentage. "When the possibility of retarded ejaculation is not taken into account, the victim's version of such multiple and extended assaults may be greeted with doubts and skepticism" (Groth, 1979, p. 88).

Conditional Ejaculation. The final type of dysfunction the authors have observed in cases submitted for profiling is one on which there has been no research conducted and which is not, to the authors' knowledge, reported in the literature. The rapist experiencing conditional ejaculation has no difficulty in obtaining or maintaining an erection, but he can ejaculate only after certain conditions are met. Most often, the conditions involve particular sexual acts, such as in the following case.

Case No. 3

A 21-year-old woman was abducted at knifepoint while walking home late one evening. Over a period of 3 hours she was forced to engage in vaginal, anal, and oral sex. Unable to ejaculate, the offender used lipstick and drew panties and a bra on the victim. Forcing her to fondle herself, he observed her, masturbated himself, and ejaculated.

This is an excellent example of conditional ejaculation and strongly suggests that the offender will have an extensive collection of pornography and/or a long history of "peeping Tom" activities for which he may have been arrested. What men desire to observe physically or through imagery (fantasy) is extremely important in the sexual gratification process. This explains why men are the primary purchasers of erotic literature, photographs, or films. It also explains why such a large number of rapes involve voyeuristic activity.

What Type and Sequence of Sexual Acts Occurred during the Assault?

"Documenting the kinds of sex acts that occur during rape helps us to more clearly understand rape" (Holmstrom and Burgess, 1980). In order to determine the motivation behind a rape assault, it is imperative to ascertain the type and sequence of sexual assault (including repetitions) that took place. This may prove difficult due to the emotional trauma experienced by the victim and/or her reluctance to discuss certain aspects of the crime because of fear, shame, or humiliation. Quite often, however, the investigator can overcome the victim's reluctance through a professional and empathetic approach. While it is common to ask about vaginal, oral, and anal acts, the authors do not frequently review reports that include information pertaining to kissing, fondling, use of foreign objects, digital manipulation of the vagina or anus, fetishism, voyeurism, bondage, or exhibitionism on the offender's part. The following case involves an act of exhibitionism.

> During the course of the attack, described earlier, on the 21-year-old, the offender kissed and fondled the victim. He also engaged in voyeurism, which enhanced his masturbation and resulted in ejaculation. Before that, he forced the victim to walk nude through the streets of her neighborhood while holding his penis.

In a sample of 115 adult, teenage, and child rape victims, Holmstrom and Burgess (1980) reported vaginal sex as the most frequent act, but also reported 18 other sexual acts. Repetitions of acts are infrequently reported. More commonly, the report is likely to state, "The victim was raped", "vaginally assaulted", or "raped repeatedly".

"Various sociopsychological meanings are attached to forced sexual acts" (Holmstrom and Burgess, 1980, p. 437). By analyzing the sequence of the assault, it may be possible to determine whether the offender was acting out a fantasy, experimenting, or committing the sexual acts to punish or degrade the victim. For example, if acts of oral and anal sex are forced on a victim and the anal sex was followed by fellatio, the motivation to punish or degrade would be strongly suggested. Anal assault is an example of a sexual act that often has underlying motivation. When anal sex has taken place in a nonconsensual relationship, the authors consider four possible reasons: acting out a fantasy and/or latent homosexuality; sexual experimentation; to punish, degrade, or humiliate; or the behavior of a former convict.

Fantasy.   In acting out a fantasy, the offender normally engages in kissing, fondling, and/or cunnilingus. He uses minimal force and engages in nonthreatening verbal behavior (apologetic, complimentary, etc.). If fellatio occurs, it generally precedes the anal sex.

Experimentation.   With sexual experimentation, the offender is moderately force-ful in his physical contact with the victim and is verbally profane and derogatory toward her. He typically engages in a variety (and repetition) of sexual acts, including the use of foreign objects. In this instance fellatio may either precede or follow anal sex.

Punishment.   When the offender's intent is to punish, degrade, or humiliate, the victim reports excessive or brutal levels of force accompanied by threatening, derogatory, and profane verbal activity on the part of the rapist. Almost invariably, the rapist will demand fellatio following the anal assault.

Exconvict.   Finally, the victim of an anal assault may have been attacked by a man who was formerly in prison. When analyzing sexual assaults involving anal sex, one should refer to the victim's description of the offender to determine the upper-body build. A muscular upper-body physique, combined with an anal assault, may be indicative of former institutionalization and regular exercise. For further indications of such offender background, the reader is referred to the portion of this chapter dealing with actions taken by the offender to facilitate escape or preclude identification.

What Was the Verbal Activity of the Rapist?

The stereotype of the male rapist's attack is that he attains power and control over the victim through strategies based on physical force. Not only do rapists use physically based strategies, but they also use a second set of strategies based on language (Holmstrom and Burgess, 1979). A rapist reveals a great deal about himself and the motivation behind the assault through verbal activity with the victim. For this reason, it becomes extremely important to elicit from the victim everything the rapist said and the manner (tone, attitude) in which it was said.

In a study of 115 rape victims, Holmstrom and Burgess (1979, p. 101) reported 11 major themes in rapists' conversation: "threats, orders, confidence lines, personal inquiries of the victim, personal revelations by the rapist, obscene names and racial epitaphs, inquiries about the victim's sexual 'enjoyment', soft-sell departures, sexual put downs, possession of women, and taking property from another male".

Preciseness is important. For example, a rapist who states, "I'm going to hurt you if you don't do what I say" has, in effect, threatened the victim; whereas the rapist who says, "Do what I say and I won't hurt you" may be reassuring the victim in an attempt to alleviate her fear of physical injury and gain her compliance without force. An offender who says, "I want to make love to you", has used a passive and affectionate phrase that is indicative of one who does not intend to physically harm the victim. Conversely, a statement such as "I'm going to fuck you" is much more aggressive verbiage with no affection intended.

Compliments directed toward the victim (attractiveness, physical attributes, etc.), politeness, expressions of concern ("Lock your doors", "Am I hurting you"?), apologies, and discussion of the offender's personal life (whether fact or fiction) suggests a relational fantasy of consent of the offender. On the other hand, derogatory, profane, threatening, and/or abusive verbiage is suggestive of anger and the use of sex to punish or degrade the victim.

When analyzing a rape victim's statement, the investigator is advised to write down an adjective that accurately describes each of the offender's statements ("You're a beautiful person" — complimentary; "Shut up, bitch" — hostile; "Am I hurting you" — concerned). The investigator will then have better insight into the offender's motivation and a verbal picture of the personality of the person being sought.

Was the Victim Forced to Say Anything?

The mind dictates what is, or is not, sexually arousing and pleasing to the person and can control the male's ability to function sexually. The involvement of the human senses is also an integral part of sexual activity, and while sexual activity is basically a biological function in animals, people depend on psychosexual involvement for arousal and gratification. When interviewing the rape victim for the purpose of preparing a crime analysis, one should be alert for atypical use of one or more of the senses.

What a person says to his/her sexual partner during intercourse can be gratifying or harmful to a relationship. A person enjoys hearing those things that are pleasing. In a rape situation, the rapist may demand from the victim certain words or phrases that enhance the act for him. The verbiage can indicate what gratifies the rapist and give the interviewer insight into the offender's needs (motivation). For example, a rapist who demands such phrases as "I love you", "Make love to me", or "You're better than my husband" suggests a need for affection or ego building. One who demands that the victim plead, or forces her to scream, suggests sadism and enjoyment of total control and domination. If the victim is forced to speak in a self-demeaning or self-derogatory manner, the offender may be motivated by anger and hostility.

Was There a Sudden Change in the Offender's Attitude during the Attack?

The victim should be asked specifically whether she observed any change in the attitude of the rapist during the time he was with her. Did he become angry, contrite, physically abusive, or apologetic, and was this a departure from his previous attitude? If the victim reports an attitudinal change, she should be asked to recall what immediately preceded the change. A sudden and unexpected behavioral change may reflect a weakness or fear on the offender's part, and it becomes important to determine what precipitated that change.

Factors that may cause such changes include offender sexual dysfunction, external disruption (phone ringing, noise, a knock on the door), victim resistance, a lack of fear on the victim's part, ridicule or scorn, or even ejaculation and/or completion of the rape.

An attitudinal change may be shown verbally, physically, or sexually. As previously mentioned, the rape is stressful not only for the victim but also for the offender. His behavioral reaction to stress may become important in future interrogations, and knowledge of the factor that precipitated the change is a valuable psychological tool to the investigator.

What Precautionary Actions Were Taken by the Offender?

The answer to this question will be a major factor in determining the experience level of the rapist. It may be possible to conclude from the rapist's actions whether he is a novice or an experienced offender who may have previously been arrested or incarcerated for rape or similar offenses.

While most rapists take at least some action (wearing a mask or telling the victim not to look at them) to mask their identity, some go to great lengths to protect themselves from future prosecution. It is the latter group to which this question is primarily addressed. As in any criminal act, the more rapes a person commits, the more proficient he becomes in eluding detection. If a person is arrested because of a mistake and later repeats the crime, it is not likely that he will repeat the same costly error.

The authors classify the offender as either novice or experienced (and/or previously arrested) based upon what protective actions he takes.

Novice.   The novice rapist is unfamiliar with modern medical or police technology and will take minimal or obvious actions to hide his identity. For example, he may wear a ski mask, wear work gloves, change his voice tone, effect an accent, order the victim not to look at him, or blindfold and/or bind the victim. These are common precautions that a person who is unaware of phosphotate tests or hair and fiber evidence would be expected to take.

Experienced/Previously Arrested.   Investigators should note factors in the experienced offender's MO that indicate a more than common knowledge of police and medical abilities. In addition to the actions above, an experienced rapist may walk through the house or prepare an escape route before the sexual assault, disable the victim's telephone before entry or departure, order the victim to shower or douche, bring bindings or gags rather than using those available at the scene, wear surgical gloves during the assault, and/or take or force the victim to wash items he touched or ejaculated on (bedding or the victim's clothing).

As in all such subjective analyses, the projected experience level of the rapist is a judgment based on the offender's actions and the investigator's interpretation of those actions.

Was Anything Taken?

Almost without exception, police record the theft of items from rape victims. All too often, however, investigators fail to probe the matter further unless it involves articles of value (pawn shop, entry in NCIC, etc.). The analyst is interested not only if something was taken, but also why it was taken. The stolen item may provide information valuable in determining a characteristic about the criminal and thereby aid the investigative process. In some cases, the victim may not realize anything was taken (one photograph from a group or one pair of panties from a drawer).

The analyst categorizes items taken as evidentiary, valuables, and personal.

Evidentiary.   As previously mentioned, the rapist who takes evidentiary items (those he has touched or on which he has ejaculated etc.) suggests experience or an arrest history for similar offenses.

Valuables.   One who takes items of value may be experiencing financial difficulties (unemployed or employed in a low-paying job). The investigator may take this a step further in categorizing the offender. It has been the authors' experience that younger rapists steal items such as stereos, televisions, etc., while the more mature offenders tend to take jewelry or items that are more easily concealed and transported.

Personal.   Personal items taken include photographs of the victim, lingerie, driver's license, etc. These types of items have no intrinsic value, but serve to remind the offender of the event and the victim. When such an item is taken, the investigator must try to determine the motivation behind the theft. Was it taken as a trophy or as a souvenir? A trophy represents a victory or conquest, while a souvenir serves to remind one of a pleasant experience. One must examine the physical, verbal, and sexual behavior of the rapist to determine what the stolen item means to the offender. The abusive, hostile, and physically assaultive rapist typically takes the item as a trophy and tends to be a "macho" type who has little respect for the female gender and is given to bragging about his sexual exploits. On the other hand, the souvenir taker is generally the "gentleman" rapist who uses minimal force and is verbally reassuring and sexually "gentle". Such an individual uses the item to fantasize later and frequently keeps the items in his home or place of work. The item, therefore, gives the police a means of connecting him to his crimes.

A final factor to consider in this area is whether the offender later returns the item to the victim. If so, why? The trophy taker does so to intimidate or frighten the victim, while the souvenir taker does so to convince the victim he meant no harm or was not really a bad person.

Has the Victim Had Any Experience That Would Suggest She Was a Targeted Victim?

Rapists quite often target or select their victims before the commission of the crime. The occurrence of a series of rapes involving victims who were either alone or in the company of small children is a very strong indication that the offender was well aware of his victim's vulnerability, either through peeping or surveillance activities. He may also have entered the home, or communicated with the victim before the offense. The investigator should determine whether the victim or her neighbors had experienced any of the following before the rape: calls or notes from unidentified persons, residential or automobile break-ins, prowlers or peeping Toms, or a feeling that she was being watched or followed. Frequently, rapists who do target or pre-select their victims have prior arrests for breaking and entering, prowling, peeping Tom activities, and/or theft of feminine clothing.

Belief as to How the Rapist's Friends Would Describe Him

The ability of the rape victim to disassociate the individual who raped her from the way he is observed to be by his friends and associates will amaze even the most experienced investigator. Having the victim so describe her attacker will benefit the investigator and the victim.

The officer conducting the investigation would be well advised to seek the victim's help in this manner, if she is reasonably intelligent. She should also be asked to list (over a period of days) any facts about the crime that she forgot earlier and that later come to mind. She should be asked to list characteristics of the rapist that she feels would be known to those who associate with him, i.e., articulate, a leader, shy, unsure of self, neat, rough, etc. Such information is very useful in the search for the rapist.

This procedure can also help in the victim's psychological recovery. The rape experience has taken from her the sense of being in control of her life; being asked to contribute in a rational, concrete, and relevant manner to the investigation returns to her some semblance of control.

A word of caution is necessary at this point. Should the victim's "profile" not describe her attacker, it may prove detrimental to the prosecution of the offender (provided to the defense under "discovery" rules). The investigator should seek guidance from his prosecutor before obtaining a "profile" from the rape victim.

Summary

Rape is a deviant sexual activity serving nonsexual needs. Through an analysis of the offender's verbal, sexual, and physical behavior, it may be possible to determine what needs were being served and to project personality characteristics of the person having such needs. It must be remembered that the only available source of information about such behavior is the victim, and therefore it is necessary to establish rapport with the victim through empathy and professionalism. One must isolate personal feelings about the crime and the criminal, and view the crime as the rapist did.

If, in fact, behavior reflects personality, it seems obvious that a set of questions designed specifically to elicit behavioral information would be the first step in the analysis of a rape. One of the authors (Hazelwood) developed and refined the questions in this article over 4 years and has found them to be of inestimable value in understanding the personality involved in rape.

References

Ault, R. L. and Reese, J. T., A psychological assessment of crime: profiling, *FBI Law Enforcement Bull.*, 22, March 1980.

Coleman, J. C. et al., *Abnormal Psychology and Modern Life,* 6th ed., Scott, Foresman, Glenview, IL, 1980.

Groth, A. N., *Men Who Rape,* Plenum Press, New York, 1979, 88.

Groth, A. N. and Burgess, A. W., Sexual dysfunction during rape, *N. Engl. J. Med.,* 297(4), 764, 1977.

Hazelwood, R. R., The behavior-oriented interview of rape victims: the key to profiling, *FBI Law Enforcement Bull.,* September 1983.

Hazelwood, R. R. and Douglas, J. E., The lust murder, *FBI Law Enforcement Bull.,* p. 18, April 1980.

Hazelwood, R. R. et al., Sexual fatalities: behavioral reconstruction in equivocal deaths, *J. Forensic Sci.,* 27(4), 764, 1982.

Holmstrom, L. L. and Burgess, A. W., Rapist's talk: linguistic strategies to control the victim, in *Deviant Behavior,* Vol. 1, Hemisphere, Washington, D.C., 1979.

Holmstrom, L. L. and Burgess, A. W., Sexual behavior of assailants during rape, *Arch. Sex. Behav.,* 9,(5), 1980.

Masters, W. H. and Johnson, V. K., *Human Sexual Inadequacy,* Little, Brown, Boston, 1970.

Reese, J. T., Obsessive compulsive behavior the nuisance offender, *FBI Law Enforcement Bull.,* p. 6, August 1979.

Ressler, R. K. et al., Offender profiles: a multidisciplinary approach, *FBI Law Enforcement Bull.,* p. 16, September 1980.

Rider, A. O., The firesetter: a psychological profile, *FBI Law Enforcement Bull.,* p. 6, June 1980.

Analyzing the Rape and Profiling the Offender

ROBERT R. HAZELWOOD

Any expertise claimed by a person is nothing more or less than a combination of one's own experience and what one has learned from the experience of others. The material set forth in this chapter is the result of reading, attendance at seminars, lectures, and courses, exchanges with others in the field, 32 years in law enforcement, and having had the opportunity of consulting on over 5000 rape cases.

While the author recognizes the impossibility of categorizing human behavior into specific classes that will be applicable to all rape situations, he is convinced that it is possible to analyze an offender's behavior during the attack and to be able to describe the type of individual who committed the crime. This description can then be set forth in such a way as to allow his friends and acquaintances to recognize him.

As addressed in Chapter 8, the first step in profiling the unidentified offender is to ascertain from the victim what behaviors the rapist exhibited. Having obtained a detailed statement, one can then proceed to the next step — analyzing what is known, to determine the purpose of the assault and to elicit behavioral information that will help prepare a criminal personality profile. The analysis should be as objective as possible, and personal feelings about the crime, criminal, and victim must not be allowed to influence the analyst's judgment. The rapist's behavior is easier to assess if it can be seen as part of a systematic pattern. To accomplish this, a typology must be established, one that the analyst believes to be valid and that is easily understood by others. This poses no small problem.

Selfish vs. Pseudo-Unselfish Behavior

In analyzing the statement of a rape victim, the first objective is to determine whether the rapist intended the assault to be "selfish" or "unselfish" in nature. To categorize a rapist as unselfish may seem contrary to everything the reader believes about sexual assault; however, the use of the term is not intended to portray the offender in a favorable light; the terms were selected to establish an easily definable starting point for the analyst to begin the necessary isolation of his/her personal feelings about the offender. It would be simple to describe the rapist as a "no-good, rotten bastard". Doing so might be satisfying, but not very analytical. Remember that a profile should describe a person as those who know him would. The reader will note that of the six classifications of rapists later described, only one exhibits "pseudo-unselfish" behavior.

As discussed in Chapter 8, the analyst considers the verbal, sexual, and physical (force) behavior of the rapist in his/her study of the crime. The same procedure will be applied in determining whether the offender intended the crime to be selfish or unselfish.

Pseudo-Unselfish Behavior

To the average person, the word "unselfish" implies sharing or caring. In the context of rape it has an entirely different meaning, but one that is important in understanding the crime. Pseudo-unselfish behavior indicates a belief on the part of the rapist that his "concern" for the victim's comfort and welfare will win her over and a hope that she will "realize" he is not a bad person at all. Therefore, he attempts to "involve" her in the act, both sexually and verbally. He wants the victim to enjoy (or pretend to enjoy) the activity, as this feeds his need for acceptance and power and fulfills his fantasy of the victim's willing compliance.

Most rapists will not exhibit all of the verbal, sexual, or physical behavior set forth below, but will demonstrate a sufficient amount to allow classification.

Verbal Behavior. The unselfish rapist will verbalize in a manner that simulates a lover rather than a criminal. He will try to reassure the victim that he does not want or intend to harm her if she cooperates. For example, he may say, "If you do as I say, I won't hurt you", "I don't want to hurt you", or "Don't make me hurt you". He is frequently complimentary with such phrases as, "You're beautiful", "You have nice breasts", "I bet you have a lot of boyfriends", or "You're so attractive, why aren't you married?" He may verbalize in a self-demeaning manner with such comments as "You'd never go out with me" or "I'm ugly, you wouldn't like me". On the other hand, he might engage in verbal activity which would indicate ego-building with such demands as "Tell me you love me", "Tell me I'm better than your husband/boyfriend", or "Tell me you want me to make love to you".

Quite often, the unselfish rapist will voice concern for his victim's welfare or comfort with such statements as "Am I hurting you?" "You should lock your doors and windows", or "Are you cold?" He may engage in what appears to be unnecessary, and potentially revealing, conversation of a personal nature. An example of this type of verbiage is present in the following case.

Case No. 1

The victim, a 27-year-old white female, reported that her assailant wakened and raped her at about 2:00 a.m. The sexual attack lasted no more than 10 min. Following the assault, the rapist lay down beside her and conversed for about 45 min. While asking her questions about her personal life (job, boyfriend, etc.), he was primarily interested in discussing himself and the events of the evening. He said that he had left his keys in his car, parked a short distance away, and that he was concerned about it being stolen. He told her that a friend of his, Jack, was outside the house, but that he wouldn't let him near the victim because Jack was drunk. He identified himself as "David" and said that he had never done anything like this before. Before leaving, he apologized and asked her not to call the police. After he left, the victim discovered that $400 was missing from her purse.

The victim reported the sexual assault and theft to the police the same morning. Two days later, she returned home from work and found an envelope in her mail box addressed to her, but bearing no stamp or postmark. Inside the envelope, she found the stolen money and an accompanying note which read:

> Fran:
>
> I'm just writing to try to express my deepest apology to you for what I put you through. I know an apology doesn't help the way you must feel right now, but I am truly sorry. I found Jack when I left, sitting on the sidewalk in front of your apartment complex. He was still pretty drunk. He took some money from a purse in your kitchen. He's really an alright guy and doesn't usually steal money. I hope this is all of it. I found my car later. Luckily, it wasn't stolen because my keys were still in it. Anyway, I just want you to know that I have never done anything like this before. I wish I could blame this on Jack, but I can't. You're really a sweet person, and you didn't deserve any of this.
>
> You can tell your boyfriend that he's a lucky guy.
>
> Good bye,
>
> David

Typically, the pseudo-unselfish rapist is nonprofane. This is not to say that he won't use profanity, but when he does, it is mild in nature and spoken without much conviction. As mentioned in the case above, he may ask questions about the victim's lifestyle, work, social life, plans, or home. Very often the victim will report that the rapist was apologetic and/or asked her forgiveness with verbiage such as "I'm sorry", "Please forgive me", "I wish it didn't have to be you", or "You didn't deserve this".

In summary, the rapist exhibiting pseudo-unselfish verbal behavior is most often (1) reassuring, (2) complimentary, (3) self-demeaning, (4) ego-building, (5) concerned, (6) personal, (7) nonprofane, (8) inquisitive, and (9) apologetic.

When analyzing a victim's statement for the offender's verbal behavior, the reader is advised to use adjectives similar to those set forth in this section.

Sexual Behavior.   As previously stated, the pseudo-unselfish rapist tries to involve the victim; this is especially true in the sexual aspect of the crime. Interestingly, he will normally do what the victim allows him to do (i.e., she does not physically or verbally resist his acts or demands). His behavior does not indicate a desire to harm the victim physically or to force her to engage in acts which she resists. This may be due to a lack of confidence on his part, or a fantasy that she has become a willing partner, which the use of force would destroy. Should the victim resist, this type of rapist may cease the demand, try to negotiate or compromise with the victim, threaten her, or leave. Very seldom will he employ physical force to gain victim compliance with his sexual demands.

He often demands that the victim kiss him "like you mean it". He fondles the sexual parts of her body and may insert his finger in her vagina. Frequently, he performs cunnilingus before penetrating the vagina, and as he rapes, he may demand that the victim kiss him back, put her arms around him, or stroke his neck or back.

As stated, he will do whatever the victim "allows" him to do, and if he is confronted with an aggressive or resistant victim, he will spend a brief amount of time with her. He will quickly discern whether his victim is thoroughly intimidated and very passive, and may take advantage of such a woman by acting out all of his sexual fantasies. In that case, the acts may include fellatio, anal sex, and the insertion of foreign objects, in addition to vaginal rape.

It is important to note at this point that it is quite possible for the pseudo-unselfish and selfish rapists to engage in or demand the same sexual acts; the former does what the victim allows, and the latter does whatever he desires. To differentiate between the two types of rapists, the analyst must closely examine the verbal and physical (force) behaviors, as they are seldom similar. One should also consider the sequence of the sexual acts to determine if there was a desire to degrade the victim (the pseudo-unselfish rapist infrequently does so intentionally).

Physical Behavior.   The amount of physical force used by the pseudo-unselfish rapist is usually minimal. The reader will recall from Chapter 8 that at this level, force is used more to intimidate than to punish the victim. While mild slapping may occur, the offender does not desire to physically hurt his victim; instead, he tends to rely on threats, the presence or threat of a weapon, or the fear and passivity of his victim to obtain her compliance.

From a behavioral standpoint, the fact that a rapist shows a weapon or tells the victim that he has one does not constitute physical force unless he uses it to inflict injury. From a legal standpoint, of course, the presence or threat of a weapon is very significant and escalates the seriousness of the offense. However, the author is aware of countless instances in which an armed assailant put the weapon aside after gaining control of the victim. He is also aware of a few instances in which the rapist turned the weapon over to the victim. Interestingly, many victims find themselves incapable of using the weapon and return it to the offender.* Most of them report that they either were afraid of the weapon, thought it might be a trick (unloaded gun), or were concerned that they might not be able to incapacitate the assailant and that he would then kill them.

Selfish Behavior

Whereas the pseudo-unselfish rapist seeks to involve the victim as an active participant and behaviorally indicates some concern for her welfare, no such actions or behavior can be credited to the selfish rapist. He neither desires nor

---

* Invariably, when the author lectures to police audiences on this subject, the attendees express amazement at the fact that the victim would not take advantage of the opportunity and shoot the rapist. This attitude is quickly changed to one of empathy when he asks how many of them have spouses at home who are afraid of their service weapons and demand that they be kept out of sight.

wants the victim to become involved. Instead, he uses the victim in much the same way an actor in a play uses a prop. He is verbally and sexually self-oriented and physically abusive. During the time he is with a victim, it is clear that his pleasure alone matters above all else. He will exhibit no concern for his victim's comfort, welfare, or feelings.

Verbal Behavior.   Verbally, this type of rapist will be offensive, abusive, and threatening. He uses a great deal of profanity throughout the attack and may refer to the victim in derogatory terms such as "bitch" or "cunt". He will attempt to demean the victim with such statements as "You've got no sex in you" or "No wonder you're not married". Frequently, this type of rapist will demand that the victim verbalize in such a manner as to humiliate herself (e.g., asking for or describing sexual activities). His communications will be consistently threatening in nature and demanding in fact. Almost invariably, his verbiage will be nonpersonal and sexual in orientation. An example of selfish verbal behavior is set forth in the following case.

Case No. 2

A young woman was kidnapped, raped, and murdered. Her killer made a tape recording of portions of the verbal interaction between himself and his young victim. The following is a brief segment of that recording.

RAPIST:	What are you doing?
VICTIM:	Nothing. I'm doing what you told me to do.
RAPIST:	What's that?
VICTIM:	I'm sucking on it.
RAPIST:	On what?
VICTIM:	This.
RAPIST:	What's this?
VICTIM:	Your dick.
RAPIST:	You're sucking on my dick?
VICTIM:	That's what you told me to do.
RAPIST:	Are you doing it?
VICTIM:	Yes.
RAPIST:	Tell me what you're doing.
VICTIM:	I'm sucking on your dick.

In summary, the selfish rapist is (1) verbally offensive, (2) abusive, (3) threatening, (4) profane, (5) demeaning, (6) humiliating, (7) demanding, (8) nonpersonal, and (9) sexually oriented.

Sexual Behavior.   Sexually, this type of rapist will do whatever he wants to do. The victim's fear, comfort, or feelings are of no significance to him. Physical, verbal, or passive resistance will not deter him in his desire to sexually dominate, punish, or use his victim. Seldom will he engage in kissing, unless he feels it will further humiliate the woman. He is not likely to fondle or stroke the victim. He is much more likely to pull, pinch, twist, or bite the sexual parts of her body. He may force the victim to perform anilingus, fellatio, or self-masturbation. The sequence of the sexual acts is more likely to be anal assault followed by fellatio than the reverse. Should the victim complain of pain or discomfort, he will be unconcerned.

Physical Behavior.   The selfish rapist may use moderate, excessive, or brutal levels of force (see Chapter 8). The amount used depends largely on the underlying motivation of the attack and is seldom directly related to the amount of resistance offered by the victim.* Case 3 illustrates this point.

Case No. 3

A 33-year-old woman and her husband returned home from an evening out and were confronted by a burglar/rapist. After binding the husband, the intruder began sexually assaulting the wife, using no force toward her and engaging in vaginal rape only. During the attack, her husband asked as to her welfare and she stated, "It's OK, he's being gentle". At that point, the rapist began to pummel her breasts. As a result of the beating, the victim underwent a mastectomy. When later interviewing the rapist, I asked why he had beaten her following the comment, and he replied, "I wanted her to know who was in charge, and she found out. Who is she to say I'm being gentle?"

Categories of Rapists

Once the rapist is broadly categorized as being either selfish or pseudo-unselfish, the rape may then be further analyzed in an attempt to learn his motivation for the assault. For this purpose, the author has chosen to use the categories of rapists

---

* What should a woman do if she is confronted by a rapist? The author is of the opinion that law enforcement officers should not provide specific recommendations when asked this question. He is not suggesting this as an "easy out", but rather as a means of dealing realistically with an impossible task. To begin with, one who is asked this question is immediately confronted with a situation having three unknown variables: (1) environment of the attack, (2) type of rapist, and (3) victim personality. The author's advice to an assertive woman confronted with an unselfish-type rapist in a parking lot would be entirely different from the advice he would give to a passive woman who is confronted with a sexual sadist on a little-used roadway after midnight. Lacking the variable information, one must proceed cautiously when giving advice. He has no hesitation in giving advice on preventive measures or recommending self-defense courses, firearms training, police whistles, or disabling gases where legal. However, as law enforcement officers, all must remember that when they speak in an official capacity, they speak not for themselves, but for their organizations. If a person following their advice is brutally beaten and requires long-term hospitalization, they or their organizations could be held liable. The author once heard a speaker advise women in the audience to defecate, vomit, or urinate if confronted with a rapist, as this would surely deter him. The author would refer the reader to Case 9 of this chapter and simply state that the only person such measures would surely deter is the individual who recommended the tactic. Case 3 illustrates the inability to determine what may or may not diminish the probability of a victim being injured (Hazelwood and Harpold, 1986).

developed by Groth et al. (1977). These classifications were developed through empirical research, and he has found them to be quite accurate when compared with the volume of cases received at the Behavioral Science Unit (BSU). They are (1) power reassurance, (2) power assertive, (3) anger retaliatory, and (4) anger excitation. The author has taken the liberty of somewhat modifying the "style of attack" in each classification and, as the reader will note, he has briefly addressed the opportunistic rapist and the gang rape. The terms "pseudo-unselfish" and "selfish" are used when describing the various styles of attack.

A word of caution is necessary here. Seldom will a rapist commit a crime in a manner that will allow the analyst to classify him clearly or simply as one of the types set forth below. More commonly, the investigator will be confronted with a mixture of types. It is at this point that common sense is to be used. The case the author has chosen to analyze and profile later in this chapter (Case 10) is an excellent example of a "mixture" of rapist types.

Power Reassurance Rapist

Purpose of Attack.   This type of rapist assaults to reassure himself of his masculinity by exercising power over women. The author asks his enforcement students to associate with this sense of power by having them recall their first patrol experience after graduation from the police academy. Entering traffic in a police cruiser, they immediately note a decrease in speed by the vehicles near them and, while not spoken, a sense of power and authority is felt by the new officer. So it is with the power reassurance rapist — the same feeling of power and control over another, a woman. Finally he's in charge! This person lacks confidence in his ability to interact socially and sexually with women, and through the use of fantasy and forced sexual activity he proves himself to himself. While he does degrade and emotionally traumatize his victim, he has no conscious intent to do so. This is the type of rapist the author has most commonly observed in stranger assaults.

Style of Attack.   The power reassurance rapist exhibits pseudo-unselfish verbal and sexual behavior and uses minimal to moderate levels of force. In police jargon, he is often described as the "gentleman rapist", the "apologist", or the "polite type". He selects his victims in advance, normally through surveillance or peeping Tom activities. He often has targeted several victims in advance, thereby explaining why, following an unsuccessful attempted rape, a second attack occurs on the same evening in the same general area.

His attacks generally occur during the late evening or early morning hours, and the victim is most often alone or in the company of small children. He uses the "surprise" approach and may exhibit (or claim that he has) a weapon. He selects victims within his own age range and typically forces them to remove their clothing, thus fueling his fantasy of the victim's willingness to participate. He generally spends a relatively short period of time with the victim. However, if he encounters a particularly passive victim upon whom he can act out all of his sexual fantasies, he will take advantage of that situation and spend more time with her. Following the assault, and consistent with pseudo-unselfish behavior, he may apologize and ask the victim for forgiveness. Occasionally, he will take a personal item (undergarment, photograph, etc.) as a souvenir.

He may recontact the victim after the assault by calling or writing her. For this reason, the author strongly recommends that a tape recorder be attached to the victim's phone for as long as 15 days after the crime.

Following an unsuccessful rape attempt, he will strike again quickly, possibly the same evening. A successful attack will reassure him, but this feeling rapidly wears off, and he finds it necessary to attack again for additional reinforcement. Therefore, his pattern of attacks will be fairly consistent and will occur within the same general vicinity or in a similar socioeconomic neighborhood. He will continue to attack until he is arrested, moves, or is incapacitated.

With the exception of the anger excitation rapist, this is the only type likely to keep records of his attacks. Such a rapist is depicted in the following case.

Case No. 4

A black male raped more than 20 black women within a short period of time. The victims were always alone or with other women who were age mates. The offender never struck his victims but relied instead on threats or the presence of a weapon. In several instances, he left the scene rather than resort to force to obtain victim compliance. Upon his identification and arrest, the investigators recovered a business ledger with the victims' names, addresses, telephone numbers, body measurements, and a scoring system for the victims' participation in various sexual acts. The ledger also contained similar information on fantasized victims, including movie stars and popular singers.

Power Assertive Rapist

Purpose of the Attack.   In contrast to the power reassurance rapist, this type has no conscious doubts about his masculinity. To the contrary, he is outwardly a "man's man". He is, in his own mind, simply exercising his prerogative as a male to commit rape. This man uses rape to express his virility and dominance over women and is the second most commonly observed type in the cases received by the BSU for profiling.

Style of Attack.   The power assertive rapist is sexually and verbally selfish in his attacks. He makes no attempt to accommodate his victims and shows no concern for their welfare or emotional comfort. He uses moderate to excessive levels of force in subduing and controlling the victim. This style of rapist most often uses the "con" approach, changing demeanor only after the victim is relaxed and at ease. Like the power reassurance rapist, he selects victims who approximate his own age.

His rapes are likely to occur anywhere that is convenient and that he considers safe. Frequently, he will rip or tear the victim's clothing from her and discard it. He will subject the victim to repeated sexual assaults, as this is a further expression of his manliness and of his imagined natural dominance over women.

If he has transported her to the assault location, he will most often leave the victim stranded there in a partial or full state of nudity, thereby delaying her ability to report the crime. While he doesn't rape as consistently as the power reassurance type, he will assault when he feels he "needs" a woman. Case 5 provides an example of this type of rapist.

Case No. 5

A female motorist was stranded with her disabled car, when a white male stopped and offered assistance. He raised the hood of her car, examined it for a few minutes, and advised her that it would have to be repaired by a mechanic. Because he was well dressed and very polite, she accepted his offer to take her to a nearby service station. Once in the car, they chatted in a friendly manner until she noticed that he had passed two exits. She inquired as to how far the station was, and he displayed a gun and told her to shut up. She screamed, and he struck her twice on the head, causing her to lose consciousness. When she awakened, she discovered her clothes had been torn off and he was raping her. When she pleaded for him not to hurt her, he cursed her, struck her again, and told her to keep quiet. During the next 2 hr, he raped her three times and forced her to perform fellatio twice. Following the assault, he threw her out of the car, keeping the clothes, and told her, "Show your ass and you may get some help". The victim was treated for severe bruises and lacerations.

Anger Retaliatory Rapist

Purpose of the Attack.   This type of rapist is identified with anger and retaliation. As Groth et al. (1977) have stated, the offenders who fall within this category are getting even with women for real or imagined wrongs. They are angry with women and use sex as a weapon to punish and degrade them. They do so intentionally, and when one interviews the victim of such an attack or reads her statement, it becomes quite clear that anger is a key component of the underlying motivation in the sexual assault. This is the third most common type of rapist observed in the BSU files.

Style of Attack.   The anger retaliatory rapist is sexually and verbally selfish and will use excessive levels of force. The analyst must recognize the application of such force as the result of intense rage and an almost frenzied attack process due to the emotional involvement of the offender.

The crime itself is not generally premeditated in the sense that a great deal of time was committed to planning or to the selection of the victim. The attack is an emotional outburst that is predicated on anger and, therefore, is an impulsive action.

This type of rapist uses the "blitz" approach, subduing the victim with the immediate application of direct and physical force, thereby denying her any opportunity to defend herself. The actual sexual assault is relatively short in duration, and the total amount of time spent with the victim is also relatively brief. The pent-up anger is vented against the female sexually and physically, and he leaves the victim following the release of tension.

The anger retaliatory rapist typically attacks women who are age mates or somewhat older than he is. Often he will assault women who, in one way or another, symbolize someone else. The similarity may be style of dress, grooming, occupation, height, weight, race, or a host of other possibilities.

As with the power assertive rapist, this offender is most likely to tear or rip his victims' clothing off. His assaults are likely to occur anytime during the day or night due to the motivational factor of anger. He tends to use weapons of opportunity, most often his feet or fists, and his attacks are sporadic in nature. That is to say, there is no pattern to his assaults. After an attack, his anger is relieved and he feels less tension. Eventually, however, his anger rebuilds and he again feels the necessity to vent his anger against the source of his problems — women! The following case provides an example of such a rapist.

Case No. 6

The victim, a woman in her late 40s, was walking toward her car in a parking lot, when a man spun her around and struck her repeatedly in the face and stomach with his fist. In a semiconscious state, the victim was placed in her car and driven to an isolated area, where the rapist ordered her to remove her clothing. As she fumbled with the buttons on her blouse, he cursed her and began tearing her clothes off and throwing them out of the car. As she held her arms up in a defensive posture, he continued to beat her severely and to scream obscenities at her. Forcing her into the rear of the car, he attempted to rape her but was unable to obtain an erection. Blaming the victim for a lack of sexuality, he decided that alcohol would "help" her and he forced her to consume a large amount from a bottle, causing her to gag. Under his control for more than 2 hr, she was repeatedly beaten and otherwise abused. He finally pushed her into a ditch and drove away. Upon being taken to a hospital, she was found to have fractures of facial and other bones, as well as multiple lacerations. She required extended hospitalization and long months of mental therapy.

Anger Excitation Rapist

Purpose of the Attack.   This type of rapist is sexually stimulated and/or gratified by the victim's response to the infliction of physical and emotional pain. His primary motivation in the assault is to inflict pain that will bring about the desired response of fear and total submission. In the cases on which this author has consulted, he has found this to be the least common type of rapist encountered. However, the rarity is more than compensated for by the viciousness of the attack and the physical and emotional trauma suffered by the victims.

Style of the Attack.   Depending on the offender's sophistication, investigators will experience no other sexual crime as well planned and methodically executed as that committed by the anger excitation rapist. Every detail of the crime has been carefully thought out and rehearsed either literally or in the offender's fantasies. Weapons and instruments, transportation, travel routes, recording devices, bindings — virtually every phase has been preplanned, with one notable exception: the victim is typically a stranger. While she will meet certain criteria established by the rapist to fill his desires and fantasies, she will generally not be associated with him in any way known to others. This is also part of his plan. He wants no ties that will connect him to the victim.

Needless to say, he is sexually and verbally selfish with his victims and typically uses the brutal level of force, often resulting in the victim's death. He most often uses the "con" approach to gain access to the victim. After gaining her confidence, he quickly immobilizes her with bindings and takes her to a preselected location that gives him the necessary privacy. He normally keeps the victim for extended periods of time (hours to days) and, during that time, may torture her with instruments and/or devices while psychologically reducing her to depths of fear difficult to imagine.

Victims often report that, while they remained bound, the rapist would cut and remove their clothing. Such rapists typically engage in sexual bondage, and the helplessness of the female is stimulating to them. The cutting of the clothing may also be a symbolic cutting of the victim. As previously mentioned, the offender will practice bondage and may also bite the victim and insert foreign objects into her vagina or rectum.

The anger excitation rapist is the most likely to record activities with the victim. The method of recording depends on the offender's desires, maturity or experience, and/or ability to afford the technology. I have seen cases in which the rapist recorded his acts with a camera, tape recorder or video recorder, or in sketches or writing.

The sexual acts forced on the victim will be varied and experimental in nature, intended to create pain, humiliation, and degradation for the victim. In some instances, the author has noted that very little sexual activity took place that involved the offender. He tends to remain emotionally detached from such acts and is almost instructional in his directions to the victim. He is particularly attuned to the visual and auditory aspects of the crime.

The victim's age and race may vary if the rapist continues to attack over a period of time. The investigator will note that there is no apparent pattern to the period of time between assaults. In other words, the rapist attacks when he wants to and when he is convinced that his plan is foolproof. Case 7 provides an example of the anger excitation rapist.

Case No. 7

The victim, a 32-year-old housewife, disappeared from a shopping center after having bought groceries. She was driving a motor home at the time of her disappearance. Her nude body was found in the motor home 5 days later; she was lying on her back on the sofa with her hands bound behind her. An autopsy indicated that she had died within the past 2 days, and her death was attributed to the continued ingestion of small amounts of arsenic accompanied by bourbon. She had been raped several times, and it was the considered opinion of those concerned with the case that she had been forced to drink the arsenic-spiked bourbon to induce convulsions of the body for the rapist's pleasure.

Opportunistic Rapist

Purpose of the Attack.   This may be the only type of rapist whose primary motivation in assaulting a woman is sexual in nature. The opportunist typically assaults as an afterthought during the commission of another crime. An example would be the burglar who discovers a woman alone after he enters the residence. He finds her to be sexually attractive and impulsively assaults her. One must not confuse this offender with the burglar who consistently rapes during other crimes.

Style of Attack.   The opportunist is in the midst of committing another crime (burglary, robbery, kidnapping, etc.) when he decides to assault sexually. He generally uses a minimal level of force and spends a relatively short period of time with the victim, leaving her bound when he leaves. He is sexually and verbally selfish and has frequently been drinking or consuming drugs before the crime. An example of this type of rapist is set forth in case 8.

Case No. 8

The victim, a 17-year-old, was normally in school at the time a burglar entered her home. Surprised to find anyone at home, the criminal bound and blindfolded the young girl, and after telling her that he wouldn't harm her, he began ransacking the home. Finding the father's liquor cabinet, he consumed a large amount of alcohol and began thinking of the attractive female who was in the house. He became mildly intoxicated and attempted to vaginally assault her, but was unable to maintain an erection. He told the crying girl to be quiet, that he hadn't hurt her, and he left quickly. Upon his arrest, he expressed regret at what happened and said that he had a daughter the same age as the victim. There was no indication that he had ever attempted such an act before.

The Gang Rape

When confronted with a rape involving two or more offenders, it is especially important to elicit information from the victim about the apparent leader of the group. In practically all rapes of this type, one person emerges as the leader, and it is this person on whom the analyst should concentrate.

It should be noted that there is generally a reluctant personality involved in gang rapes in which three or more persons participate. Frequently, this person is easy to recognize in that he indicates to the victim that he really doesn't want this to happen, but that he is powerless to stop it. Sometimes the victim identifies this person as one who tried to protect her or helped her to escape from others. This is the weak link in the group, and if such a person is evidenced, the author would apply the profiling techniques to him as well. In all such matters that the author has observed, the assault is totally selfish in nature, but the force levels have varied from minimal to brutal. The following case illustrates such a rape.

Case No. 9

A 19-year-old woman was abducted from a phone booth as she was hysterically explaining to her parents that a group a four young men were following her in a car and threatening to rape her. Four hours later, she was found and immediately taken to a hospital where she was treated for a fractured jaw, a broken arm, and severe lacerations of the vaginal and rectal regions. She later reported that she had been forcibly taken from the phone booth and placed in the back seat of the car being used by the gang. As a result of her extreme fear, she defecated and one of the youths suggested that she be released, whereupon a second male, who was the obvious leader, negated that suggestion and instead said that she needed to be taught a lesson. He then twisted her arm so severely that it broke and forced her to orally clean her soiled clothing. The youth who had objected to the rape again objected and was threatened by the leader. Following this, the leader directed the others to have sex with the young girl, and two complied; the third (the reluctant participant) was sexually unable to perform. The leader then anally assaulted the girl and forced her to perform fellatio on him. Following these acts, he vaginally assaulted her. She was later tied to the rear bumper of the assailants' car and dragged over the roadway.

A Case Study

Now that the procedures and classifications the author uses have been described, a rape case will be examined that was submitted to the BSU for analysis. The case will be presented as it was received, but with changes made to protect the victim's identity. Following the case report, the reader will find the author's analysis of the crime and the offender's behavior. Finally, the offender's characteristics will be set forth. For the reader's information, the rapist has since been identified, and the profile was found to be accurate in over 90% of the characteristics set forth.

Case No. 10

Victimology: The victim, Mary, is a white female, 24 years of age. She currently lives alone but previously lived with her parents in another part of the state. Mary attended a university and graduated 2 years before the offense. She is an active Catholic, attends church regularly, and participates in church events. After graduating, she obtained a teaching job in a junior high school. According to Mary, she is popular with the students at the school and attributes her popularity to the fact that she is young, friendly, outgoing, a nice dresser, and "is on their level". Mary is friendly with both black and white students and often attends their athletic activities. She said that students would visit her classroom during their free time even though she was not their teacher. She drives an older-model subcompact car, made noticeable by multi-colored fenders salvaged from other vehicles. Her personal life is fairly routine, but she has a boyfriend who lives a few miles from her home. She visits the Catholic church almost daily after school. She also attends a Wednesday night "happy hour" at a local bar/restaurant that attracts a respectable clientele. She is active athletically and eats out seldom. She has regular sleeping habits and is careful to draw her curtains at night. She knows of no black male fitting the physical description of her assailant.

Attack environment: Mary lives in an apartment complex, located in a middle-class neighborhood in a well-established area of the city. The complex rents to a variety of people, including elderly, singles, and young couples. Mary's apartment is at the rear of the complex and is 1 of 20 apartments. Her apartment and the two beside it are secluded and face a heavily wooded area immediately behind the complex. Her apartment is on the ground floor. A person not familiar with the area would be surprised to find the three apartments in the rear of the complex. The windows of the apartment face the wooded area. The management seems sincere in trying to screen all renters and to maintain the quiet environment of the complex; this is evidenced by their recent eviction of a tenant for creating heavy traffic in and out of the complex because of suspected drug dealing.

Assault: On the evening of Thursday, June 29, 1982, Mary went to bed around midnight. The evening was cool and clear, and she left her windows open to circulate the air. She wore a nightgown and panties to bed. Sometime after 2:00 a.m., she became aware of the sensation of something tickling her leg. Thinking it was a bug, she tried to brush it off with her hand. When it continued, she tried to brush again and felt something she believes was a hand. The room was very dark, but she could see enough to determine that a naked black male was beside her bed. When she sat up, he immediately jumped up and pushed her back down on the bed. He put a hand to her throat and told her to be quiet or he would "blow your head off". Mary began asking him to leave, and he put something, which she thought was metal, to her head and told her he had a gun. He told her he had just gotten out of prison 2 weeks ago, and not to make any trouble since he had killed the other girls he had done this with. Mary asked him how he had gotten into the apartment, and he told her he had climbed in the window. He then grabbed the sheet, but Mary kept asking him to leave. He then said he was going to kill her if she didn't let go of the sheet, because he wasn't in the mood for fooling around. Mary let go of the sheet, and he pulled her underpants off. He then told her to spread her legs, but she refused. He again threatened her, and she held her legs up. He began to perform cunnilingus and continued this for approximately 3 min. During this time, Mary tried to talk to him about his statement about just getting out of prison. She told him that she had worked in a prison and that she didn't think that he had just gotten out. He said that he was in prison in another state. She asked him to leave several times, but he told her to be quiet and continued to perform cunnilingus. He then inserted his penis in her vagina. Several times when he hurt her, she cried out, and he quickly put a hand to her throat and warned her not to do it again or he would kill her. Mary told him not to hurt her again, and he responded by telling her to take her top (nightgown) off, which she refused to do. He pushed it up and began licking her nipple. During all this time, he was careful not to raise himself above her so that, in the poor light, she might be able to get a better look at him. He "slid" up her body to lick her nipple. At one point, he bit her nipple, causing Mary to cry out. Mary told him he had hurt her, and he said, "I'll show you how I can hurt you", and inserted his penis again. He told her to "shove your ass" while he was inserting his penis, and she responded by telling him that her working was not part of the deal and that she was not enjoying this. He asked if she was only "half a woman" and she said, "Yes, that's right". At one point, he moved his penis to her anus, but she told him he was in the wrong place and he ceased that activity. Eventually he ejaculated in her vagina, and Mary began asking him to leave again.

During the rape, Mary never saw a weapon, but felt a metal object pressed to her head. He continually threatened her with death, but seemed concerned for her during the rape. When he hurt her and she let him know, he would cease the painful activity. He never struck her during the incident and his threats were not made in an angry, but rather in a stern, voice. Mary did not think he had trouble in obtaining or maintaining an erection, although he told her that he was having trouble and compared his erection with "the other". He did not ask her to do anything to help him, apart from saying, "Shove your ass", and Mary said that she did not touch him during the entire incident. She did not think that a premature ejaculation occurred, but could not be certain due to her lack of sexual experience. She felt that the actual intercourse lasted about 15 min and that he seemed to be in control of his sexual sensations during that time. He did not demand that she talk to him during the assault or that she speak any particular words to him. He was not abusive or profane at any time and, according to Mary, seemed to care about her. His demeanor changed only when he threatened her and then it was a stern tone, something Mary likened to a father correcting a child. After the rape, he leaned over the bed, closed the open window, and told her to get out of bed. She asked why, but he just repeated the order. She got out of bed, and he directed her to the living room. He told her not to turn on any lights and placed his hand on her shoulder blade and pushed her ahead. In the living room, he made her lie face down on the rug near her stereo. Mary continually asked him if he was going to leave, but he didn't say anything and she did not hear him put his clothes on. He asked her what she was going to do after he left, and she told him she would probably call her parents and cry. He asked her if she was going to call the cops, and she said no. He then asked where the phone was, and she directed him to the kitchen. She could hear him feeling against the wall but he couldn't find the phone. During the time she was on the floor, he continually ordered her to "keep that nose pressed to the floor". When he couldn't find the phone, he told her to show him where it was located. He then told her to go back and lie down. She did, and he ripped the phone out, saying he was sorry that she couldn't call her folks. He had her show him how to unlock the door (deadbolt lock, manually operated) and took her to the bathroom, keeping a hand on her shoulder. In the bathroom, he obtained a towel, telling Mary not to turn on any lights. They returned to the living room, and he made her lie down again. He ripped the towel into strips, possibly using a kitchen knife, and began to tie one strip over her eyes as a blindfold. He tied it too tight and it hurt her, so she asked him to loosen it, and he did. At this point, she noticed that he was wearing gloves, similar to those used by doctors, and work boots. He tied her hands behind her back and tied one of her ankles. Then, with a wet towel, he began wiping her vagina. He asked her if he had gotten all the "semen"; she answered that she didn't know and asked when he was going to leave. He kept asking what her name was during this time, but she wouldn't tell him. He then tied her ankles together and asked her if she had any money. She replied that she only had $1. He turned on the stereo and the announcer said it was 2:50 a.m., and he told her to give him $20 or he would take her stereo. Mary told him that she didn't have $20, but that she would write him a check. He found her purse, took a dollar and change, and asked, "Is your name Mary?"; she assumed he had found her driver's license. He then told her that he was going to take the stereo, and she told him he was going to look funny carrying a stereo around. He replied, "There are ways". Mary told him that she wanted the cassette tapes. He wanted to know if they were mood music and she said no, but that they had identification on them that might incriminate him if he took them.

He asked if she had any beer or wine in the refrigerator and she said no, but he went to the refrigerator and found a bottle of wine. She told him it was cooking wine, but he drank it anyway. He then told her that he was going to do it again and that he was going to do an "ass job". She refused, and he said, "Yes we are". She refused again and said it would hurt her too much. He then placed a knife to her throat hard enough to prevent her from speaking and told her he was going to kill her. He told her that he had a knife and was going to slit her throat. She asked him why, and he said that since she didn't want to "make it" with him that there was no point in her living at all. He then asked why he should let her live, and she told him that she needed to love, to love her parents, her husband, her children. He asked if she had a husband or kids and she said no, that she had meant her future husband. He asked if she was afraid, and she said yes. He then told her that they were going to do it again. He directed her onto her back, but it was painful and she kept rolling on her side. He put the knife to her throat and said that he didn't want any fooling around. He asked her which way she wanted it and she told him she didn't want it any way. He pressed the knife to her throat again and asked if she wanted to live, and she replied yes. At this point, he told her that he used to be a good Christian boy with a nine-to-five job until one day he came home and found his wife in bed with another guy. From then on, he just went from one girl to another. Mary told him she was sorry. He told her that if she didn't call the cops, he would be back, and she told him that she would call the police. He then told her that, even in the dark, he could tell that she had "nice features" and a "picturesque ass". Mary told him she didn't think he was from prison, and he laughed and said, "No, this is from your own neighborhood". She said she had some black friends and that she didn't know if she could treat them fairly after this. He asked what friends, and she replied that they were black students. He said, "I don't hang around those punks". Mary felt that he was so strong in his denial that it seemed as if he did hang around them. Mary asked why he had picked her, and he replied that he had heard that she was a "classy chick" and that he had seen her around. She said that didn't mean he had to do this to her, and he replied that if he had asked her to screw around, she would have said no. Mary heard him rip some paper and asked him to leave. He replied that he was leaving and slid the knife down her back and between her hands. She asked him to leave a light on, and he said he had. She then heard the door open and close. She began trying to get the blindfold off, and she felt him tapping her on top of the head. He placed the knife inside the blindfold and told her how lucky she was. She heard a big bang, and the stereo stopped playing. She heard the door slam, waited a few minutes, and then worked the blindfold off. She hopped to the door, locked it, and worked the towel from around her ankles. She opened the door and knocked on a neighbor's apartment door, and help was summoned.

Subsequent examination by a physician revealed a small laceration on her neck and towel burns on her wrists. Police investigation revealed that the rapist had removed a screen covering the point of entry (a window). Mary described the rapist as a medium-to-light-skinned black male, 20 to 30 years old, 5'8" to 5'10" in height. He had spoken in soft to normal tones and seemed to be articulate. He had been very concerned about physical evidence being left at the scene. She didn't think he had worn the gloves during the rape. The knife was a kitchen knife from her apartment. The paper she heard being ripped was determined to be newspaper he had used to light a bowl candle, which was still burning. He had also smoked a cigarette and had taken the butt with him. The "bang" she had heard was from a blow to the stereo with what is believed to have been a metal pipe.

Criminal Investigative Analysis

The investigators in the matter described above requested and used the questions set forth in the preceding chapter (question 14 had not yet been developed) as a guide during the interview with Mary. The reader will have noted that she gave an extremely detailed account of what transpired during the assault. A great deal of interaction occurred between Mary and her assailant, and it was thoroughly elicited from her. The author will now analyze the assault, following the format discussed in Chapter 8. He will also describe the significance of the behavior exhibited during the crime.

Victimology

When a case is analyzed for profiling purposes, victimology is extremely important. An absence of pertinent information about the victim may preclude an accurate analysis of the crime. Victims are categorized as either low, moderate, or high risk.

Low Risk. Low-risk victims are those whose personal, professional, and social lives would not normally expose them to crime-threatening situations. Such victims have been sought out by the criminal.

Moderate Risk. Moderate-risk victims are those who, while generally of good reputation, have escalated the possibility of becoming crime victims through their employment (working hours, environment, etc.), life-style (meeting dates through advertisement or in singles bars, etc.), or personal habits.

High Risk. High-risk victims are those whose life-styles or employment consistently expose them to danger from the criminal element (drug dealing, residential location, sexual promiscuousness, prostitution, etc.). If a victim is categorized as high risk, the probability of profiling her offender is greatly diminished because the number of potential offenders is extremely large.

Mary would be categorized as a low-risk victim. Her assailant obviously sought her out.

Method of Approach

The rapist in this case used the "surprise" approach. He entered her home at an hour when he had reason to believe she would be asleep and unprepared for an attack. In the author's opinion, the victim had been targeted in advance, through either surveillance or peeping-Tom activities. The isolated location of the apartment allowed him to observe the victim undetected. Of interest is the fact that the offender felt comfortable enough in the home to remove his clothing before approaching the victim, and did not ask whether anyone else was in the apartment or was expected. This would indicate that he was somewhat familiar with Mary's routine and knew that she lived alone. By undressing before the approach, he was able to devote himself to controlling Mary and taking precautions to disallow her seeing him sufficiently to identify him.

Method of Control

Although the rapist told Mary that he had a gun, and she felt a metal object at her head, he relied primarily on threats to control her. Of particular interest is the fact that even though he threatened physical violence if she did not comply with his demands, he did not carry out those threats. This suggests that the intent or desire to physically punish the victim was absent.

Amount of Force

The rapist had numerous opportunities to rationalize use of physical force against the victim, and yet he never struck her. The amount of force used consisted of (1) pushing her down on the bed, (2) putting his hand to her throat, (3) biting her nipple, (4) tapping her on the head, and (5) inflicting a small laceration on her neck. Of behavioral interest is the fact that when he hurt her and she told him so, he would cease the activity. The reader will recall that when she complained of the blindfold being too tight, he loosened it.

It is apparent that a battle of wills was taking place and, even though the rapist possessed Mary sexually, he failed to intimidate her emotionally. The author believes that he was aware of his failure to "control" her and that, instead of acting out against her in a physical manner, he chose to destroy something belonging to her (the stereo) in a symbolic attack.

Given the circumstances reported, the level of force exhibited in this attack would be minimal. Although the victim's neck was lacerated, it was such a minor wound that she made no mention of it in her statement and it is believed to have been inflicted unintentionally. Furthermore, she reported that the rapist seemed to care about her welfare.

Victim Resistance

There was an abundance of resistance in this case. Mary resisted the offender verbally by consistently rejecting him, questioning his demands, and asking him to leave. She resisted passively by not complying with his order to remove her nightgown, and she resisted him physically by moving away from him to avoid intercourse.

Reaction to Resistance

A very interesting pattern of resistance-reaction emerges upon analysis of the crime. As in his method of controlling the victim, he relied primarily on verbal threats to overcome her resistance. At one point, Mary refused to remove an article of clothing, and he did so himself, thereby ceasing the demand. After refusing to "shove your ass", the victim was asked if she was "half a woman". Again and again, the potential for physical violence was there, and yet it was not used. As mentioned previously, the offender failed to intimidate Mary, and his lack of violent reaction supports the author's earlier opinion that the desire or intent to physically harm the victim was absent.

Sexual Dysfunction

Mary was unable to determine if any dysfunction occurred. According to her, the rapist had no difficulty in obtaining or maintaining an erection, and he ejaculated within an average amount of time. The offender verbally indicated some difficulty, but Mary was not aware of any such problem. Her lack of sexual experience may have been a factor in her assessment regarding dysfunction.

Type and Sequence of Sexual Acts

The sexual attack included the following acts in the sequence reported by the victim: (1) cunnilingus, (2) digital manipulation of the vagina, (3) vaginal rape, (4) licked nipple, (5) vaginal rape, (6) attempted anal rape, (7) vaginal rape with ejaculation, (8) threatened anal rape, and (9) attempted vaginal rape.

The acts of cunnilingus and digital manipulation of the vagina preceded the first rape. The activity and sequencing suggests an attempt to stimulate the victim. This behavior is unnecessary in a forcible rape situation, and its presence indicates an attempt to "involve" rather than simply "use" the victim. (The reader is reminded that we examine the crime from the offender's perspective, not our own, and certainly not the victim's.) Mary told the offender that she wasn't enjoying sex, that her "working" was not part of the deal, and that she didn't want sex in any way with him. Following the vaginal rape, he attempted to enter her anally and was told by Mary that he was "in the wrong place" (resisted). Rejected, he ceased the attempt, entered her vaginally, and ejaculated. Even though he ceased his attempt to anally assault her, the desire for this type of sexual act was strong and he later told her he was going to do an "ass job". As stated in the preceding chapter, a sexual assault that includes anal sex is of interest to the analyst. His desire for this activity, combined with Mary's description of his having a muscular upper torso and his talk of prison, suggest strongly that Mary's attacker had been institution-alized. This will be more fully discussed in the criminal personality profile.

Sexually, the offender exhibits a mixture of selfish and pseudo-unselfish behavior.

Offender Verbal Activity

We are very fortunate that the victim in this case is articulate and in control of her emotions. She gave a detailed and comprehensive description of the entire episode and provided an abundance of material from which to draw conclusions. No-where is this more evident than in the victim's recollection of what the rapist said and the manner in which he said it. When originally analyzing the statement, the author wrote adjectives to describe what the rapist said. In so doing, an interesting picture of the offender began to emerge. Let's examine what he said and objectively describe it using adjectives.

1. He threatened to "blow your head off" and stated that he was "going to kill you". The adjective threatening is obvious in this situation.
2. He told her to "get out of bed", "spread your legs", and to "hold your legs up". Commanding would be appropriate here.
3. He related that he had just gotten out of prison, that he used to be a good Christian boy, and that he had been a nine-to-five person until he found his wife in bed with another man. The author would describe this verbiage as personal or disclosing.
4. He spoke in a derogatory manner when he asked if she were "half a woman".
5. He was nonprofane, as the victim clearly recalled that he had not used profanity during the course of the crime.
6. He was apologetic when he told her he was sorry she couldn't call her folks.
7. He repeatedly asked her name, if she had any kids, and if she had a husband. This would accurately be described as inquisitive.
8. He was complimentary when he told her she had nice features and a "picturesque ass".
9. He was occasionally angry when she wouldn't comply with his demands. In one instance, he told her he would show her how he could hurt her.
10. Finally, he was self-demeaning when he said she wouldn't have "screwed around" with him if he had asked her.

After examining the verbal behavior, we find that the offender exhibited a mixture of selfish and pseudo-unselfish behavior. This mixture of behavior allows us to see him as those who know him see him. The author will elaborate more fully on this in the profile.

Attitudinal Change

Mary stated that the rapist's attitude changed only when he threatened her. She described the change as being verbal in nature and said he became stern "like a father correcting a child". We see here that the victim is able to differentiate the sexual assault from the offender's attitude. Her description of his change in attitude is helpful and enlightening. The rapist is in possession of a weapon, is physically larger and stronger than Mary, and has met consistent resistance. Yet his threatening attitude is described as being "stern" — certainly not the stereotypic view of a rapist, yet very typical behavior for one not desiring to hurt his victim physically.

What Preceded the Attitudinal Change

The victim stated that only when the rapist threatened her did she perceive a change in his attitude. In each instance, the factor preceding this change was resistance by Mary. Some rapists will use physical force in such situations, others will compromise or negotiate, and still others will leave. Yet this man chose to threaten. Why? As has been pointed out earlier, the rapist engaged in a battle of wills with Mary and lost. The author believes that he is used to winning in confrontations with women, and this was a situation that should have yielded a submissive woman and didn't. His frustrations are evident in his continued threats and the physical attack on the stereo.

Precautionary Actions

This case is replete with actions taken by the offender to protect his identity, facilitate his escape, and deny investigators physical or trace evidence. These actions include: (1) removing his clothing before the attack, thereby ensuring that Mary would be unable to provide police with their description; (2) disabling the phone, which delayed her ability to report the crime; (3) readying his escape route by having the victim show him how to unlock the door; (4) blindfolding the victim before turning on a light; (5) binding her ankles and wrists before leaving; (6) wiping her vaginal area to remove semen; (7) wearing surgical gloves, which he believed would preclude the possibility of fingerprints and yet allow the sense of touch; and (8) taking the cigarette butt with him, which denies police the possibility of determining blood type from the saliva residue.

While a few precautionary measures are to be expected in such matters, the care exhibited by Mary's attacker indicates a knowledge of police forensic capabilities beyond the layman level. This area is further addressed in the "arrest history" of the criminal personality profile.

Items Taken

The rapist told the victim he wanted $20 or he would take her stereo. When told that she didn't have the money, he took a dollar and some change from her purse. These items would be classified as valuables, but the amount is so small as to be ridiculous. The author is of the opinion that he took this small amount not out of need, but rather because he could! In other words, he was showing Mary who was in control.

The reader will recall that he threatened to take the victim's stereo and she "put him down" by telling him he would look funny carrying it around, and he later destroyed it. I don't believe that he had any intention of taking it. His exhibited behavior indicates a more sophisticated and experienced individual than the petty theft of a stereo would indicate. The offender also took his cigarette butt with him, and this would be classified as evidentiary material. Nothing of a personal nature was taken.

The victim reported that there were no previous calls, notes, or break-ins prior to the offense. Follow-up investigation determined that there had been no attempt by the offender to recontact the victim.

Purpose of the Assault

As previously mentioned, most sexual assaults service nonsexual needs. It is the author's opinion that the rapist in this instance was attempting to assert his masculinity. That is to say, he was expressing his male dominance over women, which he believes is his "right". Such rapists tend to be basically selfish in their attacks. The reader will have noted, however, a vacillation between selfish and pseudo-unselfish behavior. The author is of the opinion that the "unselfish" behavior exhibited by Mary's rapist was simply another means to further exploit her. If he had been successful in having the victim even feign passion or involvement, he would have believed it was due to his ability to arouse, and thereby control, women — a characteristic of the offender that would also be found in his noncriminal associations with women.

Criminal Personality Profile

When training law enforcement personnel in the art of profiling, this author has found that the most difficult hurdle for them to overcome is their reluctance to put opinions in writing without hard facts to back them up. This is perfectly understandable, inasmuch as we have been trained not to do so. Another problem is their concern that they might be wrong in their assessment, and this is also quite natural. It must be remembered, however, that there are no absolutes in human behavior, and it is indeed rare that a criminal personality profile will perfectly match an offender. As was previously noted in Chapter 6, in some instances the profile may be completely inaccurate, and this is to be expected on occasion. However, in most cases, profiling normally is not requested until all investigative leads have been exhausted and the case is virtually at a standstill.

Some students have voiced concern that if they provide an inaccurate profile, it may mislead the investigators or cause them to overlook or disregard viable suspects who do not match the profile. While the author is aware of instances in which the profile provided did not match the identified offender, he does not know of a single instance in which the profile adversely influenced the investigation of a likely suspect. However, in an attempt to ensure that this does not happen, the following disclaimer precedes each profile prepared by members of the BSU.

> It should be noted that the attached analysis is not a substitute for a thorough and well-planned investigation and should not be considered all inclusive. The information provided is based upon reviewing, analyzing, and researching criminal cases similar to the case submitted by the requesting agency. The final analysis is

based upon probabilities. Note, however, that no two criminal acts or criminal personalities are exactly alike and, therefore, the offender may not always fit the profile in every category.

The following profile was prepared based on the preceding analysis and represented the author's opinion as to the type of person who would have committed the crime in the manner described and for the purpose set forth above. The profile is in outline format with an explanation of his reasoning for each characteristic addressed.

Personality Characteristics

As stated, the purpose of the assault was to express or assert masculinity. The rapist is confident and overly proud of his manliness and is dominant in his relationships with the women in his life. His vacillation between selfish and pseudo-unselfish behavior during the assault is indicative of how he is perceived by those who know him. He presents different images to different people in his life. Some would describe him as a respectful and pleasant individual, while others would say he is often hostile and angry. His fruitless attempts to dominate Mary suggest that he considers himself to be a macho individual and works at projecting this image to those around him.

He is a very self-centered person who does not appreciate criticism, constructive or otherwise. He is a "now" person who demands instant gratification of his needs and desires and would be described as impulsive. Because of this characteristic, his actions are often self-defeating and he seldom achieves his goals. His failures are noted by his inability to accept responsibility, and he projects the blame for them onto others or onto circumstances beyond his control. The attitudinal changes shown during the attack on Mary strongly suggest that he cannot stand losing and, therefore, those who know him would say that he is a sore loser. He dislikes authority. Law enforcement officers with whom he has had contact (see "Arrest History") would describe him as being cocky and arrogant to the extent of antagonizing them.

He exudes confidence and thinks of himself as superior to others, yet he associates with those he considers to be below him. These associates would describe him as being cool, sophisticated, and somewhat aloof. Recalling his behavior with Mary, it is obvious that he reacts negatively when his authority is challenged, whether in his imagination or in reality. Consequently, some would describe him as being easily antagonized and short-tempered.

Because of his self-centeredness, few people are allowed to get close to him. While he knows, and is known by, many people, few know very much about him. Socially, he will frequent areas he considers equal to his station in life, primarily well-known and moderately expensive establishments. He also enjoys discos or similar establishments catering to college-age crowds. The reader will recall that he told Mary he had "seen her around". She is known to frequent locations similar to those described herein.

He is a glib talker and extremely manipulative. As mentioned, he is dominant in his relationships with women. However, if he encounters a woman he cannot dominate and totally possess, he will relentlessly pursue her. Women who have dated him over a period of time will report that he was initially charming and attentive, but eventually became overly possessive and irrationally jealous, demanding that they account for the time they spent away from him.

Race

As described by the victim, the offender is a black male. While some may feel this should be an obvious factor (as in this case), numerous rape cases have been submitted for analysis in which the victim was unsure of or unable to describe the race of her attacker. In such instances, the analyst will consider the racial makeup of the assault area, victimology, racial overtones in the offender's behavior, and/ or similar attacks in which one or more victims were able to describe the offender's race.

Age

Age is the most difficult characteristic to give. Its determination depends on a number of factors including the victim's estimate, type of items taken, the maturity exhibited in the crime, and the type of rapist believed to have been responsible for the crime.

The offender in this case is between 26 and 30 years of age. Although the victim is educated and articulate, her opinion as to the age of the assailant is too general (20 to 30); therefore, the author narrowed the span to 5 years. Mary's attacker is confident of his abilities with women and, therefore, would have selected a woman who approximates his own age range. He is not the type of person that would attack helpless or hopeless people such as children or the elderly; his ego demands that he attack women he considers to be worthy of his time. With this type of rapist (and in the absence of other information), the author will generally place his age range 3 to 4 years on either side of the victim's age. In this case, however, an older person is indicated. If working on a series of rapes committed by this type of person, the author would average the age of the victims and repeat the process.

Arrest History

The precautionary actions taken by the rapist demonstrate sophistication obtained through either repeated offenses or previous arrests for similar crimes. In this instance, the offender shows an inordinate amount of forensic knowledge, which leads the author to believe he has previously been arrested for rape and/or breaking and entering. His obvious desire to assault Mary anally, coupled with a muscular upper torso, suggests that he has also been in prison and participated in upper-body exercises.

His lifestyle (see "Residence") and low income (see "Employment") indicate that he is involved in other criminal ventures. For this reason, the author believes he may be involved in the sale of narcotics and has been arrested for this in the past. The author doesn't believe he is an addict, since he did not steal items of value from Mary's residence. In fact, he destroyed a valuable (and easily fenced) stereo.

Marital Status

The behaviors exhibited by Mary's rapist reveal that he is a macho type male with a dominant attitude toward women. Such men who have come to the author's attention typically have married while in their late teens or early 20s. His attitude toward women is such that his relationships with them are relatively short-lived. For these reasons, the author believes him to be either separated or divorced. While he was living with his wife, the relationship involved a great deal of strife, and friends would have noted this. While not physically abusive toward her, he would have abused her emotionally. Typically, he would leave her stranded following an argument away from home and in the company of others.

Residence

The amount of time the rapist spent with Mary gives two significant pieces of information: (1) he was familiar with her routine and (2) he felt comfortable in the socioeconomic environment in which the assault occurred. The intelligence (see "Education") of the rapist is such that he would not assault within an area where he would be recognized or feel uncomfortable. Therefore, he lives in similar-type property (rental and middle class) in another area of town. He will live with a black female who is faithful to him but whom he regards as just one in a series of women he uses and discards. The residence is an apartment or town house and is rental property. It is nicely furnished and includes an array of video and audio equipment. It serves as a gathering point for large numbers of people at various times of the day or night, which may have caused suspicious neighbors to alert the police.

Education

The offender is educated beyond the high school level. His words during the assault, the victim's opinion of him, and his strong denial of "hanging around those punks" (students) led the author to this opinion. It is possible that he got his post-high school education while incarcerated. As a student, he achieved above-average grades and showed potential for high academic achievement. Because he dislikes authority, it is unlikely that he obtained a 4-year degree or used his education in gainful employment. Friends and associates would consider him well above average in intelligence and would often seek his advice. Because of his intelligence and disdain for having others above him, he is considered a leader rather than a follower.

Military History

In determining whether or not an offender served in the military, the author considers the age factor. The draft was eliminated in 1972, and the probability of an offender having served after that time is greatly diminished. Therefore, if he is believed to have been 18 or older in 1972, this fact would suggest a high probability of veteran status. If, however, he was born after 1954, it would be less likely that he served in the armed forces.

The offender's strong dislike for authority and regimentation diminishes the possibility of his having served in the military. If, however, he did serve, it would have been as a member of the enlisted ranks and the likelihood of his having been honorably discharged is minimal. His desire to project a macho image would indicate service in the ground forces.

Employment

If employed, he will be working in a job for which he is overqualified. His work performance will reflect an attitudinal problem, and he will complain of being bored. His supervisors will report frustration with his performance because of his potential for excellence. He is often late or absent and takes offense at being chastised. His employment is a front, and his primary source of income is from the sale of narcotics or other illegal activities.

Transportation

In keeping with his lifestyle and image, he will operate a two-door vehicle, 2 to 4 years old. It would be described as being flashy, brightly painted, and well maintained. He spends a great deal of time in his car and loves to "cruise". He is strongly associated with his car, and his friends would describe him and his car as inseparable.

Appearance and Grooming

He is a very neat person whose normal attire is contemporary, with designer jeans at the lower end of his dress style. He takes a great deal of pride in his personal and physical appearance and is critical of those who don't do the same. He exercises regularly and maintains a high level of physical fitness. The women he associates with must be equally conscious of their appearance. He has an expensive wardrobe beyond his known financial means. He has regular appointments to have his hair styled and is meticulous about body cleanliness, often bathing or changing clothes two to three times a day.

The reader will note that the profile set forth above was phrased in common terminology and in such a way that those who know the offender would be able to recognize him from this description.

Summary

The first and most important step in profiling an unidentified rapist is to obtain a detailed statement from the victim. Then the author analyzes the statement to determine whether the offender's verbal, sexual, and physical behavior exhibits a selfish or pseudo-unselfish intent. The intent shown gives information about how the rapist perceives women.

Having formed his opinion as to the offender's intent, the author then analyzes the crime behavior to determine the motivation or purpose of the sexual assault and hence the classification of the rapist.

Finally, the author describes the offender as he perceives him to be, in a manner that would enable those who know him to recognize him.

References

Groth, A. N., Burgess, A. W., and Holmstrom, L. L., Rape: power, anger and sexuality, *Am. J. Psychiatry*, 134(11), 1239, 1977.

Hazelwod, R. R. and Harpold, J., Rape: the dangers of providing confrontational advice, *FBI Law Enforcement Bull.*, p. 1, June 1986.

Collateral Materials in Sexual Crimes

10

ROBERT R. HAZELWOOD
KENNETH V. LANNING

Over the years, the authors have assisted investigators in better understanding the significance of materials seized from violent sexual offenders. Some materials, such as items stolen from rape victims, are routinely seized by police when found in the offender's possession. However, it is not uncommon to learn that the full significance of these and other materials is often not recognized by either investigators, prosecutors, or mental health professionals. Seemingly innocuous items such as newspaper articles (apparently unrelated to the crime), books, real estate listings, and detective magazines may be very significant to the crime and can provide a better understanding of the sexual offender.

Traditional Evidence in Sexual Crimes

Anyone who has participated in the investigation and prosecution of a sexual criminal will recognize that many types of evidence play critical roles in the successful conclusion of a case. However, for the purposes of this chapter, it is necessary to set forth and define the types of evidence that may be encountered in such investigations.

Forensic Evidence

Forensic evidence may be defined as physical or trace evidence which can scientifically be matched with a known individual or item. Such evidence includes fingerprints, footprints, body fluids, hairs, and fibers. Forensic evidence, if properly obtained and examined, can be powerful and reliable evidence in any type of crime (see Chapters 4 and 5).

Circumstantial Evidence

Evidence falling within this category may be defined as facts or circumstances which tend to implicate a person or persons in a crime. Examples of such evidence might include the fact that a suspect owns a vehicle similar to one reported seen in the vicinity of the crime at the time; is known to have made a threat against the victim, or is known to have engaged in similar patterns of behavior observed in the crime under investigation and had the means, opportunity, or motive to commit the crime. Although usually not sufficient to obtain a conviction, in sufficient quantity circumstantial evidence can constitute a powerful case.

Eyewitness Evidence

Evidence of this type exists when one or more individuals claim to have witnessed the crime during its commission or to have seen the suspect in the vicinity of the crime. Although this is believed by many to be the best evidence, it has historically been debated and is the subject of innumerable studies and publications.

Direct Evidence

Direct evidence may be defined as tangible items which directly implicate an individual in a crime. Most commonly this includes items *used in the crime* (handcuffs, gloves, mask) or items *taken from a victim or scene* of a crime ("fruits of the crime") and found either in the possession of a suspect or in a location (i.e., home, storage area, car) under his control.

Items taken during a sexual crime have previously been classified by Hazelwood (1983) as follows.

Personal. Items which belong to the victim and are generally of no intrinsic value (e.g., driver's license, photograph, lingerie). Such items serve to refresh the offender's memory of the crime and are used in fantasy reenactments of the offense. Behaviorally, such items are referred to as "trophies" or "souvenirs". Items in this category may or may not be kept by a sexual offender.

Evidentiary. Items which, if discovered by the police, could be used to implicate the criminal. Such items could include sheets containing seminal fluid, items with fingerprints on them, or a partly smoked cigarette. The offender is unlikely to keep such items, but that possibility cannot be ruled out.

Valuables. Items with an intrinsic value taken during the commission of a crime. Generally, the purpose of taking such things is financial gain. As with "evidentiary" materials, these items are unlikely to be retained by the sexual offender unless he has a personal need for them (e.g., television, CD player).

Collateral Materials

Webster (1988) defines "collateral" as parallel, running side by side, or auxiliary. For the purpose of this chapter, collateral material will be defined as items which do not directly associate the offender with a crime, but give authorities information pertaining to an individual's sexual preferences, interests, or sexual "hobbies". They can be valuable as evidence of intent and/or as a source of information. The finding of collateral material may also influence bail, a guilty plea, and/or the sentence eventually imposed on the offender.

Collateral materials may include those with an obvious sexual bent or those seemingly benign in nature. Items categorized as "collateral" may, on occasion, also be classified as "direct" or "circumstantial" evidence. For example, lingerie taken from a rape victim may be sexually arousing to the offender (see "Erotica" below) and simultaneously be used to link him to the crime (i.e., "direct" evidence).

The authors have identified four categories of collateral materials: *erotica* (material which serves to sexually stimulate); *educational* (material providing knowledge about criminal endeavors, the investigative process, the judicial system, or mental health); *introspective* (material providing the criminal with insight into his sexual and/or behavior disorders); and *intelligence* (materials providing information about possible future crimes or information gathered about the offender from third parties). It will not surprise the experienced investigator to learn that some materials may be categorized as more than one type of collateral material. For example, a partially clothed and bound female depicted on the cover of a detective magazine may be sexually arousing (*erotica*) and the articles in the magazine may also contain information useful for circumventing crime detection techniques (*educational*).

Types of Collateral Materials

Erotica.   Erotica is defined as any material which serves a sexual purpose for a given person. When one is trying to identify erotica, he or she should not apply their own preference for sexual stimuli, but should remain objective. For example, the average individual is not sexually stimulated by a length of rope, but for a person having a rope fetish such material can be extremely arousing. Material suspected of being erotica must be viewed and evaluated in the context in which it is found. The investigator must use good judgment and common sense. For example, in a child molestation case, possession of an album filled with pictures of the suspects's own fully dressed children probably has no significance; however, possession of 15 photo albums of fully dressed children who are not related to the suspect may be very significant. Possession of his own children's underwear may not be significant, while a suitcase containing other childrens' underwear would be quite significant. For a more complete discussion of collateral materials as it pertains to child-related offenses, the reader is referred to Lanning's work entitled "Child Molesters: A Behavioral Analysis" (1992).

In determining whether a certain item should be classified as erotica, the investigator should consider whether (1) it behaviorally relates to the crime under investigation or to possible paraphilias (i.e., fetishism) not evidenced in the crime and/or (2) there is an abnormal amount of such material present and it serves no practical purpose (e.g., three sets of handcuffs) and/or (3) the material was secreted and/or (4) the subject's financial investment in the material is large (e.g., $500 worth of pornography).

Common forms of erotica include: fetish items; literature and visual images of both a sexually explicit and nonexplicit nature which relate to demographically preferred victims; sexual paraphernalia such as inflatable dolls, vibrators, and dildos; fantasy recordings including writings, sketches, drawings, and audio/video tapes; records of crimes*; plans for future crimes; crime paraphernalia**; abused dolls (bound, burned, gagged, punctured, dissected, painted); mutilated or altered pictures of people or animals; media accounts of sexual crimes; advertisements (for clothing, lingerie, adult movies, police paraphernalia); weapons collections; and personal items taken from known victims***.

Educational. This type of collateral material is defined as items which provide the subject with knowledge enhancing his ability to commit a sexual or nonsexual crime, circumvent or thwart law enforcement and/or crime prevention efforts, or manipulate the judicial or mental health process.

Contrary to popular belief, serial sexual offenders do not necessarily have less-than-average intelligence. Research by Hazelwood and Warren (1989) refutes this belief and documents the fact that serial rapists generally have better-than-average intelligence.

Intelligent criminals often try to learn as much as possible about the crimes they are committing and resort to literature sources one would not normally associate with them. Ted Bundy, in an interview with FBI Special Agent William Hagmaier immediately before his execution, was questioned about the influence of pornography in his life. Bundy asked Hagmaier if he had read an article titled "Detective Magazines; Pornography for Sexual Sadists" (Dietz et al, 1987). Hagmaier advised that he had not and Bundy advised him to do so as it was very accurate.**** Edward Kemper, an infamous serial killer, was reported to have memorized the Minnesota Multiphasic Inventory. One of the authors (Hazelwood) began to introduce himself to a serial rapist responsible for more than 60 sexually sadistic rapes when the man said "I know who you are. When I was raping, I did a literature search on you. I've read everything you've written".

Types of educational materials commonly seen by the authors in such cases include: fictional and nonfictional crime books, newspaper articles reporting sexual and nonsexual crimes, law enforcement and mental health journal articles, textbooks on psychology and/or criminal justice, published court decisions, detective magazines, crime prevention materials, and audio/videotaped programs featuring experts on sexual crimes.

Introspective. This type of collateral material is defined as materials which give the offender information or understanding about his sexual or personality disorders, behaviors, or interests. In conducting research on serial rapists, sexual sadists, and pedophiles, the authors were surprised at the attempts of the men to gain insight into, and/or rationalize, their deviant sexuality. For example, many pedophiles spend a large portion of their lives trying to convince themselves that

---

   * Records of crime would also be classified as "direct evidence".
  ** Also "direct evidence".
 *** Also "direct evidence".
**** Personal conversation with Mr. Hagmaier, 1990.

what they are doing is not totally out of the mainstream but just happens to be politically incorrect at this time. Other offenders may be troubled by what society defines as atypical or abnormal sexual behaviors and turn to publications, college courses, seminars, and, in some cases, counseling for answers. Still others recognize that their preferences and behaviors are not normal and want to better understand, and thus cope with, their deviancy. Such actions do not minimize their responsibility for criminal behavior, but is useful information for investigators of criminal sexuality, particularly in developing interview strategies.

Introspective materials observed by the authors in sexual crimes include books and other publications on psychopathology, video/audiotapes of experts addressing the subject, self-help books, surveys in sexually oriented magazines, and newspaper, magazine, and journal articles on sexual offender research.

Intelligence. This type of collateral material is defined as information or items obtained by the offender in planning for future crimes and/or information gathered from third-party sources about the offender. Examples of "intelligence" are

1. Materials possessed by the offender which show he has planned and/or collected information for future crimes. Such information may include: automobile license plate numbers; telephone numbers or addresses of potential victims; commercial or drawn maps with notations or routes of travel; notes concerning the movements/schedules of another person; "surveillance" photographs of people or locations; written scripts for victims, and lists of materials needed for the commission of a specific crime.
2. Information obtained from interviews of current or former sexual partners of the subject. This may include spouses, lovers, or prostitutes. Hazelwood et al. (1993) have reported on the value of conducting such interviews. In sexual crimes, the investigator is specifically interested in facts and knowledge concerning the subject's sexual preferences, fantasies, habits, and/or dysfunctions. Also of interest are locations where he may have secreted additional materials, what stressors were present in his life at the time of the crimes, and whether he sexually behaved with the interviewee in a manner consistent with his criminal sexual behaviors.

Case Study

One of the authors (Hazelwood) consulted on the following case and subsequently testified at the subject's murder trial. The facts of the case, the items seized from the subject, and the discussion provide the reader with the classification of the materials as either *erotica, educational, introspective,* or *intelligence.*

> The victim, a pregnant 24-year-old housewife, was abducted from her rural home in August 1989. Her husband discovered her missing when he returned from work and found his 22-month-old infant on the floor of the home. There was no evidence of forced entry and no signs that a struggle had taken place. Missing was

the victim's car, a quilt, a telephone with a 20-ft cord, the bottom half of a swimming suit belonging to the victim, and all of her panties.

The victim's car was found the following morning about ½ mile from the home. Two days later, her decomposing body was discovered 8 miles from the point of abduction. She was dressed in the same clothing she'd been wearing when her husband last saw her, and there was no indication that the clothing had been disturbed. The autopsy revealed no evidence of sexual assault and the cause of death was determined to have been asphyxiation due to two paper towels lodged in her throat. It was the opinion of the investigators that the offender had not intentionally killed the woman.

Within 4 months, a 37-year-old man was identified as the person responsible for the crime. He was an unemployed well digger, having recently been fired. One year before the crime he had drilled a well on the victim's property. He was married, had two children, and lived in a single-family house in an adjacent county.

The man had served prison time for burglary and had been released about 3 years before the homicide. He was a high school graduate and of average intelligence. Investigation determined that he had committed a variety of crimes over a 9-month period before and after the homicide. The following is a sequential listing of those crimes:

March:	Harassing phone call to a woman
May:	Exposed genitals to a woman
June:	Obscene phone call to a woman
August:	Theft of woman's purse from a car
August:	Kidnap and murder (current case)
November:	Fondling and battery of a woman
November:	Impersonation of a police officer and attempted abduction of a woman
November:	Theft of woman's purse from a car
December:	Theft of property from a business site
December:	Kidnap and rape of a 27-year-old woman

The abducted rape victim was taken from her home, raped at an abandoned farmhouse, driven to a second abandoned farmhouse and forced to "model" a variety of lingerie, raped a second time, and then driven back to her neighborhood and released.

During a search of the killer's residence, the police seized a large volume of materials which included collateral and direct evidence. The following is a listing of those materials.

1. More than 2500 index cards containing information on women who had appeared either nude or in lingerie in *Gallery* or *Que* magazines. On each card, he had written a woman's first name, age, marital status, occupation, hobbies, the initials "GND" (Girl Next Door section of *Gallery*) or "FNL" (Friends and Lovers section of *Que*), and the month and year of the issue in which the photograph and demographic data appeared. In the upper right hand corner of each card was a numerical rating (0 to 10) of the woman.

2. A spiral notebook containing information identical to that found on the aforementioned index cards.
3. Hundreds of articles of clothing including panties, bras, nightgowns, swimsuits, slips, mesh tops, wraparounds, nightshirts, camisoles, and teddies. This apparel, bought from a mail-order firm specializing in such apparel, was estimated to have cost $3,000. Several items had been placed in plastic "baggies" and identified to allow cross-indexing to the index cards and the spiral notebook.

Discussion: Items 1, 2, and 3 would correctly be classified as *erotica*. The subject's purpose in having this information was to allow him to "have sex" (masturbatory fantasy) with any of the women whenever he chose. The amount of time and money he spent buying, indexing, and maintaining this collection is indicative of the importance he attaches to the material. It is also quite obvious that the man had a lingerie fetish. The reader will recall that the murder victim's panties and bottom half of her bathing suit were taken and that the kidnap-rape victim was forced to "model" teddies.

4. Over 100 *Gallery* and *Que* magazines.

Discussion: These magazines would be classified as *erotica*. They dated to within 1 month of his release from prison on the burglary sentence; this indicates his preoccupation with such material existed long before his known sexual crimes. Worth noting is the fact that he was particularly attracted to women who were not professional models. In the authors' opinion, such women were complementary to his fantasies in that he could mentally relate more closely to them. It is also to be appreciated that he invested over $250 in the magazines even though he was financially stressed.

5. Handwritten notes detailing specific items of lingerie and their cost if ordered from the mail order firm. The amount of the anticipated purchases would have totaled over $7000.

Discussion: These notes are *erotica*. Whether he bought the items is not as significant as his paraphilic preoccupation to possess them.

6. A library book titled *Rape: The Bait and the Trap* and a newspaper article on law enforcement tips to avoid sexual assault.

Discussion: Both these items would be classified as *educational* materials. They provide information on the crime of rape and what techniques the experts recommend to thwart it. The book would also be considered *introspective* in that it contains information on the underlying motivations of rape.

7. Numerous newspaper articles relating to the unexplained disappearances of women and runaway teenage females. These articles included

photographs, descriptive data, and investigative methodology. The police determined that the subject was not involved in any of the disappearances.

Discussion: These items would be classified as *erotica* and *educational* materials. They included photographs of the missing women and teenagers and lent reality to masturbatory fantasies. They also gave an indication of the media coverage and police procedures in such cases.

8.   Three newspaper articles pertaining to the disappearance, discovery, and autopsy of the murder victim. These articles were hidden in a paper bag behind a basement wall in the offender's home. None of the other materials were hidden.

Discussion: These media accounts of the crime would be considered *educational* collateral materials in that they would allow the man to keep up with the investigation. Recognizing that some types of sexual killers use media accounts to relive the crime for masturbatory purposes, it might seem logical to also categorize the articles as *erotica*. However, it should be remembered that the offender did not intend for the victim to die and, subsequently, released another kidnap victim. Therefore, it is highly unlikely that he would use such materials for masturbatory behavior. This material would also be considered *circumstantial* evidence in that it was hidden and related to the crime for which the man was a suspect. All other recovered materials were easily found.

9.   Several newspaper articles dealing with noncriminal activities. They included: the grand opening of a new drug store with an accompanying photograph of female employees with their names underlined, wedding announcements with photographs of the bride-to-be, the announcement of a surprise lingerie (he had underlined the word 'lingerie') shower, a photograph of an English model in a bikini.

Discussion: All of these items would be classified as *erotica*. Additionally, with the exception of the model's photograph, the items would be classified as *intelligence* gathered by the offender for a potential victim pool. He underlined the names of the drug store employees, had a photograph and identifying data on the bride-to-be in the wedding announcement, and knew the identity of the guest of honor at the lingerie shower.

10.   Several driver's licenses, license plate numbers, credit cards, and telephone numbers belonging to women.

Discussion: The driver's licenses and credit cards would be *direct* evidence as they are fruits of crimes and therefore directly link him to thefts. The driver's licenses, and license plate and telephone numbers would be categorized as *intelligence* as it was information he had gathered on potential victims.

11. The quilt taken from the murder victim's home and the bottom half of the victim's bathing suit. Because of the volume of lingerie present in the offender's home, the victim's panties (all of which were taken) could not be positively identified.

Discussion: The quilt and bathing suit bottom would be *direct* evidence. The bathing suit bottom would also be categorized as *erotica*. While it is entirely possible that the quilt also served to sexually excite the man, there is nothing to indicate that he had a fetish for such material and therefore, that assumption cannot be made.

12. A hand-drawn map depicting the route to a 27-year-old woman's residence. Notations on the map gave details such as her breast size, age of her children, and type of car she owned. Investigators followed the map and determined that the man had dug a well on her farm property about 1 year earlier.

Discussion: The map and notations would be categorized as both *intelligence* and *erotica*. It was learned that the killer had visited her farm on the pretext of checking the well. However, when her husband unexpectedly drove up, the man hurriedly left the property.

As previously mentioned, there are two types of *intelligence*: that information gathered by the offender for future crimes and/or victims, and information gathered from third parties about the offender. The wife of the subject in the murder case was interviewed extensively and provided the following *intelligence* about the man.

> She said that she was well aware of her husband's preoccupation with female attire, particularly lingerie. He had often bought teddies and nightgowns for her to wear and became sexually aroused when she wore the items. He was a chronic masturbator and would do so openly at all times of the day. He would ejaculate into condoms and leave them lying about the home. When she confronted him with this behavior, he denied the condoms were his and accused her of having affairs.

His extensive collection of lingerie led her to believe that he was having affairs and she began denying him sexual relations for fear of contracting AIDS. She also ceased wearing lingerie for his pleasure.

She gave information which showed that he was experiencing several stressors (financial, marital, health, occupational, and sexual) at the time that the known criminal behavior began.

The value of such firsthand information in a sexual crime investigation cannot be overestimated. In this case, it confirmed the subject's paraphilia (fetishism); it identified various stressors in his life, and revealed a dysfunctional marriage.

Summary

The authors have assisted investigators and prosecutors in better understanding the significance of materials found in the control of sexual offenders. In addition to forensic, eyewitness, circumstantial and direct evidence, investigators should also be cognizant of *collateral materials*.

Collateral materials can include newspaper articles, literature, viewing materials, advertisements, personal notes, fantasy recordings, sexual paraphernalia, collections, and information obtained from consenting and/or paid partners.

Collateral materials can augment "hard evidence" for investigators in presentation of their case for prosecution and by prosecutors in the use of expert testimony to educate juries as to the significance and importance of the items.

References

Dietz, P.E., Harry, B., and Hazelwood, R.R., Detective magazines: pornography for the sexual sadist?, *J. Forensic Sci.*, 31(1), 197, 1986.

Hazelwood, R.R., The behavior-oriented interview of rape victims: the key to profiling, *FBI Law Enforcement Bull.*, September 1983.

Hazelwood, R.R. and Warren, J.I., The serial rapist: his characteristics and victims, *FBI Law Enforcement Bull.*, February 1989.

Hazelwood, R.R., Warren, J.I., and Dietz, P.E., Compliant victims of sexual sadists, *Aust. Fam. Physician*, 22(4), 1993.

Lanning, K.V., *Child Molesters: A Behavioral Analysis*, 3rd ed., National Center for Missing & Exploited Children, Washington, D.C., December 1992.

Webster's II New Riverside University Dictionary, Riverside Publishing, Houghton Mifflin, Boston, 1988.

Classifying Rape and Sexual Assault

11

ALLEN G. BURGESS
ANN WOLBERT BURGESS
ROBERT R. HAZELWOOD

Professionals develop and advance their science as they are able to organize and classify their work. To this end, agents at the FBI Academy's National Center for the Analysis of Violent Crime (NCAVC) spent over 10 years in developing a Crime Classification Manual (CCM).* The purpose of this manual for classifying crimes is fourfold:

1. To standardize terminology within the criminal justice field
2. To facilitate communication within the criminal justice field and between criminal justice and mental health personnel
3. To educate the criminal justice system and the public at large to the types of crimes being committed
4. To develop a data base for investigative research

CCM Numbering System

The numbering system used to classify crimes in the CCM was developed with some memory-assist features. The basic code uses three digits, with the first digit representing the major crime category of homicide, arson, or sexual assault. The homicide category is identified by the number 1 (codes 101 to 199), arson is designated by the number 2 (codes 201 to 299), and sexual assault indicated with the number 3 (codes 301 to 399).

The second digit of the code represents further grouping of the major crimes. Sexual assault is divided into three groupings: (1) criminal enterprise, (2) personal cause, and (3) group cause. Specific classifications within these groups are represented by the third digit of the code.

Individual classifications within these three groups are further divided into subgroups, using two additional digits following a decimal point after the code.

* Sections of this chapter are reprinted from *Crime Classification Manual*, Douglas, J. E., Burgess, A. W., Burgess, A. G., and Ressler, R. R., Eds., Lexington Books, New York, 1992. With permission.

For example, entitlement rape (313) is divided into four subgroups: 313:01, social acquaintance rape; 313.02, subordinate rape; 313:03, power-reassurance rape; and 313:04, exploitative rape. Following the second decimal point, the last two digits designate the victim as an adult (.01), an adolescent (.02), or a child (.03).

Rationale for Sexual Assault Classifications

Because, currently, there are no taxonomic systems for rapists or child molesters that have achieved universal acceptance, the authors have attempted to integrate components from several typological systems that have been shown to have some empirical unity (Groth et al., 1977; Groth, 1979; Lanning, 1986; Prentky et al., 1986; Hazelwood, 1987; Knight et al., 1989). These systems continue to undergo revision (e.g., Knight and Prentky, 1990).

Rapist Classification

The taxonomic studies on which descriptions of convicted rapist types are based focus on the interaction of sexual and aggressive motivations. Although all rape clearly includes both motivations, for some rapists the need to humiliate and injure through aggression is the most salient feature of the offense, whereas for others the need to achieve sexual dominance is the most salient feature of the offense. The four major categories of rapists have been described, with case examples, in Chapter 9. Briefly, that is (1) the power-reassurance rapist whereby the assault is primarily an expression of his rape fantasies; (2) the exploitative rapist in which sexual behavior is expressed as an impulsive predatory or power-assertive act; (3) the anger rapist whereby sexual behavior is an expression of anger and retaliation; and (4) the sadistic or anger excitation rapist whereby sexual behavior is an expression of sexual-aggressive (sadistic) fantasies.

As one reads the CCM, it becomes apparent that a blend of motivations inspires many violent crimes. This is especially true when multiple offenders are involved. Essentially, one may find as many different reasons for the crime as there are offenders. The approach taken in the CCM for multiple motives is to classify the offense according to the predominant motive. The main rule when several of the categories apply (e.g., sexual assault and arson or sexual assault and murder) is that homicide takes precedence; next comes arson/bombing, and then sexual assault. The rule when several motives occur within classification, e.g., sexual assault, the dominant motive is present first. For example, abduction rape, 319 and exploitative rape, 313.04.

An outline of the major CCM sexual assault classifications with selected case examples follow.

Criminal Enterprise Rape: 300

Criminal enterprise sexual assault involves sexual coercion, abuse, or assault that is committed for material gain.

301: Felony Rape

Sexual assault committed during the commission of a felony, such as breaking and entering or robbery, is considered felony rape. The classification is made as to whether the rape was primary or secondary in intent.

301.01: Primary Felony Rape

The intent of primary felony rape is a nonsexual felony (e.g., robbery or breaking and entering). The victim is at the scene of the primary felony and sexually assaulted as a second offense. If the victim was not present, the felony would still occur. The term "opportunistic rapist" can be used.

301.02: Secondary Felony Rape

The primary intent of secondary felony rape is sexual assault, but a second felony is also planned. This implies the offender knows a person will be present for two crimes to occur.

The following is a case of an adult victim of secondary felony rape 301.02.01 and an abduction rape 319.01.

Case No. 1

Gloria is a 27-year-old single black female who was born in South Carolina. She moved to New York with her family in 1967 and has since lived in two different projects in the Bronx. She attended public school and earned average grades. Her favorite subjects were English and physical education. She left school in the tenth grade to have her first child. Before the rape, Gloria was employed as a home attendant.

Gloria was 4 months pregnant and living with her mother and daughter in a Bronx housing project. She had gone out to dinner with two friends. After dinner, she was driven home. As she was walking to her building, she saw her brother and another friend. She went into her building, passing the mailboxes, and into the elevator. She pressed the fifth floor button and heard someone coming so she held the door. She recognized this man, James. As James came into the elevator, someone else also entered the elevator. As the door closed, the unknown man grabbed her from behind and began choking her neck in an arm hold. She struggled and lost consciousness. When she awoke she was on the roof landing. The unknown male was on top of her and James was pointing a gun at her. She remembers screaming but not hearing herself. The unknown male told James not to shoot; then Gloria passed out a second time. When she awoke the men were gone. Her clothes had been ripped off except for one pant leg; her clothes were strewn about the area. She dressed, feeling very dizzy, sore and in shock. She walked down about 15 flights of stairs because she was afraid the men might still be in the elevator. She reached her mother's apartment. She had trouble talking. Her daughter woke up and came to see her. Gloria then telephoned a friend.

When her mother realized what had happened, she called the housing police. Subsequently, an ambulance took her to the hospital.

Gloria was hospitalized for 5 days. Medical reports indicated she had trauma to the head with intracranial damage, a hematoma to her forehead, and a cerebral concussion with postconcussion syndrome. This syndrome is characterized by diminished and irregular reflexes, ataxia, equilibrium disturbance, severe pressure headaches, anxiety, nausea, confusion, depression, dizziness, apprehension, nervousness, and general debility. She had flashbacks to the rape and the gun pointed at her. She worried about damage to her unborn child. She had rectal bleeding from an anal mucosal tear and needed further medical treatment for a sexually transmitted disease.

Gloria was unable to return to live in her mother's apartment and had to be relocated. She recalled two earlier crimes in the building involving a 20-year-old friend of hers who was raped and murdered on the same rooftop, and an 18-year-old man who was beaten and hanged from an exit door. She had nightmares. She was reminded of the rape when seeing military camouflage suits, as that was one of the assailant's outfit. She had aches and pains from the severe bruising. She had sexual difficulties with her boyfriend. Gloria has difficulty visiting her mother in the project. The elevator triggers frightening memories. She has difficulty socially. She finds it hard to relax; she gets into deep thought and finds herself staring into space.

The rape was a blitz method of attack. There was no prior warning; Gloria held the elevator for a friend of her brother's and an unknown man also entered. She pushed the button for her floor and was expecting to ride there when she was grabbed and choked unconscious.

Gloria was threatened with a gun that was used to control, intimidate, and terrorize her. The two assailants caused severe physical injury; both raped her and also robbed her of all her jewelry. The motivation for the felony rape was robbery. The psychological motivation was anger. She was rendered unconscious during the assault, and it is clear in terms of her psychological response to the attack that fear, intimidation, and threat to life paralyzed her and made the assailant feel powerful and in charge.

310: Personal Cause

Rape and sexual assault motivated by personal cause is an act ensuing from interpersonal aggression resulting in sexual victimization of person(s) who may or may not be known to the offender. These rape and sexual assaults are not primarily motivated by material gain and are not sanctioned by a group. Rather, an underlying emotional conflict or psychological issue propels the offender to commit rape and sexual assault. Although the case may be legally called rape, the term sexual assault is used in this classification to encompass a wide range of forced and pressured sexual activities.

312: DOMESTIC SEXUAL ASSAULT

The victim in this classification is a partner, spouse, or family member of the offender.

313.00: Entitlement Rape

In an entitlement rape, the offender forces the victim into sexual activity. Issues of power and control are underlying psychological conflict.

Classification of sexual assault and rape as either entitlement, anger, or sadism uses, as the determining criterion, the amount of aggression involved. Evidence for high expressive aggression used to determine the correct classification includes any combination of the following:

1. Injuries greater than minor cuts, scratches, and abrasions
2. Force in excess of that needed to attain victim compliance (e.g., slapping, punching, or kicking, when there is no evidence of victim resistance)
3. Specific acts in the offense (e.g., mutilation, burning, stabbing, choking to unconsciousness, biting, kicking, anal penetration, or insertion of foreign objects)
4. Desires or attempts to humiliate a victim (derogatory, demeaning remarks, any use of feces or urine, any forcing a male to observe, or evidence of forced fellatio after sodomy)

313.01: Social Acquaintance Rape

In this offense, there is prior knowledge or relationship between the victim and offender. Often the relationship is social, and for adults and adolescents the assault usually occurs on a date. Other relationships may include student/teacher or athlete/coach affiliations. For child cases, the relationship might include a neighbor or family friend.

313.02: Subordinate Rape

The relationship between the victim of subordinate rape and the offender is one of subordination and status imbalance. One person has power over another due to employment, education, or age. The offender uses this authority to take advantage of the victim.

313: Exploitative Rape

In exploitative rape, also called power assertive rape, expressed aggression is generally low and does not exceed what was necessary to force victim compliance. Callous indifference to the victim is evident.

314: Anger Rape

Sexual assault in the category of anger rape is characterized by high expressive aggression (unprovoked physical and verbal aggression or physical force in excess of that necessary to gain victim compliance must be present). Rage is evident in this offender. He may have manifested behaviors listed for sadistic sexual assault, but these must appear to be punishing actions done in anger, not to increase sexual arousal. The primary motive for the offense is anger and not sexual gratification. When the offender knows the victim, the assault on that victim appears to be the result of the offender's easy access to that victim. These offenses are predominantly impulse driven (e.g., opportunity alone, possibly coupled with impaired judgment due to drugs/alcohol).

314.01: Gender Anger Rape

The category of gender anger rape is reserved for offenders who hate women and express their rage through rape.

Case No. 2

Rita, a 40-year-old single teacher, after completing a 3-day seminar with a group of friends from work, stopped at a lounge to relax before returning home. She returned to her second-floor apartment around 8:30 p.m., unpacked and changed from her traveling clothes, listened to her phone messages, made a few phone calls, invited her boyfriend over for supper, and started a tea kettle. The doorbell rang and thinking it was her boyfriend, she went to answer it. However, it was her landlord's son, Nick, who told her he had a message from his father that would "upset her" and, therefore, had to tell her inside her apartment and not in the hallway. The essence of the message was that the landlord thought someone was using her apartment when she was out.

As Rita turned to get some cigarettes, Nick abruptly hit her on the head and she fell to the floor. The assailant held a gun to her head and threatened to "blow out her brains". He demanded money and her car keys, then ordered her to undress. She told him she had her period and he forced her to undo his pants and fellate him. Hearing noises believed to be her boyfriend, the assailant forced Rita out of the apartment, without her clothes, through a back alley to the back steps of a church. He instructed her to begin again and to "do it right" this time. His language was laced with demeaning, vulgar terms. He repeatedly hit her and held the gun to her temple. He forced vaginal sex. A noise was heard; the assailant removed his t-shirt and forced Rita to put it on, then marched her back to his father's apartment where she was ordered to clean up her face and put on a pair of his running shorts. She was then forced out of the apartment; she saw her boyfriend, ran to him, and together flagged down a passing truck to take them to a hospital. The assailant then ran away.

The dominant motive of this rapist was power, control, and displaced anger. It is clear in terms of Rita's response to the rape that fear, intimidation, and threat to life paralyzed her and made the rapist feel powerful and in charge. This can be noted by the language used and the moving of the victim from location to location. The displaced anger is noted in the extreme aggression inflicted on the victim. These dynamics are not uncommon in juveniles who rape and displace anger to someone of the same age as the ambivalent person in their life. The language used by the assailant suggests a dynamic compatible with a sadistic fantasy of domination and submission.

The juvenile was convicted.

314.02: Age Anger Rape

The motive of the offender in age anger is to seek out victims of a specific age group, usually elderly or young.

314.03 Anger Rape, Racial

This category is reserved for what appears to be racially motivated rape.

Case No. 3

Having just returned from an evening movie, Mary walked into the apartment building where she lived with her mother and sister, pushed the elevator button for her floor, and entered. As the elevator rose toward her floor, it suddenly stopped between floors. Mary tried to get the elevator to move and to get help. Suddenly she saw the elevator hatch open and a man descend. She was terrified until she realized she recognized him. She asked him for help. Then a second male came through the elevator hatch. She then realized something was wrong. A knife was flashed and she was threatened with death by a garrotte if she screamed. Mary was stripped of her clothes, sexually assaulted by both males, and forced to endure a variety of perverse sexual acts (oral, anal, and vaginal sex; urinating on her body and in her mouth; vomiting on her face; multilayered sexual acts alternating male to female and male to male). She hoped through prayer to live through the terror she was experiencing.

The assailants then forced Mary back through to the hatch of the elevator to ride to the basement. There was hesitancy by the assailants as to where to take her next (i.e., outside or the woods). She was then forced to climb 12 flights of stairs to the building roof where the sexual assaults and deviant acts were repeated (both assailants simultaneously inserting their penises into her mouth). Conversation by the assailants was interlaced with sexual questions and comments, racial slurs, orders, and threats of murder. She was held over the edge of the roof and taunted with the question: Have you ever flown? Both her life and her mother and sister's life were threatened if she told of the acts.

Eventually one assailant left. The second assailant changed his behavioral style ("he acted really crazy") as he continued the assaults. Mary managed to talk him into freeing her and she was able to return to her apartment.

She arrived at her apartment to find her mother and sister frantic with worry. She disclosed the rape and the police were immediately called. She was terrified to have to ride in the elevator. She was taken to the hospital and examined. Police followed all investigative leads and apprehended the pair; both men were convicted. However, their families live in the area and Mary has great fear for her safety when they are released from prison.

This was classified as anger racial rape due to the racial slurs made by the assailants, who are white, to Mary who is black.

314.04: Global Anger Rape

This category is reserved for offenders who appear to be globally angry at the world. This is a high expressive aggression assault with no evidence of sadism and no evidence that the offender was focally angry at women.

315: Sadistic Rape

The level of violence in a sadistic offender's rape must clearly exceed what is necessary to force victim compliance; the offender's sexual arousal is a function of the victim's suffering, fear, or discomfort; behavioral evidence may include whipping, bondage; violence focuses on the erogenous parts of the victim's body (such as burning, cutting, or otherwise mutilating the breasts, anus, buttocks, or genitals), insertion of foreign objects in the vagina or anus; intercourse after the victim is unconscious; the use of feces/urine in the offense.

Most often there is high expressive aggression with moderate to severe injury to the victim. Often, the offender uses items to inflict pain/injury (cigarettes, knives, sticks, bottles, etc.); in some cases of muted sadism, however, there is clear evidence of eroticized aggression (insertion of foreign objects, bondage, whipping, etc.) without extensive physical injury.

319: Abduction Rape

Abduction by a stranger implies transportation of a person into a vehicle, building, or a distance of more than 20 ft, for the purpose of committing a crime.

Case No. 4

Fran, a 32-year-old single white sales manager, had made reservations to stay in a hotel on a business trip. She drove from the airport to the hotel. As she entered the hotel garage she was unable to get a ticket from the automatic machine and no one was in the garage booth to give instructions or a ticket. She continued into the garage and found a parking space. As she was preparing to leave her car, she was aware of a man running over to her and thought he had the parking ticket. Suddenly, the man forced a sharp instrument to her neck, and a second man appeared. Fran was shoved into the back seat and abducted from the parking garage.

During the time she was in the back seat of the car, she tried a number of strategies to get out of the situation: she talked, pleaded, cried. All efforts failed and there was increased verbal aggression ("Shut up bitch") and physical aggression of the weapon being jabbed into her ribs. After a time period, the car stopped and Fran was blindfolded, forced out of the car, and then locked in the trunk of the car. Her immediate thoughts at this time were of death. She heard her abductors talking in the car and realized she was going to be raped. The car stopped and started several times over a 1- to 2-hr time period. Then the car stopped again and Fran was pulled out of the trunk, the blindfold was tightened, and she was shoved into the front seat of the car where she was vaginally and orally raped. She was forced to drink some liquor from a bottle. After the rape, Fran was shoved back into the car. The rapists lectured her about keeping her doors locked as they were going to leave her in a "bad" section of the city. They ordered her to count to ten and left the car. Fran removed the blindfold, calmed herself as best she could, and began driving and looking for help. She asked someone for directions and was led by another car to a hospital. At the hospital she was seen by various staff members. The police were called and she gave a statement to two officers. She telephoned her brother who came to the hospital and took her back to his apartment.

330: Group Cause Sexual Assault

This category is used for three or more offenders. When there are two offenders, each should be classified under Personal Cause. Although there are clearly group dynamics (e.g., contagion effects, defusion of responsibility) and social dynamics (e.g., highly developed gang cultures in particular communities or cities) that foster gang rape, the factors that motivate each of the offenders may well be different.

331: Formal Gang Assault

A formal gang is characterized by some internal organizational structure, a name as well as other identifying features (e.g., colors, insignias, patterns of dress), and some evidence of group cohesiveness (e.g., members owe some allegiance to the gang and gather to participate in a variety of activities). In sum, the gang must have some mission or purpose of the assault.

332: Informal Gang

An informal gang is a very loosely structured group that congregates, typically on the spur of the moment, with a common purpose of marauding or otherwise engaging in antisocial activity. Although the group may have one or more leaders, there is no formal organizational structure. This category should also include all other instances of multiple offender assault in which there is no evidence that the group constitutes a formal gang.

Case No. 5

Having spent an evening with her husband and other couples at a local restaurant, 25-year-old Nan was outside waiting for her husband to pick her up in their car. She heard a car and suddenly a man grabbed her from behind and pushed her into a car. She was thrown to the floor of the back seat, threatened if she did not stop screaming, and a foot was placed on her chest. As the car traveled, she was ordered to disrobe and when she failed to comply fast enough, the clothes were pulled off by the abductor. She was then raped orally and vaginally. The three assailants then took her to a home where four additional men were waiting. Throughout the night, Nan was forced to endure multiple sexual acts including rape and sodomy. She believed she would be murdered. Her terror was heightened with the methodical, planned manner of the assaults. She coped by being very visually aware of her surroundings and by dissociating herself from feeling what was occurring to her body. For example, after being forced to bathe with one of the rapists in a bathtub, she noted blood on the towel after drying herself. Feeling horrified, she threw the towel at the man and asked, "What have you done to me?" This major outburst illustrated her dissociation from the injuries inflicted upon her. The abductor then forced her into the car again, drove to another site, sexually assaulted her, and finally drove her to another location and released her. She sought help; the police responded and she was taken to a hospital that treated her for her physical and sexual injuries.

This rape was classified as an informal gang rape and anger racial rape, as she was white and the assailants were black.

Her major psychological defense in coping with the victimization was dissociation ("I just focused on the details of the house"). This strategy was successful in identifying the house and led to the arrest and conviction of three rapists; four rapists remain at large.

390: Sexual Assault Not Classified Elsewhere

This category is reserved for those assaults that cannot be classified elsewhere.

Summary

Over a 10-year period, the work of investigative analysts at the FBI Academy with the large number of cases seen weekly led to their expansion of traditional crime categories. The CCM is the first step to creating explicit crime categories, especially that of rape and sexual assault, that heretofore have been utilized informally. This chapter outlines the rape and sexual assault categories of criminal enterprise rape, personal cause rape, and gang rape.

References

Douglas, J. E., Burgess, A.W., Burgess, A. G., and Ressler, R. K., *Crime Classification Manual*, Lexington Books, New York, 1992.

Groth, A. N., *Men Who Rape*, Plenum Press, New York, 1979.

Groth, A.N., Burgess, A.W., and Holmstrom, L. L., Rape: power, anger and sexuality, *Am. J. Psychiatry*, 134(11), 1239, 1977.

Knight, R. A. and Prentky, R. A., Classifying sexual offenders: the development and corroboration of taxonomic models, in *Handbook of Sexual Assault*, Marshall, W. L., Laws, D. R., and Barbaree, H. E., Eds., Plenum Press, New York, 1990.

Knight, R. A., Carter, D. L., and Prentky, R. A., A system for the classification of child molesters: reliability and applications, *J. Interpersonal Violence*, 4, 3, 1989.

Hazelwood, R. R., Analyzing the rape and profiling the offender, in *Practical Rape Investigations*, Hazelwood, R. R. and Burgess, A. W., Eds., Elsevier, New York, 1987.

Lanning, K.V., *Child Molesters: A Behavioral Analysis*, National Center for Missing & Exploited Children, Washington, D.C., 1986.

Prentky, R. A., Cohen, M. L., and Seghorn, R. K., Development of a rational taxonomy for the classification of sexual offenders: rapists, *Bull. Am. Acad. Psychiatry Law*, 13, 39, 1986.

Indirect Personality Assessment

12

RICHARD L. AULT, JR.
ROBERT R. HAZELWOOD

A 19-year-old woman was abducted, raped, and murdered and her body found in a shallow creek. An investigation resulted in the development of a suspect who lived near where the body was found. The principal investigator in the case decided to interview the suspect immediately and, needing a partner, took the first detective available. Determining that the suspect was at work in a restaurant, they went there and conducted the interview in the kitchen. The suspect was immediately hostile and, while shouting at the detectives, told them that he was a homosexual. Very shortly, the principal investigator regretted his choice of partners, who was well known as a man who detested homosexuals. Predictably, the partner became increasingly angry and began shouting and menacing the suspect. Needless to say, the interview was a dismal failure and an opportunity to solve the case quickly passed.

In the above example, several obvious mistakes were made: (1) not learning in advance that the suspect was homosexual, (2) insufficient care in the selection of the partner, and (3) selection of the suspect's place of work for the interview. Many factors should have been considered before the interview, such as: (1) What environment would be best suited for the interview? (2) What time of day (or night) should the interview take place? (3) What sex, race, age, and size of interviewer would have the most success with the suspect? These are but a few of the significant questions that might have been answered, had an assessment of the suspect's personality been done before conducting the interview.

Every investigator has experienced failure in interviewing suspects, subjects, or witnesses. Often this failure is caused by inadequate preparation on the interviewer's part. The propensity to interview an identified suspect without proper preparation is a critical mistake. Admittedly, the rush to interview is often attributable to external sources such as case load, administrative pressures, or interference from superiors. All too often, however, the investigator doesn't take the time to get the behavioral and psychologically based information about the suspect that may make the difference between success and failure in an interview or trial situation.

The goal of this chapter is to give the investigator information on the application of indirect personality assessment (IPA) — a behavioral science technique — in rape investigation. The reader will also find an assessment protocol that may help in gathering information necessary for the application of this technique. This chapter will not teach the reader how to prepare an IPA; it is intended to famil-iarize him/her with the type of information that should be collected, and what the best sources of information will be.

It should be noted at the outset that often a great deal of time and effort is involved in gathering information and preparing an IPA. Therefore, the decision to have an assessment prepared should be a judicious one. Because of the invest-ment of time and effort, it is recommended that this technique be considered for use only in major investigations. However, any investigator who takes the time to gather the type of information recommended in the Appendix will find his or her ability to conduct the interview greatly enhanced. It is for this reason that the investigator is encouraged to gather the information about the suspect, witness, or other person being interviewed. Remember, too, that while information gathering is performed *by* the investigators and others, it is important that the IPA be prepared by persons trained in the behavioral sciences who are not directly in-volved in the case.

Behavioral Science and Law Enforcement

Traditionally, law enforcement has not trusted the behavioral sciences. One has only to hear any five mental health professionals testify in court to see that behavioral scientists often do not agree among themselves. Time and again, inves-tigators have heard contradictory or even unrealistic testimony from those who purport to be experts in mental health. Nevertheless, investigators can and should make use of advances in the behavioral sciences for the benefit of the law enforce-ment profession.

An excellent example of the successful union of behavioral science and law enforcement is an application that was, at one time, called "profiling" (Ault and Reese, 1980; Porter, 1983; Ault et al., 1994). The technique is currently referred to as "criminal investigative analysis" (CIA) (NCAVC, 1989). CIA has become widely used through the Federal Bureau of Investigation's (FBI) National Center for the Analysis of Violent Crime (NCAVC) at the FBI Academy, Quantico, VA. NCAVC investigative analyses, which set forth characteristics and traits of unidentified offenders ("profiles"), are usually quite accurate and become increasingly so as data improve through the increasing number of cases analyzed every year.

A profile is the end result of a behavioral assessment of a crime scene or, in the case of rape, the interaction between the offender and his victim. The analyst interprets the evidence to produce a vivid outline of the salient characteristics of the offender. In a rape case, for example, the behavioral evidence left by the rapist allows the investigative analyst to determine a variety of information about the assailant (Chapter 9). As he demonstrates, Hazelwood encourages rape investiga-tors to solicit information about the offender's behavior that may give "the officer better insight into the (psychological and social aspects of) the type of person he is seeking". While Hazelwood's statement concerns criminal investigative analysis, it applies also to IPA. If the investigator's experience in the field is enhanced by behavioral principles, he or she will be able to eliminate unlikely suspects and limit the scope of the investigation.

It has been stated that CIA is now a widely used technique in rape and other crimes of violence. A lesser-known, but equally valuable, behavioral science technique is the indirect assessment of a suspect or offender's personality for investigative or trial purposes.

What is Indirect Personality Assessment (IPA)?

Although definitions of assessment abound, most behavioral scientists agree that it is not something that can be reduced to a "cookbook" technique. Maloney and Ward (1976) describe assessment as a "variable process, depending on the questions asked, the person involved, time commitments, and myriad other factors. As such, it cannot be reduced to a finite set of specific rules or steps" (p. 5). Sundberg, in his book *Assessment of Persons* (1977), states that "knowing others and ourselves is still largely an art, though certainly it is aided by an emerging science".

There is no simple answer to the question "What is assessment?". Assessment has always been an integral process of human existence. All of us are involved, somehow, in assessing others. We select close friends from our acquaintances, we trust our money to one bank or another, and we have our car repaired by one mechanic over another. In all these selections, we involve ourselves in an assessment. The friend may have been chosen because of his or her attitude, appearance, humor, or for many other reasons. The bank may have been chosen because of its location, convenient hours of operation, and monetary reserves. The mechanic may have been selected because of his reputation for good work at a reasonable price. In each case, the evaluation process required information about the person or firm involved. *Assessment* is also the term used by mental health professionals when they attempt to determine the mental state of persons charged with a crime or when screening applicants for employment in law enforcement.

For law enforcement purposes, IPA may be defined as an evaluation of behavioral information about a particular person in an attempt to determine areas of personality that are susceptible to investigative techniques. The purpose of all assessment processes is to determine what makes people "tick" — what type of person the individual is. *Indirect* assessment is the specialty of making the evaluation about a person based on information that was not gathered directly from that person. There are several types of indirect assessment used in the mental health profession. The most commonly known of these is the so-called "psychological autopsy". The psychological autopsy is conducted by mental health professionals to attempt to determine the mental state of persons who may have committed suicide.

In law enforcement, indirect assessments do not always serve the same goals as those of mental health. Law enforcement assessors are attempting to determine areas of vulnerability in the personality, while mental health professionals are attempting to diagnose and treat. While the goals are different, law enforcement can use the tools of the behavioral sciences to identify those components of the suspect's personality that will be susceptible to the knowledgeable investigator.

Assessment Techniques

There are three basic techniques used by mental health professionals to assess individuals: objective, projective, and behavioral. The following descriptions are necessarily brief; readers interested in a more detailed discussion are referred to the recommended readings following this chapter.

Objective techniques seek to evaluate aspects of the personality that can be measured by tests that are usually administered by psychologists. The technique is called *objective* because it asks the person to respond to specific questions; the answers do not require much interpretation. The term "cookbook" is often applied to this technique because the final product, the analysis, is a direct result of the answers that went into it. There is no latitude in the scoring for administrator interpretation.

A number of problems limit the use of objective techniques in law enforcement, the most obvious being the difficulty of asking a suspect to take a test. Another problem is that the validity of all objective tests requires the respondent to be truthful and not to sway the test in one direction or another. Law enforcement officials would not want to depend solely on such a test to determine personality factors of a suspected rapist for interview purposes.

The objective techniques, therefore, are not often applicable in the assessment of suspects or offenders. However, investigators should never rule out the possibility of obtaining the results of tests which suspects or offenders have previously taken.

Projective techniques are based in part on the theory that a person, faced with an unstructured situation or stimulus, will reveal some unconscious thoughts and/ or emotions as he attempts to make sense of the stimulus (Maloney and Ward, 1976; Sundberg, 1977). The most widely known projective technique is the Rorschach, which, like the objective tests, is usually administered by a psychologist.

Projective techniques are controversial. Enthusiasm for their use depends on the examiner's particular school of thought and the use to which the test will be put. One problem with projective tests is that a person's responses to ambiguous situations depend on much more than unconscious impulses and needs.

However, law enforcement officers can effectively appropriate the theory of the projective hypothesis to practical situations. When they gather information about a suspect, they must be aware that the quality of that information may depend on the source from which it was obtained. For example, information received from a suspect's ex-girlfriend or wife may be more valuable than the same type of information obtained from his employer. The suspect, because of the often unstructured aspects of daily involvement in an emotional relationship, will relax his defenses and show more (or less) of his thought structure to his girlfriend than to his employer. These principles may help evaluate contradictory information from several sources by enabling the investigator to prioritize information based on which informant was "closer" to the suspect and might have better insight.

Behavioral techniques are the type most used by investigative analysts in the preparation of personality assessments. They are based on reported or actual observations of what a person does and/or says. They do not rely on self-reported material other than to note how it may contrast with how the person behaves. Personality assessments for law enforcement purposes are based on observations of behavior accompanied by such questions as: "When was the behavior first observed?" "How frequently did it occur?" "How long did it last?" and "What was going on in the person's life at the time?".

Observation of behavior is not a new concept to law enforcement, but determining baselines of behavior is. An analyst is concerned not only with what behavior is occurring but how long it has been taking place. For example, if an officer determined during a rape investigation that a suspect was reported to have increased his alcohol consumption, the officer should try to learn when the increased consumption began (e.g., following the rape[s]). Significant events can cause a person to alter his behavior to such an extent that the changes would be noticed by those around him. The increase in alcohol intake may be indicative of additional stress on the suspect. If the behavior change was noticed shortly after the rape(s), it would be a significant behavioral change and, therefore, of interest to the investigator and the assessor.

The Assessment Process

Often the assessment process will yield information about a suspect that the investigator already knows. This is not necessarily wasted or useless information; it is external confirmation and will reinforce the investigation's direction. Occasionally the analyst's conclusions will clash with the investigator's, and this may also have positive results. The reasoning by which the investigative analyst arrived at his/her conclusions should always be included so the investigator can observe the suspect from a different perspective. The decision to accept the analyst's evaluation and recommendations is left entirely up to the principal investigator in the case, and the assessment should never be allowed to replace the investigative process or overrule the investigator's decisions. For purposes of this chapter, the analyst is a person with an advanced degree in behavioral sciences (i.e., social worker, forensic nurse, psychologist, clinical psychologist, psychiatrist, etc.), experienced in criminal investigations, who studies a person's behavior to determine where he or she may be vulnerable to diverse investigative techniques.

To facilitate the process, the investigator must keep in mind certain fundamentals.

First, the investigator must determine the specific purpose of the assessment; assessments are done with the understanding that a specific problem must be addressed. Each assessment is unique because each is designed to achieve a specific goal or series of goals (e.g., how to best approach a subject for interview, what type of interviewer should be used). Some of the ways in which assessments may help the investigator will be discussed in the section "Uses of Indirect Personality Assessments".

Second, the most time-consuming and critical step in the process is collecting information. The appendix to this chapter sets forth a suggested protocol for the gathering of information. While it may not be necessary to have all the information listed in the protocol, it is imperative that the officer, or whoever assists him, collect the behavioral information in a structured manner to assure quality results. The following suggestions will help provide the necessary structure for quality results:

1. **Ask the same question of many sources.** For example, if a question concerning the suspect's fears is asked (i.e., "Do you know of anything that frightens John?"), then the question should be spoken identically to all who are questioned. This is necessary because once an officer has learned something about a person, he tends to file it away as a fact unless someone contradicts it later on. However, if the same question is asked, the reliability issue is resolved rather quickly.

2. **Determine how the source knows the information.** Information about a person gains value when the investigator determines how the source became aware of the information provided. For example, if the source reports that he or she actually observed the behavior (subject drinking himself into a stupor shortly after the rape), it would certainly be much more significant than if the source merely heard about the behavior.

3. **Determine when the information was obtained by the source.** A "baseline" for the subject's behavior can be established if the analyst is aware of when it began, and if the behavior has changed over a period of time. Therefore, the investigator should attempt to pinpoint behavioral time factors. One method of doing so is to determine when the source acquired the information being reported.

4. **Determine how long the subject has exhibited the behavior.** To further help the analyst in determining a behavioral baseline, the officer should ask whether the reported behavior (e.g., compulsive gambling) is a recent activity of the subject or one that has been noted over a period of time, and, if the latter, over what length of time. To learn that a suspect in a rape and torture case reads bondage magazines is very significant if he has been doing so for 2 years. It becomes much less significant, however, if he was seen looking through such a magazine on only one occasion.

Uses of Indirect Personality Assessments

Generally speaking, investigators are not aware of what an indirect personality assessment can provide. Typically, they will ask, "What can I expect?". The answer to that question depends on what the investigator intends to do with the assessment and on the quality of information that can be collected and given the analyst. For example, an assessment may be requested in planning an interview, and the investigator may want to know what type of approach should be made, how questions to the subject should be phrased, what areas should be emphasized or avoided, or what environment would be most beneficial to the investigator, or he may request that all of the above areas be addressed. Depending on the quantity and quality of information available, the analyst will advise the requesting officers on how best to address these problems. Hopefully, the analyst will suggest additional uses for the information from the assessment that will further advance the investigation.

While the potential for assessment used by law enforcement is virtually unlimited, rape case assessments have proven most helpful in the following ways: (1) preparing for the initial interview of a suspect, (2) assisting in the planning of prosecutive strategy, and (3) reducing the number of suspects.

Preparing for the Initial Interview

It is extremely important to note that this investigative technique is most useful in the initial interview of a suspect or an offender. It is much less helpful in subsequent interviews. The reason is that the psychological advantage lies with the investigator in the first confrontation with the subject. The person being interviewed is uneasy and unaware of the extent of the investigative effort, how much is known (or remains unknown), and how long he has been a suspect. The initial interview may also be crucial to the case if direct evidence linking the suspect to the crime is not available.

Case No. 1

A 12-year-old girl had been reported missing, and several days of searching failed to locate her. Her body was found 3 weeks later in a deserted shack several miles from her home. Evidence indicated that she had been killed elsewhere and her body transported to the shack. Investigators identified one suspect during the period the victim was missing. The suspect, convicted previously on charges dealing with abduction and rape of minors, had served time in prison before returning to the area in which the victim lived. The investigators were fairly certain that the suspect had killed the victim and were about to conduct their initial interview. Realizing they had little evidence to link the suspect to the crime, they wanted to assure that, if he had committed the crime, he would confess. They requested an assessment of the subject.

Collecting the necessary information, the officers learned that the subject was not well educated, but did have average intelligence. They discovered that although he was a loner, he had briefly worked as a security guard. His employment, and his previous exposure to police, made the suspect well versed in police methods. The investigators were gratified that they had not rushed into the interview with little preparation. It was obvious to them that a routine interview would have been unsuccessful.

The personality assessment provided them with suggestions for pre-interview and interview techniques. The suggestions included interview environment (lighting, seating arrangements, and location); a specific time for the interview to begin; composition of the interview team (age, sex, race, height, dress, and educational level); method of introduction; topics to be avoided or emphasized; and props to be in view of the suspect. The interview was successful, and the offender was later convicted.

Reducing the Number of Suspects

In some cases, more than one person may emerge as a suspect in a rape or series of rapes. Once the investigation has narrowed them to two or three, the assessment technique may be of value to the investigation.

Case No. 2

A series of 20 rapes occurred in an 11-month period, all within a large housing complex. Police became convinced, correctly, that at least 18 of the rapes were committed by one person, and requested a CIA. After the profile was prepared, five suspects were developed. The assistance of the CIA and investigation eliminated all but two suspects and, at this point, an IPA of these two was requested. Data on the two were collected, and an evaluation of this information showed that certain significant behavioral changes should have been shown by one of the suspects during the series of rapes. Additionally, the investigators had noticed these changes themselves during the information-gathering stage of assessment, and had begun to concentrate their investigative efforts on the one man before receiving the assessment. This case clearly illustrates the value of gathering information, whether an assessment is requested or not, since the investigators would not have noticed the behavior change unless they had been gathering the background information.

Planning Prosecutive Strategy

The value of personality assessment in the trial situation has been proven repeatedly. It has proven useful in the development of opening and closing remarks to the jury, as well as in the development of questions for cross-examination.

Case No. 3

A 28-year-old man brutally raped and murdered a 21-year-old woman, hid the body, and left the area. When the body was discovered and the young man became the prime suspect, he was arrested. He told the police that the victim was raped and killed by intruders, who then threatened to kill him if he talked to the police. According to investigators, the circumstantial evidence linking the suspect to the crime was very strong and indicated that the young man had committed the murder. The prosecutor requested an assessment in order to understand the motives of the criminal and the crime so that he might make a strong and logical argument to the jury in the event the suspect took the stand. Two analysts first studied the crime behavior, then compared it to the information available about the subject's personality. A logical and comprehensive assessment was prepared that provided the prosecutor with an opinion on the murderer's reasons for the attack and on the victim's behavior that triggered the crime. The assessment also designed specific questions to exploit the offender's weaknesses should he take the witness stand. Following a successful trial, the prosecutor expressed his appreciation for the usefulness of the assessment technique.

Information Required for an Assessment

As mentioned, the appendix to this chapter contains a protocol to be used by investigators desiring a personality assessment. Information generally of interest to an analyst includes: (1) demographic data, (2) religion, (3) education, (4) hobbies or pastimes, (5) physical characteristics, (6) marriages, (7) employment, (8) specific types of behavior, and (9) mental and physical health. While the protocol is quite comprehensive, much of the information may not be needed; it, therefore, behooves the investigator to ascertain from the analyst what will be required for the process. It is also obvious that it may not be possible to obtain some of the information, a limitation clearly understood by the analyst.

In some instances, investigators may be legally or administratively prohibited from obtaining such information or providing it to outside consultants. It is recommended, therefore, that before requesting an IPA the officer consult with his superiors and the responsible prosecutor, explaining the time and effort required and the intended use of the assessment. Ideally, the investigator who is most knowledgeable about the suspect/offender should be involved in the information gathering. It is imperative that he prepare the information summary that is to be provided to the analyst.

Sources of Information

The information necessary for the preparation of an IPA can be obtained from many sources. The following have proven valuable in past assessments.

Records. Written documentation often gives insight into a subject's personality. For example, a poor credit record might indicate that a sense of responsibility is lacking or that the subject is inclined to impulsiveness. Employment records reflecting disciplinary problems may indicate a dislike for authority. Medical records that reflect numerous, but undiagnosed ailments may indicate a need for attention. Arrest records and incident reports may provide information about the suspect's attitude toward women. The type of documentation that may prove helpful is limited only by the imagination of the one seeking the information. Officers should not restrict their search for information only to their geographical area of responsibility, but should consider sources that may be found in areas where the person previously resided.

Suspect's Friends and Associates. This source of information, while potentially rich in nature, should be approached cautiously, unless it is the investigator's intention to let the subject know of the investigative interest in him (this may be an investigative suggestion of the analyst). If this is not the intent, associates having the least contact with the subject should be questioned first, followed by those slightly closer to him, and so on.

Former Spouse or Girlfriend. Experience has shown that this source is potentially the most valuable to an investigator who wants to become more knowledgeable about a subject (Hazelwood et al., 1993). Often, the termination of the relationship was not pleasant, and feelings of anger or a desire for revenge may motivate such a source to divulge information of immense value to an assessment. A word of caution is necessary at this point: anger or a desire for revenge may cause the source to exaggerate or lie about the subject. The investigator should be alert to this possibility and prepared to deal with it. Regardless, the former spouse or girlfriend often has knowledge about the subject that no one else has. Specifically, she can tell the investigator about the subject's strengths, weaknesses, fears, sexual habits, what makes him happy or sad, and at what time of day or night he is most alert. This is by no means all-inclusive of the information she may have.

Criminal Behavior. The behavior exhibited by the offender during the commission of previous sexual crimes should also be provided to the person preparing the assessment. As addressed in Chapter 8, a carefully conducted interview of the rape victim can yield invaluable information about the offender's personality, motivation, and attitudes toward women.

Summary

For law enforcement purposes, an IPA is the evaluation of behavioral information about a particular person in an attempt to determine his strengths and weaknesses, as well as other areas of personality that may be susceptible to specific investigative techniques. Assessments can be used in preparing for the initial interview of suspects or subjects, to reduce the number of suspects, and in the preparation of trial strategy.

The appendix to this chapter gives a protocol useful in gathering information for the preparation of a personality assessment. Since all of the information may not be needed, the investigator should consult with the assessor before collecting the information. Sources of information about the suspect/subject include records and other documentation, friends and associates, former spouses and/or girlfriends, and the subject's behavior during the commission of previous or current sexual crimes.

IPA is a useful tool in investigating rape and other cases. A great part of the usefulness of IPA is that information about the suspect will be gathered that might not normally be collected. While this helps the behavioral scientist to assess the person, more importantly it gives information to the investigator about the subject being assessed. Thus, while IPA itself may be another tool in the investigative repertoire, its use enhances the opportunity for successful conclusion of the case.

Appendix
Principles

1. Ask the same question of many sources.
2. Determine how the source knows the information.
3. Determine when the information was obtained by the source.
4. Determine how long the subject has exhibited the particular behavior being reported.

Assessment Information

General

Date of birth
Place of birth
Race

Family

Socioeconomic status of family (upper, middle, lower)
Number of brothers
Number of sisters
Subject's place in birth order (oldest, youngest, middle, etc.)
Parents still living? If no, when did each die? If yes, where are they living?
To what degree was (is) family involved in religion?
What is (was) subject's relationship with parents?
  a. Was it always like this?
  b. When did it change?

Subject

Is subject currently involved in a religion? What faith?
To what degree?
Is this involvement recent?
How do associates describe subject?
Are school records available for review by assessor?

Education Level

What is the highest level of schooling subject obtained?
Why did subject leave school?

Hobbies

What are subject's former hobbies?
What are subject's current hobbies?

What are subject's current special interests?
What are subject's former special interests?
What type of movies does the subject enjoy?
What type of reading material does subject enjoy (i.e., spy novel, pornography, adventure stories)?

Residence and Associates

Where does subject currently live (rental apartment, trailer, house, etc.)?
Type of neighborhood (middle class, upper class, ghetto, etc.)?
Does subject live alone? If not alone, with whom?
Does subject have any friends?
How do they compare to him (higher/lower class, more/less educated, more/less money, more/less intelligent, any other striking comparisons)?
Has the subject ever belonged to any groups or organizations (motorcycle clubs, volunteer police, special deputy, volunteer fireman, Explorer Scout, etc.)?

Mobility

What is the subject's general mode of transportation (walking, bicycling, public transportation, own vehicle, etc.)?
Are there any unusual circumstances connected with subject's selection of mode of transportation?
If the subject has his or her own vehicle, how well is it maintained?

Physical Characteristics

What is subject's dress style compared with others in the subject's group (neater, sloppier, uncaring about appearance, stylish, etc.)?
What are your overall impressions of subject's personal appearance?
How long has subject had this appearance?
How is the subject's physical health and well-being? If subject has had any major illnesses or injuries, what were they?
Does subject have any unusual physical features (limp, hairlip, cast in eye, stutter, lisp, etc.)?
Does subject wear a beard and/or mustache? How long has the subject had it? Did subject say why he grew it?
Does the subject smoke? What does subject smoke? For how long has subject smoked? How often?
Does subject drink alcoholic beverages? What does subject drink? How often? Does subject drink to excess?
How would you describe subject's overall physical appearance (handsome, pretty, fat, skinny, a "hunk", ugly, etc.)?
Does subject have any distinguishing scars, marks, or tattoos?

Marriage

Is subject currently or previously married? How long? How many times?

Was there anything unusual in any of the subject's marriages (i.e., divorced because of "extreme cruelty", marriage lasted very short time)?

What are subject's sexual preferences?

Does the subject have any sexual perversions? What are they? (Be specific.)

Did the subject engage in any extramarital affairs? Was subject blatant, or a braggart, about extramarital affairs? Please interview former spouses and lovers, if possible.

Employment

Is subject employed? Where? How long?

Is subject skilled in any area (welder, auto mechanic, electrician, machinist, professional, typist, etc.)?

How does subject relate to co-workers (leader, loner, agitator, etc.)?

How does subject relate to superiors (subservient, defiant, angry, unconcerned, etc.)?

How does subject relate to subordinates?

How many jobs has the subject held in the past 5 years? What type of jobs?

Behavior

What makes the subject angry?

What makes the subject happy?

Whom does subject turn to for advice

What sorts of things seem important to subject?

How does subject relax?

How does subject spend free time?

How does subject react to the loss (by death, separation, alienation, etc.) of people important to him/her?

What events seem to shake subject's self-confidence?

Has the subject ever been violent?

Health

Has subject had any major illnesses in past 5 years? If so, what?

Has subject sustained any injuries in past 5 years? If so, what?

Does subject have any history of mental health care?

What are subject's sleep patterns (early riser, up all night, sleep all day, etc.)?

Does subject use drugs? What type? How often?

References

Ault, R. L., Jr. and Reese, J. T., A psychological assessment of crime: profiling. *FBI Law Enforcement Bull.*, p. 22, March 1980.

Ault, R.L., Hazelwood, R.R., and Reboussin, R., The epistemological status of equivocal death analysis: a reply to Poythress et al. *Am. Psychologist*, January 1994.

Hazelwood, R.R., Warren, J.I., and Dietz, P.E. Compliant victims of sexual sadists, *Aust. J. Med.*, 22, 474, 1993.

Maloney, M. P. and Ward, P., *Psychological Assessment: A Conceptual Approach*, Oxford University Press, New York, 1976.

Porter, B., Mind hunters: tracking down killers with the FBI's psychological profiling team, *Psychol. Today*, p. 44, April 1983.

Sundberg, N. B., *Assessment of Persons*, Prentice-Hall, Englewood Cliffs, NJ, 1977.

Suggested Readings

Bristow, A. P., *Field Interrogation*, 2nd ed., Charles C. Thomas, Springfield, IL, 1964.

Bull, R., Bustin, B., Evans, P., and Gahagan, D., *Psychology for Police Officers*, John Wiley & Sons, Bath, England, 1983.

Duncan, S., Jr. and Fiske, D. W., *Truth and Deception*, Williams & Wilkins, Baltimore, 1977.

Eysenck, H. J., *The Structure of Human Personality*, John Dickens & Co., Great Britain, 1970.

Groth, A. N., *Men Who Rape*, Plenum Press, New York, 1979.

Hazelwood, R. R., The behavior-oriented interview of rape victims: the key to profiling, *FBI Law Envorcement Bull.*, p. 8, September 1983.

Holt, R. R., *Assessing Personality*, Harcourt Brace Jovanovich, New York, 1971.

Johnson, W. C., Snibbe, J. R., and Evans, L. A., *Basic Psychopathology: A Programmed Text*, Spectrum Publications, New York, 1975.

Knapp, M. L., *Nonverbal Communication in Human Interaction*, Holt, Rinehart & Winston, New York, 1978.

Lanyon, R. L. and Goodstein, L. D., *Personality Assessment*, John Wiley & Sons, New York, 1971.

Maloney, M. P. and Ward, P., *Psychological Assessment: A Conceptual Approach*, Oxford University Press, New York, 1976.

National Center for the Analysis of Violent Crime (NCAVC), *Deviant and Criminal Sexuality; 2nd Ed.*, NCAVC, FBI Academy, Quantico, VA, 1993.

Nirenberg, G. I. and Calero, H. H., *How to Read a Person Like a Book*, Hawthorne Books, New York, 1971.

Rada, R. T., Ed., *Clinical Aspects of the Rapist*, Grune & Stratton, New York, 1978.

Reed, J. E. and Inbau, F. E., *Truth and Deception*, Williams & Wilkins, Baltimore, 1977.

Rider, A. O., The firesetter: a psychological profile, *FBI Law Enforcement Bull.*, p. 6, June 1980.

Samenow, S. E., *Inside the Criminal Mind*, New York Times Book, New York, 1984.

Simpson, K., *Police: The Investigation of Violence*, MacDonald & Evans, London, 1978.

Sundberg, N. B., *Assessment of Persons*, Prentice-Hall, Englewood Cliffs, NJ, 1977.

Wiggins, S., *Personality and Prediction: Principles of Personality Assessment*, Addison-Wesley, Menlo Park, CA, 1970.

False Rape Allegations

13

MARGARET M. AIKEN
ANN WOLBERT BURGESS
ROBERT R. HAZELWOOD

Compared to other serious crimes, rape has a number of unique characteristics. First, it is difficult to know how frequently rape occurs because of the low reporting rate for this crime. Accurate estimates of the incidence and prevalence of rape are not readily available, as the majority of victims do not report to the police and do not receive medical attention from hospitals or seek help from service agencies such as rape crisis centers (Kilpatrick et al., 1985). Second, rape is the only serious crime in which victims are generally thought to be responsible for their own assault. It is believed by many that people like to be overpowered sexually, that women say "no" but mean "yes", and that women issue false reports regarding rape to "save face", "get even", or conceal pregnancy (Burt, 1980). Third, rape is treated distinctively in the courtroom from property crime, for example. Further, rules of evidence have been unique and stringent (e.g., signs of resistance required as a proof of nonconsent, the need for third-party corroboration). Fourth, rape and abuse are selectively perpetrated by the male segment of the population and are selectively borne by the female segment of the population. Fifth, rape instills fear in women and serves to limit women's freedom by placing constraints on their activities (Riger and Gordon, 1988). Sixth, unlike other crimes, there is considerable variation in what constitutes a "real" rape. Law enforcement agents and child protective service workers use the term "unfounded" when there is insufficient evidence or use the term "false allegation" to dismiss the complaint of a "non-believable victim".

This last point is the focus of this chapter. Although most experienced investigators have taken false crime reports of one type of another, they are always sensitive to the possibility. Surprisingly, even though the phenomenon of the false rape report is well recognized, there has been little careful research into the problem. This chapter clarifies the concept of false allegation, develops parameters for its use along with precise operational definitions (Walker and Avant, 1983; Rodgers, 1989), examines types of motivation, and offers strategies for interviewing.

False Allegation*

The term "false allegation" is composed of two terms which will be defined separately from dictionary sources. Dictionaries in common use define "false" as

* This section is reprinted from Aiken, M.M., False allegation, *J. Psychosoc. Nursing,* 31(11), 16, 1993. With permission.

0-8493-8152-1/95/$0.00+$.50
© 1995 by CRC Press, Inc.

follows: "not true, incorrect, wrong, untruthful, lying, unfaithful, misleading, not real, artificial" (Woolf, 1973; Guralnik, 1984). In reading through these definitions, one gets the sense of deliberateness rather than of being in error. *Black's Law Dictionary* (1968) gives the above definitions as well as the following: "deceitful, designed to deceive, intentionally untrue, dishonest, fraudulent, and not according to truth or reality". From this we may conclude that that which is falsified is done so knowingly, for some deceitful intent. Under this assumption, care must be taken to distinguish between mistakes and deceit.

Dictionary sources define "allegation" as "a positive assertion, an assertion unsupported and insupportable, an assertion without proof or to be proven, an assertion to be used as a reason or excuse, and an assertion which is questionably true or so-called" (Woolf, 1980; Guralnik, 1984). *Black's Law Dictionary* (1968) defines the term in more neutral terms: "the assertion, declaration or statement of a party... what he expects to prove".

In summary, a false allegation is simply a statement which is unproven and untrue in the spirit of deliberateness or deceit. Here, questions must be asked: Must the entire allegation be false to be considered a false allegation? How false must it be? Is it more grievous to make false accusations against a person than to falsify other aspects of the crime?

Definitions by College Students

In an informal survey conducted by one of the authors (Aiken), college juniors (n = 23) were asked to briefly define false allegation. The class was predominantly white and female. The majority of the group (n = 14) said that the term meant to be "wrongly accused". A smaller number (n = 8) included "wrongly accused" but added that there was "no proof". One student defined it as a "statement made without evidence or proof". None of the statements made is completely correct, nor completely incorrect. This demonstrates the lack of precision and common meaning of the term as perceived by students.

Definitions from the Literature

Little is published which addresses the issue and concept of false allegation. Several approaches to literature review were employed: computer, ancestral, and manual. Most existing literature addresses false allegation as it applies to children and sexual abuse. A computer search by the Bureau of Justice found only two citations. A visual and manual search of library shelves at a major university found four books which had "rape" in the title and which included some discussion of false reporting and false allegation.

The studies describing false allegation in child sexual abuse were uniform in reporting sparse literature in the area and the rare occurrence of the phenomenon (Green, 1986; Fuller, 1984; Rosenfeld et al., 1979; Benedek and Schetky, 1984). These same authors concurred that when child custody is a predominant issue, the frequency of the occurrence of false allegation rises dramatically. Vindictiveness and psychological dysfunction on the part of parents may underlie such false accusations (Fuller, 1984; Benedek and Schetky, 1984). None of the sources reviewed presented a precise definition of the term, but indicated that there were possible variations. For example, Rosenfeld et al. (1979) suggested that it is possible that the specified act did occur, but that the wrong person was accused. Goodwin et al. (1978) used the terms "false accusation" and "false denial", which suggests two variations which are in no way specified by the term "false allegation".

Peters (1976) and Goodwin et al. (1978) found that they could not substantiate allegations of sexual abuse in approximately 6% of cases. This rate of occurrence rises dramatically when allegations are made against a backdrop of custody and visitation disputes (Benedek and Schetky, 1984; Brant and Sink, 1984). It is of interest to note that in none of the studies reviewed was false allegation defined in any way.

Katz and Mazur (1979) defined "false report" as "... deliberate lie by the 'alleged victim' accusing a man of a rape that did not occur. It may also be a fantasy report that the female believes to be true" (p. 207). This definition is clear and captures the spirit of deceitful intent but is limited in the variations which could be classified as false allegations. These same authors wrote that wide discrepancies in the reported frequency of false allegation are due to differences in definitions and criteria, and due to the source of the judgments in these situations.

McDowell and Hibler, in the first edition of *Practical Aspects of Rape Investigations: A Multidisciplinary Approach* (1987), presented a sensitive treatment of the issue of false allegation, which includes the role of defense mechanisms, secondary gain, and other psychological aspects. They asserted that investigators can make sense of these false claims once they discover the purpose served for the victim by such an allegation. However, a precise definition of the very phenomenon they described was omitted.

McDowell (March 1990), in another source, again failed to define the concept, but described three conditions used to classify cases as false allegations:

1. Victim recants complaint.
2. Victim fails polygraph.
3. Investigation reveals allegation to be false.

These criteria are very broad and imprecise, thereby leaving a wide margin for discretionary interpretation and action. McDowell (1990) has published a checklist for use by investigators which is intended to help determine the validity of claims of sexual assault. According to the key to this instrument, the best that a victim can "do" or be classified as, is "equivocal".

Lefer (1992) reported that there is a primary myth about women and sexual offense: they lie about it. Lefer (1992) wrote, "It is as though the victim is the one on trial; every gesture,... word can be held against her" (p. 198). Further, she asserted that by reporting sexual assault women lose credibility, and where there is any inconsistency in the report, validity of the entire allegation comes into question. Credibility for victims is elusive. Women who are unemotional may also be conveying that they were not disturbed by the "alleged" event, hence, the absence of harm. Women who are overwrought come across as emotionally unstable, and thus not credible.

Investigators suspect false allegation when victims repeatedly change accounts of the assault. Care must be taken to distinguish "changing the story" from recollection of "additional data". In both true and false claims, new facts and more detail may be added in subsequent interviews. The false claimant wishes to "shore up" her allegation to make it more believable, while the genuine victim may remember more detail and descriptive data in the days following the assault, as composure and equilibrium are regained. This situation places investigators in very delicate positions. Worst-case scenarios are that the false claimant successfully manipulates the system for personal gain or that the legitimate claimant is further traumatized by aggressive attempts on the part of investigators to elicit the ultimate "truth".

Related to this same discussion is the distinction between deliberate deceit and an honest mistake. The person making a false allegation may offer data which differ from the original report to further deceive and mislead the authorities. A legitimate rape victim, in the initial stages of the investigation, because of stress and psychic pain, may offer wrong information related to altered ability to accurately process information.

When a rape or, for that matter, any crime occurs, there must be three elements: perpetrator(s), act(s), and a setting or set of conditions. One can make a false allegation with reference to any or all of these elements. To further complicate the situation, a false allegation can consist of a false accusal or a false denial (Goodwin et al., 1978). Taking all of these variables into consideration, there are 14 possible variations in the concept: false allegation (seven cases of false accusal; seven cases of false denial). If and when the term "false allegation" is used, there needs to be "more to it". A false allegation can be a false accusal/denial with respect to perpetrator(s), act(s), and/or setting.

A Model of False Allegation

A model of the concept, false allegation shows the relationships among the motivation antecedent, defining attributes, empirical referents, intervening variables, and the concept itself.

Motivation: The Antecedent

An antecedent must occur before the concept and provide the environment in which the concept occurs. The unique antecedent of the concept, false allegation, is "motivation to deceive", which distinguishes this concept from errors, misperceptions, delusions, and other relatively benign sources of erroneous reporting as previously discussed.

Defining Attributes

Defining attributes are criteria to assist in the identification of the phenomenon under study (Walker and Avant, 1983). For a false allegation to occur, a statement of perpetrator(s), act(s), and setting must be made which is unproven and lacks truth in at least one aspect.

Intervening Variables

Intervening variables represent context. Variables influence our thinking and behavior. The list presented is not exhaustive but includes age of victim, sex, race, marital status, mental health status, socioeconomic status, lapse of time, life-style variables, relationship to assailant, secondary gain. These variables have a direct effect on any consequences which occur.

Empirical Referents

Empirical referents are the phenomena or events whereby a concept may be evaluated. Empirical referents do not represent confirmation of false allegation, for even the self-admission by the claimant of a false allegation may, in fact, be a false denial. Empirical referents may even be representative of contrary situations whereby the concept may be excluded. For example, in a case where a confession is proffered by the accused, variables associated with a valid claim could be observed and measured. Some empirical referents include alteration in story, failure to indict, self-admission by claimant, acquittal, refusal to prosecute, lie detector test, confession by perpetrator, unfounded cases.

Consequences

Consequences of the concept can be positive and/or negative. Positive consequences include perceived solution of a personal problem, decreased risk to life, and changed relationships. Negative consequences include loss of credibility, increased risk to self, perpetuation of unhealthy behavior, violence in community, revenge, secondary gain, changed relationships, system failure, shame, guilt, erosion of social support, miscarriage of justice, and prosecution of claimant.

There are serious consequences to making a false statement of rape. In some states, a proven false allegation can result in the claimant being charged with "abuse of process", the conviction of which may lead to fines and incarceration.

Classification of Unfounded Rape Cases

Prosecutors and investigators find the term *false allegation* of little use unless the claimant says in some way that the account is untrue. It is more common to use general terms such as unfounded, refusal to prosecute, and the like. These categories allow law enforcement to close cases without completing the investigations. Cases of false allegation are included in these categories. Some jurisdictions have reported that 35 to 40% of all cases are relegated to this disposition. This is one way in which rates of false allegation have been inflated and misrepresented. It may be reported that false allegations of rape occur at the rate of 30%, for example, when what is really meant is that 30% of cases are "unfounded".

The following categories represent common reasons for "unfounding" a rape complaint. Careful classification by police departments would be a beginning in determining how rape complaints are categorized and whether or not the FBI Uniform Crime Reports of a 50% clearance rate nationwide for rape cases is accurate.

Three of the categories represent a determination based on the psychological evaluation of a victim; three of the classifications are determined through investigation.

Psychological Determination

Sex Stress Situations

Sex stress situations are cases where, as the story unfolds, the male and female initially agreed to have sexual relations but then something "went wrong". Usually, what went wrong was that a third party became aware of the situation and defined the situation as rape or caused the female to say it was rape as a way out of a dilemma. Also, in some of these sex stress cases, the person who referred to the problem as rape in reality wanted some service from the hospital and felt she could not directly ask for it. For example, a young teenager, having had sex the evening before, may be frightened of becoming pregnant and needs medication to prevent pregnancy (Burgess and Holmstrom, 1974).

It is important to understand sex stress cases for several reasons. First, they greatly influence how the system deals with rape. Staff members tend to become obsessed with trying to determine whether a case is rape. A tremendous amount of energy goes into this "diagnosing" rather than helping the victim with her request for aid. Second, sex stress cases deserve counseling in their own right. These women are victims in their own way and have many emotional concerns over what to them has been an upsetting experience.

The two main types of sex stress cases the authors identified are (1) mutual agreement and (2) financial gain.

In one type of mutual agreement case, both parties agree to have sex but then one person wishes to deny the act or becomes repulsed by her behavior. The following case illustrates true setting, true act, and false perpetrator.

Case No. 1

Roberta, a 27-year-old civilian employee of a state police department, made a report of rape. She disclosed the alleged rape to a male co-worker. Roberta told a very detailed and complex story. She reported that when she was walking to her car from a disco club, a known male, a police sergeant, jumped out from behind a car and grabbed her from behind. He forced her into a van and ripped her clothes off. When she refused to spread her legs he cut her thighs repeatedly (all cuts were superficial and within the reach of the victim). He also slashed at her breasts. As she gave this account, she showed her co-worker the injuries. She said the assailant succeeded in having vaginal sexual intercourse with her.

A formal complaint was made to internal affairs, which initiated a full investigation. The officer in question was suspended from duty. After the initial disclosure to the co-worker, Roberta became markedly uncooperative and resistant to investigative efforts. She refused to submit material evidence and refused the polygraph test. Eventually she did turn in her dress which was liberally stained with semen.

The investigating police officer sought consultation regarding the possibility of this being a false rape allegation for two reasons. First, the alleged assailant was outraged, categorically denying everything, and readily agreed to forensic evaluation and a polygraph test. Second, concurrent to this complaint was a highly publicized rape case involving a police officer who was eventually convicted of raping a woman he had stopped for a motor violation. Consultation supported the investigating officer's suspicions and suggestions for proactive interviewing techniques were made.

Roberta, on re-interview, admitted to having made a false allegation. She admitted to repeated sexual intercourse with a male previously unknown to her whom she had picked up at the disco; the acts were all consensual. When she awoke the next morning she felt "dirty". Additionally, she had overslept and was consequently late for work. She then inflicted the mutilating injuries on herself and fabricated her story. The falsely accused officer was a believable suspect because he had shown considerable interest in Roberta at work. Fortunately for Roberta, no charges were brought against her. She was referred for counseling and remains in therapy.

In another type of sex stress mutual agreement case, the woman agrees to have sex and the male becomes violent or perverted and frightens the woman. Sex was agreed upon, but the setting and/or acts cause the victim to seek protective assistance through the police.

A third type of mutual agreement is where parental intervention occurs. A parent may suspect sex occurred and perceives some danger to the daughter's reputation and assumes responsibility in the matter; or the teenager reports the sex to the parent as rape in order to get pregnancy prevention advice. The following is such a case where the setting and perpetrator were false and the act was true.

Case No 2

Samantha was a pretty 15-year-old girl. She came home well past her curfew on a Friday night. She tearfully and reluctantly told her parents that she had gone to the skating rink with her friends. At closing time, she and her friends left the building to walk home. According to Samantha, a young man who worked at the rink called her aside and offered to drive her home. She said she accepted his offer and went with him to his car. Samantha reported that he drove to a deserted area and forced her to have intercourse with him. The parents immediately contacted the local police (they lived in a small town in the South). Samantha and her parents were brought to the regional rape crisis center by the local police. The nurse was summoned. She completed the examination and evidence collection without incident.

The case was evaluated as being a possible sex stress situation. A female supervising officer conducted a second interview. At this time, Samantha retracted her allegation, stating that she had consensual sex with her boyfriend and was late coming home. Because of her fear of punishment from her parents, she created the fiction.

In sex stress cases involving a money motive, prostitutes may encounter a situation in which the customer does not live up to the contract. The customer may persevere, become violent, rob her or him, or not pay for services obtained. As a result, prostitutes often feel they are in danger and, as a result, sometimes turn to police for protection. The police, in turn, bring the woman to the hospital for medical attention.

False Rape Allegation

In false rape allegations, all three components of an allegation are false, e.g., the act, the perpetrator, and the setting. These are situations where the complainant is motivated to deceive by psychological needs for attention, or by financial motives. The complainant has conscious understanding that the complaint is false.

In the following false rape allegation case the act was false but the setting and perpetrator were true.

Case No. 3

Julie, a 16 year old, presented at the trauma center having been severely beaten in the head and face. She reported being abducted from the street in her neighborhood by an unknown male. She reported that he dragged her into a park and repeatedly raped her vaginally and orally. He kept her in his apartment for 2 days. When the forensic nurse arrived at the trauma unit, the staff nurses asked repeatedly whether she really had been raped. Thinking this to be strange, the forensic nurse inquired further into their concerns. The staff nurses reported that Julie's mother had called several times saying that Julie deserved a good beating, as she had been missing from the home for 5 days.

The examination revealed no vaginal trauma. Microscopic examination of a slide prepared from vaginal secretions revealed no sperm. When confronted with the discrepancy between mother's report of her being missing 5 days and her statement of 2 days, Julie changed her story. She actually knew her assailant; in fact, she had had consensual sex with him several months before the alleged rape. She further admitted that there had been no rape nor even sex, but that he had beaten her as she had previously reported.

The following case illustrates false act, false perpetrator, and false setting. The motive was financial.

Case No. 4

Dorina was a single mother living in public housing. She brought her two young girls to the rape crisis center for evaluation following allegations of child molestation. No physical evidence of the allegation was found in either child. The child advocate informed her of "victim's compensation". Under this provision, victims of violent crime may apply to the state for compensation in amounts up to $3000. The only requirement is that a police report be filed. Dorina was awarded $2000 for each child. Approximately 6 months later, Dorina presented at the center stating that two unknown males had broken into her home, raped her, and left. She was unable to provide any usable description, and neither trauma nor physical evidence was found. She was again advised of the availability of victim's compensation. She made application and was compensated in the amount of $3000.

Approximately 18 months later Dorina again reported a rape to the police. She was taken to the rape crisis center where she was again evaluated. As before, she was unable to describe adequately her assailant, and again neither trauma nor evidence was found. Under the provisions of the victim's compensation program, compensation can only be awarded one time per individual. Several months after the second assault, Dorina brought suit against the city public housing authority seeking punitive damages in the amount of $150,000. Her claim was that both criminal assaults occurred because of a faulty lock on her door. She claimed to have made a formal report requesting appropriate repair. No record of such a report was ever found. The determination is that all of the allegations made by Dorina were false and motivated financially.

The following false rape allegation case is a false act, false setting, and false perpetrator with a financial motive.

Case No. 5

Micaela, a teenage single mother, was brought to the rape crisis center by a police officer. She claimed to have been abducted from the street in her neighborhood by an unknown assailant who dragged her into a vacant house and forced her to have vaginal sex. During this commentary, she mentioned several times that the assailant had stolen her food stamps. She seemed more concerned about the food stamps than about the rape. Micaela was unable to give an meaningful description of the assailant. Although she had reported the crime promptly, neither trauma nor physical evidence was identified.

While Micaela was dressing, the nurse asked the police officer if he knew about the theft of the food stamps. He said that had been her primary concern since she first had made the complaint. He went on to say that there was a lively black market in food stamps for drugs. The officer explained that lost or stolen public subsidies can only be replaced if a police report is made.

After several attempts to complete the investigation, the case was designated as unfounded. The police were of the opinion that it was a false allegation made to obtain additional food stamps.

Delusional Rape Allegation

In delusional rape allegations, all three components of an allegation are false (the act, the perpetrator, and the setting). These are situations where the complainant is psychotic and/or delusional. The complainant may not be consciously aware of the multiplicity of complaints being made as the delusion is a continuous part of his or her thinking. It is important to carefully evaluate the complaint since it will be obvious that the person is suffering major mental illness. There may be an ongoing abuse situation that the person is trying to communicate. The problem is that it becomes repetitious in nature and represents a chronic ongoing unresolved trauma, as in the following case.

Case No. 6

Ann, a 37-year-old white, homeless woman, was admitted to a large, busy emergency department for the sixth time in a 3-month period reporting she had been sexually assaulted. She had dirt and leaves in her vagina, superficial cuts and scratches on her inner thighs, and a vague description of the man who raped her, stating he had been stalking her for a while. When the nurse examiner came into the examining room, Ann cried and reached for her hand saying she just wanted to talk to someone who understood and cared. While waiting to be seen by the nurse, Ann was angry and volatile with severe mood shifts and little control over her anger.

Ann claimed six times that this man had stalked and raped her. The nurse examiner's assessment was that Ann was probably an incest victim who had not dealt with and resolved her incest issues. Her reports of rape were seen as a cry for help for the incest she could not yet address. The goal was to get Ann into counseling where, over time, the incest or childhood abuse issues could be discussed (Ledray, 1994).

Investigator Determination

Problematic Life Style

These are situations where there is a determination that attributes of a person will be perceived negatively by juries. Lifestyle stereotypes may be of sexual preference or work, as with a prostitute. The person may have a long history of alcoholism or mental illness, or the behavior may be perceived as negatively influencing the credibility of the person. For various reasons, the decision is made not to move forward with the case.

Insufficient Evidence

Law enforcement and prosecutors may close an investigation because of insufficient evidence or lack of corroborative evidence. The complainant may have been unable to supply adequate information as to the assailant's physical description, or there is no workable description of an assailant. A delayed report may also account for minimal evidence.

There may be no collaborative evidence. The complainant states the assailant ejaculated or injured her and there is no collaborating forensic evidence. The forensic examination does not match the person's statement.

Nol Pros

Nol pros comes from the Latin term "nolle prosequi". *Black's Law Dictionary* defines nol pros as a formal entry upon the record by a prosecuting officer in a criminal action by which it is stated he will not prosecute the case any further.

The victim may not be able to be found. She may have moved without a forwarding address. There may be a host of other reasons which impede or prevent completion of the investigation.

Victim Drops Charges

Often the victim drops charges when the assailant is an acquaintance or known. She does not want the consequences of following through with the case to court. Sometimes the victim does not want to go through a lengthy trial, wanting to move on with her life. The victim may refuse to testify and charges are dropped. Dropping of charges does not mean it was a false allegation.

The Psychology of False Rape Allegations*

Those who make false allegations may have legitimate problems worthy of attention in their own right. Yet if their false allegations are accepted at face value (rather than as symptoms of psychological needs), the actual problems may go untreated and can result in future difficulties. It goes without saying that a false allegation, especially when it is based on malice, can result in grievous injustice. Only by understanding the psychology of those making false allegations can investigators hope to increase the possibility of convicting rapists, while at the same time giving needed assistance and protection to everyone involved.

Need for Attention

While there are several reasons for a person to falsely claim to have been raped, one motive is a need for attention. Persons making false complaints for this reason usually have overwhelming feelings of inadequacy. They desperately want and need attention, usually in the form of concern and support. In their suffering, a claim of rape may seem a likely method to force a favorable response from friends and relatives as well as the authorities. Besides, they have probably tried a number of lesser methods of getting attention, and these have failed. Although false reports for this reason are relatively rare, it is important for the investigator to be aware

* This section through the end of the chapter was written by Charles P. McDowell, D.ED. and Neil S. Hibler, Ph.D. and is recopied with permission from the 1st edition of *Practical Aspects of Rape Investigation*, Elsevier Publishers.

of the possibility. The most significant fact in these cases is their reaction to the concern and support exhibited by friends, relatives, and the criminal justice community. In most rapes, even the most compassionate and supportive response from all concerned cannot fully alleviate the horror experienced by the victim. However, for the person desperately seeking attention this solicitude may very well fill her/his needs.

Self-Esteem

Perhaps the central feature of human personality is the concept of self-image. How one views oneself colors one's vision of the rest of the world. As Schlenker (1980) has noted, "One's self-concept and social identity are composed of numerous interrelated images of oneself; each image is discrete yet part of the whole".

Since a positive self-image is desirable, people strive for a sense of self-esteem, a belief in their own worthiness. As a developmental process, self-esteem in a person must first be created and then maintained. A set of values, beliefs, and expectations becomes internalized and is then reinforced through the approval and acceptance the person gains from others by living up to those values and expectations. The "others" from whom the person seeks external approval consist of his or her parents, friends, co-workers, and others whom the person respects and admires (and whose respect and admiration he or she values). Self-esteem is maintained by behaving in ways that earn the approval of both the person's "external audience" and his/her own conscience. Unfortunately, life is not always fair or easy, nor are people perfect; people occasionally violate their own values as well as those of their role models, and in so doing threaten their sense of self-esteem. When this happens, the need to reestablish a satisfactory level of self-esteem results in one or more of a variety of corrective responses. Thus, when people do something that is in conflict with their values, either they can maturely accept responsibility for their act, they can protect their self-image by offering excuses to others (or themselves), or they can deny the act ever occurred. For people with highly internalized value systems, the reality of an act such as a casual sexual encounter can be so disturbing that the person may not be able to accept responsibility for it. When this happens the mind activates one or more of a number of possible defense mechanisms (Snyder et al., 1983).

Protecting Self-Esteem: The Use of Defense Mechanisms

Defense mechanisms are the methods the mind uses to protect its self-esteem. They do so by allowing the mind to selectively "forget" what happened, deny responsibility, project blame to someone (or something) else, overcompensate, or seek escape in a world of fantasy. These reactions most often occur spontaneously and are not usually a matter of conscious desire or awareness. Through their use the mind is given a way of not having to face a sense of failure or feelings of inadequacy, and thus they help to maintain a positive sense of personal worth. Defense mechanisms naturally change the person's perception of reality and encourage self-deception. Unfortunately, when used too often, the defense mechanisms not only do not solve the problem, but add another dimension to the original one. On rare occasions, activation of the right combination of defense mechanisms can result in a false claim of rape.

When a person using this system falsely claims to be the victim of a rape, the mind has literally created an alternative reality with the crime itself as the focal point. This effectively changes one's role from participant to innocent. In this way the false claim enables people to recover, at least in the short term, their self-esteem and, at the same time, avoid responsibility for their own unacceptable conduct. When a false allegation is made in an effort to preserve the person's self-esteem, the following defense mechanisms are usually involved.

Denial. At the very core of the false allegation is the denial of responsibility. A key to understanding false allegations therefore lies in understanding what really threatens the victim. This usually revolves around the person's internalized beliefs about his or her own courage, integrity, honesty, competence, loyalty, decency, and so on. When a person engages in acts that are so much in violation of his values that they threaten to destroy his entire system of beliefs about himself, the mind can choose to protect itself by denying the person's consensual participation.

Projection. Denial works best if it is accompanied by projection. If the mind chooses to deny responsibility for some act or failure, blame must be placed elsewhere. Through the use of a false allegation of rape, the responsibility and control is shifted to another person, someone whose actions were beyond the victim's ability to control. Thus, responsibility is "projected" or displaced to the criminal.

Escape. Denial is closely associated with escape. By denying responsibility, the mind seeks to escape accountability for actions that are unacceptable to it. By claiming to be the victim of rape, one shifts corrective responsibility to the police. Furthermore, if the "crime" cannot be solved, then the ultimate responsibility for failure lies with the police rather than the victim. The result is that the false claim allows the mind to "escape" the responsibility for the behavior and thus to maintain a positive self-image.

Rationalization. For a false allegation to be credible, it must be logical and believable. This requires the construction of a story that "explains" the crime. Rationalization is the mind's ability to find justification for something the person has done or plans to do; it provides the superego with a logical reason that absolves the actor of blame and makes the action appear reasonable under the circumstances. The vulnerability of this manipulation lies in the fact that a person who falsely claims to have been raped may have no understanding of what it really means to be a victim of rape. As a result, the report is based on what she believes happens in a rape situation. Imperfect understanding of rape is often transparent and thus provides valuable clues to experienced investigators who are seeking to provide effective support for the person while taking the complaint.

Self-Handicapping (Secondary Gain). In self-handicapping, the mind creates a situation in which the person is in some way injured or at a disadvantage, in such a manner as to allow the person to evade responsibility. The result is that being injured or sick is actually advantageous. The effect of the deception can be more potent and effective than their own interpersonal skills (Snyder et al., 1983). For example, the person who claims inability to meet some obligation because of illness defers responsibility to a circumstance over which there is no control. To be effective, the handicap must, of course, appear to be beyond the person's control, but must eventually result in his or her favor. In a false claim of criminal victimization, it is automatically implied that the claimant is at a disadvantage by virtue of being harmed. Their innocence (lack of responsibility) is assumed because of the presumed actions of others who exploited them. In some cases, the mind may further defend itself by indicating that circumstances such as being lost, intoxicated, frightened, or confused further reduced the person's normal ability to avoid victimization. By claiming to be the victim of a crime, the person is thus able to derive support, care, and a degree of social control from a situation that was "beyond his or her control".

False Allegations and the Adaptation Continuum

The creation of a fictitious crime to avoid personal responsibility for some act or failure obviously represents an extreme departure from the way mature people normally deal with problems. The extent to which false claims capitalize on actual events is unknown. However, there appears to be a rough continuum of inaccurate claims, ranging from a slightly distorted report of an actual event to the completely false report of an assault or rape. In its most extreme manifestation, the report can include bizarre scenarios supported by self-inflicted injuries and even self-mutilation. There have actually been incidents in which elaborate props, such as threatening letters or even messages written in blood, were used. Cases such as this at the far end of the continuum are extremely rare. Fictitious claims of criminal victimization at the more "normal" end of the continuum may be more frequent.

While the pathology involved in self-mutilation to support the false claim of rape is extremely rare, fictitious claims of illness or injury on a much lower level are a well-recognized phenomenon in medical literature.

Severe cases of self-inflicted injuries or illnesses in which medical attention is sought have been termed "Munchausen's syndrome" (Asher, 1951). The name derives from the central figure in a book of tall tales and fabulous adventures who was named after Hieronymus Karl Friederich, Freiherr von Munchausen, a retired soldier known for his generosity and graphic conversations that took the form of the "serious narration of palpable absurdities". The key to understanding Munchausen's syndrome lies in awareness that the patient is trying to use hospitals and clinicians in the service of pathologic psychological needs under the guise of seeking medical treatment for an ostensibly legitimate illness.

Munchausen's syndrome is based on a preoccupation with manipulation. These patients appear to be compulsively driven to make their complaints. As Gawn (1955) has noted, "While he is aware he is acting an illness,... he cannot stop the act". Therefore, reports may capitalize on circumstances and occur only occasionally, or they may be a well-developed means of adapting and part of an extensive history. The degree to which Munchausen's patients defend their claims is in direct proportion to their need to be seen as victims. Dramatic, extreme cases are not likely to confess to the hoax, and those who present such cases are prone to become enraged at the suggestion that their illnesses are anything but genuine (Nadelson, 1979; Pankratz, 1981).

In much the same way that Munchausen patients manipulate hospitals and doctors, a fraudulent claim of rape might be interpreted as a form of manipulation directed at the criminal justice system. This kind of manipulation is conceptually similar to other kinds of behavior (malingering, hysterical conversion reactions, and self-mutilation) that are well documented as medically achieved coping mechanisms (Ford, 1973). In Munchausen patients there is also a continuum, ranging from exaggerated claims of infirmity to actual self-induced illness (Grinker, 1961). At the extreme end of this continuum, life-threatening injuries are masqueraded as being legitimately contracted (Carney, 1980; Carney and Brown, 1983). Even child abuse, disguised as natural illness, is suspected of being an underrecognized means of gaining attention (Hodge et al., 1982; Kurlandsky et al., 1979; Meadow, 1982; Waller, 1983; Vaisrub, 1978).

Although police officers and investigators are used to seeing people who have been harmed or injured by others, they are less accustomed to seeing those who have harmed themselves. Most such instances involve a suicide or attempted suicide. However, since self-inflicted injuries used to support a claim of rape or assault are rare, it is "logical" for police to accept them at face value, at least initially. Where self-inflicted injuries are recognized as such and either are serious or appear to be very painful, it is understandable that police officers may look upon the victim as being mentally ill; yet, even those who reinforce their claims with severe self-inflicted injuries are seldom insane. Nevertheless, these people are psychiatrically impaired and should be helped in getting professional help. The following case illustrates this phenomenon.

Case No. 7

A 25-year-old housewife reported receiving obscene phone calls and threatening letters that were made out of words cut from magazines and newspapers and pasted on a blank sheet. A short while later, she reported being raped by an unidentified intruder who threatened to come back and kill her in a particularly brutal manner if she reported the rape to the authorities. She had numerous bruises and a bite mark on her left breast. During the course of a subsequent polygraph examination she admitted to fabricating the entire series of events. She also inflicted rope burns on her hands, bit her own breast, and ran face-first into a support post in her basement in order to acquire the injuries she thought would support her claim of rape. She said her husband did not understand her or pay attention to her, and she wanted to "test his love".

As one proceeds along the continuum, the amount of violence the person claims was used against her can reach fantastic levels, and the presenting dynamics of the case can become increasingly extraordinary. Keep in mind, however, that legitimate rapes may also incorporate varying levels of misperception. Because of this, every aspect must be scrutinized. For example, physical evidence and patterns of injury are always vital aspects in rape cases, and they require their own careful analysis. Appropriate support and assistance can only be given by a careful objective examination of both the information and the physical evidence available.

This woman's self-esteem had been eroded over time by her insensitive and uncaring husband. By claiming to be the recipient of obscene phone calls and letters, and by claiming to have been raped, she was effectively making a desperate statement of her worth, both as a person and as a sexually desirable partner. Her willingness to engage in self-injurious behavior to support her claim underscores the seriousness of her emotional problems.

Red Flags of False Rape Allegations

There is, of course, no simple way to determine the legitimacy of any criminal complaint. This is true whether the report concerns a rape, a burglary, or any other offense. All complaints must, of necessity, be taken at face value and, unless there is some specific reason to believe otherwise, handled accordingly. False criminal reports are relatively common in law enforcement. It is well known that victims frequently exaggerate the value of items taken in burglaries, and robberies are occasionally reported to explain the absence of money and other valuables to the victim's family. In most instances, it is impossible to determine whether the crime actually occurred unless the victim is moved to admit that the report was false. However, as in the false burglary or robbery complaint, certain characteristics are found with greater frequency in false rape reports than in actual rape cases. In and of themselves, none of these characteristics are significant, but taken together, they indicate a possibility that the facts may be different from those reported.

The key to any successful criminal investigation is knowing what to look for and how to construct a logical sequence of the investigative steps (Kirk, 1974; O'Hara, 1977). If at some point in a rape investigation the allegation itself becomes suspect, immediate efforts should be made to resolve this question. Both the potential for false imprisonment and the need for objectivity demand this. To continue to work a case when the truthfulness of the victim is suspect will invariably result in a poor investigation and reduced cooperation, both then and in the future.

It is extremely important to remember that no single element is significant; it is only the combination of factors that may suggest the possibility that an allegation may be exaggerated or false.

The Initial Complaint

The manner in which a rape allegation comes to the attention of law enforcement authorities is significant. In our experience, the filing of a false report is usually somewhat delayed. Several other variables are also frequently associated with the filing of false complaints:

- Complaint is usually first made to friends, associates, or medical authorities along with requests for tests for pregnancy or venereal disease.
- Complainant is indifferent to apparent injuries.

Nature of Allegation

The concept of rape is deceptively simple, and women who make false allegations often structure their complaints in a fashion that seems to meet the "requirements" of rape but ignore its reality. False allegations, therefore, often contain less common elements, such as:

- Complainant states she cannot describe her assailant because she kept her eyes closed.
- Complainant alleges she was assaulted by more than one person, but cannot offer descriptions.
- Complainant claims she offered vigorous resistance but was forcibly overcome.
- Assailant was a total stranger or a person whom she can only describe in vague and nonspecific terms.
- Complainant claims she received threatening notes or phone calls before or after the assault.
- Complainant was unable to describe details and sequence of the sexual activities to which she was subjected.

Evidence

Law enforcement authorities correctly place a premium on the evidence supporting an allegation, because it often provides information needed to prosecute the case. Because of the nature of a rape case, evidence is particularly important. Moreover, the consistency or inconsistency of the evidence may suggest that a rape complaint has been exaggerated or is completely false. An absence of the kind of evidence usually associated with rapes can sometimes be as revealing in identifying false allegations as its presence is in establishing that a rape has taken place. Some of the types of evidence that appear to suggest a false allegation are:

- Complainant cannot recall where the crime took place even though she does not report being blindfolded, under influence of drugs or alcohol, or moved from location to location.
- Crime scene does not support story (i.e., ground cover not disturbed; no footprints where there should be; no signs of struggle when they should logically be present).
- Damage to her clothing is inconsistent with any injuries she reports (i.e., cuts or scratches inconsistent with tears or cuts in clothing).

- Complainant presents cut-and-paste letters allegedly from the rapist in which death or rape threats are made. Note or letter is identifiable with pseudovictim (via handwriting analysis, indented writing, typewriter comparison, paper stock, or fingerprint comparison).
- Confirming laboratory findings are absent.

Injuries

The nature of the person's injuries can yield a great deal of information about what did or did not happen. Women who make false rape allegations and try to support them with injuries tend to present a consistent picture in terms of the cues suggested below:

- Injuries were made either by fingernails or by sharp instruments usually not found at the scene. Fingernail scrapings of victim reveal her own skin tissue.
- Injuries are extensive, but do not involve sensitive tissues (i.e., lips, nipples, genitals, etc.).
- Complainant reports seemingly painful injuries with an air of indifference.
- Complainant's statement states wounds were incurred while she tried to protect herself, yet the location and angle of injury are inconsistent with defense wounds.
- Practice or hesitation marks are present (sometimes appear as older marks, indicating earlier attempt or rehearsals).

Personality and Life-Style Considerations

In false rape allegations, extensive and important information on the complainant is often available. In general, this information suggests that the pseudovictim has experienced numerous personal problems and that her ability to cope is seriously impaired. For example, in temporal sequence, the "rape" follows one or more escalating incidents revealing difficulties in her personal relationships.

- Complainant has history of mental or emotional problems (particularly referencing self-injurious behavior, with hysterical or borderline features).
- Complainant has previous record of having been assaulted or raped under similar circumstances.
- Allegation was made after a similar crime received publicity (suggesting modeling or "copycat" motive in which the similarity to the publicized crime offers credibility).
- Complainant has extensive record of medical care for dramatic illnesses or injuries.
- Friends or associates report that the complainant's postassaultive behavior and activities were inconsistent with her allegation.

- Complainant becomes outraged when asked to corroborate her victimization.
- Complainant tries to steer the interview into "safe" topics or those that tend to engender sympathy.

A Second Opinion

A second opinion, through the use of a second interviewer, is an important strategy when a false rape allegation is suspected. Another investigator should be used only when there are serious questions concerning the truth of the report. Confronting a person suspected of making a false complaint is always a difficult matter. The critical issue is that if the doubts are incorrect, this would greatly compound the victim's trauma. Such a confrontation will also undoubtedly destroy any relationship that may have been developed between the victim and the investigator. One way to handle this challenge to the victim's credibility without sacrificing the investigator's rapport with the victim is to introduce a second party, a person who can act as a buffer. The principal investigator needs to be available to the person alleging rape and should maintain a nonjudgmental, supportive, and sympathetic relationship with her. It would be counterproductive for this person to voice any doubts as to the veracity of her report. Issues regarding unresolved inconsistencies, conflicts, or the lack of supporting data should be made by an investigative supervisor or co-worker. In this way, the vital relationship between the complainant and the principal investigator can be maintained and perhaps even improved.

The supervisor's style of confrontation should also be supportive, however, since false allegations are usually desperate attempts to protect self-esteem. Any harsh challenges to the person's credibility will increase her defensiveness. It is often effective to simply present doubts to the victim in a way that makes it clear they are based on the information she herself has provided. This decreases personal conflict while conveying an impression that investigators have been thorough and objective. It also allows for adjusting investigative hypotheses and gives the victim an opportunity to provide additional information without having to place herself in a psychologically threatening position.

The reaction of fictitious victims to this approach varies. At the low end of the adaptation continuum there is usually an emotional confession, mixed with both despair and relief. The amount of energy required to maintain her story is exhausting, and this becomes a time for her to cooperate and to seek solace. Exaggerators and malingerers often provide great detail as to how and why they masqueraded as a rape victim. For those who adhere to their statements in the face of overwhelming contradictory evidence, it may be advantageous to request they take a polygraph examination.

At the extreme upper end of the adaptation continuum, the complainant's distortions will have been internalized and for her own well-being she will need to believe what she is saying because she is unconsciously terrified of losing control.

Consequently, her denial will be intensified no matter how the confrontation is handled. Predictably, she will react with outrage. If the family is told of the findings, they may be of great help in her eventual recovery. Unfortunately, because of the disordered life of such people, they are often estranged from their families.

Summary

False accusation is a term frequently used and heard in discussions of interpersonal crime. Though simple on the surface, this concept becomes vague and complex under scrutiny. This chapter explores and explicates the concept of false allegation in the context of rape, which usually occurs in isolated places where there is no one to support or refute a person's claims.

False allegations of rape are occasionally unrecognized by investigators and are almost totally neglected in the literature. The reason for this is obvious. These are acts that are designed to appear plausible. The key to understanding false allegations lies in determining how a false allegation "helps" the complainant manipulate, control, or mentally recoup her self-esteem. Therefore, it is the context in which the allegation occurs that provides the framework for understanding the dynamics of the problem. A final word of caution: it must be remembered that even those who are emotionally prone to make a false allegation can be raped. Basic principles of police professionalism require that officers who investigate rapes remain objective and compassionate. If they do not, the veracity of the allegation may never be known, and the victim, for she is a victim in either case, may never receive the help and support she needs.

Acknowledgments

The authors thank the following for contributing case examples: Eddie Grant, David Muram, M.D., Robin Jones, Patricia Speck, and Nola Mendenhall.

References

Aiken, M.M., False allegation, *J. Psychosoc. Nursing*, 31(11), 16, 1993.
Asher, R., Munchausen's syndrome, *Lancet*, p. 339, 1951.
Benedek, E. and Schetky, D., Allegations of sexual abuse in child custody cases, paper presented at the Annu. Meet. American Academy of Psychiatry and the Law, Nassau, Bahamas, October 1984.
Black, H., *Black's Law Dictionary*, 4th ed., West Publishing, St. Paul, MN, 1968.
Brant, R. and Sink, F., Dilemmas in court-ordered evaluation of sexual abuse in child custody cases, paper presented at the Annu. Meet. American Academy of Child Psychiatry, Toronto, Canada, October 12, 1984.
Burgess, A.W. and Holmstrom, L.L., Sex stress situation, in *Rape: Victims of Crisis*, Brady, Bowie, MD, 1974.
Burt, M.R., Cultural myths and supports for rape, *J. Pers. Soc. Psychol.*, 38, 215, 1980.
Carney, M. W. P., Artifactual illnesses to attract medical attention, *Br. J. Psychiatry*, 136, 542, 1980.

Carney, M. W. P. and Brown, J. P., Clinical features and motives among 42 artifactual illness patients, *Br. J. Med. Psychol.*, 56, 57, 1983.

Fuller, K., Is the child victim of sexual abuse telling the truth?, *Child Abuse Neglect*, 8, 473, 1984.

Ford, C. V., The Munchausen syndrome: a report of four new cases and a review of psychodynamic considerations, *Psychiatry Med.*, 4(1), 31, 1973.

Gawn, R. A. and Kauffmann, E. A., Munchausen syndrome. *Br. Med. J.*, 2, 1068, 1955.

Goodwin, J., Sahd, D., and Rada, R., Incest hoax: false accusations, false denials, *Bull. Am. Acad. Psychiatry Law*, 5(3), 296, 1978.

Green, A., True and false allegations of sexual abuse in child custody disputes, *J. Am. Acad. Child Psychiatry*, 25(4), 449, 1986.

Grinker, R. R., Imposture as a form of mastery, *Arch. Gen. Psychiatry*, 5, 53, 1961.

Guralnik, D., Ed., *Webster's New World Dictionary of the American Language*, Warner Books, New York, 1984.

Haddy, R. I., Weber, R. M., and Joglekar, A. S., Munchausen's syndrome, *Am. Fam. Physician*, 27(2), 193, 1983.

Hodge, D., Schwartz, W., Sargent, J., Bodurtha, J., and Starr, S., The bacteriologically battered body: another case of Munchausen by proxy, *Ann. Emergency Med.*, 4, 205, 1982.

Katz, S. and Mazur, M., *Understanding the Rape Victim*, John Wiley & Sons, New York, 1979.

Kilpatrick D.G., Veronen, L.J., and Best, C.L., Factors predicting psychological distress among rape victims, in *Post-Traumatic Therapy and Victims of Violence*, Brunner/Mazel, New York, 1985, 113.

Kirk, P. O., *Crime Investigation*, 2nd ed., Wiley, New York, 1974.

Kurlandsky, L., Lukoff, J. Y., Zinkman, W. H., Brody, J. P., and Kessler, R. W., Munchausen syndrome by proxy: definitions of factitious bleeding in an infant by Cr labeling of erythrocytes, *Pediatrics*, 63(2), 228, 1979.

Ledray, L.E., Rape or self-injury?, *J. Emergency Nursing*, 20(2), 88, 1994.

Lefer, H., Women and the truth: who says we're lying? *Elle*, p. 194, September 1992.

McDowell, C. and Hibler, N., False allegations, in *Practical Aspects of Rape Investigations: A Multidisciplinary Approach*, Hazelwood, R. and Burgess, A., Eds., New York, 1987, 275.

McDowell, C., Rape Allegation Checklist, North Carolina Justice Institute, 1990.

McDowell, C., "False alligators" and fuzzy data: a new look at crime analysis, *Police Chief*, p. 44, March 1990.

Meadow, R., Munchausen syndrome by proxy, *Arch. Dis. Child.*, 57, 92, 1982.

Meadow, R., Munchausen syndrome by proxy, *Lancet*, 8033(2), 343, 1977.

Nadelson, T., The Munchausen spectrum: borderline character features, *Gen. Hosp. Psychiatry*, 1(1), 11, 1979.

O'Hara, C. E., *Fundamentals of Criminal Investigation*, 4th ed., Charles C. Thomas, Springfield, IL, 1977.

Panken, S., *The Joy of Suffering*, Jason Aronson, New York, 1983.

Pankratz, L., A review of the Munchausen syndrome, *Clin. Psychol. Rev.*, 1, 65, 1981.

Peters, J., Children who are victims of sexual assault and the psychology of offenders, *Am. J. Psychother.*, 30, 398, 1976.

Riger, S. and Gordon, M.T., The impact of crime on urban women, in *Rape and Sexual Assault*, Vol. 2., Burgess, A. W., Ed., New York, 1988.

Rodgers, B., Concepts, analysis and the development of nursing knowledge: the evolutionary cycle, *J. Adv. Nursing*, 14, 330, 1989.

Rosenfeld, A., Nadelson, C., and Krieger, M., Fantasy and reality in patients' reports of incest, *J. Clin. Psychiatry*, p. 159, April 1979.

Schlenker, B. R., *Impression Management: The Self-Concept, Social Identity, and Interpersonal Relations*, Brooks/Cole, Monterey, CA, 1980.

Snyder, C. R., Higgins, R. L., and Stucky, R. J., *Excuses: Masquerades in Search of Grace*, John Wiley & Sons, New York, 1983.

Vaisrub, S., Baron Munchausen and the abused child, *J.A.M.A.*, 239(8), 752, 1978.

Walker, L. and Avant, K., *Strategies for Theory Construction in Nursing*, Appleton-Century-Crofts, Norwalk, CT, 1983.

Waller, D. A., Obstacles to the treatment of Munchausen by proxy syndrome, *J. Am. Acad. Child Psychiatry*, 22(1), 80, 1983.

Woolf, H., *Webster's New Collegiate Dictionary*, G. & C. Merriam, Springfield, MA, 1980.

Rape Investigators: Vicarious Victims

14

JAMES T. REESE

Rape investigators can and often do become vicarious victims — stressed, altered, and in some cases destroyed by the crimes they investigate. The job of the investigator pushes and pulls at him from many directions, forcing him to play the "hard nut" in one situation, then to move smoothly into the role of a sympathetic helper in the next. Often he will choose to ignore or repress the emotional concerns of role conflict, ambiguity, and stress caused by "shifting gears" into the various roles. When he does this, the conflicts within him can only intensify. He would do well to understand in broad terms why and how his job is stressful, and how to bring sensible coping strategies to bear on his problems.

The rape investigator's life is taxing for many reasons. In the course of his work, he sees the worst manifestations of human behavior — and consequently feels compelled to hide his professional life from his family for its own protection. Moreover, his work with victims of rape on a daily basis emotionally drains him; and he is emotionally strained by dealing regularly with emergencies. All such variables add up to stress, and stress produces (1) family problems, (2) unsystematic and often counterproductive defense mechanisms, and ultimately (3) burnout. If the investigator looks for the early warning signs of stress in himself, however, and learns some effective stress management techniques, he will be able to maintain his physical and mental health in spite of the demands of his profession.

Professional Demands

Rape investigators routinely see the worst manifestations of human behavior. They deal with molested children, sexual assault of the elderly, and defenseless, senseless beatings and murders, rape, and mutilated bodies. The sum total of these experiences can lead to depression, despair, and discouragement. At some point in time a sort of "hardening process" occurs, the method by which an officer can deal with all the human misery he sees. Reiser (1974) has referred to this process as the "John Wayne syndrome". This syndrome allows an officer to protect himself by becoming cynical, overly serious, cold, authoritarian, and emotionally withdrawn, especially from his family. Because he loves his family, he builds a protective "bubble" around them. He dares not tell them of the human suffering he has witnessed at work for fear they will become frightened. Yet his very attempt to protect his family often alienates him from it and leads to lack of communication.

0-8493-8152-1/95/$0.00+$.50
© 1995 by CRC Press, Inc.

Another difficult pressure on rape investigators stems from their constant exposure to victims of crime. The investigator must face their shocked relatives and friends, then deal with his own emotional response to the crime. If the victim is left alive, he must deal with her at the most traumatic time, the period immediately following the crime. Victims of rape and other violent crimes often are extremely emotional and draw on the officer's every resource to calm them. The investigator's own emotional reaction festers as he tries to comfort the victim, knowing his words matter little in light of what she has just undergone. Then he must face seeing the rapist in court wearing a three-piece suit and accompanied by his entire family, all of whom avow his innocence despite evidence to the contrary. When the sentence seems inadequate to the officer, as it often does (see Chapter 3), he must simply swallow his anger.

Although police officers are periodically killed in the line of duty, police psychologists say that the emotional dangers are far greater than the physical dangers. The fact is that police officers routinely respond to situations that would be emergencies to others (Wilson, 1968). Although statistically the chances of being killed in the line of duty may be slight, the *threat* of being killed takes a huge emotional toll.

For rape investigators, dealing with terrible situations, traumatized victims, and possibly the threat of physical danger can result in overwhelming stress; and it is this unusual amount of stress that explains the fact that police officers have unusually high rates of problem drinking, suicide, and divorce (Somodevilla, 1978).

Stress

Stress has been defined as "the nonspecific response of the body to any demand placed upon it" (Selye, 1974, p. 14). More simply, it is described as the wear and tear on the body caused by living — which correctly implies that to eliminate all stress one would have to die. Stressors — those stimuli that place demands on the body — force people to readjust or readapt constantly to new situations. Toffler (1970) estimated that man, historically, has faced these readjustments for 800 lifetimes since the beginning of human existence. Toffler, in fact, credits man's unique ability to adapt to change as the reason for human survival. Yet, while man continues to adapt, his rate of adaptation may not be fast enough to keep pace with modern times. Man's traditional response to the events of life has been "fight or flight". In the modern world, and particularly in the context of an investigator's profession, flight is not usually an option. With these reduced or frustrated options, a policeman's stress necessarily increases.

Police stress is universal. It has no geographical boundaries or political affiliations, and it is found wherever there are police officers functioning in their enforcement roles. In America, however, such stress may be heightened by the unusual violence found in some cities, which reportedly have more armed citizens than armed police officers.

The concern with police work is underlined in a survey conducted by the Training Division of the Federal Bureau of Investigation (FBI) on the training needs of state and local law enforcement agencies. The respondents represented, by sample, 90% of all sworn officers in the U.S., and the majority of these rated the category "handle personal stress" as the number one training priority (Phillips, 1984).

Stress and its consequent impact on the body and mind have long been explored in scientific and quasiscientific studies. More work needs to be done, however, on the specific relationship between stress and the day-to-day job of the police officer. How exactly does stress cause attitude and behavior changes, impair family and social relationships, and develop cynicism, apathy, and an unwillingness to seek help? These concerns will be explored here, together with the early warning signs of poor adaptation. Also, some techniques to combat poor adaptation will be outlined.

The Family

Rape investigators may hear from their spouses: "You're different". "You've changed". "You've become cold, callous, almost emotionless and unfeeling". "Whatever happened to the kind, considerate, patient, understanding person I used to know?". Experienced officers have almost certainly heard comments like these because their profession affects the way they live, impacts their emotions, and consequently affects their relationships with others, especially family members.

Family members thus need to be educated to identify the early warning signs of maladaptation to investigative stress, for they are in a position to see the changes in attitude as they occur. The hardened attitudes that officers develop to get through the workday will stand out dramatically as inappropriate at home (Reese, 1982b). First, family members should be aware of being deliberately excluded from the investigator's life as, for example, when the officer identifies himself primarily as a member of a closed law enforcement community and adopts the attitude "silence is security, sex is survival, keep your cool, and stay on top" (Bennett, 1978). Second, the spouse should take note if the officer has increasing difficulty in relating to members of the family or is less able to respond emotionally or talk about feelings. Third, the spouse should be on the lookout for the defense mechanisms discussed in the next section.

At the same time, because the integrity of the family is affected by stress on the officer, the investigator and his department should be educated in ways to prevent damaging it. Above all, the family members, including the officer, must be regarded as a whole unit or support system. All members use the family unit as a resource pool for support and strengthening, and a change in the status of any of them will alter the balance of the whole unit. Thus, to keep the officer a vital and healthy member of the law enforcement community, he must be maintained as a vital and healthy member of his family.

Defense Mechanisms

Defense mechanisms arise as a response to stress and become habits through use. As the officer begins to succumb to the stress of his job, he begins to perceive that the offenders are winning, that everything that is meaningful to him is slipping out of his reach, that his family is upset, and that he doesn't seem to care about the public he serves. On the basis of these perceptions, he alters his behavior and attitudes to make them less threatening. In other words, he adopts defense mechanisms.

Defense mechanisms, in fact, may be thought of as mental functions that protect a person from internal and/or external threats, conflicts, impulses, and hurts. They include isolation of affect, "sick" humor, displacement, substitution, repression, rationalization, and projection. While a person can attack, compromise, or withdraw on a conscious level, on an unconscious level he will use these defense mechanisms to protect the integrity of the self — that picture or image of self without which he cannot function.

The process by which defense mechanisms are developed hinges on the person's perception. For an event to be stressful, it must be perceived as such in the mind; and how one perceives a situation will largely dictate one's response. The mind goes through three basic steps when confronted with a problem. First, the problem is perceived; then an analysis is conducted; and, finally, a decision is made. The first step, perception, is a variable that can be manipulated and that, accordingly, can influence the remaining steps. One way to change perception is to adopt defense mechanisms.

Defense mechanisms were first identified by Sigmund Freud in 1894 in his study "The Neuro-Psychosis of Defense". Anna Freud later identified 10 defenses by name (1966), and by 1979 Laughlin had differentiated 22 major defenses, 26 minor defenses, and 3 special reactions and combinations. Of these, several are adopted most frequently by police officers.

Perhaps one of the most deceptive and, if uncontrolled, emotionally dangerous defenses used by officers is that of *isolation of affect*. Although extremely effective for the investigator while on the job, this defense is most responsible for domestic conflict, marital unhappiness, and divorce.

Isolation is in use when "an idea or object is divorced from its emotional connotation" (Laughlin, 1979, p. 476). Investigators see it in rapists who speak about their crimes expressionlessly. They see it in hospitals where doctors and nurses cope with rape victims with such detachment that they seem cold and indifferent; and they see it in themselves when they interview a victim and calmly order an investigation.

This altered perception of reality, this ability to view events less intensely, lets the officer appear in control at all times, live up to his image, and deny any emotional stake in the situation. At the same time, however, it necessarily carries over into his social roles as father, husband, and neighbor. The emotional divorcement that allows him to perform well on the job cuts his ties at home. He will hear: "Why are you always so detached from what you're doing?" "I can't seem to get through to you any more", or "You have no feelings!".

An adjunct to emotional isolation is grotesque humor — the kind that is not funny and is not meant to be. "Sick" humor works; it maintains an investigator's sanity because it acts as a safety valve and lessens the emotional impact of the crime. The officer, in effect, reaches out to others instead of sitting on his emotions. By speaking the unspeakable and being understood, he can vent his wounded feelings and share his pain.

Using such humor as a release, however, is usually very controlled. It is expressed only within earshot of fellow investigators who are directly involved, and only veterans can get away with it — as if they have paid their dues through the years, have no more emotions to invest, and have all but dried up their coping resources. Lazarus (1977) notes a similar defense mechanism among laboratory technicians at work on dissections.

So long as "sick" humor is tightly controlled by investigators, it performs a useful function. Once it finds its way out of the locker room, however, and into the public eye, it is a clear sign of maladaptation to stress.

Displacement is in operation when "an emotional feeling is transferred, deflected, and redirected from its internal object to a substitute external one. The emotion is thus displaced to a new person, situation, or object" (Laughlin, 1979, p. 86). Investigators often see this phenomenon in the course of their work, as when a rape victim will revile the police for not arriving in time; but officers are often not aware of using such a defense themselves — of taking their anger and job stress home and venting it on their spouses or children.

Displacement, in fact, is usually the defense most to blame for strife in the investigator's home. If the officer could recognize the symptoms, however, he could consciously use a more acceptable defense. "Displacement frequently, if not universally, operates in conjunction with *substitution* [a defense mechanism], through which an unacceptable or unobtainable goal, emotion, drive, attitude, impulse, interest, or need, which is consciously intolerable or repugnant, is replaced by a more acceptable one" (Laughlin, 1979, p. 402). In everyday life, substitution may be as simple as chopping wood to release hostility.

Repression has been referred to as the primary and most important ego (self) defense (Snyder, 1976, p. 186). Laughlin (1979) defines it as "the automatic, effortless, and involuntary assignment or relegation of consciously repugnant or intolerable ideas, impulses, and feelings to the unconscious" (p. 359). For example, a rape victim, when questioned by investigators, might not remember any details relating to the attack, even though the assailant was unmasked and the attack was in broad daylight. If the information is truly repressed, the victim will not be aware that she knows it, for her mind has protected itself by keeping this information out of her consciousness.

Although investigators may not use this defense themselves, they often see themselves victimized by it. Nothing is more trying to an investigator attempting to solve a crime than a victim (his best witness) who cannot recall a single thing.

Rationalization as defense is used when "the ego (self) justifies, or attempts to modify, otherwise unacceptable impulses, needs, feelings, behavior, and motives into ones that are consciously tolerable and acceptable" (Laughlin, 1979, p. 251). It is one of the most often used defense mechanisms. Officers rationalize why they became officers, why they work sex crimes, why rapes occur, and why they have become the type of people they are. Daily, investigators rationalize why they work long hours, spend long hours separated from their families, and even risk their lives. Too often these rationalizations are left unexamined and upset the lives of the very egos they are supposed to defend.

Finally, *projection* is a defense mechanism of major importance. Known as the defense of "blaming others", projection occurs when "consciously disowned aspects of self are rejected or disowned and thrown outward, to become imputed to others… a mirror-defense" (Laughlin, 1979, p. 221). Thus, people who are never neat will accuse others of being messy, and persons who swear will often be unduly offended when someone swears in their presence. In rape investigations, the investigators who can't seem to solve a crime will find it easier to blame their lack of success on someone or something than to face the fact that they may not be clever enough to sort out the evidence and conduct a proper and orderly investigation.

Defense mechanisms are used daily and productively by all people — so it's all right if readers have identified some of these defenses in their lives. However, these defenses can become counterproductive if they are habitually used to excess, for the wrong reason, or in the wrong place, and they can lead to burnout.

Burnout

The complexities of the tasks and the many demands, responsibilities, and deadlines placed on rape investigators force them to be on alert throughout the workday. They are expected to be constantly energetic, self-motivated, independent, and task-oriented, as well as strong team members (Reese, 1982a). When the officer cannot meet these expectations, when he no longer has energy or interest in his work, chances are he suffers from *burnout.*

Burnout is a common affliction of those employed in human services and is easier to observe than to define. Cherniss (1980, p. 16) defines it as "to fail, wear out, or become exhausted by making excessive demands on energy, strength, or resources". Unfortunately, such a definition pays little attention to the emotional and attitudinal effects of burnout. Burnout often includes psychological withdrawal from work in response to excessive stress or dissatisfaction; loss of enthusiasm, excitement, and a sense of mission in one's work (Cherniss, 1980), and a change in attitude from empathy to apathy (Edelwich, 1980). Burnout has been called a disease of overcommitment, which, ironically, causes a lack of commitment. Above all it is a coping technique as regards occupational stress and, as such, it uses defense mechanisms of projection, withdrawal, detachment, avoidance-oriented behavior, and lowering of goals.

"What's it all for?" "Why am I doing this?" "I hate to go to work". "I have nothing to offer anymore". Statements such as these are frequently made by victims of burnout. They are not adjusting or coping well. They remain in a state of disequilibrium and they strain to make it through each day. Studies have shown that burnout correlates with other damaging indices of human stress, such as alcoholism, mental illness, marital conflict, and suicide (Maslach, 1976).

The 1980s have seen an increased interest in the concept of burnout and in the supportive role peer counseling can play in an officer's career. "Employees who experience short-term crises need to be heard, need to have the opportunity to feel understood, and need to receive peer recognition of the extent of the problems they face" (Capp, 1984). Such counseling formalizes the locker-room sessions that are in force in most police departments, but it improves them by using time-tested professional skills.

Early Warning Signs

The numerous symptoms that may relate to stress disorders can be grouped in three categories: (1) emotional, (2) behavioral, and (3) physical. The number of symptoms a person may exhibit is not important, but rather the extent of changes noted from the person's normal condition. Furthermore, the combined presence of symptoms determines the potency of the problem. Indicators range from isolated reactions to combinations of symptoms from the three categories. Finally, the duration, the frequency, and intensity of the symptoms indicate the extent to which the person is suffering (Hibler, 1981).

In the *emotional* category, symptoms include apathy, anxiety, irritability, mental fatigue, and overcompensation or denial. Persons afflicted with these symptoms are restless, agitated, overly sensitive, defensive, preoccupied, and have difficulty concentrating. These officers will overwork to exhaustion and may become groundlessly suspicious. They may be arrogant, argumentative, insubordinate, and hostile. Their feelings of insecurity and worthlessness lead to self-defeat. Depression is common and chronic.

Behavioral symptoms are often more easily detected than emotional ones, for their sufferers withdraw and seek social isolation. Such people are reluctant to accept responsibilities and/or tend to neglect current ones. They often act out their misery through alcohol abuse, gambling, promiscuity, and spending sprees. Much of their desperate behavior is a cry for help and should be recognized as such. Other indications could be habitual lateness, poor appearance, and poor personal hygiene, both at work and at home. These patterns can lead to domestic disputes and spouse/child abuse.

The *physical* effects of stress are extremely dangerous. The person may become preoccupied with illness or may dwell on minor ailments, taking excessive sick leave and complaining of exhaustion during the workday. Among the many somatic indicators are headaches, insomnia, recurrent awakening, early morning rising, changes in appetite resulting in either weight loss or gain, indigestion, nausea, vomiting, and diarrhea. Such psychophysical maladies may be a direct result of excessive stress upon the officer.

Coping Strategies

Rape investigators could perform well under stress and reduce their chances of falling prey to stress-related disorders if they (1) monitored their own stress reactions and (2) learned skills that would help them cope with stress effectively.

Unfortunately, many resist such procedures, believing that to admit the need for stress management is to admit they can't cope and thus appear weak to their friends.

The philosophy of stress management, however, emphasizes two reasonable techniques: exercise and relaxation, both normal means to good general health. Moreover, it recommends seriously and ruthlessly structuring one's life so that time is systematically allotted for various important needs. Depue (1981) recommends a division into work time, family time, and the one most difficult to find, personal time.

Effective stress management practices include the following:

1. Eat three meals a day, including breakfast.
2. Avoid sugar, salt, animal fat, and processed white flour in your diet.
3. Pursue a regular program of physical exercise or other leisure activities.
4. Form new friendships and maintain old ones.
5. Get enough sleep each night (6 to 8 hr).
6. Practice abdominal breathing and relaxation.
7. Schedule time and activities for yourself, by yourself, and schedule the same to spend with others socially.
8. Stop smoking.
9. Limit your alcohol and caffeine intake.
10. Pace yourself and allow for an even flow of demands.
11. Identify and accept emotional needs.
12. Recognize early warning signs of stress.
13. Allocate time and energy to allow for outside interests and stimulation.
14. Take appropriate dietary supplements, if needed.
15. Avoid self-medication.
16. Take one thing at a time.
17. Give in once in a while.
18. Talk out your worries.
19. Make yourself available.
20. Learn to accept things you cannot change.

Summary

Law enforcement officers have long lived, and sometimes died, with the knowledge that their occupation seems to breed alcoholism, divorce, and suicide. Many, in fact, hold their jobs directly accountable for much of the misery in their lives, not reflecting that they might change the trends themselves. Today we know that, as a rule, personal problems stem not from the job itself, but from the officer's failure to deal effectively with the stress created by the job. Thus, rape investigators must "self-diagnose" their problems, measuring their level of happiness, job satisfaction, personal growth, family relationships, and other subjective concerns. Above all, they must assume responsibility for their own mental and physical health.

Rape investigators are involved in an important and rewarding job. Although its negative aspects are often highlighted, no one should ever doubt its value to the person and to society. One should, however, understand thoroughly and systematically how to cope with the negative aspects of the task.

Rape investigators must realize that they don't have to become vicarious victims. They must be willing to assume responsibility for their own mental and physical health, and they must face the fact that there are no shortcuts to stress management. They must commit themselves strongly to understanding stress, its symptoms, and its causes, in order to achieve and maintain their personal and professional health.

References

Bennett, B., The police mystique, *Police Chief*, p. 46, April 1978.

Capp, F. L., Peer counseling: an employee assistance program, *FBI Law Enforcement Bull.*, p. 2, November 1984.

Cherniss, C., *Staff Burnout*, Sage Publications, Beverly Hills, CA, 1980.

Depue, R. L., High risk lifestyle: the police family, *FBI Law Enforcement Bull.*, August 1981.

Edelwich, J., *Burn-Out*, Human Sciences Press, New York, 1980.

Freud, A., *The Writings of Anna Freud, Volume II, The Ego and the Mechanisms of Defense*, rev. ed., International Universities Press, New York, 1966.

Hibler, N., Early Warning Signs and Symptoms, U.S. Air Force Office of Special Investigations, Washington, D.C., 1981.

Laughlin, H. P., *The Ego and Its Defenses*, 2nd ed., Jason Aronson, New York, 1979.

Lazarus, R. S., Cognitive and coping processes in emotion, in *Stress and Coping: An Anthology*, Monat, A. and Lazarus, R. S., Eds., Columbia University Press, New York, 1977.

Maslach, C., Burned-out, *Hum. Behav.*, September 1976.

Phillips, R. G., Jr., State and local law enforcement training needs, *FBI Law Enforcement Bull.*, August 1984.

Reese, J. T., Life in the high-speed lane: managing police burnout, *Police Chief*, June 1982a.

Reese, J. T., Family therapy in law enforcement: a new approach to an old problem, *FBI Law Enforcement Bull.*, September 1982b.

Reiser, M., Some organizational stresses on policemen, *J. Police Sci. Adm.*, No. 2, 1974.

Selye, H., *Stress without Distress*, Lippincott, New York, 1974.

Snyder, S. H., *The Troubled Mind: A Guide to the Release from Distress*, McGraw-Hill, New York, 1976.

Somodevilla, S. A., The psychologist's role in the police department, *Police Chief*, April 1978.

Toffler, A., *Future Shock*, Random House, New York, 1970.

Webster, W. H., Crime in the United States 1983, U.S. Department of Justice, Federal Bureau of Investigation, Washington, D.C., 1984.

Wilson, J. Q., *Varieties of Police Behavior: The Management of Law and Order in Eight Communities*, Harvard University Press, Cambridge, MA, 1968.

III

MEDICAL AND NURSING ASPECTS OF RAPE INVESTIGATION

Medical Exam of the Live Sexual Assault Victim

15

JOSEPH A. ZECCARDI

Overview

The medical system becomes involved in the sexual assault investigation for two reasons: therapy involving the physical and emotional consequences of the assault, and evidence gathering to corroborate the initial charges or to be used in the adjudication of the complaint. Although these medical responsibilities have existed for years, it is only recently that sexual assault has been introduced into medical school curricula. Therefore, it is unusual that a physician is versed in the investigation of sexual assault without special training. Pediatricians, gynecologists, emergency physicians, and some family physicians are introduced to the subject of sexual assault during their training after medical school, but it is rare for them to have significant experience in sexual assault cases except as a member of a community response team. Medical personnel should have a procedure to follow in sexual assault cases so that victims receive proper attention and evidence is preserved. Persons in all areas involved in the matter — medicine, prosecution, crime investigation, rape crisis, crime laboratory — need to proceed in a coordinated manner. They must educate each other as to the needs of the sexual assault victim from their various vantage points and agree on such particulars as the specific handling of historical and evidentiary matters within their jurisdiction.

The physician's role in sexual assault cases should be clearly defined before involving the patient in a medical evaluation. The physician's responsibilities, as mentioned above, are both medical and evidentiary. The medical responsibilities include treatment of any trauma involved, prevention and treatment of any possible venereal disease or pregnancy, and adequate follow-up for counseling to reduce emotional trauma.

Physicians and other medical staff members should be educated about common misconceptions and attitudes concerning sexual assault. They should also be advised of the definitions of sexual assault and rape in local jurisdictions. A medical definition of penetration, for example, usually assumes that there has been penetration into the vagina, whereas many legal jurisdictions consider penetration between the labia as rape.

The type of physician or facility used in sexual assault cases varies. Emergency departments, because of their 24-hr, 7-day-a-week availability, have a certain attractiveness that is counterbalanced by the realities of shifting priorities for

0-8493-8152-1/95/$0.00+$.50
© 1995 by CRC Press, Inc.

medical crises; e.g., a cardiac arrest must take priority over a sexual assault victim. Depending on the size and complexity of the emergency service, it may be possible to have a section that deals with sexual assault and/or emotional emergencies. These special kinds of facilities usually will be able to arrange a more appropriate waiting space and the necessary personnel to deal with the victim. Large facilities may use physicians from the disciplines of emergency, gynecology, or pediatrics, or residents in training may handle these cases. Each of these groups has advantages and disadvantages that need to be considered. In a busy sexual assault program it is unlikely that a single physician can deal with all sexual assault cases. However, in a smaller jurisdiction where this is possible, a single physician would have the advantage of being able to coordinate information.

The medical personnel should be trained as to the scope of activity and responsibility of the district attorney's office, law enforcement officers, the crime lab, rape crisis workers, and rape treatment facilities. The medical facility itself should be able to support a quick reception and registration process and a secure waiting space where information may be obtained from the patient and shared with the patient about the process about to occur. Rape crisis workers should be involved in this activity and thus will extend the ability of the medical facility to give informed and caring support. The victim should be given visual and acoustical privacy and provided with printed material explaining the role of each member of the sexual assault team and the medical process. The victim's emotional state will make it difficult for her to absorb information being given to her. Thus, she will be given the same information in print to refer to later.

It is not unusual to have a nurse, physician, social worker, police, and rape crisis workers all interviewing the patient. These interviews should be coordinated so that duplication of effort does not become another harassment and infringement of the patient's rights. It is not reasonable that the patient should be interviewed while in various stages of undress in preparation for the medical evaluation. Preplanning can allow coordination of these various activities so that the patient is not made to feel vulnerable again.

Consent

Consent must be obtained for examination and treatment of the sexual assault victim, as well as for the release of information obtained during the medical examination to legal authorities so that prosecution may proceed.

Written permission for medical examination and treatment is obtained from all patients, and the staff is usually familiar with the process. In a true emergency, permission for medical examination and treatment is assumed and treatment may proceed without written consent. In the area of sexual assault, however, special issues are raised, mostly pertaining to the victim's age. Many victims are adolescents and may, therefore, fall below the legal age of consent. Minors are variously defined by individual states as emancipated by marriage, if they have been pregnant, or have graduated from high school. Some states permit medical treatment of venereal disease or pregnancy in a minor without parental permission.

In most cases, it is advisable to obtain parental consent since successful long-range treatment of the minor depends on parental involvement and support. Moreover, parental consent is needed for the dispensing of estrogen hormonal therapy as emergency treatment against pregnancy, after informing the patient of possible side effects of such therapy (these side effects are discussed later in this chapter).

Rape is a crime, and the law in certain jurisdictions requires physicians to report any injury inflicted in violation of a penal code. Moreover, whether the patient claims sexual assault or not, if the physician has reason to believe it has occurred, reporting to local agencies may be not only advisable, but required. In addition, most municipalities have ordinances requiring reporting of sexual assault against children and adolescent victims to a multidisciplinary group that reports to child welfare agencies, especially if the assault has occurred within the household.

Apart from written consent for examination and treatment, the sexual assault victim must give authorization for the release of information gathered during the medical exam to law enforcement agencies. Should the patient refuse to press charges or share medical information with the legal system, the medical facility must retain the information that may then be released only upon written consent of the parent or guardian or upon subpoena by the court. In the absence of consent or court order, the only information that may be released is a report of the injury to police, the patient's name and address, and, in the case of a minor, a report to the child welfare agency.

Medical Examination

Before outlining the mechanics of the medical examination, several general factors regarding the approach to the sexual assault victim must be addressed. This is often the first interaction of the victim with society after the crime. While it is important that the medical examination be thorough, it must also be sensitive. Thus, medical personnel should respect the limits that the victim needs to set in order to maintain her integrity.

The mechanics of the evaluation should be reviewed with the patient before the examination by a nurse, crisis worker, or physician. The evaluation should, of course, take place in an acoustically and visually private area. A nurse should be present throughout the evaluation to provide emotional support and to assist the physician. A friend or caseworker may also be present during the examination if the patient so desires. If photographs are to be taken as evidence, their purpose should be discussed with the patient and a specific separate written consent obtained.

The medical examination includes history, physical examination, and collection of specimens for laboratory analysis.

History

The purpose of the history is to gather information that will aid in the medical and legal management of the case. Emphasis is placed on ascertaining a general medical history, a sexual history, and a history of the incident and postincident events.

General Medical History

A past medical history of injury or illness should be documented with emphasis on those disorders that may adversely affect the assault victim, e.g., bleeding tendencies. Any medications taken as well as known allergies to medications should be noted, since medical therapy may be indicated, e.g., for the prevention of venereal disease. A history of past immunizations, especially tetanus, is important since booster shots may be required when injury has been sustained and immunizations are not up to date.

Sexual History

Inquires must be made to determine whether the female assault victim is menarchal (has begun menstruating), and, if so, the date of the patient's last normal menstrual period should be documented. Also, a history of sterilization or the use of any type of birth control method should be noted. The number of pregnancies and the results of these pregnancies (live birth, stillbirth, miscarriage, abortion) should be recorded. In addition, the patient must be questioned about her most recent consensual sexual intercourse, as well as the existence and time of onset of any symptoms of pregnancy. Finally, it is necessary to assess the patient's attitude concerning pregnancy and its prevention or termination by hormonal or mechanical means. All of these questions will aid in evaluating the possibility of pre-assault or assault-related pregnancy, as well as any course of action that should be taken if pregnancy exists.

The patient's venereal disease history should be ascertained. If the patient has been treated for syphilis, it is helpful to know whether her blood titers returned to normal. The facility at which the patient was treated should be noted so that results of past blood tests can be compared with present laboratory analysis.

History of the Incident and Postincident Events

The history of the event, for legal purposes, should include statements regarding several aspects of the assault that may be further corroborated by physical or laboratory examination. The time and place at which the assault took place should be recorded. Such information will lead the physician to look for the presence of grass stains, dirt, etc. during physical examination. The specific nature of the physical/sexual assault should be noted. The physician must know if any body fluids (through ejaculation, urination, defecation) were left on the patient or if vaginal, oral, or anal penetration occurred during the incident, so that proper lab specimens can be obtained. It is helpful to know if any instruments, such as restraints, were used. By impeding blood return from the vein, restraints often lead to bruises and broken blood vessels (petechiae), which will be evident on physical examination.

Postincident events that should be noted include any activities that may interfere with the collection of evidentiary facts and specimens during the physical examination, such as bathing, douching, urinating, defecating, drinking, or changing clothes.

As a final word, it should be emphasized that the history should be conducted in a sensitive, caring manner, using language familiar to the patient. If the victim is a child, the interviewer should talk to other family members to determine what terminology is used for various body parts. Furthermore, it may be necessary to use other techniques to obtain a history from a child, such as the use of anatomically correct dolls or the use of illustrations depicting the events as constructed by the child. It is noteworthy that children seldom lie about explicit sexual behavior. Accusation by a child of sexual abuse should, therefore, be taken at face value.

Physical Examination

The approach to the victim for the physical examination should be gentle and empathic. Ideally, the mechanics of the examination should be previewed with the patient by a nurse, caseworker, or physician. Nevertheless, during the examination it is helpful for the physician to explain, in a calm and mannerly voice, step by step, what he/she is doing. A young child may be examined on a mother's lap or, like the older patient, on the examining table. If supportive, the parent should be allowed to remain with the patient during the examination. An adolescent can be given the option of having anyone she wishes present. In all cases, the examination should be performed with a hospital employee, preferably a nurse, who can also assist the physician, as chaperon. Of course, the examination should take place in an acoustically and visually private area. Finally, a gown and drapes should be used as appropriate to preserve the patient's modesty and decrease feelings of vulnerability.

The physical examination must be complete enough to note any abnormalities that have occurred as a result of the sexual assault. The physician should assess and record the patient's general appearance before she disrobes (e.g., patient appears disheveled, clothes torn). The physician should also note the patient's demeanor, emotional distress, or depression which may manifest itself by inappropriate laughing, agitation, or withdrawal. Vital signs (blood pressure, pulse, temperature, or respiratory distress) should be taken and documented. Abnormalities such as elevated pulse may reflect emotional stress or major trauma. Foreign material such as blood or dried semen should be scraped and submitted for evidence as described in Chapter 5. Any sign of trauma should be documented on the medical record.

The patient's description of the assault may indicate parts of the physical exam requiring special consideration. For instance, the use of restraints may produce broken superficial vessels (petechiae). These may be especially notable on the inside of the eye if restraints about the neck were used. When a history of oral or rectal intercourse is elicited, these sites should be meticulously inspected. Bruises (ecchymoses) should be described in terms of location, size, shape, and color. Bruises evolve over a period of time and their age may be estimated from their appearance. Thus, early on, a bruise appears as a reddened area which, with time, evolves into the more traditional black and blue mark.

Later, the bruise changes color again to various shades of green, reflecting the degradation and uptake of blood by the healing body. The physician's assessment of the age of a bruise by its appearance may be used in the courtroom to corroborate or dispute the victim's claim by comparing it to the historical timing of the alleged assault. Another physical finding of legal significance, soft tissue injury or contusion, is diagnosed by the physician by the ability to elicit pain on palpation of the traumatized body area.

Genital exam is required in order to assess the degree (if any) of trauma and to collect specimens for evidentiary purposes. Initially, the external genitalia and surrounding area are inspected. Signs of trauma such as a bruising on the inner thigh may result from attempts to pry or pull the legs apart. Combing the pubic hair for specimens of free foreign hair and clippings of a few of the patients's pubic hair for comparison may be done at this point of the examination. While an integral part of the examination in the older female patient, internal (vaginal) examination may not be required for children. However, if blood is seen coming from the vagina in a child, a vaginal exam is indicated and is preferably performed under general anesthesia to permit adequate inspection and repair of physical trauma without inflicting further psychological trauma.

The internal examination begins with an inspection of the vaginal opening, the introitus. The presence of an intact hymen at this site should be documented but does not rule out vaginal penetration. Evidence of recent disruption of the hymenal ring, such as reddening, laceration, or bleeding, is rarely found, but should nevertheless be sought. In practice, hymenal tissue is difficult to identify in the majority of patients, a fact that has been attributed to masturbation during childhood or to the active lifestyle of the modern-day woman, but not necessarily signifying previous intercourse. Thus, the status of the hymenal ring has minimal legal significance. In some centers, the findings of a relaxed vaginal opening in a child is used as evidence of sexual abuse; however, no objective data can be found in the literature to support this conclusion. Direct visualization of the vaginal vault and cervix is accomplished with the aid of a nonlubricated, water-moistened speculum of the smallest size to avoid further trauma of the tissue after the assault. Again, inspection for signs of trauma and collection of appropriate specimens from the cervix and from the deepest, most dependent portion of the vagina, the posterior fornix, is performed. In children, when a vaginal exam is not performed, a small catheter with a syringe on one end may be inserted into the vagina in order to withdraw a specimen for forensic testing.

The final portion of the physical examination is the bimanual examination. The physician performs the examination after withdrawing the speculum by inserting the first and second fingers of one hand into the vaginal vault and placing the other hand on the abdomen. The purpose of the examination is to assess by means of palpation (1) the size and consistency of the uterus and adjacent organs, the adnexa (ovaries and tubes), looking for signs of pre-existing pregnancy; and (2) the presence of tenderness resulting from trauma sustained during the assault.

Rectal examination is indicated if a history of rectal intercourse is elicited and, similar to the genital examination, includes external examination for signs of trauma and foreign material and internal examination using an anoscope with inspection for signs of trauma and foreign material, collection of specimens for evidentiary and medical purposes, and palpation with a gloved finger for signs of tenderness and trauma.

Laboratory Evaluation

Evidentiary material should be collected and held for possible release to the law enforcement officer. As previously mentioned, release of this material requires the consent of the patient (or guardian in the case of a minor) or a court subpoena. In the absence of such consent or court order, specimens should be set aside, preferably in a locked refrigerator or box.

Similar to the physician's report of the examination, specimens obtained from the assault victim have both medical and legal significance. It is therefore essential to properly label all specimens (patient's name, date, time of collection, area from which the specimen is collected, collector's name) and to establish written documentation of the custody of evidentiary material, a so-called written "chain of evidence" in which specimens are accounted for during every step, from collection to possible introduction into courts. Failure to properly label specimens or to maintain written documentation when custody is transferred may render any evidence legally worthless.

The type of evidence to be collected, as well as the method of collection and handling of evidence, will vary depending on the patient's history and the specific legal jurisdiction. If there is time for preplanning, medical facility staff should meet with crime laboratory personnel to discuss these issues. The law enforcement officers should also alert medical personnel to any specific evidence they have noted so that it will be collected with other specimens. Specimens collected routinely include any clothing that is torn, bloody, or soiled in the course of the assault, any foreign debris (e.g., hair fibers) or dried secretions adhering to the patient's body, and fingernail scrapings. Routine studies performed on these specimens include analysis for the presence and concentrations of acid phosphatase, an enzyme present in the ejaculate. The presence of this enzyme in a specimen serves as an indirect verification of the presence of semen. Specimens are also tested for the identification of blood group substances (ABO, Rh). Blood and saliva samples obtained from the victim are used to determine her blood type and whether she secretes her blood type in other body fluids. By comparing blood group substances found in various specimens to the patient's blood group, a secretion (e.g., semen) may be identified as foreign.

Other routine studies are performed to detect sperm, either live sperm in a wet mount or dead sperm or sperm products on a dry slide. It is possible to estimate the length of time the sperm were present in their current state at the site of examination. Studies performed for the detection of venereal disease include gram staining and culture of secretions for gonorrhea and baseline serology for syphilis. It should be noted that it takes about a month from the time of infection before the blood test becomes positive for syphilis, and that the blood test is not always negative after successful treatment or prior syphilis infection. The test thus serves only as a baseline in recent assaults. Pregnancy tests may be required in the postmenarchal female if the history (missed period, symptoms of pregnancy) or physical (increased size and softening of the uterus) indicates the possibility of a pre-existing pregnancy.

Additional specimens should be obtained from any orifice which, by history, has been violated. Genital violation, therefore, would require the collection of any foreign material adhering to the external genitalia, free hairs, reference hair clippings, and swabbings from the vaginal pool.

Medical Therapy

As previously mentioned, medical therapy requires attention to life-threatening conditions first. In the absence of such conditions, prophylactic treatment for venereal disease and pregnancy should be addressed. It is a common practice in sexual assault centers to treat most adult victims for incubating gonorrhea and syphilis. This is due to several facts: a slightly increased incidence of venereal disease reported in victims of sexual assault, the poor medical follow-up of victims, and the frequency of asymptomatic gonorrheal infection in adult females who consequently serve as a reservoir for spreading the infection or develop significant complications before the infection is diagnosed. In contrast to the adult, however, the prepubertal female infected with gonorrhea is usually symptomatic, largely due to a difference in anatomy and physiology which localizes the infection and inflammation to the vagina with a resulting external discharge. For this reason, in some facilities only symptomatic children are treated for gonorrhea.

Treatment for the prevention of a potential pregnancy as a result of sexual assault should also be considered. An existing pregnancy, however, must first be ruled out, and the patient's attitude toward pregnancy and its prevention/termination should be assessed. Information on alternative methods of pregnancy prevention as well as the possible short and/or long-term effects of such treatment should be offered. Diethylstillbesterol (DES), the "morning after pill", has traditionally been used as a medical prophylactic against pregnancy. When administered within the first 72 hr following unprotected intercourse, DES prevents implantation of the fertilized egg and, therefore, pregnancy — in 99.9% of the cases. Such therapy is not, however, without adverse effects; significant nausea and vomiting are common following administration. Furthermore, there is the highly publicized risk of vaginal adenocarcinoma in the female offspring of mothers exposed to DES in the first trimester. It is wise, therefore, to obtain signed, informed consent before administering DES and to follow-up treated patients in order to detect the 0.1% in whom DES intervention failed. In such patients, abortion might be discussed.

As a result of the problems associated with DES, many facilities have switched to other forms of hormonal therapy for the prevention of pregnancy. It must be emphasized, however, that while reasonably effective, the long-term consequences will only be determined with time and may prove to be more devastating than those of DES. One such alternative is Premarin (conjugated Estrogen). A single dose of 50 mg, administered intravenously, assures 100% compliance in spite of such adverse effects as nausea. Other nonhormonal options for pregnancy interruption that should be offered to the sexual assault victim include the insertion of an intrauterine device (IUD), elective abortion, or carrying potential pregnancy to term.

Medical Records

The medical facility staff should be advised of the medical record requirements in sexual assault cases. They must understand that their records should be nonjudgmental, use standard terms, and be legible. It is also important to notify the medical facility that the final diagnosis may be a sexual assault complaint and that society, in the form of a jury or its other agents, will decide whether sexual assault has occurred. The medical records should not reflect any conclusions as to whether or not a crime has taken place and the final diagnosis should be "sexual assault complaint" rather than "sexual assault". The frequency of physician court appearances can be significantly reduced if the medical record is properly kept and legible.

Psychological Aspects

Rape trauma syndrome (described in Chapter 3) is of concern. The appropriate management of the patient in the facility may minimize additional stress. Victims are seeking assurance from the facility about their medical condition, emotional support, and external control. Patients should be prepared for events in the emergency department. This preparation need not be by physicians, and there may be some advantage to using female crisis workers. The patient should be assured she is in a secure environment and will not be left alone, and the crisis worker, if available, should accompany the patient through the entire process. It is important to be sensitive to the importance of repetition because of multiple participants. Privacy after an assault is a sensitive issue and questioning must be approached carefully. Assurances of safety are important, as patient fear of injury or death is common. Despite the need for sensitivity, it is important to ask about specific acts that the rapist performed, since the patient's embarrassment may lead to minimal responses.

Patient control during the examination is important and the patient should be told of her physical condition immediately following the examination and reassured during such an examination. It is helpful, as mentioned earlier, to have written descriptions of the emotional reactions that accompany sexual assault, in addition to printed medical instructions and descriptions of what to expect of the process following the reporting of the sexual assault. This material then can be reviewed by the patient later to refresh her memory. Some crisis workers provide outreach services on the next day or so to talk with the victim and discuss her feelings. If a sexual assault treatment unit is available, the patient should be referred there with assurances that she is not required to go, but that these experts have been helpful to other victims.

Rape crisis workers who are organized for families of sexual assault victims are also helpful. There is a tendency to look for a negative cause for a negative result, and friends and family sometimes consider that the victim must have been at fault. Follow-up mental health consultation should be sought not only for the victim, but also for significant others.

Any additional medical contact necessary for obtaining evidentiary material is accompanied by careful explanations of emotional sequelae, as well as written materials and referrals to support therapeutic agencies, which can do much to optimize the outcome for the patient.

Summary

This chapter outlines the medical examination as conducted in the emergency department for a sexual assault investigation. Types of tests and examinations with rationale are discussed.

Victim Care Services and the Comprehensive Sexual Assault Assessment Tool

16

ANN WOLBERT BURGESS
JACQUELINE FAWCETT
ROBERT R. HAZELWOOD
CHRISTINE A. GRANT

The history of victim care services, in general, and the antirape movement, in particular, began over 30 years ago. Largen (1985) credits two forces for finally bringing the problem of rape to the attention of U.S. citizens in the late 1960s. First, primary credit is given to the women's movement for initiating consciousness-raising groups and then "speak outs", where women began saying publicly what they had not dared say before about rape. Second, in response to a rising crime rate and the growing community concern over the problem of rape, Senator Charles Mathias of Maryland introduced a bill in September 1973 to establish the National Center for the Prevention and Control of Rape. The purpose of this bill was to provide a focal point within the National Institute of Mental Health from which a comprehensive national effort would be undertaken to conduct research, develop programs, and provide information leading to aid for the victims and their families, to rehabilitation of the offenders, and, ultimately, to curtailment of rape crimes. The bill was passed by overwhelming vote in the 93rd Congress, vetoed by President Ford, and successfully reintroduced. The National Center was established through Public Law 94-63 in July 1975.

Parallel with these political forces, the early 1970s were a time of major efforts to organize services for rape victims, including community-based and hospital-based programs. Although most of the pioneer services were in the form of grass roots self-help programs, now widely known as rape crisis centers, nurses practicing in hospital emergency departments began to develop programs to provide rape counseling services. Boston City Hospital, Boston's Beth Israel Hospital, and Santa Monica Hospital were among the first hospital-based programs; they represent the roots of forensic nursing programs (Lynch, 1993).

This chapter, which is a companion to Chapter 15, presents a description of a comprehensive multidisciplinary victim care service program and sexual assault nurse examiner (SANE) programs. These programs may be viewed as prototypes for agencies to consider for their own communities. The chapter also presents a

0-8493-8152-1/95/$0.00+$.50
© 1995 by CRC Press, Inc.

263

new Comprehensive Sexual Assault Assessment Tool (CSAAT) that was developed by the authors for forensic and/or research purposes.

Victim Care Service

In 1972, a victim counseling program was developed as a nurse-managed service at the Boston City Hospital by Burgess and Holmstrom (1986). The counseling approach, developed in the early years of this program, expanded in the mid-1980s into a six-phase Victim Care Service (VCS) coordinated by an advanced practice psychiatric nurse (Minden, 1989). These six phases represent various health care providers that network to communities throughout a state.

> Phase 1: Standards are set and treatment providers are trained in victim care; also, coordination with other programs in the city and state is arranged.
> Phase 2: Acute intervention is provided to the victim entering the emergency department as well as any other patient unit in the hospital system.
> Phase 3: Crisis intervention follow-up of victim is provided by appropriately prepared psychiatric nurses or social workers.
> Phase 4: Education regarding sexually transmitted disease, including HIV, is provided according to the age and verbal requests of the victim.
> Phase 5: Ongoing therapy is arranged through referral to psychiatric clinicians.
> Phase 6: Evaluation and research relevant to sexual victimization is conducted.

The VCS is organized around the following six fundamental assumptions:

1. *There is a continuum of sexual victimization.* The continuum ranges from rape to sexual assault. Although states and jurisdictions legally define rape differently, three criteria are generally present: sexual penetration of the victim's vagina, mouth, or rectum that occurs without the individual's consent and involves the use or threat of force. Sexual assault refers to a wider range of forced or pressured sexual contact; specifically, child sexual assault, incest, acquaintance rape, and marital rape. Furthermore, there are situations involving relationships of unequal power in which the person in authority violates the normal bounds of the relationship and abuses and sexually pressures or forces the subordinate. Such abusive relationships include husband/wife, therapist/patient, parent/child, teacher/student, and employer/employee. A basic premise of the VCS is that a patient does not need to meet any stringent legal criteria for rape in order to be considered sexually victimized. The legal system bears the burden of determining the validity of a given charge of rape, whereas the primary responsibility of the VCS is to care for the patient reporting sexual victimization.
2. *Sexual victimization is not a rare event.* Rape is a serious public health problem (Kilpatrick et al., 1992). Since 1977, the rate of forcible rape has increased by 21%, which is the largest increase of all violent crimes. In

1990, three separate reporting units described the incidence of rape: the FBI Uniform Crime Report cited 102,560 cases of forcible rape to women of consenting age; the U.S. Department of Justice, Bureau of Justice Statistics (NCS) reported 130,000 forcible rapes; and the National Women's Study estimated 683,000 cases of forcible rape (Kilpatrick et al., 1992).

3. *Responses to sexual assault victims have frequently been based on myths and stereotypes.* The stereotype that rape victims are somehow responsible for their victimization is based on the belief that women have rape fantasies and that it is acceptable for men to fulfill such fantasies. This belief is also noted in the attitudes that women who dress provocatively, stay out late, or frequent unsafe areas get what they deserve. Although engaging in certain behaviors may increase one's risk of victimization, the VCS maintains that it is the offender who is responsible for the victimization. Other myths include: rape is a crime that is prone to false complaints, rape only happens to other people, and rape occurs in dark alleys at the hands of strangers. To the contrary, studies suggest that victims of rape are disinclined to make complaints under current laws and that those who do so frequently refuse to continue their testimony because of the manner in which they are treated (Schwartz and Clear, 1980). Also, contrary to popular belief, confidence rape or assault by someone known to the victim is more frequent than stranger rape, and often happens in the victim's home or another familiar place. Furthermore, sexual assault and abuse cross all boundaries of class and culture. The fact that victims can be of either sex helps to negate the myth that women are naturally better equipped than men to care for sexual assault victims. The clinician, whether male or female, must be accepting of the patient. A female clinician caring for a female victim might defend against her own feelings of vulnerability by rejecting the patient. In contrast, that same patient might benefit from interaction with a male clinician who acts in a caring manner. Attitude rather than gender determines a clinician's ability to provide victim care (Minden, 1989).

4. *Rape or sexual assault represents a trauma or crisis that results in a disruption of the victim's physical, emotional, and social life-style.* People who have been raped usually describe it as an extremely traumatic event in their life. Whether or not a person is able to cope with the trauma depends on a number of factors, including the nature of the assault, the presence of other stressors, the patient's precrisis functioning and coping skills, and the available support system. The clinician who can communicate a sense of optimism for recovery may help nullify the chronic negative effects of sexual assault. Rape trauma, a clinical term, describes a clustering of biopsychosocial and behavioral symptoms exhibited in varying degrees by victims of rape. Most victims develop a pattern of moderate to severe symptoms described as *rape trauma syndrome* (see Chapter 3); a minority of victims report no or mild symptoms. Rape trauma is an acute reaction to an externally imposed situational crisis. The victim's trauma results

from being confronted with a life-threatening and highly stressful situation; the resulting crisis is in the service of self preservation. The victim's reactions to the impending threat to his or her life is the nucleus around which such an adaptive pattern may be noted. In many rape victims, responses during and after the rape correspond to the critical symptoms of post-traumatic stress disorder (PTSD). Diagnostic criteria are found in the CSAAT (see this chapter).

5. *Rape trauma is a traumatic stressor.* Crisis intervention encourages a positive resolution of the victimization experience. Patterns of coping after the assault can be adaptive or maladaptive. The purpose of crisis intervention is to direct the victim into therapeutic coping patterns rather than defensive positions. The forte of VCS is *crisis intervention;* the emphasis is moving the patient from being a victim to being a survivor. A salient feature of victimization is a loss of control. Emergency department clinicians can easily mirror the patient's crisis and may also experience feelings of being overwhelmed by the trauma. Consequently, the VCS implements a very structured process for providing victim care, which has helped to reestablish a sense of control for the clinician who can then put energies into stabilizing the patient. Two phases of care are provided the rape victim (Minden, 1989). The first phase of care includes implementation of the sexual assault protocol described in Chapter 15. The second phase is victim follow-up by telephone over a 3- to 4-day period, when a counseling referral to ease the victim's recovery from the acute phase is discussed.

6. *Multidisciplinary approach to victim care is used.* Rape is a complex, multifaceted problem that no one person or group can resolve alone. Indeed, dealing with sexual victimization requires the collaborative and cooperative efforts of a network of services. Thus, a multidisciplinary team approach helps to meet the victim's diverse needs and also provides the caregivers with a support system for dealing with the stress of victimization. The VCS provides continuous victim care training for various community agencies and joins with other programs in offering workshops to enhance community awareness of sexual victimization (Minden, 1989).

7. *Victim care providers experience compassion fatigue.* Compassion fatigue, a term coined by trauma expert Charles Figley, describes how working with victims can take a psychological toll on the providers of care. Clinicians working in emergency departments of large city hospitals have very direct and frequent exposure to trauma. Ever escalating economic constraints and patient acuteness present care providers with increasing challenges that are physically, intellectually, and emotionally stressful. Discussion of burnout and the vulnerability of law enforcement agents and clinicians who work with victims is given in Chapter 14.

Nurses have taken a leadership role in the care of rape victims. The following section describes current services.

Sexual Assault Nurse Examiner Services

SANE programs developed in the late 1970s in Memphis (1976), Minneapolis (1977), and Amarillo (1978). In 1992, the first national meeting bringing forensic nurses together was hosted by the Sexual Assault Response Team of Minneapolis. The International Association of Forensic Nurses (Ledray and Arndt, 1994) was established as an outgrowth of that meeting.

SANEs are specially trained registered nurses who provide comprehensive care to sexual assault survivors. Certification is usually by the local institution after completing a 40-hr training program and demonstrating competence in conducting a comprehensive evidential examination. Although sexual assault nurse examiners work cooperatively with medical facilities, most are from independent nursing programs or agencies that contract with the hospital to provide the specific services on an on-call basis. Some hospitals that provide services to large numbers of rape victims have their own programs (Ledray and Arndt, 1994).

Variations in the collection procedure and treatment components exist because hospitals and SANE programs have each developed their own sexual assault protocols. Seventeen states have developed statewide protocols and 14 additional states have adopted a protocol developed by the U.S. Department of Justice. Most states have developed rape examination kits that allow for consistency in evidence collection and ensure a proper chain of evidence. Although some variation is likely to continue, all forensic nursing examinations of sexual assault victims include the following five essential components:

Treatment and documentation of injuries
Treatment and evaluation of sexually transmitted diseases
Pregnancy risk evaluation and prevention
Crisis intervention and arrangements for follow-up counseling
Collection of medicolegal evidence while maintaining the proper chain of evidence

In some states, the nurse examiner collects the evidence and does the crisis intervention. In other states the nurse works in conjunction with a rape crisis counselor, usually a volunteer from a local crisis center. Frequently, the nurse examiner will be called upon to testify in legal proceedings.

One of the purposes of the International Association of Forensic Nurses is to coordinate research on rape. To that end, the following assessment tool, the CSAAT, has been devised and is published here for law enforcement and other professionals to use, and to be aware of the existing national data set being coordinated at the University of Pennsylvania School of Nursing. The CSAAT can be used for: (1) compilation of statistics for use at an agency, (2) program development, (3) research data, and (4) victim evaluation reports for clinical or forensic purposes.

Comprehensive Sexual Assault Assessment Tool

The CSAAT is comprised of four major areas for data collection. Items for the first area, investigative data, are identified in Chapter 8 as behavioral aspects of the offender. Items for the second area, victim forensic data, are described in Chapter 15. Items for the third area, legal/services information, and fourth area, psychosocial assessment for PTSD, are included in this chapter. Each area of data collection may be completed separately.

Investigative Data

Information basic to the background of the victim includes age, date of birth, gender, race, marital status, education, occupation, employment status, presence and/or type of disability, living arrangements, primary language, and if multiple victims were involved.

Information basic to the offense includes time of the rape, day of the week, and location (residence, place of employment, inside, outside). Data on offender characteristics include race, gender, approximate age, weight and height, unique features, and if there were multiple offenders. Other information includes offender relationship to victim, weapon brought to the scene, telephone disabled, bindings brought to the scene, use of gloves, washing up of the scene, evidence taken from scene, items of value taken, or victim's personal items taken.

The offender's method of approach is recorded as to whether it was a con (verbal coercion), blitz (injurious force), or surprise (no force). The control of the victim is recorded as to mere presence, weapon of opportunity, threats used, victim use of alcohol or drugs, victim bound or blindfolded, battery of the victim, abduction of the victim, bribery, psychological coercion, and percentage of clothing removed from the victim. Information is requested about the offender's use of drugs or alcohol and level of physical force used. Questions about the victim's resistance (passive, verbal, or physical) and offender reaction to victim resistance (cease demand, compromise/negotiate, flee, threats, or increased force/beatings) are asked. Information is requested about the assailant's sexual dysfunction (such as erectile insufficiency, premature ejaculation, retarded ejaculation, and conditional ejaculation) and type and sequence of sexual acts during the offense. In addition, information about the offender's verbal activity and victim's verbal activity, as well as offender's initial attitude and behavior, and any change during assault and attire, is requested because these are crucial aspects of victim interviews and crime investigations.

Victim Forensic Data

The second area, victim forensic data, includes information on height, weight, vital signs (blood pressure, pulse, temperature), and postassault activities as to urination, defecation, vomiting, bathing, or shower. Questions are asked to determine whether the pelvic examination was performed by direct visualization, bimanual, speculum, or colposcopic exam, the number of photographs taken and areas of body, and the use of the evidence kit. Microbiology findings from vagina, anus, or pharynx are recorded, as are the results of VDRL and HIV testing, findings about sperm presence/motility in vagina, anus, or mouth, as well as DNA testing results. Treatments given for sexually transmitted disease and pregnancy prevention are recorded.

In addition, rape examination findings are documented regarding genital trauma to female (labia majora, labia minora, clitoris, posterior fourchettes, fossa nacicularis, periurethral, vestibule, vagina, hymen, cervix, perineum, anus, and rectum) and to male victims (penis, periurethral, perineum, anus, rectum, and scrotum).

A knowledge of the various emotional states and responses experienced by victims can provide additional details of the offender's behavior for suspect apprehension. Information is, therefore, requested about the victim's behavior during interview as quiet or tense, trembling or tearful, agitated or verbally upset. Victim responses to questions as brief, reluctant, or readily responsive and behavior during examination as controlled, expressed, fearful, or angry are also recorded.

The victim's prior history can be important for planning referrals and follow-up counseling. Information as to prior history of assault or victimization and the victim's prior psychiatric history is also important; thus, these data are also recorded.

Legal and Services Information

The needs of victims for help and support require that they have access to a comprehensive system of services and resources. Provision of eight services, which are intended to help victims to deal with the short-term, long-term, and/or delayed effects of victimization, are documented in the third area of the CSAAT.

Emergency Response. A set of services are to be provided by the first person(s) coming in contact with the victim after the crime, e.g., a law enforcement dispatcher, a crisis line operator, family members, or a neighbor. The services should aim to ensure the physical safety of the victim and to make him or her feel safe and secure.

Forensic Services. Forensic services include treatment and documentation of injuries, treatment and evaluation of sexually transmitted diseases, pregnancy risk evaluation and prevention, and rape examination for the collection of medicolegal evidence while maintaining the proper chain of evidence. Forensic medical and nursing services should include victim stabilization and immediately follow the emergency response.

Resource Mobilization. Resource mobilization services are designed to help the victim in his or her recovery and include crisis intervention or other kinds of emotional support following the trauma as well as the provision of protection, shelter, food, or other emergency aid as necessary. Arrangements for follow-up counseling are included. Additionally, resource mobilization includes a broad array of help ranging from filling out insurance forms and filing for victim compensation to short-term counseling or long-term therapy. With some victims, this stage may last for years.

Suspect Arrest. When a suspect is arrested, the victim automatically becomes involved in the criminal justice system. The victim needs to be informed of the investigation and the arrest, the potential and actual charges that may be filed, and any bail considerations. Interaction with the victim may also include consultation over such decisions and emotional support during this period.

Preparation for Court. Services at this stage focus on preparing the victim for his or her involvement in the court process. Examples include providing the victim with an orientation to the courthouse and the courtroom, telling him or her what to expect in a hearing or trial and what she/he will be expected to do. Victim assistance programs linked to the county prosecutor's office are best equipped for this service.

Court Appearance. Victims who become involved in a court appearance may need a number of tangible services — transportation, child care, parking, and separation from the accused while waiting for their appearance. Often overlooked is the need for escort and supportive court counseling both in the courtroom and after the appearance is over.

Sentencing Process. Most states have legislation which allows the victim to be involved in the sentencing process. Services at this stage include helping the victim with a victim impact statement or alternative expression of his or her concern, escort and support for victims wishing to give testimony at the sentencing hearing, and short-term counseling following the sentencing outcome.

Postsentencing. Often the services needed after a sentencing are ignored. Yet victims may need to be kept informed about probation revocation hearings, parole hearings, escapes, appeals, and other issues related to the criminal justice system. They also may need continued short-term counseling or long-term therapy now that the case "is over".

A crime classification for rape and sexual assault is found in Chapter 11. The classifications include whether the offense was criminal enterprise, felony rape; personal cause of domestic sexual assault, entitlement rape, social acquaintance rape, subordinate rape, exploitative rape, anger rape, sadistic rape, abduction rape; group cause of formal gang rape or informal gang rape. Chapter 13 discusses unfounded cases, including insufficient evidence, nolle pros, charges dropped, sex stress situation, and false rape accusation.

Psychosocial Assessment for PTSD

Clinicians evaluating rape victims generally use the *American Psychiatric Association's Diagnostic and Statistical Manual* (1994) for determining a psychiatric diagnosis. An assessment for post traumatic stress disorder (PTSD) is defined by the following criteria:

> The experience of an event that involved actual or threatened death, serious injury, or threat to one's physical integrity
> Reexperiencing the trauma by external cues, memories, or dreams
> Avoidance of stimuli associated with the trauma
> Numbed responsiveness, e.g., feelings of detachment from others, constricted feeling, or diminished interest in significant activities
> Persistent symptoms of increased arousal as in sleep disturbance, irritability, difficulty concentrating, hypervigilance, and/or exaggerated startle response

Other related symptoms requested on the CSAAT and noted since the assault include increased perspiration or heart rate, changes in appetite, increased nervousness, body image disturbance, unusual body sensations, sexual problems with partner, blames self, low self-esteem, afraid to be alone, prior victimization, and prior psychiatric history.

A multiaxial evaluation report as suggested by the DSM-IV is recommended. Axis I includes diagnoses, the most common of which will be PTSD. Other DSM-IV diagnoses may also be used, especially if there is a pre-existing condition. Axis II includes diagnoses from the list of personality disorders and mental retardation in the DSM-IV. Axis III includes any diagnosed medical conditions. Axis IV includes a list of psychosocial and environmental problems such as problems with primary support group, social environment, schooling, work, hobbies/activities, finances, access to health care, and legal problems. Axis V asks for the highest level of functioning for the past year. An assessment scoring for symptoms is included at the end of the CSAAT.

The CSAAT is found in the Appendix to this chapter.

Summary

The history of victim care services began in the early 1970s. The organizing fundamental assumptions provide direction for the care of the rape victim. The late 1970s witnessed the development of sexual assault nurse examiner programs and the early 1990s note the emergence of an international association of forensic nurses. The chapter includes a Comprehensive Sexual Assaults Assessment form for agency use as well as research and data collection purposes.

References

American Psychiatric Association, *Diagnostic and Statistical Manual*, Vol. 4, Washington, D.C., 1994.

Burgess, A. W. and Hartman, C. R., *Exploitation of Patients by Health Professionals*, Praeger, New York, 1988.

Burgess, A. W. and Holmstrom, L. L., *Rape: Crisis and Recovery*, Awab, West Newton, MA, 1986.

Kilpatrick, D. G., Edmunds, C. N., and Seymour, A., *Rape in America*, National Victim Center, Arlington, VA, 1992.

Largen, M. A., The anti-rape movement: past and present, in *Rape and Sexual Assault*, Burgess, A. W., Ed., Garland Publishing, New York, 1985, 1.

Ledray, L. E. and Arndt, S., Examining the sexual assault victim: a new model for nursing care, *J. Psychosoc. Nursing*, 32(2), 7, 1994.

Lynch, V.A., Forensic nursing: diversity in education and practice, *J. Psychosoc. Nursing*, 31(11), 7, 1993.

Minden, P. B., The victim care services: a program for victims of sexual assault, *Arch. Psychiatr. Nursing* 3(1), 41, 1989.

Rieker, P. P. and Carmen, E., *The Gender Gap in Psychotherapy*, Plenum Press, New York, 1984.

Schwartz, M. D. and Clear, T. R., Toward a new law on rape, *Crime Delinquency*, 4, 129, 1980.

Appendix

Comprehensive Sexual Assault Assessment (CSAAT)*

Facility _____ City _____ State _____
Case Number:_____ Date:_____

I. INVESTIGATIVE DATA

1. Age of victim: _____ 2. Date of birth: _____
3. Gender: Male____ Female____
4. Race: Asian___ Black___ Caucasian___ Hispanic___ Other___
5. Marital status: Single____ Married/cohabitating____
   Divorced/separated_____ Widow____ Other____
6. Education by highest level completed: _____
7. Occupation:_____
8. Employment status: Full time_____ Part time_____
   Unemployed____ Retired____ Looking for work____
9. Disability: No____ Yes____
10. Living arrangements: Self____ Parents/relatives____
    Spouse/partner____ Other____
11. Primary language: _____
12. Multiple victims: No____ Yes____

Offense Data

13. Time of rape: AM____ PM____
14. Day of week: Sun___ Mon___ Tue___ Wed___ Thu___ Fri___ Sat___
15. Date: / /
16. Location: Residence No____ Yes____
    Place of employment: No____ Yes____
    Outside: No____ Yes____ Describe _____
    Inside: No____ Yes____ Describe_____
    Other: No____ Yes____ Describe_____

Offender Characteristics

17. Race: Asian___ Black___ Caucasian___ Hispanic___ Other___
18. Gender: Male____ Female____
19. Approximate age (in years): _____ to _____
20. Approximate weight: _____

*© Ann W. Burgess, Jacqueline Fawcett, Robert R. Hazelwood, and Christine A. Grant.
Address inquiries to:
Dr. Ann W. Burgess, University of Pennsylvania School of Nursing, 420 Guardian Drive,
Philadelphia, PA 19104-6096

21. Approximate height: _____
22. Unique features: No____ Yes____ Describe_____
23. Multiple offenders: No____ Yes____ No data____

Offender Relationship to Victim

24. Known: No____ Yes____ If known, relationship
    ___ Acquaintance/friend   ___ Current or former cohabitant
    ___ Dating relationship   ___ Supervisor/authority figure
    ___ Relative or in-law   ___ Other _____

25. Weapon bought to scene: No____ Yes____ Type_____
26. Telephone disabled: No____ Yes____ No data____
27. Bindings brought to scene: No____ Yes____ No data____
28. Use of gloves: No____ Yes____ Type_____
29. Wash up scene: No____ Yes____ No data____
30. Evidence taken from scene: No____ Yes____ No data____
31. Items of value taken: No____ Yes____ No data____
32. Victim personal items taken: No____ Yes____ No data____

Offender Method of Approach

33. Con (subterfuge or a ploy): No____ Yes____ No data____
34. Blitz (injurious force):   No____ Yes____ No data____
35. Surprise (no force):   No____ Yes____ No data____

Offender Control of the Victim

36. Mere presence: No____ Yes____ No data____
37. Weapon of opportunity: No____ Yes____ Type_____
38. Threats: No____ Yes____ No data____
39. Victim alcohol or drug use: No____ Yes____ No data____ Type_____
40. Victim bound: No____ Yes____ No data____
41. Victim blindfolded: No____ Yes____ No data____
42. Battery/beating: No____ Yes____ No data____
43. Abducted: No____ Yes____ No data____
44. Bribery: No____ Yes____ Describe_____
45. Psychological coercion: No____ Yes____ Describe_____
46. Percentage victim clothed (0% for nude): _____ %
47. Offender alcohol or drug use: No____ Yes___ No data___ Type_____
48. Physical force by the offender: No____ Yes____ If yes, type:
    ___ Minimal (little/no physical force)
    ___ Moderate (repeated slaps/hits)
    ___ Excessive (beaten, bruises, lacerations)
    ___ Brutal (sadistic torture)

49. Victim resistance: No____ Yes____ If yes, type:
    ___Passive
    ___Verbal
    ___Physical
50. Offender reacted to victim resistance: No____ Yes___
    ___ Cease demand
    ___ Compromise/negotiate
    ___ Flee
    ___ Threats
    ___ Increased force/beatings

Sexual Acts

51. Sexual dysfunction: No____ Yes____ No data____
52. Erectile insufficiency: No____ Yes____ No data____
53. Premature ejaculation: No____ Yes____ No data____
54. Retarded ejaculation: No____ Yes____ No data____
55. Conditional ejaculation: No____ Yes____ No data____

Type and Sequence of Sexual Acts during the Assault

56. Kissed: No____ Yes____ Sequence____
57. Breasts fondled: No____ Yes____ Sequence____
58. Vaginal: No____ Yes____ Sequence____
59. Oral (offender to victim):   No____ Yes____ Sequence____
60. Oral (victim to offender):   No____ Yes____ Sequence____
61. Anal: No____ Yes____ Sequence____
62. Foreign object: No____ Yes____ Sequence____
63. Offender masturbates self: No____ Yes____ Sequence____
64. Offender masturbates victim: No____ Yes____ Sequence____
65. Condom used: No____ Yes____ Sequence____
66. Experimentation: No____ Yes____ Sequence____
67. Punishment: No____ Yes____ Sequence____
68. Other: No____ Yes____
                                   Describe/sequence_____

Offender Verbal Activity

69. Apologies: No____ Yes____ Describe____
70. Compliments to victim: No____ Yes____ Describe____
71. Personal inquiries of victim: No____ Yes____
72. Reassurance to victim: No____ Yes____ Describe____
73. Affectionate phrases: No____ Yes____ Describe____
74. Profanity toward victim: No____ Yes____ Describe____
75. Demeaning statements toward victim: No____ Yes____

76. Threats: No____ Yes____ Describe_____
77. Orders   No____ Yes____ Describe_____

Victim Verbal Activity

78. Forced to talk to offender: No____ Yes____ Describe_____
79. Forced to state affection for offender: No____ Yes____
80. Self-demeaning statements: No____ Yes____
81. Talk to calm offender: No____ Yes____
82. Negotiate out of sex act: No____ Yes____ Describe_____

Offender's Initial Attitude/Behavior

83. Angry: No____ Yes____
84. Abusive: No____ Yes____
85. Quiet: No____ Yes____
86. Offender changed during rape: No____ Yes____
    Describe_____
87. Offender wore mask/disguise: No___ Yes___ Describe____
88. Percentage offender clothed (0% is nude): _____ %

II. VICTIM FORENSIC DATA

89. Height_____
90. Weight_____
91. Blood Pressure_____
92. Pulse_____
93. Temperature_____

Actions Postassault

94. Urination: No____ Yes____
95. Defecation: No____ Yes____
96. Vomit: No____ Yes____
97. Bath/shower: No____ Yes____

Method of Pelvic Examination

98. Direct visualization: No____ Yes____
99. Bimanual exam: No____ Yes____
100. Speculum exam: No____ Yes____
101. Colposcopic exam: No____ Yes____
102. Photographs taken: No____ Yes____ Number____
     Area(s) of body_____
103. Evidence kit collected No____ Yes____

Microbiology

104. Vaginal: GC____ CT____ Other____ Not done____
105. Anal: GC____ CT____ Other____ Not done____
106. Pharyngeal: GC____ CT____ Other____ Not done____
107. VDRL: Positive____ Negative____ Not done____
108. HIV: Positive____ Negative____ Not done____
109. Sperm presence/motility: Vaginal____ Anal____ Oral____
     None present____
110. DNA: No____ Yes____ No data____

Genital Trauma Noted

111. Labia majora   No____ Yes____
112. Labia minora   No____ Yes____
113. Clitoris   No____ Yes____
114. Posterior fourchette   No____ Yes____
115. Fossa navicularis   No____ Yes____
116. Periurethral   No____ Yes____
117. Vestibule   No____ Yes____
118. Vagina   No____ Yes____
119. Hymen   No____ Yes____
120. Cervix   No____ Yes____
121. Perineum   No____ Yes____
122. Anus   No____ Yes____
123. Rectum   No____ Yes____
124. Other site of injury/or injury to male victims_____
_____

Victim's Behavior during Examination/Interview

125. Controlled demeanor: No____ Yes____ If yes,
     ___ Quiet/tense
     ___ Trembling
     ___ Brief response to questions
     ___ Reluctant response to questions
     ___ Other_____
126. Expressive demeanor: No____ Yes____ If yes,
     ___ Tearful/sobbing
     ___ Agitated
     ___ Anxious smiling
     ___ Angry
     ___ Responsive to questioning
     ___ Other_____

Treatment Provided

127. Pregnancy prevention: No_____ Yes_____
128. STD prevention: No_____ Yes_____
     Other_____ (describe)_____

III. LEGAL/SERVICES INFORMATION

129. Emergency response: No_____ Yes_____ Type _____
     __ Police   _____ Crisis line
     __ Family member   _____ Friend
     __ Other
130. Forensic services: No_____ Yes_____
131. Resource mobilization: No_____ Yes_____ Type:_____
     __ Crisis intervention   __ Completing forms
     __ Victim compensation   __ Counseling
132. Preparation for court: No_____ Yes_____
133. Court appearance: No_____ Yes_____
134. Sentencing of offender: No_____ Yes_____
135. Postsentencing: No_____ Yes_____
136. Assailant(s) in custody: No_____ Yes_____ No data_____
137. Crime classification; circle one of the following:
     301:    Criminal Enterprise, felony rape
     312:    Domestic Sexual Assault
     313:    Entitlement Rape
     313.01: Social Acquaintance Rape
     313.02: Subordinate
     313.03: Power-Reassurance Rape
     313.04: Exploitative Rape
     314:    Anger Rape
     315:    Sadistic Rape
     319:    Abduction Rape

     Assault

     331:    Formal Gang Sexual Assault
     331.01: Informal Gang Sexual Assault
     390:    Sexual Assault Not Classified Elsewhere
     399:    Unfounded Case; select all that apply:
             _____ Insufficient evidence
             _____ Nolle pros
             _____ Charges dropped
             _____ Sex stress situation
             _____ False rape allegation
             _____ Delusional rape allegation
             _____ Other Describe_____

138. Victim testified at Grand Jury: No____ Yes____ No data____
139. Victim testified in Superior Court: No____ Yes____ No data____
140. Defendant convicted: No____ Yes____ No data____
141. Sentence: _____
142. Civil court trial: No____ Yes____ No data____
143. Settlement: No____ Yes____ No data____
     Verdict amount:_____

IV. PSYCHOSOCIAL ASSESSMENT FOR PTSD

Time interval since rape_____
Item Present = Yes, Absent = No; Intensity 1 = Low to 5 = High

144. Event involving actual/witnessed threatened death
     or injury   No____ Yes____ 1 2 3 4 5
145. Felt intense fear, helplessness, or horror   No____ Yes____ 1 2 3 4 5

One or more of the following reexperiencing symptoms:

146. Involuntary intrusive thoughts   No____ Yes____ 1 2 3 4 5
147. Recurrent upsetting dreams   No____ Yes____ 1 2 3 4 5
148. Flashback episodes   No____ Yes____ 1 2 3 4 5
149. Psychological distress to trauma cues No____ Yes____ 1 2 3 4 5
150. Physiological distress to trauma cues No____ Yes____ 1 2 3 4 5

At least three of the following avoidant symptoms:

151. Avoids thoughts, feelings, or talk associated
     with the trauma   No____ Yes____ 1 2 3 4 5
152. Avoids activities, places, or people associated
     with the trauma   No____ Yes____ 1 2 3 4 5
153. Amnesia to aspects of the trauma   No____ Yes____ 1 2 3 4 5
154. Decreased interest in activities   No____ Yes____ 1 2 3 4 5
155. Feeling estranged from others   No____ Yes____ 1 2 3 4 5
156. Restricted emotions   No____ Yes____ 1 2 3 4 5
157. Feeling of a foreshortened future   No____ Yes____ 1 2 3 4 5

At least two symptoms of increased arousal:

158. Difficulty sleeping   No____ Yes____ 1 2 3 4 5
159. Irritability or mood swings   No____ Yes____ 1 2 3 4 5
160. Difficulty concentrating   No____ Yes____ 1 2 3 4 5
161. Hypervigilance   No____ Yes____ 1 2 3 4 5
162. Exaggerative startle response   No____ Yes____ 1 2 3 4 5

Other symptoms since assault:

163. Increased perspiration	No____ Yes____	1 2 3 4 5
164. Increased heart rate	No____ Yes____	1 2 3 4 5
165. Changes in appetite	No____ Yes____	1 2 3 4 5
166. Increased nervousness	No____ Yes____	1 2 3 4 5
167. Body image disturbance	No____ Yes____	1 2 3 4 5
168. Unusual body sensations	No____ Yes____	1 2 3 4 5
169. Sexual dysfunction	No____ Yes____	1 2 3 4 5
170. Blames self	No____ Yes____	1 2 3 4 5
171. Low self esteem	No____ Yes____	1 2 3 4 5
172. Afraid to be alone	No____ Yes____	1 2 3 4 5
173. Prior victimization	No____ Yes____	1 2 3 4 5
174. Prior psychiatric history	No____ Yes____	1 2 3 4 5

Multiaxial Evaluation Report Form (DSM-IV)

Axis I: Clinical Disorders _____

308.3 Acute Stress Disorder (symptoms less than 1 month)
309.81 PTSD Acute (symptoms less than 3 months)
309.81 PTSD Chronic (symptoms 3 months or more)
309.81 PTSD Delayed (Symptoms begin after 6 months)
Other DSM-IV Diagnoses

Axis II: Personality Disorders_____
Mental Retardation _____

Axis III: General Medical Conditions

Axis IV: Psychosocial and Environmental Problems

__ Problems with primary support group _____
__ Problems related to social environment _____
__ Educational problems _____
__ Occupational problems _____
__ Housing problems _____
__ Economic problems _____
__ Problems with access to health care services _____
__ Problems related to legal system/crime_____
__ Other _____

Axis V: Global Assessment of Functioning Score_____Time frame _____

GAF Scale

100–91	Superior functioning	50–41	Serious symptoms
90–81	Absent or minimal symptoms	40–31	Some impairment in reality or communication
80–71	Transient symptoms	30–21	Serious impairment
70–61	Some mild symptoms	20–11	Some danger of hurting self or others
60–51	Moderate symptoms	10–1	Persistent danger of hurting self or others

IV

PROSECUTION OF RAPE

Prosecuting Rape Cases: Trial Preparation and Trial Tactic Issues

17

WILLIAM HEIMAN

Revised and Updated by
ANN PONTERIO and GAIL FAIRMAN

The focus of this chapter is the preparation and presentation of rape cases for trial. The trial of a rape case, like any other criminal case, is a series of connected parts dependent on one another. A trial is a network of interrelated pieces, all making up a discernible pattern. Everything that is done in the preparation stage must serve a purpose in terms of setting up the closing argument. From the start of jury selection, 90% of the closing statement should already have been prepared mentally and/or on paper. The remaining 10% is filled in based on material that is unforeseen at the start and that is developed during the course of the trial.

Whether trying an identification case, consent case, or an imperfect victim case, the prosecutor should begin to educate the jury in his or her opening remarks, during the *voir dire,* and during the opening statement. In closing, he or she should tie together all of the pieces of the argument that were developed in the preparation stage and established through the other stages of trial.

Process of Trial

The process of trial is a series of specific phases that will be described as follows: preparation, jury selection, opening statement, defense opening, cross-examination, rebuttal, and closing arguments.

Preparation

The key to presenting a well-organized, logical, smooth-running case in court is careful and thorough preparation. A case can be destroyed if the trial attorney is surprised by damaging information in the midst of trial. The prosecutor should also use the preparatory period to organize the file and trial exhibits. Avoid fumbling with papers and exhibits throughout the trial in order to gain the jury's confidence and to impress them with your preparedness, competence, and thorough knowledge of the case.

Preparation for a rape case should begin at the earliest encounters between the prosecutor and the rape victim and other witnesses. Usually this will occur at the

0-8493-8152-1/95/$0.00+$.50
© 1995 by CRC Press, Inc.

preliminary hearing. At this early stage the prosecutor will probably not have a complete file, but can begin preparing the victim to deal with anticipated cross-examination and can observe the victim on the witness stand to detect demeanor and articulation problems that can be smoothed out prior to trial. The prosecutor should also use this opportunity to identify any possible "prompt complaint" witnesses, witnesses to whom the victim reported the rape before the first report to police. These corroborating witnesses are usually permitted to testify by statutory exceptions to the hearsay rule.

The next step in preparing a case for trial is to gather all the statements made by the witnesses. For a rape victim, this may mean gathering as many as nine different partial or full statements. They could include: (1) the transcript of the telephone call to police emergency and the actual tape of the call, if preserved; (2) the brief interview by the first officer on the scene; (3) the nurse's interview at the hospital; (4) the examining physician's interview at the hospital; (5) the "formal" interview with the assigned investigator; (6) the notes of testimony from the preliminary hearing; (7) the notes of testimony for the pretrial motion to suppress; (8) any statements to prompt complaint witnesses; and (9) any statement given to a private investigator working on behalf of the defendant or on behalf of a third party who may have civil liability to the victim.

After obtaining and reviewing all these statements, a list of the inconsistencies should be compiled concerning such issues as the physical details of the defendant's appearance, time of day, amount of alcohol or drugs consumed, etc. Reviewing these discrepancies with the victim and attempting to reconcile them as much as possible are essential. In most cases such differences can be found to have a logical explanation.

Without exception, the trial attorney should interview all potential witnesses personally. In order to avoid the risk of the trial attorney becoming a witness, the investigating officer should be present during preparation sessions. The investigator may be an important witness at trial if the witnesses report any threats or other contacts from the defense at the prep session. Additionally, in the event that one of the witnesses recants either at the prep session or later at trial, the investigator will be able to testify regarding the circumstances of the interview, including the witness' demeanor and statements, or to refute any allegations by the witness that he or she was threatened or intimidated by the prosecutor.

After the witnesses' statements are reviewed and the discrepancies are explored, the victim should be informed about the areas of cross-examination that will come up. All the sensitive, unpleasant, and embarrassing issues that will come out at trial must be thoroughly reviewed. A review of the actual sexual acts should be avoided to prevent the victim from losing a genuine emotional edge when she recounts these acts on the stand and to avoid her appearing blase or overrehearsed.

It is important to review all other areas of her testimony in which it is likely that she will become emotionally upset or angry, such as drug or alcohol use or prior, admissible sexual contact with the defendant. This helps give her an awareness of these issues and prevents her from losing self-control or dignity on the witness stand. However, explain that if she feels as though she is going to break down and cry on the witness stand it is all right to do so, and that she should take a moment to regain her composure.

Whenever possible the prosecutor should visit the scene of the crime. A thorough understanding of the physical setting will help the attorney in preparing witnesses and in cross-examining defense witnesses and may help explain apparent improbabilities in testimony. The attorney should try to observe the viewpoints of any eyewitnesses to understand the relevant lines of sight, obstructions, and lighting.

The trial attorney should be creative in the preparation and use of demonstrative evidence. The key rule in the area of demonstrative evidence is to provide the jury with clear, visible exhibits. Pictures should be enlarged or mounted on cardboard so that they can be seen and handled easily by the jury. During the preparation sessions with the witnesses the photographs and any other physical evidence should be reviewed to ensure that the witness is not surprised at trial.

Try to learn as much as possible about the defendant in order to effectively cross-examine and to prepare for any defense. Subpoena and obtain any available material including prior criminal files, prison records, prison visitor logs, work or school records, and health records.

Once the case has been dissected and analyzed, it is time to put it together for trial. Make a list of the order of witnesses to be called. It is often effective to use an articulate prompt complaint witness or the first officer on the scene as the initial witness to set the scene for the jurors and then follow with the victim. List the major points each witness is expected to make and any physical evidence they will identify. Review the information or bills of indictment to determine the bills on which you will move to trial. Deleting the minor bills will help the jury by simplifying the case and will help avoid a compromise verdict. The testimony of the witnesses on your list should cover all of the elements of all of the crimes that are moving to trial. Avoid duplicative witnesses who may contradict each other.

At this point, the case should be thought through carefully to pinpoint the areas in which there will be a serious issue with respect to admissibility. Do the legal research and obtain cases that will support the theory of admissibility of evidence. If necessary, prepare a short memorandum on the point.

After the preparation is completed and the trial is ready to begin, the rule of thumb is to have, in outline form, 90% of the closing argument prepared. Rape trials are not won by the prosecutor "winging it"; they are won by careful, meticulous preparation.

Jury Selection and the Voir Dire Process

Entire books have been written on jury selection. Purported experts and psychologists have designed and employed personality profiles and all types of analyses in an effort to pick the perfect jury for one side or the other. As a word of caution, most experienced trial lawyers can't agree on most issues in jury selection. For example, the two most experienced and successful trial lawyers in the author's office once gave a lecture on jury selection. The first attorney said that a prospective juror should be struck unless there is some specific positive reason why you want him. The second attorney said if you are neutral about the person, take him. Obviously, there are few rules in jury selection that apply in all cases.

People who have roots and a stake in the community, the "solid citizen" types, are good progovernment jurors. Working people from high-crime neighborhoods are excellent jurors who understand the dynamics of crime and victimization. People from the victim's neighborhood or the area where the crime was committed may understand the particular problems in your case, such as why neighbors wouldn't respond to screams or a struggle or why a witness might initially lie to officials.

Always be conscious of the nature of your particular case or victim in selecting jurors. Try to pick people who will identify or relate to your victim or to you and who will not identify with the defendant. Remember that the U.S. Supreme Court has ruled that peremptory strikes cannot be used to eliminate jurors solely on the basis of race or gender. See *Batson v. Kentucky*, 476 U.S. 79, 106 S.Ct. 1712, 90 L.Ed.2d (1986); *Georgia v. McCollum*, __ U.S.__, 112 S.Ct. 2348, 120 L.Ed.2d 33, (1992); and *J.E.B., Petitioner v. Alabama ex rel. T.B.*, __U.S.__, 114 S.Ct. 1419, __L.Ed.2d__ (1994).

Avoid people who are on the fringes of society, who are drifting through life, who act and dress in a bizarre manner, or who answer questions inappropriately. Look for the mainstreamers and achievers in the group. Try to select at least two strong progovernment jurors who can control jury deliberations.

Avoid picking jurors who would be naturally antagonistic toward one another. The jury will have enough to discuss and argue about when they examine the case. It only takes one intransigent juror to hang a case.

The voir dire process varies among jurisdictions and among individual judges. It is therefore impossible to recommend any one style. However, the following are some factors to keep in mind:

- Voir dire is the first time that you have any opportunity to influence the jury. Speak to them as much as the judge will allow. This will permit you to educate them about crucial points of law in your case and to establish a personal rapport. If the judge limits your opportunity to ask questions directly of the juror try to establish eye contact as much as possible.
- In the "imperfect victim" case, extract from the jurors a promise that they will follow the law, even if they don't agree with it.
- Avoid embarrassing, humiliating, or insulting the jurors. They won't forgive you and they certainly won't forget.
- If the case depends heavily on police work, explore the juror's feeling about law enforcement. A person who believes he has been mistreated by the police will likely use your trial to "get even".
- If a juror is obviously not acceptable, thank him or her politely and abort the questioning. Don't provide a forum for the juror to espouse ideas and possibly influence the others on the panel.

- Show utmost respect at all times for the judge and the panel. Don't appear friendly to the defense counsel in front of the jury. Your tone should be dignified and professional. Any attempts at sarcastic remarks or humor are inappropriate in a rape trial. Be conscious of your behavior and the behavior of your witnesses in the hallways surrounding the courtroom if jurors may roam in that area.
- Always keep in mind the number of peremptory strikes that are left and the types of people remaining on the panel. A person who did not initially appear to be a good selection might begin to look great when there is only one strike left and the remaining group is even less promising.

Opening Statement

An opening statement is the first opportunity for a prosecutor to reveal to the jury the essence of the case. A prosecutor should create with words a clear image of the facts of the case for the jury. In preparing an outline of an opening statement, write down all of the strengths and weaknesses of the case. Foremost, be confident in presenting an opening statement. Bring out the best points and defuse the worst points of the case. Do not be afraid to address the weaknesses. Never apologize to the jury for the lack of evidence. (Juries, unlike judges, are unfamiliar with inadequacies of a case.) A prosecutor should strive for a fluid opening statement. Use language the jury will understand. While evidence in a trial may be introduced out of turn because of scheduling difficulties, you should structure an opening statement so that the evidence flows and is not confusing.

The following are some suggested guidelines for delivering an effective opening statement:

- Speak slowly.
- Reintroduce yourself. Tell the jury the main charge of rape. Do not outline every lesser included offense.
- Be brief, avoid relating minute details or quoting specific conversation.
- Personalize your victim. Don't address her by her first name; rather, say, "Donna Jones will tell you" or "Miss Jones cried for help".
- Depersonalize the defendant. Refer to him as the defendant. Never refer to him as "that gentleman".
- Promise the jury only what you know you will be able to deliver to them. If you are not sure that a certain witness will testify, don't tell the jury that the witness will definitely testify.
- Don't tell the jury your entire case.
- Focus in on the key and crucial issue(s) of the case. If it is an "ID" case, urge the jury to pay particularly close attention to the victim's opportunity to observe her assailant.
- If the victim is, for example, a drug user or met the defendant when she was frequenting a bar, be tactful, but firm (without being insulting), in stating

to the jury that the life-style of the victim is not the issue; remind the jurors of their solemn oath to be fair and impartial and not to prejudge the facts until they hear from the victim herself, relating to the jury what happened to her. No woman should ever be made to feel apologetic or shameful as to the circumstances that led up to her being raped.

- Avoid law-school-esque phrases such as "I welcome the awesome burden of the Commonwealth" or "the government will prove to you beyond a shadow of a doubt that the defendant committed this heinous, dastardly act". They may sound good on television shows, but they are less persuasive in a real courtroom before real jurors. On the other hand, telling the jury that they are about to begin their "search for the truth" has a good ring to it and is effective.
- Save the dramatics, the flamboyance, and the clever phrases for your closing. Be controlled and straightforward in your delivery of the opening statement.
- Most importantly, **be yourself**. No one style is better at communicating to juries than another. Your own style, whether it be soft spoken or energetic, is something you cannot fake. Being comfortable with who you are and how you speak will make you credible to a jury.

Defense Opening

After a prosecutor opens to the jury, the defense may make an opening statement. The purpose of any opening statement is to inform the jury of the facts of the case and what each side intends to prove as evidence. Many defense openings are dramatic, mini-closing arguments that rehash reasonable doubt and state nothing of the facts of the case. While most judges give defense attorneys considerable leeway, don't sit there listening to a defense attorney have two bites at a closing argument; stand up and object. Don't get carried away and object continuously, but set the tone with an objection.

Cross-Examination

Cross-examination of the defendant or any of his witnesses is obviously a crucial part of the truth-seeking and fact-finding process. It is also fraught with danger for the prosecutor. An excellent book on this subject is Francis Wellman's *The Art of Cross Examination*. It provides valuable background and a foundation. Another excellent resource is the writings (and some video tapes) of Professor Irving Younger, particularly his famous piece, "Ten Commandments of Cross Examination".

Following are some suggestions:

- Avoid rehashing the witness' direct examination. Have specific areas of the direct examination in mind to challenge on cross. Repeating the direct examination is boring to the jury, and it allows the witness to emphasize the points a second time which is very damaging to the prosecution's case.

- Ask as many leading questions as possible. Have in mind the answer you are looking for. Don't ask the "key" question early on in cross-examination. Set up your cross with preliminary questions, then focus in on the "key" question the witness/defendant does not have an answer for. When your point has been made to the jury don't ask another question along that line. Invariably, attorneys have a bad habit of asking one too many questions. It only gives the witness an opportunity to explain his or her previous answer.
- Two traditional rules of cross-examination are never to ask questions to which you don't know the answer and rarely ask a witness a question beginning with the word "why". There may be instances where a question beginning with a "why" is appropriate; more often than not, it gives the defense witness another opportunity to tell his or her story.
- Not all cross-examinations are hostile, heated retorts between a witness and a prosecutor. It depends on who the witness is, e.g., defendant's grandmother, and what the witness says and how damaging it is to your case. A cross-examination may illustrate to the jury that although the witness believes what he or she is saying, the witness is mistaken in that belief.
- Often the hardest thing for a prosecutor to do is not to cross-examine a witness. Do not cross-examine a witness who does not hurt your case.
- Before cross-examining the defendant, outline all possible avenues the defendant may take on the witness stand. The defendant can admit or deny sexual intercourse with the victim. If he admits sexual intercourse, then his defense is most likely to be consent. If he denies sexual intercourse, then his defense can be one of the following: the victim is mistaken in her identification of the defendant; the victim is fabricating the rape; the defendant has an alibi for his whereabouts at about the time of the (most often used word by the defense attorney during a trial) **alleged** occurrence.
- Be prepared to cross-examine the defendant thoroughly depending on which avenue he chooses. (A prosecutor should always be prepared to cross-examine a defendant on the rare occasion when he testifies at a motion to suppress. Never take much credence in a defense attorney who tells you that the defendant will not be testifying at trial.)
- Always know the extent of any prior sexual relationship the defendant had with the victim.
- It is important to bring out questions to demonstrate to the jury the defendant's motive to lie on the witness stand.
- Often an overlooked, important piece of cross-examination is cross-examining the character witness. In many jurisdictions, a defendant can introduce character only through reputation and not through specific good acts. Bring out any bias the character witness has such as being a family

member or a close friend. If the witness is a co-worker, demonstrate how the witness only knows the defendant from work and not from any social setting. Ask the character witness when was the last time he or she spoke about the defendant's character in the community — before or after his arrest — and with whom. You may choose not to ask the defendant's mother any questions regarding character, and if you do, only ask one or two questions.

- In prepping your victim for cross-examination tell her not to be sarcastic in answering the defense attorney's questions.
- Tell the victim that the defense attorney's tone may be sarcastic and the attorney does that so that she will respond in a sarcastic fashion. The prosecutor's job is to not let this happen and object when the defense does this.
- Have the witness remain as calm as possible and not show a temper to the jury.
- Tell the victim that when you object, she is to stop answering the question until the judge indicates otherwise.
- Remind the witness to only answer the question and not to volunteer any additional information.
- Explain to the witness that if she doesn't understand the question to say she doesn't understand the question.
- Know the terminology of the victim. A victim may not comprehend what words like, e.g., ripped and torn, mean, as illustrated in the following exchange:

> **Defense attorney**: Are you telling this jury that my client ripped your panties off of you?
> **Victim**: He most certainly did.
> **Defense Attorney**: And he did it with as much force as he could muster, he ripped your panties apart in getting them off of you?
> **Victim**: I told you already that he did.

Defense attorney then argues to the jury that the jury heard from the witness that the defendant ripped her pants apart getting them off of her and introduces a report from the forensics laboratory that the panties are intact and show no tears. The victim, on the other hand, understood the expression "ripped" as being taken off forcibly, not actually "ripped apart".

This is nothing more than a game of semantics. Prepare the witness that the defense attorney may use words that she is not familiar with and may not understand their meaning. Tell her not to be embarrassed in saying to the attorney that she does not understand his question. Make the defense attorney rephrase it. Attorneys get flustered when they have to repeat or rephrase questions.

- Every attorney must be comfortable with his or her style of cross-examination. Many prefer to stand through all of cross-examination; others prefer to stand when they make their key points. If time permits, discuss your cross-examination with fellow colleagues and ask for their input.

Rebuttal

The government's rebuttal to certain parts of the defense case is an explosive part of the prosecutor's package. Keep in mind the following points:

- Rebuttal testimony should be very brief, pointed, direct, and specific. It should be aimed at challenging a specific point presented by the defense. Stay away from recalling a witness on rebuttal unless it's compelling evidence, to avoid the risk of opening the door on issues that are ancillary to the case.
- Rebuttal evidence is particularly persuasive to the jury because it is usually the last evidence presented to them.
- The jury already has a frame of reference in which they can evaluate the credibility of the evidence offered; that is, they know what defense evidence is being directly challenged by the rebuttal evidence.
- Documents and records make particularly strong rebuttal evidence. By presenting records, the prosecutor doesn't have to worry about credibility factors, which are present when a live witness is being evaluated. The records are cold, unemotional facts that speak for themselves.
- The way to present rebuttal evidence effectively is first to lock the witness into his testimony regarding a particular fact. Make sure the fact to be challenged is on the record in a clear, unambiguous manner. Then put on your rebuttal witness in as short and succinct a manner as possible — get in and get out. Examples of documentation of record that are particularly effective include time cards from work records proving that the defendant was not, in fact, at work when he said he was; records from a television station showing that the program the witness was supposed to have been watching that night was preempted, etc. The point is that when the jury has to evaluate a witness' testimony against a cold business record, they will invariably resolve any factual dispute in favor of the business record.
- In rebutting an alibi defense, consider the alibi witnesses like links in a chain that is only as strong as the weakest link. You don't have to explode the entire testimony of every alibi witness. Search for the inconsistent part of one alibi witness' testimony and then argue to the jury that when the weak link in the chain breaks, the entire alibi crumbles.
- If the defendant testifies to materially different facts from those the victim has already testified to, you must decide whether to recall her in rebuttal. This may not be wise if she is an "imperfect victim". However, if the defense raises a fact that the victim did not testify to (drug use, for example), it is incumbent on the prosecutor to bring the victim back on rebuttal to deny it. Be careful not to have the victim rehash her whole testimony on rebuttal. Raise the specific point and stop. This type of rebuttal is particularly effective as it gives the jury one last opportunity to see, hear, and evaluate the victim.

Closing Argument

The closing argument is a crucial part of every criminal trial. Countless cases are won or lost based upon the quality of the summation.

The first point to keep in mind is preparation. As mentioned above, you should have about 90% of your closing argument outlined in your head or on paper at the time you begin the trial; the remaining 10% of the content is based on materials that came to light for the first time during the course of trial.

The length of your closing will vary with the length and complexity of the case. In general, however, anything under 15 min is probably too short; 30 to 45 min is a good period of time; and anything over an hour in length may very well be too long.

The following is a general outline of a closing argument in a rape trial:

- Do not read your closing verbatim from a tablet or cards.
- Speak **to** the jurors and not at them. Don't speak quickly; take your time. Jurors cannot understand or absorb your points if you rattle them off. Forget big legal words — they are not impressive.
- Have a general outline with keywords to remind you of the areas to cover.
- Answer the most offensive or fallacious arguments made by the defense attorney in his closing. Mention to the jury that before you begin the merits of your argument, you feel obliged to respond to a few comments made by your opponent that you cannot let pass. Avoid the trap of spending your whole time responding to the defense's argument.
- Cover the main thrust of your case.
- In an identification case review the witnesses' opportunities to observe, one by one. In reviewing your notes from trial, write down every fact that helps you in identifying the defendant — distance, lighting, time period to observe, height, prior descriptions — and match these facts to the defendant. In a consent case, highlight issues such as the lack of a motive for the victim to lie, and any other evidence in the case that supports her testimony.
- Emphasize all corroboration of the rape victim's testimony. Review the key portion of each witness' testimony and point out how it adds to the government's overall case or how it supports the victim's testimony.
- If the victim is an "imperfect victim" argue that the jury has been summoned to decide the issue of rape, not to decide a popularity contest as to whether they like the victim as a person or approve of her life-style. Emphasize that negative opinions regarding the victim's life-style or personality are never an excuse for the defendant to have raped her.
- Use the emotional aspects of rape — that the dignity of the person has been attacked.
- It is helpful to have the victim sitting in the front row of the courtroom so that you can gesture toward her as you speak. Make sure to have someone sit next to the rape victim such as a police officer or a rape crisis counselor.
- It is particularly important to stress the credibility of the testimony of the neutral or unbiased witness: the examining physician or the bystander

stranger who obviously has no "axe to grind". These unbiased corroborating witnesses lend strong support to the victim's credibility.

- Where the defense has offered evidence in the case, particularly if the defendant testified, remind the jury that they must evaluate this testimony by the same yardstick they did the victim's testimony.
- Mention the defendant's strong motive to lie to avoid conviction and pick apart any inconsistencies in his testimony. Appealing to the jury's collective common sense and logic is more effective than appealing to their passion. Usually in the "he said vs. she said" type of case, there is one witness or piece of evidence that can be indicative of which side is telling the truth.

After the facts have been analyzed in the closing and the jury has been urged to resolve credibility issues in favor of the victim and the government witnesses, mention the definition and elements of the crimes charge. Be deferential to the judge by stating to the jury that the judge will instruct them on the law, but you would like to take a few moments to discuss it and how it applies to the facts of this case. Often juries become bored and confused during the judge's charge when he or she reads legal definitions to them. If the prosecutor in his or her closing argument uses similar words without all the legalese attached, the juries will have a better understanding of the elements rather than just hearing the legal definition once. Carefully analyze any key issues of your case, such as the sufficiency of a "substantial step" in an attempted rape case or the definition of sufficient force, and the lack of any requirement that the victim offer physical resistance in the face of a substantial threat. Remind the jury of their solemn oath to obey the law, even if they don't agree with it or approve of it.

It is often useful to reserve to the very end of your closing a summary of how the crime occurred. Do not repeat the testimony. During the course of a trial, witnesses are not presented chronologically. There are many breaks and jurors can forget parts of the testimony. Summarizing the testimony in a coherent narrative gives the jurors a clearer understanding.

It is often effective to reserve the last section of the closing argument for a jurors' call to duty. Remind jurors that they represent the spirit and the conscience of the community and that all of us have a right to expect that they will act fairly and impartially and will seek to do justice. As always during the course of the trial, be proud to be a prosecutor and be proud to represent the interests of the victim and the community at large. Never apologize for the lack of evidence. If the prosecutor is confident, then that confidence transcends to the jury.

Difficult Cases

Identification Issue Case

The identification issue case is the most straightforward type of rape case to try. The issue is not "Was she raped?" but, rather, "Is the defendant the one who did it?".

The identification case is an excellent example of how the prosecutor should weave different parts of the trial into a coherent whole. Basically, the identification case breaks down into three distinct issues: (1) the victim's opportunity to observe the assailant, and barring some unusual physical characteristic, specifically his face; (2) the accuracy of the physical description made by the victim to the authorities; and (3) the identification or confrontation of the defendant by the victim, whether by photograph, in person, in a lineup, or in a one-on-one confrontation.

The first key to successfully prosecuting this type of case is the preparation session with the victim. Having all of the prior statements in hand, review with her in minute detail each and every opportunity she had to see the defendant during the commission of the crime. Focus in on the victim's observations of the defendant's face. For each opportunity ask her the following questions: How far from his face were you when you saw his face? What were the lighting conditions? What were you thinking of at the time? List each and every specific opportunity and the surrounding information separately. These small, isolated chips of information must be ascertained. Work with the victim carefully and help her to recall each and every opportunity.

Also, at the preparation session you must review with the victim why she is certain it was the defendant who assaulted her. If the victim merely says, "Yes, the defendant", when asked if she sees the person who attacked her in the courtroom, the jury won't know if "yes" means "I know that's him and I'll be positive until the day I die", or whether the "yes" means "I guess that must be him. After all, they arrested him didn't they?". The prosecutor must review this question with the victim very carefully. She must be prepared to tell you at the end of your direct examination, and stress during cross-examination, the basis or reason why she is able to swear under oath it was the defendant and no one else who attacked her.

During your opening statement to the jury tell the jurors that while they must pay close attention to all of the testimony, they should listen very carefully to the victim as she describes each and every opportunity to see the defendant's face. They should also note carefully the accuracy of her description to the authorities and her certainty during the identification confrontation that occurred.

The next important step occurs during direct examination of the victim. As soon as the victim mentions the presence of the assailant on the scene, immediately ask her if she sees the man she is describing physically in the courtroom. Indicate on the record that she has identified Mr. Jones, the defendant. From then on, she should refer to him as the "defendant".

As mentioned earlier, let the victim testify in a narrative, flowing form on her direct testimony. Interrupt her with specific questions only when necessary. You want the jury to hear her dramatic account of what happened in a narrative manner, without constantly being interrupted. After the victim has finished recounting the assault ask her to go back to the point at which she first saw the defendant and tell the jury about that and about the first time that she saw the defendant's face. Take her through the accompanying detailed questions just as you reviewed them in the prep sessions. Then go through the same series of questions with each opportunity to observe. The effect of letting the victim describe the incident in narrative form and then filling it in with specific opportunities to observe is twofold: first, it organizes her opportunities to observe the defendant for the jury and makes it easy for you to argue the point in your closing; and second, it gives you two "bites of the apple", in that the jury will hear the violent aspects of the victim's testimony repeated again as she explains her opportunities to observe the defendant. Emphasize any unusual features of the defendant that the victim noted and used in making her identification. The victim should also note any significant changes in appearance that may be efforts on the part of the defendant to conceal his identity and evidence a consciousness of guilt.

In closing, emphasize that the trauma of the assault has emblazoned the defendant's face into the brain of the victim. Argue to the jury that the case is not an identification case but a recognition case. Stress any consistent out-of-court identification and the absence of any misidentification. Review each and every opportunity the victim had to observe the defendant's face. The cumulative effect of listing every single opportunity impacts significantly on the jury. Argue that it is these many opportunities that are the foundation of an accurate, reliable, in-court identification.

Consent Issue Case

The consent issue case presents several difficult problems for the prosecutor. The issue in the case is not whether the sexual activity occurred; most often the defendant will readily admit sexual contact with the victim. The issue is whether the act occurred by direct force or threat of force, or whether it happened with the victim's consent.

One of the problems presented by this type of case is that extraneous issues find their way into the record about the prior relationship between the parties or the nature of the activities of the victim and the defendant prior to the assault. Rape Shield Statutes that preclude the introduction of evidence of prior sexual activity on the part of the victim do not usually preclude the evidence of a sexual relationship between the parties when consent is the issue. When you have this type of case, it is better to bring out the scope of the prior relationship in your opening statement and on direct examination rather than wait for the defense attorney to spring it on the victim on cross-examination.

When the facts show that the victim and the defendant were engaged in an "unpopular" type of activity prior to the assault, such as drug or excessive alcohol use, follow the suggestions outlined in the "imperfect victim" section of this chapter.

The key to successfully prosecuting the consent defense case is to corroborate the testimony of the victim with as much supporting evidence as possible. The following are suggestions for handling the consent issue type of case:

- If the victim claims she was slapped, choked, or in some manner physically abused by the defendant introduce evidence of her physical injuries from the medical records custodian, from the examining physicians, the first officer on the scene, or a prompt complaint or other witness. This documentation of her physical injuries, even minor scratches or bruises, becomes crucial in arguing to the jury in your closing that the victim's version of what happened can and should be believed.

- If the victim claims she was screaming during the incident, it is important to bring in the neighbor or the person who heard her scream. This again corroborates the victim's testimony that the sexual contact was without her consent.

- Any type of *res gestae* or excited utterance statement that is admissible is very valuable and should be introduced.

In a consent case where the victim has not suffered any trauma to her vaginal area, the defense attorney will try to argue to the jury during his closing that the lack of vaginal injury is consistent with the defendant's version of consensual intercourse. After all, he will argue, if the victim had been forced, she would have suffered some type of injury to her vagina. To a lay person this argument is persuasive. However, it is not valid. Therefore, in a consent case without vaginal trauma consider bringing in an expert medical witness, preferably the examining physician, to educate the jury on this issue. The doctor should explain the female pelvic anatomy and how rarely visible bruises or tears are noted even in confirmed sexual assault cases. The medical expert should conclude by offering his expert medical opinion that the lack of trauma is entirely consistent with the victim having been forced to submit to intercourse.

Imperfect Victim Case

The "imperfect victim" is a label used to describe a victim who, by virtue of her background or life-style in general, or because of the particular activity in which she was engaged just before the rape, can be expected to elicit biased or negative feelings from the average juror. Examples of this include prostitutes, drug and alcohol abusers, and runaways.

The prosecutor should file a motion in limine before trial to obtain a ruling regarding any information concerning the victim's activities that is inadmissible and thus preclude a suggestive and improper defense question. Once the defense attorney asks a question in front of the jury regarding one of these unpopular activities it is too late to object. The jury will suspect that you are trying to conceal some unpleasant facts and will not disregard the question regardless of how many times they are told that questions are not evidence. If you obtain a pretrial ruling in your favor be sure to review the parameters with your witness to insure that she does not open the door on the inadmissible and potentially damaging information through their testimony.

Much of the unpopular information will be admissible, however, and because you will be unable to disguise the victim's unpopular activities or life-style it is better to bring the matter to the jury's attention as soon as possible. You must be totally honest, without being apologetic, about the victim's imperfections through-out the trial. You must emphasize to the victim that, while she should not offer inadmissible information, she must be forthright no matter how bad she thinks the admissible information will make her seem to the jurors. The already "imperfect victim" cannot afford to be caught in an obvious lie by the defense. Additionally, the prosecutor can argue in closing that the victim was not concealing anything from the jurors in her quest for justice, and use this point to highlight her credibility regarding the entire incident.

If the judge will permit you to participate in voir dire, it is crucial in this type of case to extract a promise from the jurors before they are selected that, notwithstanding the fact that they do not approve of the victim's life-style or of what the victim was doing before the rape, nevertheless, they will keep an open mind as they hear the testimony and not reach any conclusions until the appropriate time. Also, the jurors must promise that, like it or not, they will follow the law as it is stated by the judge in his charge.

One important benefit of bringing the unpopular facts out during voir dire is that you can judge whether or not the juror can be fair and impartial and will give the government a fair trial, notwithstanding the imperfect aspects of the victim. If the juror indicates that he can't be fair or is hesitant in stating that he will be fair, it is obviously far better for the prosecutor to know that during voir dire rather to accept a juror and run the risk of poisoning the other jurors during deliberations.

During the opening statement don't be afraid to state again the negative aspects of the victim. Be sure to remind the jurors of the promise they made when they were selected, both to you individually and on their oath, to keep an open mind and follow the law as the judge states it to them in his charge. As you present your case, at least the jury is not shocked when they actually hear the victim testify. Highlight any type of corroboration, as this evidence will be crucial when you argue, in closing, that the victim's testimony was credible and worthy of the jury's belief.

This is the type of case where it would be particularly effective to use a witness other than the victim to set the stage. If an initial witness effectively describes a distraught, injured, or desperate victim seeking help, then the jury will be sympathetic to the victim from the start of the testimony and may be more forgiving of the unpopular aspects of her testimony.

When the victim testifies, be sure to bring out on direct examination the nature and extent of the unpopular activity, assuming, of course, that it is admissible and would be brought out on cross-examination. The purpose of this approach is to be "up front" with the jury and not hide any unpopular aspects of the victim's activities. This will "take the wind out of the sails" of your opponent by leaving no new material in these areas to develop on cross-examination. Use every piece of corroborating evidence available, including physical aspects of the scene, torn, dirty, or disheveled clothing, weather, and anything else a creative prosecutor can think of to hit hard that the victim is worthy of belief.

In closing argument, again remind the jury of the promise they made to be fair and impartial. Tell them that the issue in the case is not whether they approve of the victim's life-style or activities. Advise them that the only issue is whether the evidence proves, beyond a reasonable doubt, that the defendant assaulted her.

Remind them of their oath to follow the law, whether or not they like or approve of it. Explain that when the judge defines the law they must follow and obey, they will hear nothing that says a drug addict can't be raped or that it is a defense to the crime of rape that the victim had been drinking in a bar alone, etc. You must have the jury focus on the true issues in the case and move them beyond the imperfect aspects of the victim.

It is also effective in closing to point out that this type of flawed victim is "easy prey" or the "perfect victim" for the defendant, as she would be less likely to go to the police and less likely to be believed if she did. Remind the jury that she, as well as the defendant, is entitled to equal protection under the law.

General Policy Issues

The prosecutor's office should also set general policies to govern the handling of rape cases within the office and should use available resources to help to set policies with the law enforcement and civilian communities concerning rape cases.

In the category of policy issues external to the prosecutor's office, the prosecutor can have a direct impact by lobbying, primarily at the state level, for new statutes concerning issues ranging from mandatory minimum prison sentences for repeat offenders to the protection of the confidentiality of rape counseling records. Other external policy issues include dealing with members of the press who publish rape victims' names, pictures, and addressees; coordinating a sexual assault coalition in the local community made up of the treating hospitals, police departments, and rape crisis and victim counseling centers; and supporting in various ways the right of the rape crisis center to existence and financial viability.

In the category of internal office policies, the prosecutor should develop clearly defined standards for negotiating guilty pleas, nol-prossing charges (withdrawing from prosecution of cases), and administering polygraph tests to defendants or victims. There should be a regularly scheduled series of training sessions for the staff covering the legal, medical, and psychological issues involved in trying rape cases.

Summary

This chapter provides practical suggestions regarding the process of trial including preparation, jury selection and the voir dire process, opening statement, defense opening, cross-examination, rebuttal, and closing argument. Difficult cases include identification issue cases, the consent issue case, and the imperfect victim. The importance of general policies to govern the handling of rape cases within the prosecutor's office is discussed.

Rape Trauma Syndrome: A Review of Case Law and Psychological Research*

18

PATRICIA A. FRAZIER
EUGENE BORGIDA

Rape Trauma Syndrome:
A Review of Case Law and Psychological Research

Psychologists and other mental health professionals have contributed their expertise to court proceedings for many years on such topics as insanity and competency to stand trial. However, both the frequency of the use of expert psychological testimony and the types of issues about which psychologists testify have increased in recent years. Controversy surrounding the admissibility and ethics of such testimony also has escalated (see, e.g., Elliott, 1991; Ellsworth, 1991; McCloskey et al., 1986).

An example of a relatively new and controversial type of evidence is expert testimony on rape trauma syndrome (RTS). This testimony typically consists of a description of the common aftereffects of rape (i.e., RTS) and an opinion that a particular complainant's behavior is consistent with having been raped. The testimony is most often used to corroborate the complainant's claim that intercourse was not consensual when the defendant claims consent.

Previous reviews of the case law on RTS evidence revealed that appellate courts initially were divided sharply regarding its admissibility (Borgida et al., 1987; Frazier and Borgida, 1985). Several appellate courts have addressed the admissibility of RTS evidence since these initial reviews were published. While the issues have changed somewhat, courts continue to be divided, with some ruling in favor of expert testimony on RTS (*Lessard v. State*, 1986; *People v. Hampton*, 1987; *People v. Taylor*, 1990; *Simmons v. State*, 1987; *State v. Allewalt*, 1986; *State v. Bubar*, 1985; *State v. Gettier*, 1989; *State v. Huey*, 1985; *State v. Robinson*, 1988) and

* This chapter is reprinted from Frazier, P.A. and Borgida, E., Rape trauma syndrome: a review of case law and psychological research, *Law Hum. Behav.*, 16, 293, 1992. With permission. Some citations in this reprinted version have been updated. For an analysis of how the recent Supreme Court decision in *Daubert v. Merrell Dow Pharmaceuticals* (1993) may influence the admissibility of expert testimony on rape trauma syndrome, see a forthcoming chapter by Frazier, P. and Borgida, E., *Scientific Evidence Reference Manual*, Farigman, D. L., Kaye, D., Saks, M. J., and Sanders, J., West Publishing.

some rulings against the admissibility of the testimony (*Commonwealth v. Gallagher,* 1988; *People v. Coleman,* 1989; *State v. Black,* 1987; *State v. Brodniak,* 1986; *State v. McCoy,* 1988). That dissenting opinions were filed in several cases (*Commonwealth v. Gallagher,* 1988; *State v. Allewalt,* 1986; *State v. Black,* 1987; *People v. Hampton,* 1987) and that several courts explicitly noted that they were *not* ruling on RTS evidence, can be interpreted as additional evidence of the controversial nature of the testimony.*

The purpose of this chapter is, first, to review recent appellate court decisions on the admissibility of RTS evidence (i.e., cases decided since the authors' earlier reviews). The second purpose is to describe psychological research relevant to concerns expressed by the courts in these recent decisions about the scientific reliability, helpfulness, and prejudicial impact of RTS evidence. This review provides the background for an evaluation of the expert testimony and judicial decision making in recent cases. These evaluations focus on the use of psychological research both by experts and by the courts. Finally, the authors provide suggestions for future psychological research that could inform discussions of the admissibility of RTS evidence. This chapter thus differs from law review articles on RTS that focus more specifically on the case law (e.g., Buchele and Buchele, 1985; Donohue, 1987/1988; Dwyer, 1988; Fischer, 1989; Lawrence, 1984; Massaro, 1985; McCord, 1985).

Admissibility Criteria

Prior to reviewing the case law on RTS evidence, it is necessary to discuss briefly the criteria for the admissibility of expert psychological testimony. Unfortunately, there is no uniformly accepted standard by which courts evaluate such testimony. There are, however, a few basic requirements that must be met in order for expert testimony to be admissible. First, the expert must be qualified "by knowledge, skill, experience, training, or education" (Rule 702, Federal Rules of Evidence, 1984).** Second, the evidence must assist the trier of fact (i.e., be helpful to jurors in their decision making). Third, the evidence must be scientifically reliable. In determining reliability, some courts rely on *Frye v. United States* (1923) which requires that scientific evidence be "generally accepted" within the relevant scientific community in order to be admissible. Other courts rely on the Federal Rules of Evidence

---

* These cases involve testimony that (1) the complainant's reactions were typical of sexual assault victims (*People v. Farley,* 1987), (2) the complainant's behavior was not unusual (*State v. Horne,* 1986), (3) the complainant had been penetrated against her will (*People v. Mays,* 1986), and (4) the complainant had been sexually assaulted (*People v. Smith,* 1986).

** The American Psychology-Law Society *Specialty Guidelines for Forensic Psychologists* recommends that "forensic psychologists provide services only in areas of psychology in which they have specialized knowledge, skill, experience, *and* education" [emphasis added] (Committee on Ethical Guidelines for Forensic Psychologists, 1991). Thus, whereas the Federal Rules allow experts to be qualified on one of several grounds, these guidelines recommend that psychological experts be qualified on all four grounds.

which do not require "general acceptance". The final criterion for admissibility is that the expert testimony be probative and not unfairly prejudicial to the defendant. Further clarification of these criteria is provided in the ensuing discussion.

Rape Trauma Syndrome Case Law

Qualitative reviews of the early case law (i.e., decisions made prior to 1985) revealed that arguments against the admissibility of RTS evidence have been made in regard to all four of these criteria (Borgida et al., 1987; Frazier and Borgida, 1985). The primary objections to the testimony in the early decisions concerned its helpfulness (e.g., whether the testimony is beyond the common knowledge of the jury), prejudicial impact (e.g., whether the testimony improperly bolsters the credibility of the complainant), and scientific reliability (e.g., whether the evidence can reliably determine whether a rape occurred). The authors' analysis of recent case law will assess whether the same concerns continue to be raised regarding the admissibility of RTS evidence.

Expert Qualification

As was true in earlier cases, the qualification of the expert was rarely a determining issue in the more recent cases. The defense objected to the qualifications of the expert in three cases; the expert was a rape crisis counselor in each (*State v. Bubar*, 1985; *State v. McCoy*, 1988; *State v. Robinson*, 1988). The courts upheld the qualification of the expert in all three cases on the basis that experts can be qualified on several grounds (e.g., training or experience). In cases where the qualifications of the experts were not questioned, the experts have been psychologists (*People v. Hampton, 1986; State v. Brodniak*, 1986; *State v. Gettier*, 1989); psychiatrists (*State v. Huey*, 1985); social workers (*Simmons v. State*, 1987; *State v. Black*, 1987); rape crisis counselors (*People v. Coleman*, 1989); physicians (*People v. Coleman*, 1989); and academic professionals (*Commonwealth v. Gallagher*, 1988). Rape crisis counselors thus seem to be more vulnerable to objections about their qualifications than other experts. This may be because they lack the educational credentials and research background of other experts or because they are more likely to be perceived as advocates for victims.

Scientific Reliability

The scientific reliability* of RTS evidence was not often raised as an issue in the more recent appellate court decisions. Unlike concerns about expert qualification, however, the issue appeared to be a major factor in the evaluation of the testimony

---

* Consistent with its use in judicial decisions, the authors' use of the term "reliability" encompasses the psychometric concepts of both reliability and validity.

when it was raised. The cases that addressed the scientific reliability of the evidence will thus be discussed in some detail.

In *People v. Hampton* (1986), the Colorado Court of Appeals reversed a conviction on the grounds that RTS evidence had been improperly admitted by the trial court. The Colorado Supreme Court reviewed the case and reinstated the original conviction based on its finding that the testimony had been properly admitted at the trial court level (*People v. Hampton*, 1987). The difference between decisions lies in the differing standards imposed on the testimony by the two courts. Specifically, the Court of Appeals ruled that the testimony did not meet the criteria for admissibility outlined in *Frye v. United States* (1923) because it did not reliably establish that a rape occurred. On the other hand, the Supreme Court argued that the appellate court erred in applying the *Frye* test and that the Federal Rules more properly apply to this type of evidence. According to the Federal Rules, any weaknesses in the evidence should affect the weight given the evidence by the jury rather than the admissibility of the testimony itself. Whether the *Frye* test properly applies to this type of testimony is an ongoing debate in the literature (see, e.g., Frazier and Borgida, 1985; Lawrence, 1984; McCord, 1985).

The Washington Court of Appeals also reversed a conviction on the grounds that expert testimony on RTS had been improperly admitted by the trial court (*State v. Black*, 1987). Unlike the Colorado Supreme Court, the Washington Supreme Court affirmed the appellate court decision. Relying on the *Frye* test to determine the admissibility of the evidence, the Washington Supreme Court ruled that RTS is not a scientifically reliable means of proving that a rape occurred. This decision was based on the fact that their review of the scientific literature on rape trauma suggested that there is no typical response to rape and that the symptoms of rape trauma are not unique because they can be caused by other traumatic events (see Dwyer, 1988, for further discussion of this case).

The New York Court of Appeals also has discussed the reliability of RTS evidence (*People v. Taylor*, 1990). The New York Court concluded that although RTS is associated with a broad range of symptoms and there are individual differences in patterns of recovery, the relevant scientific community has generally accepted that rape is a traumatic event that triggers the onset of identifiable symptoms in many women. Unlike the Washington Supreme Court, they did not frame the question of scientific reliability in terms of whether RTS evidence proves that a complainant was raped.

In sum, two of the three courts that have addressed this issue have decided that RTS evidence is scientifically reliable. Differences between courts reflect that questions about scientific reliability have been framed in two very different ways. Some courts are concerned with whether there is a consistent and generally accepted body of knowledge on the aftereffects of rape, whereas others are concerned with whether a diagnosis of RTS "proves" that a rape occurred. Courts that have framed the question in terms of whether the symptoms associated with rape trauma can prove that a rape occurred have tended to decide that the evidence is not reliable (e.g., *State v. Black*, 1987). Several commentators have noted that this interpretation sets an unreasonably high standard for the admission of expert testimony (Donohue, 1987/1988; Massaro, 1985; McCord, 1985). According to the Federal Rules of Evidence (1984), expert testimony must tend to make the existence of a fact more or less probable, rather than "prove" the fact in question. Although there is debate regarding whether the Federal Rules or the *Frye* test is the appropriate standard for determining reliability, as well as whether these two standards really differ (Salzburg, 1983), neither requires that evidence be determinative proof.

Helpfulness

The helpfulness of RTS evidence was raised as a concern in only two recent decisions. Specifically, in *State v. Gettier* (1989), the expert testified in general terms about the characteristics exhibited by people who have experienced traumatic events. The defendant argued that the testimony was irrelevant because it did not "assist the trier of fact to understand the evidence or to determine a fact in issue" (p. 4). The Iowa Supreme Court ruled that the evidence was relevant to show that the complainant had been traumatized, but added that it did not add much to the jury's common understanding.

In *State v. Robinson* (1988), the expert testified that it was not unusual for a victim to exhibit little emotion immediately following an assault. This testimony was offered to rebut the defendant's assertion that the complainant's lack of emotion was inconsistent with her claim of rape. The Wisconsin Supreme Court ruled that the testimony was helpful in "disabusing the jury of some widely held misconceptions about sexual assault victims" (p. 173). Similarly, the New York Court stated that patterns of responses of rape victims are not within the common understanding of lay jurors (*People v. Taylor*, 1990).

Thus, in cases where the helpfulness of the testimony has been in issue, courts have ruled that the testimony is indeed helpful, particularly when used to educate jurors regarding common misconceptions about rape. That the issue was raised in only two cases suggests that the helpfulness of the evidence was of less concern in more recent cases than it was in earlier cases.

Prejudicial Impact

By far the most common objection to expert testimony on RTS in recent cases is that it is unfairly prejudicial to the defendant. Courts have been divided fairly evenly on this issue, with approximately half of the courts deciding that the testimony was not unfairly prejudicial (*Lessard v. State*, 1986; *Simmons v. State*, 1987; *State v. Allewalt*, 1986; *State v. Gettier*, 1989; *State v. Huey*, 1985) and half of the courts reaching the opposite conclusion (*Commonwealth v. Gallagher*, 1988; *People v. Coleman*, 1989; *State v. Black*, 1987; *State v. Brodniak*, 1986; *State v. McCoy*, 1988). These differences of opinion partly reflect differences in the exact nature of the testimony provided, as described below.

First, testimony can differ in regard to whether or not the expert used the term "RTS". For example, the expert in *State v. Allewalt* (1986) testified regarding the characteristics of post traumatic stress disorder (PTSD), stating that PTSD could be caused by several kinds of traumatic events, and gave an opinion that the complainant was suffering from PTSD. The Maryland Court of Appeals ruled that avoiding the term RTS is "more than cosmetic" (p. 751) and that the potential for unfair prejudice is largely reduced when the terminology does not equate the syndrome exclusively with rape. Conversely, the Washington Supreme Court found "such semantic distinctions unpersuasive" (*State v. Black*, 1987, p. 19) and ruled that the testimony is unfairly prejudicial because it constitutes an opinion regarding the guilt of the defendant.

A second distinction made by the courts is whether or not the testimony is used to rebut claims by the defendant that the complainant's behavior was inconsistent with her claim of rape. Courts have admitted testimony regarding a wide range of behaviors for this purpose, including failure to recall details of the assault (*Simmons v. State*, 1987), asking the defendant not to tell anyone about the assault (*Lessard v. State*, 1986), delayed reporting (*People v. Hampton*, 1986), and lack of emotion following the assault (*People v. Taylor*, 1990; *State v. Robinson*, 1988). In fact, the New York Court of Appeals ruled that RTS testimony is admissible *only* to explain behavior that may seem inconsistent to the jury (*People v. Taylor*, 1990; see, also, *People v. Bledsoe*, 1984).

It also should be noted, however, that other courts have *excluded* testimony offered to rebut a defendant's claim that a complainant's behavior was inconsistent with that of a rape victim. This includes testimony (1) explaining a complainant's inability to identify the defendant until years after the rape (*Commonwealth v. Gallagher*, 1988), (2) on the frequency of false accusations among rape victims (*State v. Brodniak*, 1986), and (3) that the complainant was still traumatized by the experience (*State v. McCoy*, 1988). The courts in *Brodniak* and *McCoy* both ruled that expert testimony on RTS generally is admissible, but that the testimony offered in the particular case at hand went beyond what was proper.

Finally, the testimony has varied in terms of how specifically it is related to the case at hand. The evidence appears to be more acceptable to courts if the expert discusses the symptoms experienced by victims as a class rather than those experienced by a particular complainant (e.g., *State v. Gettier*, 1989). More often, the expert testifies about the typical behaviors of rape victims and offers an opinion that the complainant's behavior is consistent with that of a rape victim (e.g., *State v. Black*, 1987). This opinion can be given by an expert who has interviewed the complainant solely for the purpose of providing the testimony or by an expert who has provided counseling to the complainant. Whether the expert actually interviewed the complainant does not appear to be a major factor in determining prejudice. Nonetheless, some legal scholars recommend that, in order to reduce the risk of prejudice, experts not interview complainants (Dwyer, 1988).

In sum, the potential prejudicial impact of RTS testimony has become its most controversial aspect. Both the content and the purpose of the testimony are crucial factors in determining prejudice. In regard to content, courts seem to prefer testimony that refers to victims in general, but are divided regarding whether the use of the term "RTS" is unfairly prejudicial. In regard to purpose, the testimony seems to enjoy somewhat greater acceptance if it is used to rebut a defendant's claim that the complainant's behavior was inconsistent with having been raped.

Psychological Research Relevant to Concerns about Admissibility

As this review of the case law suggests, decisions regarding the admissibility of expert testimony on RTS are based on judicial evaluations of the scientific litera-ture on rape trauma as well as on judicial assumptions regarding the presumed helpfulness and/or prejudicial impact of the testimony. Because the issues that arise in making decisions about admissibility often are empirical questions, the purpose of this section is to review psychological research bearing on these issues. Specifically, the authors discuss research relevant to judicial concerns about the scientific reliability of RTS evidence as well as recent studies designed to test judicial assumptions regarding its helpfulness and prejudicial impact. Note that, rather than being a comprehensive review of the literature on rape trauma, this chapter focuses on research that addresses the specific concerns raised by the courts.

Scientific Reliability

Before discussing judicial concerns about reliability and the research relevant to these concerns, it is important to mention that evaluations of reliability are made difficult by the fact that the term "RTS" has several meanings in the literature. The term was coined by Burgess and Holmstrom (1974) to describe a two-stage model of recovery from rape (i.e., an acute and a reorganization phase). Although this study was very important in heightening awareness about the traumatic effects of rape, it was quite limited methodologically, and many of its results have not been replicated. Subsequent research, which is much more rigorous, conceptualizes rape trauma in terms of specific symptoms rather than more general stages of recovery. Finally, RTS often is described as a specific type of PTSD (DSM-III-R, APA, 1987). Equating RTS with PTSD also can be misleading because the symp-toms listed in DSM-III-R are not identical to those described by Burgess and Holmstrom or those studied in most research on rape. Thus, RTS can refer to the stage model of recovery described by Burgess and Holmstrom, more recent studies on postrape symptoms, or rape-related PTSD. It seems most appropriate, how-ever, to base assessments of scientific reliability on the entire, evolving body of research on rape.

Three general concerns have been raised by the courts regarding the scientific reliability of RTS evidence. First, questions have been raised about the notion of a "syndrome" given the wide range of symptoms experienced by rape victims. For example, one court argued that "because the symptoms associated with 'rape trauma syndrome' embrace such a broad spectrum of human behavior, the syndrome provides a highly questionable means of identifying victims of rape" (*State v. Black*, 1987, p. 16). This conclusion was based on the fact that victims can experience such "varied" symptoms as fear of being alone, fear of crowds, fear of the outdoors, and fear of the indoors.

In response to this concern, it should be noted that the symptoms described in *State v. Black* (1987) merely illustrate that victims develop fears related to the nature of the rape. In addition, that victims experience varied symptoms is consistent with the notion of a syndrome, which does not preclude variability. Finally, although victims can and do experience a range of symptoms, only a relatively few symptoms have been studied consistently (for reviews, see Frazier and Cohen, 1992; Koss and Burkhart, 1988). These include fear and anxiety (e.g., Kilpatrick et al., 1979), depression (e.g., Frank and Anderson, 1987), social maladjustment (e.g., Resick et al., 1981), and sexual dysfunction (e.g., Orlando and Koss, 1983). Recent studies (Burge, 1988; Kilpatrick et al., 1989; Rothbaum et al., 1992) also have documented that many victims experience the symptoms of PTSD outlined in DSM-III-R (APA, 1987) (e.g., recurrent nightmares, irritability, hypervigilance).

A second concern about the reliability of RTS evidence is that, because the symptoms experienced by rape victims are not unique, they could be caused by numerous other stressors. A closer look at the data suggests that this concern may be unwarranted. First, although the DSM-III-R (APA, 1987) lists rape as only one of several stressors that can cause PTSD, different stressors produce different types and levels of symptoms (Wilson et al., 1985). In addition, the particular manifestation of the disorder will differ across events. That is, a woman who has been raped may have recurrent nightmares about the assault, whereas a combat veteran may have recurrent nightmares about combat experiences. Rape-related PTSD thus can be distinguished easily from PTSD caused by other stressor events. Second, although the symptoms of PTSD do overlap with those of other disorders, particularly depressive and anxiety disorders, it is also the case that certain symptoms are unique to PTSD. For example, unlike other diagnostic categories, several of the symptoms of PTSD relate directly to a specific traumatic event (e.g., intrusive recollections and dreams of the event, avoidance of activities that arouse recollection of the event).

A final concern is that the concept of a rape trauma syndrome is not viable because not all victims respond to an assault in the same way. Individual differences in levels of postrape trauma clearly exist, and several factors associated with these differences have been identified (see, e.g., Frank and Anderson, 1987; Frazier, 1990, 1991; Meyer and Taylor, 1986). Research on individual differences in levels of postrape distress need not negate the helpfulness of the testimony to a jury. Rather, it could be incorporated into the testimony to help explain the response of a particular complainant. For example, in addition to describing the typical aftereffects of rape, the expert could describe research on factors affecting the degree of trauma experienced by victims. If one of these factors was relevant to a particular complainant, research on the relation between this factor and postrape recovery could be incorporated into the testimony to further explain the complainant's response.

In sum, the specific concerns raised by the courts about the reliability of RTS evidence may not be warranted. The symptoms identified in recent research are relatively circumscribed, and at least some symptoms of rape trauma are unique. Research on individual differences in responses to rape can be incorporated into expert testimony and thus can add to, rather than detract from, its helpfulness.

On the other hand, as noted, the authors have addressed only the specific concerns about reliability raised by the courts in these recent decisions. These may not actually be the most important concerns. The basic issue in evaluating the scientific status of RTS is not the range of symptoms experienced by victims, the uniqueness of the symptoms, or individual differences in levels of distress. Rather, the basic issue is whether there is a consistent body of evidence, based on well-designed research, about the aftereffects of rape. When a finding has been sufficiently established in the literature is a difficult question to answer (see Elliott, 1991 and Ellsworth, 1991 for a discussion of this issue in a different context). In the authors' opinion, although early studies were plagued by numerous methodological problems (see Katz and Mazur, 1979), several studies have since been conducted that are much more sophisticated methodologically (see Resick, 1993 for a review). These studies have assessed victim recovery at several points after the assault using standardized assessment measures and have employed carefully matched control groups. This research has established that rape victims experience more depression, anxiety, fear, and social adjustment and sexual problems than women who have not been victimized. Research on PTSD among rape victims is more recent but consistently suggests that many victims experience PTSD symptoms following an assault. Initially high symptom levels generally abate by 3 to 4 months postassault, although significant levels of distress continue for many victims.

Helpfulness

The primary concern about the helpfulness of RTS evidence in judicial decisions is whether the testimony is "beyond the ken" of the average juror. For example, in one of the first decisions on the admissibility of RTS evidence, the Minnesota Supreme Court ruled that the evidence is not helpful because most jurors are adequately informed about rape and rape victim behavior (*State v. Saldana*, 1982). Whether jurors are likely to be informed about rape is a question that can best be answered empirically.

In order to test judicial assumptions about the extent of juror knowledge about rape, Frazier and Borgida (1988) administered an 18-item Sexual Assault Questionnaire (SAQ) to two expert and two nonexpert groups. The expert groups consisted of 22 experts on rape and 20 experts on PTSD. The two nonexpert groups were 87 students and 55 nonacademic university employees. Results indicated that both nonexpert groups scored significantly lower on the SAQ than did the experts. The employee and student groups answered at almost chance levels (57 and 58% correct, respectively). For example, the nonexperts were not aware of the frequency of multiple victimization experiences or the behavioral changes often apparent following a rape. Both of these could be important factors in jurors' assessments of the credibility of a complainant. That is, jurors may perceive a complainant who has made a number of life changes as unstable rather than as exhibiting a normal reaction to a crisis.

In addition to completing the SAQ, both expert groups were asked for their opinions about the admissibility of RTS evidence and its helpfulness to jurors. There was almost complete agreement among the experts that jurors are not sufficiently knowledgeable about rape and its aftereffects. Thus, both the responses to the SAQ and the experts' opinions about juror knowledge suggest that expert testimony on rape trauma could be helpful in educating jurors and that the judicial assumption that jurors *are* adequately informed about rape victim behavior may not be well founded.

Prejudicial Impact

Courts have expressed various concerns about the potential for expert testimony on RTS to unfairly prejudice the defendant. For example, courts have argued that expert testimony unfairly prejudices the defendant by "creating an aura of special reliability and trustworthiness" (*State v. Saldana*, 1982, p. 324). The evidence also is more likely to be seen as prejudicial if the expert (1) uses the term "RTS", (2) does not testify about "unusual behaviors", and (3) links the testimony specifically to the case at hand. Whether jurors give expert testimony undue weight and whether the above-mentioned factors affect the prejudicial impact of the testimony also are empirical questions.

One study that directly assessed whether jurors give expert testimony undue weight examined the impact on juror decision making of two types of expert psychological testimony (polygraph or RTS) as well as the presence or absence of an opposing expert (Brekke, 1985). A nonexpert control group also was included. Mock juries listened to an audiotaped reenactment of an actual rape trial (in which type of expert testimony was varied) and deliberated to a unanimous verdict. Jurors also completed various measures evaluating both the complainant and the defendant (e.g., credibility ratings).

Brekke reasoned that if jurors give undue weight to expert testimony, jurors exposed to such testimony also should be extremely likely to vote for conviction, have poor recall of case facts, and offer few criticisms of the expert during deliberations. Results indicated, first, that jurors exposed to expert testimony rendered more guilty verdicts, considered it more likely that the defendant committed rape, and recommended longer sentences than jurors not exposed to expert testimony. The effects of the expert testimony on juror decisions were quite small, however (e.g., the largest effect accounted for 8% of the variance in judgments). Other evidence suggested that there were no significant effects of expert testimony on recall of case facts. Finally, jury deliberation analyses indicated that discussions of the experts were not consistently positive.

Brekke also examined whether the expert testimony was unfairly prejudicial to the defendant. Unfair prejudice was operationalized as derogation of the defendant in conjunction with enhanced evaluations of the complainant. Results suggested that there were no differences across conditions on ratings of the defendant's credibility or honesty. Analyses of jury deliberations also failed to reveal effects of expert testimony on evaluations of the defendant. There was some suggestion, however, that expert testimony enhanced evaluations of the complainant. For example, jurors exposed to expert testimony rated the complainant as more credible than did other jurors.

A study by Brekke and Borgida (1988) provides some data regarding the impact of the specificity of RTS testimony on juror decisions. Mock juries listened to an audiotaped reenactment of an actual rape trial containing either (1) no expert testimony, (2) standard expert testimony providing general information about rape, or (3) expert testimony linked to the specific case. Whether the testimony was presented early or late in the trial also was varied.

Results suggested that juries exposed to the specific testimony were more likely to convict and to recommend harsher sentences for the defendant than those exposed to the standard expert testimony. In addition, the testimony had greater impact when it was presented early in the trial. The testimony with the greatest impact was always the specific hypothetical version presented early in the trial. Under these circumstances, the expert testimony seemed to function as a filter through which jurors interpreted subsequent case facts. When the expert testimony came late in the trial, jurors tended to interpret the case in light of their preconceived notions and biases about rape. Though it could be argued that these data indicate that the evidence unfairly prejudices the defendant, analyses of jury deliberations found that expert testimony did not affect the favorability of the discussions of the defendant's credibility. Rather than being prejudicial to the defendant, the expert testimony seemed to counteract the otherwise pervasive effects of rape myths on juror judgments (see Borgida and Brekke, 1985).

In sum, these two studies suggest that expert testimony does exert some influence on jury decision making in rape trials. Jurors do not, however, appear to give the testimony undue weight nor does the testimony appear to unfairly prejudice the defendant. Testimony that is specifically related to the case at hand has more impact, but appears to counteract juror biases against the complainant rather than prejudice the defendant.

Evaluation of Expert Testimony and Judicial Decisions on Rape Trauma Syndrome

This review of the relevant psychological research provides a basis for evaluating both the expert testimony provided and judicial decision making in recent RTS cases. First, we evaluate whether the expert testimony provided in recent cases is supported by existing research. Second, we address the manner in which courts use psychological research in their decision making. Although there are other criteria by which judicial decisions could be evaluated (e.g., consistency in applying admissibility criteria), we focus specifically on the extent to which courts seem to be aware of and informed by relevant psychological research. Our evaluation of these issues is based on information available in appellate court decisions. These

decisions do not provide complete information about either the testimony provided or the bases for the judicial decisions, although they are the best indicators
available (Hafemeister and Melton, 1987).

Expert Testimony

As mentioned previously, expert testimony on RTS can take several forms. Experts
can testify in general terms about the symptoms of posttraumatic stress without
interviewing the particular complainant. More commonly, experts provide testimony about posttraumatic stress responses as well as testimony that the particular
complainant's behavior is consistent with such responses. This more specific
testimony can be based on interviews with the complainant performed for the
purpose of providing testimony or as part of a counseling relationship.

Whatever particular form the testimony takes, the expert should be qualified,
and the testimony should be helpful, scientifically reliable, and not unfairly prejudicial. We will focus in this section on the scientific reliability of the testimony.
Whether the specific testimony provided is based on reliable data is a different
question than whether research on RTS generally is reliable. In other words, expert
testimony provided in specific cases varies in terms of how well it conforms to the
research literature.

Unfortunately, the information available in the appellate decisions about the
content of the expert testimony provided in these cases suggests that some of the
testimony may not have a firm basis in the research literature. This seems particularly true of testimony used to explain complainant behaviors that seem inconsistent with having been raped. Several examples follow. In *Lessard v. State* (1986) the
expert stated that it is "very common" for a victim to ask an assailant not to tell
anyone about the assault. To our knowledge, this particular behavior has not been
documented in the research literature on responses to rape. Statements by the
experts in both *Simmons v. State* (1987) and *Commonwealth v. Gallagher* (1988)
concern behaviors that also have not been documented in the research literature,
although they can be seen as consistent with the acute trauma experienced by
victims immediately following an assault (i.e., failure to recall details of the assault
and inability to identify the defendant until years after the rape). Testimony in
People v. Hampton (1986) that victims of acquaintance rape are more likely to
delay reporting is supported in the research literature (e.g., Williams, 1984);
whether this behavior is part of RTS is questionable, however. The expert testimony in *People v. Taylor* (1990) and *State v. Robinson* (1988) concerned the
controlled style of responding in the immediate postrape period described by
Burgess and Holmstrom (1974). Few other researchers have documented this style
of responding because they have not interviewed victims in emergency rooms.

In sum, experts in recent cases have described a broad range of symptoms and
behaviors as consistent with RTS, some of which do not appear to be based on
research. Testimony that is not research based often seems to be prompted by a
defendant's claims that a complainant's behavior was inconsistent with having
been raped. If virtually any victim behavior is described as consistent with RTS, the

term soon will have little meaning. Indeed, some critics have argued that this already is the case (e.g., Lawrence, 1984).

The ethical issues that arise here are the same as those that arise in regard to other types of expert psychological testimony. It is the ethical responsibility of each expert "to present the science of psychology... fairly and accurately... [and to be] guided by the primary obligation to aid the public in developing informed judgments... " (APA, 1990, p. 392). In other words, it is incumbent upon experts to be familiar with the existing research and only to describe victim behaviors that have been reliably established in the literature. If testimony is not research based, it is very important that the basis of the testimony be stated clearly. Which victim behaviors have been reliably established is, of course, open to interpretation and experts are bound to disagree (see, e.g., Elliott, 1991 and Ellsworth, 1991). Surveys of experts regarding the reliability of different aspects of the research can provide an objective means of determining consensus in the field (Kassin et al., 1989). On the other hand, these experts may have a vested interest in portraying their own work as reliable (for a discussion of this issue, see Fiske et al., 1991).

There also are pragmatic issues to consider in providing expert testimony on RTS that should be mentioned. First, the term "PTSD" generally is viewed as less prejudicial than "RTS" because the former does not equate symptoms exclusively with rape. The term "PTSD" also is preferable because, as discussed previously, the term "RTS" has no clear referent. Second, expert testimony consisting of a general description of research on the aftereffects of rape is seen as less prejudicial than testimony by an expert who also states that a particular complainant's behavior is consistent with that of a rape victim. Using nontreating expert witnesses and limiting the testimony to research on victims as a class has several advantages (see Buchele and Buchele, 1985; Dwyer, 1988). For example, it reduces the risk that the testimony will lead to compulsory examinations of complainants by defense experts (Massaro, 1985) and lessens concerns about the extent to which the expert's testimony depends on the veracity of the particular complainant.

General testimony describing research on the aftereffects of rape is not without its critics, however. It has been argued that expert testimony on RTS lacks relevance because existing research does not compare "true" victims to "false" victims, which is the crucial issue in consent defense cases. Rather, existing research compares rape victims to *nonvictims*. If false victims are indistinguishable from true victims, and different from nonvictims, expert testimony may not be helpful. For example, a complainant who is a false victim may have engaged in consensual sex with a defendant but later regret having done so. Although the experience would not be defined as rape, she may nevertheless exhibit stress-related symptoms (e.g., depression) that are similar to the symptoms experienced following a "true" rape. To our knowledge, however, no research on this issue currently exists and, because of the infrequency of false claims, may never develop. In general, it appears unlikely that a false victim (i.e., one who engaged in consensual sex that she later called rape) would exhibit the specific symptoms of rape-related PTSD exhibited by true victims (e.g., recurrent and intrusive thoughts about the event, exaggerated startle response, hypervigilance to danger). If expert testimony were offered in such a case, the expert would testify about typical characteristics and behaviors of rape victims, including the symptoms of rape-related PTSD. Other testimony would be offered about the victim's behavior following the incident, and it would be up to the jury to determine the complainant's credibility. Thus, expert testimony would still serve to educate jurors about rape and aid them in their decision making.

Judicial Decisions

In addition to evaluating the content of the expert testimony provided, it is instructive to assess the bases for judicial decisions on the admissibility of RTS testimony. There are many criteria by which these decisions could be evaluated (e.g., consistency in applying admissibility criteria, definition of what constitutes RTS evidence). We will focus specifically on the extent to which judicial decisions seem to be informed by the relevant psychological research.

In order to examine this issue, they performed a count of psychological research articles cited in recent appellate court decisions.* This count suggested that courts may not be particularly well informed regarding the most recent research on rape. For example, although these decisions were published between 1985 and 1990, the most recent research article cited was published in 1983. The 1974 Burgess and Holmstrom study was by far the most frequently cited (in 7 out of 16 decisions). Only two other studies were cited more than once and both represent rather early research (Kilpatrick et al., 1979; Notman and Nadelson, 1976). The DSM-III (APA, 1980) and DSM-III-R (APA, 1987), which list the symptoms of PTSD, also were cited frequently.

It is somewhat ironic that State v. Black (1987), which contained the most complete research review, was the only recent case in which a court ruled that the evidence was not scientifically reliable. Their discussion of reliability concluded with the following quote from an article published in 1979: "To date, investigations of how a rape experience affects women over time have been scarce and methodologically poor.... Therefore these studies provide little, if any, scientifically valid data regarding the effects of a rape experience" (Kilpatrick et al., 1979, p. 658). Thus, although the court in Black cited the most recent research, their conclusion about the adequacy of the research was drawn from an article published several years prior to most of the research they reviewed.

As discussed previously, some research exists that could inform judicial decisions about the helpfulness (Frazier and Borgida, 1988) and prejudicial impact of RTS evidence (Brekke, 1985; Brekke and Borgida, 1988). This research has not yet begun to influence decisions on RTS. The Frazier and Borgida study was, however, cited by the Minnesota Supreme Court (State v. Hall, 1987) to support its decision that expert testimony on adolescent sexual abuse was helpful to the jury. This study also has been cited in recent law review articles (e.g., Dwyer, 1988; Fischer, 1989), which may make it more accessible to the courts.

---

* The authors did not count citations included as part of references to other cases or articles.

In sum, although the authors' review of the case law suggests that recent decisions reflect less concern about the scientific reliability of RTS evidence, this change may not necessarily reflect an awareness by the courts of the increased sophistication of the research. Indeed, the citation count suggested that courts may review only a small portion of the available research. On the other hand, that research relevant to helpfulness and prejudice has not informed judicial decisions is not surprising given the limited number of studies and the recency of their publication.

It also should be mentioned that researchers need to pay more attention to how they disseminate their work if it is to have an impact on the legal system. As Melton (1987) notes, the influence of psychology on the legal system is less than it should be because (1) the diffusion of knowledge into the system is slow; (2) psychologists have failed to address questions of interest to the law; and (3) even when research has been designed explicitly to test legal questions, insufficient attention has been paid to ensuring that it reaches the proper audiences. Use of social science research by the courts is substantially more likely when researchers make a concerted effort to make their research accessible to the legal system. Several recent articles provide excellent suggestions for how that can be accomplished (e.g., Grisso and Melton, 1987; Hafemeister and Melton, 1987; Melton, 1987).

Future Research

Psychological research directly relevant to the admissibility of RTS evidence is rather limited. We, therefore, would like to present some suggestions for research that could inform future discussions of its scientific reliability, helpfulness, and prejudicial impact.

Scientific Reliability

Most research on the aftereffects of rape was not conducted for the purpose of establishing the scientific reliability of expert testimony on RTS. Several types of research would be useful for this purpose. For example, one of the concerns about RTS evidence is that the symptoms of rape trauma are not unique. Most research to date has focused on symptoms that are more *common* among rape victims (e.g., fear, anxiety, depression) but not necessarily *unique* to rape. Additional research on the unique symptoms of rape-related PTSD would be particularly helpful in addressing this concern. Studies that assess differences in PTSD symptomatology across events also would be useful. Translation to a legal context would be facilitated by reporting percentages of victims experiencing each symptom rather than mean scale scores.

Another way to assess the uniqueness of rape trauma is to conduct prospective studies of symptomatology prior to, and following, the rape. This type of study would address concerns that the symptoms of rape trauma could have been present prior to the rape. Research of this type obviously would be very difficult to conduct. One possibility would be to administer measures of symptoms and victimization experiences at several points in time among samples of women who are known to be at risk, such as college students (Koss et al., 1987). Comparisons could be made between victims and nonvictims and between prerape and postrape functioning among victims. This design also would provide information on factors associated with increased risk of being victimized.

Finally, surveys of experts regarding their opinions about the degree of research support for various aspects of rape trauma would provide another basis for evaluating scientific reliability (see Kassin et al., 1989). In a previous study (Frazier and Borgida, 1988), the authors asked experts for their general opinions about the reliability of RTS evidence. They did not, however, ask about the reliability of research on specific topics or whether the evidence on each topic was reliable enough to present in court. This information would be helpful to courts in evaluating the evidence and to experts in preparing their testimony.

Helpfulness

To date, only one study has assessed common knowledge about rape and rape victim behavior (Frazier and Borgida, 1988). This initial research could be expanded in several ways. First, the SAQ, or a similar measure, could be administered to nonexpert samples that are more representative of average jurors. In addition, the expert samples could be asked for their opinions regarding juror understanding of each separate issue (Kassin et al., 1989). Other methods of assessing juror common understanding have been used in the eyewitness area and could be used to assess common knowledge about rape trauma. For example, in addition to administering questionnaires similar to the SAQ (e.g., Deffenbacher and Loftus, 1982), investigators interested in juror knowledge about eyewitness accuracy have conducted mock jury studies (Hastie, 1980; cited in Wells, 1984) and have asked subjects to estimate the results of prior research on eyewitness accuracy (Brigham and Bothwell, 1983).

These studies would provide information on the extent of knowledge about rape among jurors. The question of how much knowledge is sufficient remains, however. Although they are unlikely to establish absolute standards of common understanding, it would be interesting to survey judges regarding their attitudes about RTS evidence and how much knowledge they feel is sufficient.

Prejudicial Impact

Judicial concerns about the prejudicial impact of expert testimony on RTS also suggest several testable questions that have not yet been addressed. These questions are generally concerned with how variations in the content of expert testimony influence juror judgments. For example, do juror evaluations differ as a function of whether the expert uses the term "RTS" or the more neutral "PTSD"? Is the testimony more prejudicial when the expert has interviewed the complainant and links the symptoms of rape trauma directly to the case at hand? Is the testimony less prejudicial when it is used to rebut claims by the defendant that the complainant's behavior was inconsistent with having been raped? All of these questions could be addressed using designs similar to those employed by Brekke (1985) and Brekke and Borgida (1988). In light of Monahan and Walker's (1988) recommendations, studies also could assess the effect of the method of presentation of RTS evidence (i.e., expert testimony vs. jury instructions) on juror judgments. Careful attention should be paid to defining "unfair prejudice" to the defendant in this research.

Although we hope we have provided an impetus for future research relevant to expert testimony on RTS, one caveat needs to be mentioned. That few studies have been designed to address questions concerned with the admissibility of expert testimony may be because very few cases ever go to trial (Chandler and Torney, 1981; Frazier et al., 1994; Galvin and Polk, 1983). Although very little systematic evidence exists, available data suggest that there is considerable attrition in the processing of rape cases from the time of the initial police report to sentencing (Galvin & Polk, 1983) and that extraneous variables (e.g., defendant race) affect the severity of charges filed (Bradmiller and Walters, 1985; Chandler and Torney, 1981; LaFree, 1980). Research is thus needed on all aspects of the legal processing of rape cases, including expert testimony.

Authors' Notes

The authors would like to thank Anne Byer for her assistance and David Faigman, Stephen Golding, Roger Park, Steven Penrod, and Ronald Roesch for their comments on an earlier draft of this chapter.

References

Alphonso v. Charity Hospital of Louisiana, 413 So.2d 982, 1982.

American Psychological Association, Ethical principles of psychologists, *Am. Psychol.*, 45, 390, 1990.

American Psychiatric Association, *Diagnostic and Statistical Manual of Mental Disorders*, 3rd ed., Washington, D.C., 1980.

American Psychiatric Association, *Diagnostic and Statistical Manual of Mental Disorders*, 3rd ed. revised, Washington, D.C., 1987.

Borgida, E. and Brekke, N., Psycholegal research on rape trials, in *Rape and Sexual Assault: A Research Handbook*, Burgess, A. W., Ed., Garland, New York, 1985, 313.

Borgida, E., Frazier, P., and Swim, J., Prosecuting sexual assault: the use of expert testimony on rape trauma syndrome, in *Practical Aspects of Rape Investigation: A Multidisciplinary Approach*, Hazelwood, R. and Burgess, A., Eds., Elsevier, New York, 1987, 347.

Bradmiller, L. and Walters, W., Seriousness of sexual assault charges, *Criminal Justice and Behavior*, 12, 463, 1985.

Brekke, N., Expert Scientific Testimony in Rape Trials, unpublished doctoral dissertation, University of Minnesota, 1985.

Brekke, N. and Borgida, E., Expert psychological testimony in rape trials: a social-cognitive analysis, *J. Pers. Soc. Psychol.*, 55, 372, 1988.

Brigham, J. and Bothwell, R., The ability of prospective jurors to estimate the accuracy of eyewitness identifications, *Law Hum. Behav.*, 7, 19, 1983.

Buchele, B. and Buchele, J., Legal and psychological issues in the use of expert testimony on rape trauma syndrome, *Washburn Law J.*, 25, 26, 1985.

Burge, S., Post traumatic stress disorder in victims of rape, *J. Traumatic Stress*, 1, 193, 1988.

Burgess, A. and Holmstrom, L., Rape trauma syndrome, *Am. J. Psychiatry*, 131, 981, 1974.

Chandler, S. and Torney, M., The decisions and the processing of rape victims through the criminal justice system, *Calif. Sociol.*, 4, 155, 1981.

Committee on Ethical Guidelines for Forensic Psychologists, Specialty guidelines for forensic psychologists, *Law Hum. Behav.* 15, 655, 1991.

Commonwealth v. Gallagher, 547 A.2d 355, 1988.

Daubert v. Merrill Dow Pharmaceuticals, 113 S. Ct. 2786, 1993.

Deffenbacher, K. and Loftus, E., Do jurors share a common understanding concerning eyewitness behavior?, *Law Hum. Behav.*, 6, 15, 1982.

Donohue, M., Another door closed: rape trauma syndrome, *Gonzaga Law Rev.*, 23, 1, 1987/1988.

Dwyer, D., Expert testimony on rape trauma syndrome: an argument for limited admissibility — *State v. Black,* 109 Wash.2d 336, 745 P.2d 12 (1987), *Wash. Law Rev.*, 63, 1063, 1988.

Elliott, R., Social science data and the APA: the *Lockhart* brief as a case in point, *Law Hum. Behav.*, 15, 59, 1991.

Ellsworth, P., To tell what we know or wait for Godot?, *Law Hum. Behav.*, 15, 77, 1991.

Federal Rules of Evidence, West, St. Paul, MN, 1984.

Fischer, K., Defining the boundaries of admissible expert psychological testimony on rape trauma syndrome, *Univ. Ill. Law Rev.*, 3, 691, 1989.

Fiske, S., Bersoff, D., Borgida, E., Deaux, K., and Heilman, M., Social science research on trial: the uses of sex stereotyping research in *Price Waterhouse v. Hopkins, Am. Psychol.*, 46, 1049, 1991.

Frank, E. and Anderson, P., Psychiatric disorders in rape victims: past history and current symptomatology, *Compr. Psychiatry*, 28, 77, 1987.

Frazier, P., Victim attributions and postrape trauma, *J. Pers. Soc. Psychol.*, 59, 298, 1990.

Frazier, P., Self-blame as a mediator of postrape depressive symptoms, *J. Soc. Clin. Psychol.*, 10, 47, 1991.

Frazier, P. and Borgida, E., Rape trauma syndrome evidence in court, *Am. Psychol.*, 40, 984, 1985.

Frazier, P. and Borgida, E., Juror common understanding and the admissibility of rape trauma syndrome evidence in court, *Law Hum. Behav.*, 12, 101, 1988.

Frazier, P., Candell, S., Arikian, N., and Tofteland, A., Rape survivors and the legal system, in *Violence and the Law,* Costanzo, M. and Oskamp, S., Eds., Sage, Thousand Oaks, CA, 1994, 135.

Frazier, P. and Cohen, B., Research on the sexual victimization of women: implications for counselor training, *Counseling Psychol.*, 20, 141, 1992.

Frye v. United States, 293 F. 1013, 1923.

Galvin, J. and Polk, K., Attrition in case processing: is rape unique?, *J. Res. Crime Delinquency,* 126, 1983.

Grisso, T. and Melton, G., Getting child development research to legal practitioners: which way to the trenches?, in *Reforming the Law,* Melton, G., Ed., Guilford, New York, 1987, 146.

Hafemeister, T. and Melton, G., The impact of social science research on the judiciary, in *Reforming the Law*, Melton, G., Ed., Guilford, New York, 1987, 27.

Kassin, S., Ellsworth, P., and Smith, V., The "general acceptance" of psychological research on eyewitness testimony: a survey of the experts, *Am. Psychol.*, 44, 1089, 1989.

Katz, S. and Mazur, M., *Understanding the Rape Victim*, Wiley, New York, 1979.

Kilpatrick, D., Saunders, B., Amick-McMullan, A., Best, C., Veronen, L., and Resnick, H., Victim and crime factors associated with the development of crime-related post-traumatic stress disorder, *Behav. Ther.*, 20, 199, 1989.

Kilpatrick, D., Veronen, L., and Resick, P., The aftermath of rape: recent empirical findings, *Am. J. Orthopsychiatry*, 49, 658, 1979.

Koss, M. and Burkhart, B., A conceptual analysis of rape vicitimization: long-term effects and implications for treatment, *Psychol. Women Q.*, 13, 27, 1988.

Koss, M., Gidycz, C., and Wisniewski, N., The scope of rape: incidence and prevalence of sexual aggression and victimization in a national sample of higher education students, *J. Consult. Clin. Psychol.*, 55, 162, 1987.

LaFree, G., The effect of sexual stratification by race on official reactions to rape, *Am. Sociol. Rev.*, 45, 842, 1980.

Lawrence, R., Checking the allure of increased conviction rates: the admissibility of expert testimony on rape trauma syndrome in criminal proceedings, *Univ. Va. Law Rev.*, 79, 1657, 1984.

Lessard v. State, 719 P.2d 227, 1986.

Massaro, T., Experts, psychology, credibility, and rape: the rape trauma syndrome issue and its implications for expert psychological testimony, *Minn. Law Rev.*, 69, 395, 1985.

McCloskey, M., Egeth, H., and McKenna, J., Eds., The ethics of expert testimony [special issue], *Law Hum. Behav.*, 10(12), 1986.

McCord, D., The admissibility of expert testimony regarding rape trauma syndrome in rape prosecution, *Boston Coll. Law Rev.*, 26, 1143, 1985.

Melton, G., Bringing psychology to the legal system: opportunities, obstacles, and efficacy, *Am. Psychol.*, 42, 488, 1987.

Meyer, C. and Taylor, S., Adjustment to rape, *J. Pers. Soc. Psychol.*, 50, 1226, 1986.

Monahan, J. and Walker, L., Social science research in law: a new paradigm, *Am. Psychol.*, 43, 465, 1988.

Notman, M. and Nadelson, C., The rape victim: psychodynamic considerations, *Am. J. Psychiatry*, 133, 408, 1976.

Orlando, J. and Koss, M., The effect of sexual victimization on sexual satisfaction: a study of the negative-association hypothesis, *J. Abnorm. Psychol.*, 92, 104, 1983.

People v. Bledsoe, 203 Cal.Rptr. 450, 1984.

People v. Coleman, 768 P.2d 32, 1989.

People v. Cruikshank, 484 N.Y.S.2d 328, 1985.

People v. Farley, 746 P.2d 956, 1987.

People v. Hampton, 728 P.2d 345, 1986.

People v. Hampton, 746 P.2d 947, 1987.

People v. Mays, 387 N.W.2d 814, 1986.

People v. Pullins, 378 N.W.2d 502, 1985.

People v. Smith, 387 N.W.2d 814, 1986.

People v. Taylor, 552 N.E.2d 131, 1990.

Resick, P., The psychological impact of rape, *J. Interpers. Violence*, 8, 223, 1993.

Resick, P., Calhoun, K., Atkeson, B., and Ellis, E., Social adjustment in victims of sexual assault, *J. Consult. Clin. Psychol.*, 49, 705, 1981.

Rothbaum, B., Foa, E., Riggs, D., Murdock, T., and Walsh, W., A prospective examination of post traumatic stress disorder in rape victims, *J. Traumatic Stress,* 3, 455, 1992.

Salzburg, S., *Frye* and alternatives, *Fed. Rules Decisions*, 99, 188, 1983.

Simmons v. State, 504 N.E.2d 575, 1987.

State v. Allewalt, 517 A.2d 741, 1986.

State v. Black, 745 P.2d 12, 1987.

State v. Brodniak, 718 P.2d 322, 1986.

State v. Bubar, 505 A.2d 1197, 1985.

State v. Gettier, 438 N.W.2d 1, 1989.

State v. Hall, 406 N.W.2d 503, 1987.

State v. Horne, 710 S.W.2d 310, 1986.

State v. Huey, 699 P.2d 1290, 1985.

State v. McCoy, 366 S.E.2d 731, 1988.

State v. Robinson, 431 N.W.2d 165, 1988.

State v. Saldana, 324 N.W.2d 227, 1982.

United States v. Moore, 15 M.J. 354, 1983.

United States v. Tomlinson, 20 M.J. 897, 1985.

Wells, G., How adequate is human intuition for judging eyewitness testimony, in *Eyewitness Testimony,* Wells, G. and Loftus, E., Eds., Cambridge University Press, Cambridge, 1984.

Williams, L., The classic rape: when do victims report?, *Soc. Probl.,* 31, 459, 1984.

Wilson, J., Smith, W., and Johnson, S., A comparative analysis of PTSD among various survivor groups, in *Trauma and Its Wake,* Figley, C., Ed., Brunner/Mazel, New York, 1985, 142.

V

SPECIAL OFFENDER POPULATIONS

Child Molestation: A Law Enforcement Typology

19

KENNETH V. LANNING

Too often the terms *child molester* and *pedophile* are used interchangeably or without definition. In fact, not all child molesters are pedophiles, and there is a clear need for a typology to clear up the confusion. Law enforcement has frequently accepted offender categories and characteristics developed by therapists and criminologists; these typologies, however, primarily serve the needs of mental health professionals and have limited application to those of law enforcement. These typologies are usually developed from data collected *from* offenders *after* arrest or conviction and often reflect unsubstantiated information about pre-arrest behavior. It is the pre-arrest or pre-identification behavior of child molesters that is of most value to law enforcement.

In addition, law enforcement usually does not have the luxury of having a known, confessed offender in front of them. Law enforcement and prosecutors need a typology that can be applied before the perpetrator is identified or the case is proven in court.

Needs of Law Enforcement

Child sexual abuse cases can be difficult to prove. Frequently there is only the word of a child against that of an adult. Many factors combine to make it difficult and possibly traumatic for children to testify in court. In spite of some recent advances that make testimony easier for the child victim or witness, an important objective of every investigation of child sexual abuse should be to prove the case without resorting to the courtroom testimony of the child. This is best done by building such a strong case that the perpetrator pleads guilty and there is no trial. This may not always be possible, but it should be the investigative goal. Many children can testify in court if necessary.

The child victim should be carefully interviewed. The information obtained should be evaluated and assessed, and appropriate investigative action taken. The investigator, however, should proceed as though he or she has information about a crime from a reliable source whose identity cannot be revealed. The investigator should be an objective fact finder attempting to determine what happened.

One way to avoid child victim testimony is to avail yourself of other evidence that may help prove the case. Frequently, more evidence is available than the investigator realizes; much of this evidence can be identified and located only if the investigator has a solid understanding of offender behavior patterns and the kinds of child molesters.

Kinds of Child Molesters

Dietz (1983) divides sex offenders into two broad categories: *situational* and *preferential*. This concept can be of great practical value to law enforcement. After consulting on hundreds of cases in his work at the FBI Behavioral Science Unit and not finding a typology that fits law enforcement needs, the author decided to develop his own. Expanding on Dietz's idea, the author developed a typology of child molesters for criminal justice professionals. The author has deliberately avoided all use of diagnostic terminology and used descriptive terms instead. The purpose of the typology set forth here is not to gain insight or understanding about *why* child molesters have sex with children in order to help or treat them, but to recognize and evaluate *how* child molesters have sex with children, in order to identify, arrest, and convict them. What evidence to look for, whether there are additional victims, how to interview a suspect, and so on depend on the type of child molester involved.

Situational Child Molesters

The situational child molester does not have a true sexual preference for children, but engages in sex with children for varied and sometimes complex reasons. For such a child molester, sex with children may range from a "once-in-a-lifetime" act to a long-term pattern of behavior. The more long-term the pattern is, the harder it is to distinguish from preferential molesting. The situational child molester usually has fewer different child victims; other vulnerable people such as the elderly, sick, or the disabled may also be at a risk of sexual victimization by him or her. For example, the situational child molester who sexually abuses children in a day care center might leave that job and begin to sexually abuse elderly people in a nursing home. It is the author's opinion that the number of situational child molesters is larger and increasing faster than that of preferential child molesters. Members of lower socioeconomic groups tend to be overrepresented among situational child molesters. Within this category at least four major patterns of behavior emerge (see also Table 1).

Regressed.   Such an offender usually has low self-esteem and poor coping skills; he turns to children as a sexual substitute for the preferred peer sex partner. Precipitating stress may play a bigger role in his molesting behavior. His main victim criterion seems to be availability, which is why many of these offenders molest their own children. His principal method of operation is to coerce the child into having sex. This type of situational child molester may or may not collect child or adult pornography. If he does have child pornography, it will usually be the best kind from an investigative point of view: homemade photographs or

Table 1   Situational Child Molester

	Regressed	Morally indiscriminate	Sexually indiscriminate	Inadequate
Basic characteristics	Poor coping skills	User of people	Sexual experimentation	Social misfit
Motivation	Substitution	Why not?	Boredom	Insecurity and curiosity
Victim criteria	Availability	Vulnerability and opportunity	New and different	Nonthreatening
Method of operation	Coercion	Lure, force, or manipulation	Involve in existing activity	Exploits size, advantage
Pornography collection	Possible	Sadomasochistic; detective magazines	Highly likely; varied nature	Likely

videos of the child he is molesting. Although this type of child molester may be very common, not many cases involving this pattern of behavior are referred to the FBI Behavioral Science Unit for case consultation.

Morally Indiscriminate.   In the author's experience, this is a growing category of child molesters. For this person, sexual abuse of children is simply part of a general pattern of abuse in his life. He is a user and abuser of people. He abuses his wife, friends, co-workers. He lies, cheats, or steals whenever he thinks he can get away with it. He molests children for a simple reason: "Why not?". His primary victim criteria are vulnerability and opportunity. He has the urge, a child is there, and so he acts. He typically uses force, lures, or manipulation to obtain his victims. He may violently or nonviolently abduct his victims. Although his victims frequently are strangers or acquaintances, it is important for the investigator to realize that the victims can also be the offender's own children. The incestuous father or mother might be this morally indiscriminate offender. He frequently collects detective magazines or adult pornography of a sadomasochistic nature. He may collect some child pornography, especially that which shows pubescent children. Because he is an impulsive person who lacks conscience, he is an especially high risk to molest pubescent children. Such acts may be criminal but not necessarily sexually deviant.

Sexually Indiscriminate.   This pattern of behavior is the most difficult to define. Although the previously described morally indiscriminate offender often is a sexual experimenter, this person differs in that he appears to be discriminating in his behavior except when it comes to sex. He is the "try-sexual" — willing to try anything sexual. Much of his behavior is similar to and is most often confused with the preferential child molester. While he may have clearly defined paraphiliac or sexual preferences — bondage or sadomasochism, etc. — he has no real sexual preference for children. His basic motive is sexual experimentation, and he appears to have sex with children out of boredom. His main criteria for such children are that they are new and different, and he involves children in previously existing sexual activity. Again, it is important to realize that these children may be his own. Although much of his sexual activity with adults may not be criminal, such a person may also provide his children to other adults as part of group sex, spouse-swapping activity, or even as part of some bizarre ritual. Of all situational child molesters, he is by far the most likely to have multiple victims, be from a higher socioeconomic background, and collect pornography and erotica. Child pornography, however, will only be a small portion of his potentially large and varied collection.

Inadequate. This pattern of behavior is also difficult to define and includes those suffering from psychoses, eccentric personality disorders, mental retardation, and senility. In layman's terms he is the social misfit, the withdrawn, the unusual. He might be the shy teenager who has no friends of his own age, or the eccentric loner who still lives with his parents. Although most such people are harmless, some can be child molesters and, in a few cases, even child killers. This offender seems to become sexually involved with children out of insecurity or curiosity. He finds children to be nonthreatening objects with whom he can explore his sexual fantasies. The child victim could be someone he knows or a random stranger. In some cases the victim might be a specific "stranger" selected as a substitute for a specific adult (possibly a relative of the child) whom the offender is afraid of approaching directly. Often his sexual activity with children is the result of built-up impulses. Some of these people find it difficult to express anger and hostility, which then builds until it explodes — possibly against their child victim. Because of mental or emotional problems, some may take out their frustration in cruel, sexual torture. His victims, however, could be among the elderly as well as children — anyone who appears helpless at first sight. He might collect pornography, but it will most likely be of adults.

Almost any child molester is capable of violence or even murder to avoid identification. In spite of a few notable exceptions, however — Theodore Frank in California and Gary Arthur Bishop in Utah — most of the sexually motivated child murderers profiled and assessed by the FBI Behavioral Science Unit have involved situational child molesters, especially the morally indiscriminate and inadequate patterns of behavior. Low social competence seems to be the most significant risk factor in why a child molester might abduct his victims (see "References"). Sadistic and morally indiscriminate preferential molesters (pedophiles) who kill will be discussed later in this chapter.

Preferential Child Molesters

The preferential child molesters have a definite sexual preference for children. Their sexual fantasies and erotic imagery focus on children. They have sex with children not because of some situational stress or insecurity, but because they are sexually attracted to and prefer children. They can possess a wide variety of

Table 2 Preferential Child Molester

	Seduction	Introverted	Sadistic
Common characteristics	Sexual preference for children Collects child pornography or erotica		
Motivation	Identification	Fear of communication	Need to inflict pain
Victim criteria	Age and gender preferences	Strangers or very young	Age and gender preferences
Method of operation	Seduction process	Nonverbal sexual contact	Lure or force

character traits but engage in highly predictable sexual behavior. These highly predictable sexual behavior patterns are called "sexual ritual" and are frequently engaged in even when they are counterproductive to getting away with the criminal activity. Although they may be smaller in number than the situational child molesters, they have the potential to molest large numbers of victims. For many of them, the problem is not only the nature of the sex drive (attraction to children), but also the quantity (need for frequent and repeated sex with children). They usually have age and gender preferences for their victims. Members of higher socioeconomic groups tend to be overrepresented among preferential child molesters. More preferential child molesters seem to prefer boy rather than girl victims. Within this category at least three major patterns of behavior emerge (see also Table 2).

Seduction. This pattern characterizes the offender who engages children in sexual activity by "seducing" them — courting them with attention, affection, and gifts. Just as one adult courts another, the pedophile seduces children over a period of time by gradually lowering their sexual inhibitions. Frequently his victims arrive at the point where they are willing to trade sex for the attention, affection, and other benefits they receive from the offender. Many of these offenders are simultaneously involved with multiple victims, operating what has come to be called a "child sex ring". This may include a group of children in the same class at school, in the same scout troop, or in the same neighborhood. The characteristic that seems to make this individual a master seducer of children is his ability to identify with them. He knows how to talk to children, but, more important, he knows how to listen to them. His adult status and authority is also an important part of the seduction process. In addition, he often selects as targets children who are victims of emotional or physical neglect. The biggest problem for this child molester is not how to obtain child victims, but how to get them to leave after they are too old. This must be done without the disclosure of the "secret". Victim disclosure often occurs when the offender is attempting to terminate the relationship. This child molester is most likely to use threats and physical violence to avoid identification and disclosure or to prevent a victim from leaving before he is ready to "dump" the victim.

Introverted. This pattern of behavior characterizes the offender who has a preference for children, but lacks the interpersonal skills necessary to seduce them. Therefore, he typically engages in a minimal amount of verbal communication with his victims and usually molests strangers or very young children. He is like the old stereotype of the child molester in that he is more likely to hang around playgrounds and other areas where children congregate, watching them or engaging them in brief sexual encounters. He may expose himself to children or make obscene phone calls to children. He may use the services of a child prostitute. Unable to figure out any other way to gain access to a child, he might even marry a woman and have his own children, very likely molesting them from the time they are infants. He is similar to the inadequate situational child molester, except that he has a definite sexual preference for children and his selection of primarily children as victims is more predictable.

Sadistic. This pattern of behavior characterizes the offender who has a sexual preference for children, but who, in order to be aroused or gratified, must inflict psychological or physical pain or suffering on the child victim. He is aroused by his victim's response to the infliction of pain or suffering. They typically use lures or force to gain access to their victims. They are more likely than other preferential child molesters to abduct and even murder their victims. There have been some cases where seduction molesters have become sadistic molesters. It is not known whether the sadistic needs developed late or were always there and surfaced for some reason. In any case, it is fortunate that sadistic child molesters do not appear to be many in number (see "References").

The Role of Law Enforcement

In our typology the term preferential child molester is synonymous with the pedophile who sexually molests or exploits children. Since there are federal, state, and local laws that deal with such crimes as the possession and distribution of child pornography, law enforcement officers will sometimes be involved in the investigation of pedophiles and others who have not technically molested children but who have sexually exploited them by collecting or trading child pornography. Therefore, pedophiles who do not physically or legally sexually molest children might become of investigative interest to local or federal law enforcement. Any person, however, who collects or distributes child pornography actually perpetuates the sexual abuse or exploitation of the child portrayed. It is no different than the circulation of sexually explicit pictures taken by a rapist of his victim during the rape. Such collectors and distributors of child pornography are, in essence, child molesters.

Identifying Pedophiles

Sexual exploitation is a term used to describe the sexual victimization of children, involving child pornography, child sex rings, and child prostitution. While offenders using the services of a child prostitute may be either situational or preferential child molesters, those involved in child pornography and child sex rings are predominately preferential child molesters; and, although a variety of persons sexually abuse children, preferential child molesters, or pedophiles, are the *primary* sexual exploiters of children. (For the purpose of our law enforcement typology, *pedophile* is used interchangeably with *preferential child molester*.)

An important step in investigating the difficult cases of child sexual victimization is to recognize and identify, if present, the highly predictable sexual behavior patterns of preferential child molesters or pedophiles. First, it is essential that the law enforcement investigator try to determine whether an offender is a situational or preferential child molester.

There are most likely more situational than preferential child molesters. Each situational child molester, however, is likely to abuse only a small number of children in a lifetime. A preferential child molester might molest 10, 50, 100s, or even a 1000 children in a lifetime, depending on the offender and how broadly or narrowly you define child molestation. In his study of 561 sex offenders, Dr. Gene Abel found that pedophiles who targeted young boys outside the home committed the greatest number of crimes, with an average of 281.7 acts involving an average of 150.2 partners. Molesters who targeted girls within the family committed an average of 81.3 acts with an average of 1.8 partners. He also found that 23.3% of the 561 subjects offended against both family and nonfamily targets. Although pedophiles vary greatly, their sexual behavior is repetitive and highly predictable. Knowledge of these sexual behavioral patterns or characteristics is extremely valuable to the law enforcement investigator.

These highly predictable and repetitive behavior patterns make cases involving preferential child molesters far easier to investigate than those involving situational child molesters. If enough of these characteristics can be identified through investigation, many of the remaining ones can be assumed. Most of these indicators mean little by themselves; however, as they are identified and accumulated through investigation, they can constitute reason to believe a given offender is a preferential child molester. You do not have proof beyond a reasonable doubt, but you may have *probable cause.*

The Preferential Child Molester (Pedophile)

The four major characteristics of the preferential child molester (pedophile) are (1) long-term and persistent pattern of behavior, (2) children as preferred sexual objects, (3) well-developed techniques in obtaining victims, and (4) sexual fantasies focusing on children. These characteristics, together with the listed indicators, will assist the investigator in identifying the preferential child molester and collecting the evidence necessary to arrest and convict him. At the outset, it must be stated and emphasized that *the indicators alone mean little.* Their significance and weight come as they are accumulated and come to form a pattern of behavior. If the investigator determines the existence of enough of these indicators, there is probable cause to believe the individual is a preferential offender. In order to identify these indicators, the investigator must be willing to go beyond the typical background check of date of birth and credit and criminal histories and learn everything legally possible. Indicators and counterindicators must be identified and evaluated.

Long-Term and Persistent Pattern of Behavior

Sexual Abuse in Background.   Although most victims of child sexual abuse do not become offenders, research indicates that many offenders are former victims. It is well worth the investigator's time and effort to determine if a suspect had ever been the victim of sexual abuse and what the nature of the abuse was (age it occurred, relationship with offender, acts performed, etc.).

Limited Social Contact as Teenagers.   The pedophile's sexual preference for children usually begins in early adolescence. Therefore, during his teenage years he may have exhibited little sexual interest in people his own age, but, as with several of these indicators, that fact *alone* means little.

Premature Separation from Military.   If an individual was dishonorably discharged for molesting children, there is not much doubt about the significance. It was far more common, though, for this type of individual to be prematurely separated from the military with no specific reason given or available. The military, like most organizations, was frequently only interested in getting rid of such people and not necessarily in prosecuting them. Fortunately, this attitude seems to be changing.

Frequent and Unexpected Moves.   When they are identified, pedophiles are often "asked" to leave town by someone in authority, by the parent of one of the victims, or by an employer. This was, and still is, a common way to deal with the problem. The result is that pedophiles frequently show a pattern of living in one place for several years with a good job and then suddenly and for no apparent reason moving and changing jobs. Chances are the investigator will find no official record of what happened. The pedophile will usually have an explanation for the move, but it probably will not reflect the true circumstances. This moving pattern can sometimes be determined from examination of driver's license records.

Prior Arrests.   In some cases, pedophiles have previously been arrested for child molestation or sexual abuse. Certainly such an arrest record is a major indicator, particularly if the arrest goes back many years or is repeated. Investigators must also be alert to the fact that pedophiles may have arrest records for actions that do not appear to involve sexual abuse. These might include impersonating a police officer, writing bad checks, violating child labor laws, or other violations that may indicate a need to check further. Any arrest of an adult in the company of a child not his own should be evaluated with suspicion. The investigator should try to get copies of the reports concerning the arrests in order to evaluate their significance properly.

Multiple Victims. If investigation reveals that an individual molested many different victims, that is a very strong indicator that the offender is a pedophile. More important, if other factors also show that he is a pedophile, then a concerted effort should be made to identify the multiple victims. If you know of only one victim but have reason to believe the offender is a pedophile, then begin looking for the other victims. For instance, if a teacher who is a suspected pedophile molests one child in his class, the chances are high that he has molested or attempted to molest other children in the class as well as children in all the other classes he has taught. This is also true of incest offenders suspected of being preferential child molesters.

Planned, Repeated, or High-risk Attempts. Bold and repeated attempts to obtain children that have been carried out in a cunning and skillful manner are a strong indication that the offender is a pedophile.

Children as Preferred Sexual Objects

Over 25, Single, Never Married. By itself, this indicator means nothing. It has significance only when combined with several other indicators. Because they have a sexual preference for children, pedophiles usually have some difficulty in performing sexually with adults; therefore, they typically do not marry. Some pedophiles, though, do enter into marriage for specific reasons, and these will be discussed below.

Lives Alone or with Parents. This indicator is closely related to the above. Again, by itself, it has little meaning: the fact that a man lives alone does not mean he is a pedophile. The fact that a person who possesses many of the other traits discussed here and also lives alone might be significant.

Limited Dating Relationships if Unmarried. A man who lives alone, has never been married, and does not date should arouse suspicion if he also possesses other characteristics discussed here.

If Married, "Special" Relationship with Spouse. When they do marry, pedophiles often marry either a strong, domineering woman or a weak, passive woman-child. In any case, they will marry a woman who does not have high sexual expectations or needs. A woman married to a pedophile may not realize that her husband is a pedophile, but she does know he has a "problem" — a sexual performance problem. Because she may blame herself for this and because of the private nature of people's sex lives, most wives will usually not reveal this information to an investigator. However, a wife, ex-wife, or girlfriend should always be considered as a possible source of information concerning the sexual preferences of an offender. Pedophiles sometimes marry for convenience or cover. Pedophiles marrying to gain access to children are discussed below.

Excessive Interest in Children.   How much interest is excessive? This is a difficult question. The old adage "if it sounds too good to be true, maybe it is" may apply here. If someone's interest in children seems too good to be true, maybe it is. This is not proof that someone is a pedophile, but it is a reason to be suspicious. It becomes more significant when this excessive interest is combined with other indicators discussed here.

Associates and Circle of Friends are Young.   In addition to sexual activity, pedophiles frequently socialize with children and get involved in youth activities. They may hang around schoolyards, arcades, shopping centers — any place that children frequent. Their "friends" may be male, female, or both sexes, very young, or teenagers, all depending on the age and gender preferences of the pedophile.

Limited Peer Relationships.   Because they cannot share the most important part of their life (their sexual interest in children) with most adults, pedophiles may have a limited number of close adult friends. Only other pedophiles will validate their sexual behavior. If a suspected pedophile has a close adult friend, the possibility that the friend is also a pedophile must be considered.

Age and Gender Preference.   Most pedophiles prefer children of a certain sex in a certain age range. The older the age preference of the pedophile, the more exclusive the gender preference. Pedophiles attracted to toddlers are more likely to molest boys and girls indiscriminately. A pedophile attracted to teenagers is more likely to prefer either boys or girls exclusively. The preferred age bracket for the child can also vary. One pedophile might prefer boys 8 to 10, while another might prefer boys 6 to 12. A pedophile's age preference might not even correspond exactly with the legal definitions of a child or minor. For example, a pedophile might prefer sexual partners 13 to 19. How old a child looks and acts is more important than actual chronological age. A 13-year-old child who looks and acts like a 10-year-old child could be a victim target for a molester preferring 8 to 10 year olds. For the introverted preferential child molester, how old the child looks is more important than how old the child acts. Puberty seems to be an important dividing line for many pedophiles. This is only an age and gender preference, not an exclusive limitation. Any person expressing a strong desire to care for or adopt only a child of a very specific sex and age (other than an infant) should be viewed with some suspicion.

Refers to Children as "Clean, Pure, Innocent, Impish," etc., or as Objects.   Pedophiles sometimes have an idealistic view of children that is expressed in their language and writing. Others sometimes refer to children as if they were objects, projects, or possessions. "This kid has low mileage" and "I've been working on this project for 6 months" are typical comments.

Well-Developed Techniques in Obtaining Victims

Skilled at Identifying Vulnerable Victims.   Some pedophiles can watch a group of children for a short time and then select a potential target. More often than not, the selected child turns out to be from a broken home or the victim of emotional or physical neglect. This skill is developed through practice and experience.

Identifies with Children (Better than with Adults).   Pedophiles usually have the ability to identify with children better than they do with adults — a trait that makes most pedophiles master seducers of children. They especially know how to *listen* to children. Many pedophiles are described as "pied pipers" who attract children.

Access to Children.   This is one of the most important indicators of a pedophile. The pedophile will surely have a method of gaining access to children. Other than simply hanging around places where children congregate, pedophiles sometimes marry or befriend women simply to gain access to their children. Pedophiles are frequently the "nice guys" in the neighborhood who like to entertain the children after school or take them on day or weekend trips. Also, a pedophile may seek employment where he will be in contact with children (teacher, camp counselor, babysitter, school bus driver) or where he can eventually specialize in dealing with children (physician, dentist, minister, photographer, social worker, police officer). The pedophile may also become a scout leader, Big Brother, foster parent, little league coach, and so on. The pedophile may operate a business that hires adolescents. In one case known to the author, a pedophile married, had a daughter, and molested her. He was the "nice guy" in the neighborhood who had the neighborhood girls over to his house for parties at which he molested them. He was a coach for a girls' softball team, and he molested the players. He was a dentist who specialized in child patients, and he molested them.

Activities with Children, Often Excluding Other Adults.   The pedophile is always trying to get children into situations where there are no other adults present. On a scout hike he might suggest the fathers go into town for a beer. He will "sacrifice" and stay behind with the boys.

Seduces with Attention, Affection, and Gifts.   This is the most common technique used by pedophiles. They literally seduce the children by befriending them, talking to them, listening to them, paying attention to them, spending time with them, and buying gifts for them. If you understand the courtship process, it should not be difficult to understand why some child victims develop positive feelings for the offender. Many people can understand why an incest victim might not report his or her father, but they cannot understand why a victim not related to the offender does not immediately report molestation. There are many reasons for a victim not immediately reporting molestation (fear, blackmail, embarrassment, confusion), but the results of the seduction process are often ignored or not understood at all.

Skilled at Manipulating Children.   In order to operate a child sex ring involving simultaneous sexual relations with multiple victims, a pedophile must know how to manipulate children. The pedophile uses seduction techniques, competition, peer pressure, child and group psychology, motivation techniques, threats, and blackmail. The pedophile must continuously recruit children into and move children out of the ring without his activity being disclosed. Part of the manipulation process is lowering the children's inhibitions. A skilled pedophile who can get children into a situation where they must change clothing or stay with him overnight will almost always succeed in seducing them. Not all pedophiles have these skills; the introverted preferential child molester is an example of a pedophile who typically lacks these abilities.

Has Hobbies and Interests Appealing to Children.   This is another indicator that must be considered for evaluation only in connection with other indicators. Pedophiles might collect toys or dolls, build model planes or boats, or perform as clowns or magicians to attract children. A pedophile interested in older children might have a "hobby" involving alcohol, drugs, or pornography.

Shows Sexually Explicit Material to Children.   Any adult who shows sexually explicit material to children of any age should be viewed with suspicion. This is generally part of the seduction process in order to lower inhibitions. A pedophile might also encourage or allow children to call a dial-a-porn service, or send them sexually explicit material via a computer as part of this process.

Sexual Fantasies Focusing on Children

Youth-Oriented Decorations in House or Room.   Pedophiles attracted to teenage boys might decorate their homes the way a teenage boy would. This might include toys, games, stereos, rock posters, and so on. The homes of some pedophiles have been described as shrines to children or as miniature amusement parks.

Photographing of Children.   This includes photographing children fully dressed. One pedophile bragged that he went to rock concerts with 30 or 40 rolls of film in order to photograph young boys. After developing the pictures, he fantasized about having sex with them. Such a pedophile might frequent playgrounds, youth athletic contests, child beauty pageants, or child exercise classes with his camera.

Collecting Child Pornography or Child Erotica.   Pedophiles use this material for their sexual arousal and gratification, to lower a child's sexual inhibitions, to "blackmail" the victim child into keeping the "secret" of their sexual activity, and as a medium of exchange with other pedophiles.

If, after evaluating these indicators, the law enforcement investigator has reason to suspect that a particular subject or suspect is a preferential child molester, the investigator should use the three most important pedophile indicators to his or her investigative advantage. These three indicators are access to children, multiple victims, and collection of child pornography or erotica.

The investigator must try to identify additional victims to strengthen the case against the offender. The more victims identified, the less likely that any of them will have to testify in court. But, even more important, *as soon as legally possible* the investigator must obtain a warrant to search for child pornography or erotica, which is invaluable as evidence. There is a certain urgency in this because the more interviews conducted to obtain the needed probable cause for a search warrant, the greater the chance the pedophile will learn of the investigation and move or hide his collection. Child pornography, especially that produced by the offender, is *one of the most* valuable pieces of evidence of child sexual abuse that any investigator can have. The effects on a jury of viewing seized child pornography is devastating to the defendant's case. The investigator must also attempt to develop a good interview strategy based on knowledge of the preferential offender's need to rationalize and justify his behavior.

Acknowledgment

This material is excerpted from *Child Molesters: A Behavioral Analysis for Law Enforcement Officers Investigating Cases of Child Sexual Exploitation* © 1986, 1992; authored by Kenneth V. Lanning in cooperation with the Federal Bureau of Investigation, U.S. Department of Justice; and published by the National Center for Missing and Exploited Children. It is reprinted with permission of the National Center for Missing and Exploited Children, Arlington, VA. All rights reserved.

References

Abel, G. G. et al. Multiple paraphilic diagnoses among sex offenders, in *Bull. Am. Acad. Psychiatry Law*, 16(2), 153, 1988.

Abel, G. G. et al., Self-reported sex crimes of nonincarcerated paraphiliacs, *J. Interpers. Violence*, 2(1), 3, 1987.

Dietz, P. E., Sex offenses: behavioral aspects, in *Encyclopedia of Crime and Justice*, Kadish, S. H. et al., Eds., Free Press, New York, 1983.

Hazelwood, R. R. et al., The criminal sexual sadist, *FBI Law Enforcement Bull.*, February 1992.

Lanning, K. V. and Burgess, A. W., *Child molesters who abduct*, National Center for Missing and Exploited Children, Arlington, VA, March, 1995.

The Serial Rapist

20

ROBERT R. HAZELWOOD
JANET I. WARREN

In early 1981, a husband and his wife celebrated their 15th wedding anniversary by going out to dinner. They hired a 13-year-old neighbor girl to babysit their two small children and left for the evening. Two hours later, a 29-year-old white male entered the house and subdued the babysitter and her young wards. Using threats, he forced the young girl to fondle him and perform fellatio. Learning that the parents were due to return shortly, he decided to wait for them. On their return, he displayed a gun and forced the wife to handcuff her husband's wrists, after which the perpetrator bound the woman's wrists behind her back. In the presence of the husband, he raped and brutalized the woman so severely she required hospitalization. This man raped more than 50 women before he was arrested.

Research Project

In 1984, the Office of Juvenile Justice and Delinquency Prevention* (OJJDP) provided grant money for a collaborative effort by the FBI National Center for the Analysis of Violent Crime (NCAVC) and Dr. Ann Wolbert Burgess of the University of Pennsylvania's School of Nursing to conduct research on serial rape. As reported elsewhere (Hazelwood, 1983), the study included interviews with 41 imprisoned serial rapists who had raped at least 10 times and who, as a group, were responsible for 837 sexual assaults and over 400 attempted rapes. The inclusion criterion of ten rapes was established as it signified continuing success at eluding law enforcement, an aptitude that warranted further investigation. The study of multiple rapes by a single person also allowed for an assessment of change over time on a number of important variables, i.e., in the amount of force used, the sexual activities enacted, and the details of the *modus operandi.*

Members of the NCAVC and other selected FBI Agents conducted each of the 41 interviews. Before the interviews all available documentation, including police investigatory reports, victim statements, presentence reports, medical and mental health records, and pertinent prison records were reviewed. The interviews were open-ended and unstructured and ranged from 4½ to 12½ hr. They included a detailed review of the rapist's developmental, familial, sexual, marital, educational, employment, and military history as well as his current hobbies and pastimes. The interview also focused on the offender's pre-offense, offense, and

* This research was funded in part by grant #84-JN-AX-KO from the Office of Juvenile Justice and Delinquency Prevention to the University of Pennsylvania School of Nursing in conjunction with the FBI National Center for the Analysis of Violent Crime.

postoffense behavior as well as any advice he might provide law enforcement regarding investigation, interrogation, and rape prevention. Following the interviews, a 70-page protocol was completed by the interviewers. While the research interviews, conducted under the auspices of the OJJDP grant, were concluded in 1986, the research and interviews of serial rapists continues to the present. To the authors' knowledge, this research represents the only body of information on this type of serial sexual offender.

Who is the serial rapist? At what age does he begin to assault and how does he select his victims? In what other types of deviant sexual activities does he engage? Drawing from these interviews, this chapter outlines for the reader information about the serial rapist, his victims, and his criminal behavior. In assessing these data, it is important for the reader to remember that the data refer to a special category of serial rapist and may not be generalized to a more undifferentiated group of rapists.

Serial Rapist Demographics

The sample consisted of 35 white males, 5 black males, and 1 Hispanic. At the time of interview, the subjects' ages ranged from 23 to 55 years, with a mean of 35.2 years. The mean age of the subjects at the time of their first, middle, and last rape was 21.8, 25.8, and 29 years, respectively.

The youngest rapist interviewed also assaulted for the shortest period of time before his first arrest. That rapist, who will be referred to as "Jess", was 20 years old when he was apprehended for a series of 12 rapes over a 3-month period.

Case No. 1

Jess said that he had never consciously thought about rape until a month before he began his crimes. On that occasion, he and a male friend were discussing the friend's disappointment with a date the previous evening which had not culminated in sexual relations. The friend stated that he was so angry, he considered raping the woman. Jess asked why he didn't and the friend said that he wasn't willing to go to jail for sex. Jess reported that he thought about rape that evening and decided to commit one about a month later.

Although he was relatively young at the time, his method of obtaining victims was thoughtful: he would go to a singles bar and wait for an unaccompanied woman over 40 years of age. His rationale for selecting a victim of that age was that women over 40 had been raised during a time when it was believed that women who went to bars alone were looking for sexual liaison. Jess was young and attractive, and therefore the women were flattered when he approached them. After spending time with the woman, he would suggest that they go to his place. If she agreed, he would ask himself, "I wonder what her face will look like when I tell her I'm going to rape her?" After leaving the bar, he would drive to an isolated area, stop the car, and tell her to take her clothes off saying, "I'm going to rape you". The victim would be incredulous, and he would strike her face, force her to remove her clothing, rape her, and leave her stranded.

Jess had no previous history of criminal activity before his arrest for rape. He was raised in an advantaged socioeconomic environment; from all accounts, his family was close-knit, and the parents were involved in their children's lives. He was an outstanding athlete in high school and had been voted most popular student and senior class president.

Employment

Twenty (54%) of 37 who responded described their employment history as "generally stable", 14 (38%) stated that it was "unstable", and 3 (8%) described themselves as "chronically unemployed". The respondents said that at the time of their most recent arrest, they had been employed at their last job for a mean period of 2.4 years. They had held from 1 to 35 jobs, with a mean of 5.4, during the previous 15 years. Their reported annual income ranged from $5000 to $52,000, with a mean of $16,446 a year.

The types of employment held by the rapists included skilled jobs (e.g., cardiovascular technician) and white collar occupations (e.g., business manager). Of particular interest is the fact that the majority of serial rapists were generally stable in their employment; only a small minority were chronically unemployed. With few exceptions, the serial rapists were employed at the time they were committing their assaults.

Marital History

Twenty-nine (71%) of 41 respondents had been married at least once, with 14 of them (34%) having been married more than once. These findings confirm earlier studies (Rada, 1987), which suggest that the marital status of a person or the presence of consensual sexual relationships, is not directly related to whether a person commits rape. All but one of the rapists interviewed had participated in consensual sexual activities.

One of the serial rapists, "Mike", commented on the irony of raping when a consensual partner is readily available.

Case No. 2

On being released from prison after serving a sentence for rape, Mike got a job managing a business and moved back in with his wife of 7 years. Before leaving work late one evening, he called his wife, suggested an intimate dinner, and hinted at sexual activities to which she responded positively. While driving home, he observed a woman driving alone. Pulling in behind her, he flashed his lights, and the victim, believing him to be a police officer, pulled over. He walked to her car, asked for her driver's license and registration, and requested that she accompany him back to his car. She did so, and he subdued and raped her.

After relating the details of the crime, Mike shook his head and said, "I mean, my God, there I was on my way home to have sex with my wife, and I ended up back here".

Military History

Twenty-one (51%) of the 41 rapists served in the Armed Forces. Of these, 18 were in the ground forces, and all were in the enlisted ranks. It is worth noting that the mean age of the men at the time of interview was 35.2, therefore being eligible for the draft which ended in 1972. Future studies may include fewer veterans.

Of 20 veterans, 10 received honorable discharges and 10 received other than honorable discharges. Information was not available on one veteran.

Information on military performance was available for 18 veterans; 9 of them reported that they had encountered "occasional difficulties" in the military. Eight veterans indicated that they had been charged with a criminal offense while in the service.

The large number of other-than-honorable discharges and the high incidence of noncriminal and criminal problems experienced by the interviewees are in keeping with a general pattern of antisocial behavior observed in the serial rapists' background.

Intelligence

In 33 instances, formal intelligence test scores were available for review. The serial rapists demonstrated an unusually high level of general intelligence. Only 4 (12%) scored below average, while 12 (36%) scored within the average range of intelligence. Seventeen (52%) scored above average (i.e., 9 scored "bright normal" and 8 "superior" or "very superior"). It is important to note that 88% of those tested scored average or better.

The educational level of the men ranged from 5 to 17 years, with a mean of 11.3 years of formal education. Twenty-five (61%) of the 41 respondents had obtained a GED or high school diploma and 9 (22%) held either an associate or bachelor's degree.

"Ted" was one of the most intelligent rapists interviewed during the research. He had a measured full scale IQ of 139. Interestingly, he was the only man in the sample who had never experienced a consensual sexual relationship.

Case No. 3

Ted was steadily employed, earned well over $30,000, and considered himself to be socioeconomically advantaged. The manner in which he committed his crimes showed a great deal of forethought. In preparing for a series of rapes, he would drive far from where he lived or worked and select a residential area into which he would easily blend. Through peeping activities, he would select a minimum of six women who lived alone, and would begin observing their homes in order to learn their patterns of behavior. He explained that he always maintained a minimum of six potential victims, and after raping one, he would select another to replace her. He did this in the event he was, for one reason or another, unsuccessful in his first attempt. On some occasions, after unsuccessfully attempting a rape, he would subdue an alternate victim and rape her while the police were responding to the first victim's complaint.

Ted was a very ritualistic rapist. Before entering the victim's home he would dress in his "going in clothes", which consisted of work gloves, loose-fitting dark coveralls, oversized sneakers, and a ski mask. Using a glass cutter and a suction cup, he would noiselessly make entry through a patio door or window. After ensuring that the victim was asleep and alone, he would disconnect the telephone and any light-emitting devices in her bedroom. He would then leave the residence; but prior to doing so, he would raise a window or leave the door ajar. Returning to his vehicle, he would change into his "rape clothes", which consisted of oversized coveralls, tight-fitting surgical gloves, a differently sized pair of sneakers, and a ski mask. Upon approaching the home, he would check to see if the window or door had been closed. If it had, he would know that the victim had awakened, and he would leave and go to another victim's home. If the window or door had not been closed, he would go to the victim's bedside and count to ten in increments of one half (i.e., one half, one, one and one half, two, etc.). He would then leap upon the victim, rape her, and depart within 2 min.

When questioned as to the meaning of this ritualistic behavior, Ted explained that he "was putting off the rape" because "that was the least enjoyable part of the whole thing". When asked why he didn't leave if that was the case, he said, "Pardon the pun, but after all I had gone through to get there, it would have been a crime not to rape her".

In assessing the intelligence of these offenders, it is important to remain aware of problems inherent in relying too heavily on documented intelligence test scores. The first rapist interviewed had a documented test score of 108. During the interview, it became obvious that the score did not accurately reflect his intelligence. Commenting on this, the rapist said that when first imprisoned, he was advised by older inmates to score intentionally low on such tests so that the authorities would not expect too much of him. At the interviewer's request, he agreed to be retested and scored 128, a full 20 points higher.

Formally measured intelligence may not always be the best indicator of one's ability to be a successful criminal. While the vast majority of the people in this study were average or above average in intelligence, some scored below average, and yet they were very successful in eluding law enforcement. "Street smarts", while not something that can be measured through standardized testing, is well recognized by criminals and police. Perhaps it is best defined as the ability to survive by applying what has been learned through one's own experiences or the experiences of others.

Representative of this concept is the case of "Jack", an impulsive serial rapist who harbored a sincere and earnest hatred of women. Jack's measured intelligence was only 79 (full scale), yet he was a successful criminal because of his ability to anticipate and manipulate others.

Case No. 4

One sunny afternoon, Jack was walking across a food store parking lot and observed a woman placing groceries in her car. He approached the woman, shoved her into the front seat of her car, beat and raped her, and walked away.

Following that crime, he left that city and traveled to his home town. Aware that the FBI had a warrant for his arrest (under the Unlawful Flight to Avoid Prosecution statute) and would surely be looking for him in his hometown, he entered a drug rehabilitation program. He did so knowing that these programs do not have to divulge the identities of the participants to law enforcement or any member of the criminal justice system. Even though he had no drug problem, he knew enough about drug addiction to be able to evidence the necessary symptoms.

After a month in the program, he decided that he "wanted a woman" and asked when he would be allowed to leave the center unescorted. On learning he could not do so for at least 6 months, he said, "I wasn't gonna wait no damn 6 months for a woman". He thought about it and decided to use a medical ploy to get away from the confines of the center. He feigned abdominal pains, knowing they were not easily diagnosed, and was taken to a hospital by a counselor. After being examined by a physician, he told the counselor that he would have to take a series of tests, each being on a different floor of the hospital. The counselor told Jack that he would wait for him on the ground floor of the hospital.

Now on his own, Jack set out for the one location where he was guaranteed to find women — the restroom area. Observing a woman enter the lavatory, he followed her in and, seeing no one else was present, he took a paper towel from the dispenser and, using a marking pen and tape he had brought with him, printed "Out of Order" on it. He affixed it to the front of the restroom door. He then re-entered the room and proceeded to assault the victim. Another woman, ignoring the sign, entered the restroom, at which time the victim screamed. The second woman ran out of the room and yelled that a woman was being assaulted, and a crowd gathered outside the door. Jack grabbed the victim by her hair, opened the door, and screamed at her, "If I ever catch you screwing around again, I'm not only gonna kill him, I'm gonna kill you, too". Believing that Jack and the victim were involved in a domestic argument, the crowd parted and Jack moved through them with the victim in tow. Fortunately the woman's doctor recognized her, and Jack ran down the stairwell and to his counselor. They returned to the treatment center, and Jack later fled to Canada.

Arrest History

The rapists reported diversified criminal histories, including a variety of property offenses, nuisance sexual offenses, and other sexual assaults. Only one rapist had no prior arrests when he was apprehended for his 3-month spree during which he had raped 12 women (see case 1). The majority of the rapists (24 or 58%) had been institutionalized in either a correctional center (46%) or a mental facility (12%) at least once before their arrests for their most current offenses.

When asked about previous sexual assaults, the respondents reported they had been convicted of a mean of 7.6 sexual assaults, although they were, in fact, responsible for a mean of 27.8 assaults. Prior sexual offenses committed by 38 of the respondents included rape only (37%), sexual nuisance offenses only (8%), a combination of rape and sexual nuisance offenses (42%), and "other" types of offenses (13%). The number of actual sexual assaults committed by the rapists ranged from 10 to 78. (According to the respondents, they also had been convicted of a mean of one sexual assault of which they were not guilty.) The most commonly reported nonsexual offenses included burglary and breaking and entering.

The rapists were asked how they responded to being confronted by an arresting officer. The majority surrendered without resistance and, when interrogated, close to a half admitted fully to the offense. By the last offense, more than a half of the respondents tried to deny their guilt. For the last offense, 30 (79%) out of 38 respondents reported surrendering without resistance, 3 (8%) attempted to escape, 1 (3%) resisted physically, and 4 (11%) reported some other type of response. Following their arrest, 21 (52%) out of 40 respondents denied committing the offense, 18 (46%) confessed to being responsible, while 1 (3%) qualified his admission by minimizing his guilt.

Residence

At the time of the first, middle, and last offense, most respondents were living in single-family dwellings, although a significant minority also resided in apartments. In a small number of instances, the offender was institutionalized at the time of the offense. The majority were living with parents, spouses and/or children, or a roommate. During the first and last rape, only 9 (22%) out of 41 respondents were living alone.

These findings certainly contradict popular stereotypes which characterize the serial rapist as a lonely, isolated person who lives alone and has little or no contact with his family. Rather, in most cases, the rapist is living either with his parents or spouse at the time of the offense.

Use of Vehicle

The serial rapists often used a vehicle in the commission of their crimes, either to get to and from the scene or to transport the victim. The type and ownership of vehicles used by the rapists in their assaults were examined. In no instance was a stolen vehicle involved. In the majority of the assaults (62%) the perpetrators used their own vehicles. In only seven (8%) rapes did the offenders use the victim's vehicle, while in six (7%) instances a borrowed vehicle was used.

Most frequently (46%), the body type of vehicles used was a sedan or hardtop. The next most frequently used vehicle was a pickup truck (19 crimes or 19%).

In only 14 (15%) assaults were the vehicles described as being in poor condition. At the time of the last assault, there were nine reports of the offenders' vehicles being equipped with a CB radio, police scanner, spotlight, or police antenna.

Personality Characteristics

The information presented here is based on self-reported data and the observations of the interviewing FBI Agents. Not all serial rapists interviewed were represented by the descriptions set forth below.

The vast majority of the rapists could be described as neat and well-groomed men who obviously took pride in their personal appearance. They exhibited a range of emotions from "cold and aloof" to "agitated and tearful". The largest proportion of them, however, were observed to be expressive, though guarded and controlled. The rapists indicated that they were not trustworthy persons. They were, however, able to hide this aspect of their personality from friends and associates.

They conversed in an articulate and conversational manner frequently punctuated with profanity. They used a precise and concise manner to ensure that their thoughts were being conveyed and in order to maintain control.

When asked how their friends would have described them at the time they were committing the assaults, they responded with descriptions such as "average", "friendly", "a leader", and "willing to help out a friend". Further discussion brought out the fact that while they tended to meet people easily, they eventually attempted to dominate the relationship. They displayed a good sense of humor, but were manipulative and cunning. While able to convince people of their ability to achieve, they were impulsive and always seemed to be having one type of problem or another.

The rapists described themselves as being perceived by others as macho and suggested that they worked at maintaining this image through their dress, attitude, speech, and mode of transportation. They were intelligent and consequently tended to lead rather than follow.

While this was the image or "service personality" that others saw, many of the rapists related a sense of inadequacy, immaturity, and irresponsibility to the interviewers. As one rapist said, "I was expected to decide what my group was going to do or where we were going to go. I really didn't feel comfortable in that role and would have liked having someone else make the decision. I didn't see myself as others saw me".

Hobbies and Activities

Thirty-seven of the 41 rapists reported having pastimes or hobbies. Twenty-three of them reported outdoor activities, while 14 mentioned a variety of indoor interests. Of 35 pastimes reported, physically oriented activities included fishing (12), hunting (7), swimming (5), and baseball (5). Nonphysical types of activities included music, model building, reading, woodworking, coin/stamp collecting, chess, and antiques.

When asked what types of books and magazines they preferred to read, the respondents listed *Playboy*, *Penthouse*, other sex magazines, crime novels, as well as a variety of spy novels and science fiction books. Newspapers, *Time* magazine, *Reader's Digest*, and entertainment magazines were also reported.

Developmental Characteristics

Socioeconomics

Table 1 summarizes various aspects of the rapists' family structure. As indicated, slightly over one half grew up in homes that were socioeconomically average

(37%) or advantaged (17%). Approximately one quarter (27%) were raised in marginal but self-sufficient homes, while 20% were raised in submarginal homes and were, at times, on welfare.

The significance of these findings is that 54% of the serial rapists were brought up in average or above-average socioeconomic environments. While it is recognized that the results of this research cannot be generalized to the undifferentiated rapist population, these findings would seem to contradict long-held beliefs and theories that the majority of such persons come from economically deprived families.

Parental Relationships

The rapists were asked questions pertaining to their relationship with their parents (see Table 1). When asked who was the dominant parental figure, 20 (50%) reported the mother, 16 (40%) the father, and 4 (10%) some other adult figure.

"Kenny" provides the reader with an example of a young man who was raised in an unusual interpersonal environment.

Case No. 5

When Kenny was 8 years old, his mother was convicted of murder, and he was sent to live with an aunt who had recently been released from prison for stabbing a man to death. The aunt was an alcoholic and a chronic gambler, and all of the family's money went to support these activities. At the age of 14, he ran away from home and was taken in by a pimp. The pimp was in his mid-20s and a college graduate. The man allowed Kenny to help in his business by collecting money from the female prostitutes in his stable. Of interest is the fact that the pimp insisted that Kenny continue his education and not "run the streets". The pimp stressed the value of education and said that when he could no longer "work the girls", he could always fall back on his college degree. Kenny advised that while he was with the pimp, he never got into trouble with the law. Eventually, the man was arrested and sentenced to a long prison term, and, unfortunately, Kenny returned to the streets.

Within the sample, only 14 (36%) of the men described their relationship with their mothers as "warm/close". Twelve (31%) stated that it was a "variable" relationship, seven (18%) said it was "hostile/aggressive", four (10%) that it was "uncaring, indifferent", and two (5%) described it as being "cold/distant". Even fewer of the men (7 or 18%) described the relationship with their fathers as "warm/close". Twelve of the respondents (31%) indicated that it was "cold/distant", ten (26%) reported it to be "variable", seven (18%) as "hostile/aggressive", and three (8%) as "uncaring/indifferent".

Childhood Abuse

Abusive behavior in the families of the serial rapists was well documented. As noted in Table 1, 15 (30%) of the rapists reported being physically abused. One man said that his mother would "hit me with anything that was handy, a belt, a broom handle, iron, whatever". Scars on his back were evidence of the truthfulness

Table 1   Family Structure of Serial Rapists

Assessment of socioeconomic level of subject's preadult home (N = 41)	N	%
Advantaged	7	17
Comfortable, average	15	37
Marginal, self-sufficient	11	27
Submarginal	8	20
Variable	—	—
Dominant Parental Figures (N = 40)		
Mother	20	50
Father	16	40
Other	4	10
Quality of Relationship to Mother or Dominant Female Caretaker (N = 39)		
Warm, close	14	36
Variable	12	31
Cold, distant	2	5
Uncaring, indifferent	4	10
Hostile, aggressive	7	18
Quality of Relationship to Father or Dominant Male Caretaker (N = 39)		
Warm, close	7	18
Variable	10	26
Cold, distant	12	31
Uncaring, indifferent	3	8
Hostile, aggressive	7	18
Evidence That Subject Was Physically Abused by Parents/Caretakers (N = 40)		
Yes	15	38
No	25	62
Evidence That Subject Was Psychologically Abused by Parents/Caretakers (N = 41)		
Yes	30	73
No	11	27
Evidence That Subject Was Sexually Abused (N = 41)		
Yes	31	76
No	10	24

of his statement. Another rapist explained that his mother caught him fondling his penis through his pants and reported it to his father. The father made the boy put his penis over the back of a chair and whipped it with a belt.

Thirty (73%) of the subjects described psychological abuse. However, obtaining this information was not always easy. One man, when asked if he had been emotionally abused as a child, replied negatively; but later, when asked what his mother said to him when she was angry, he replied, "She would call me a bastard, son-of-a-bitch, asshole. Things like that".

In a separate analysis of the same 41 rapists, Burgess et al. (1988) found that 31 (76%) of them reported experiencing some type of unusual sexual experience either in childhood or during their teen years. Eight (26%) of 31 subjects described being forced to witness disturbing sexual occurrences. Seven (22%) stated that they were fondled or were involved in the fondling of another, and 16 (52%) recalled being forced to submit to penetration of their body. "Ray" (Burgess et al., 1988), a progressively violent offender, was repeatedly raped by his father and later initiated by him into raping women.

Case No. 6

Ray described his father as being cold and distant, until he began anally raping him at the age of 9. From that stage of his life to the present, Ray described his father as being hostile and aggressive. Ray's father raped him until the age of 12, and as his age increased, so did the aggressiveness of the assaults. He said that when he reached 11 years, his father began taking him to bars where he would pick up women, take them to an isolated area, sadistically beat and rape them, and then force them into the back seat with Ray and tell them to "take care of my son". Ray would be told by his father what part of the victim's body he was to hit, bite, pinch, or pull. He stated that at the age of 12, he began anticipating his father being finished with the woman, so that he could gain access to her. Ray maintained that until 14, he believed that this was the way men and women had sex. He continued to rape with his father until, when he was 16, his father raped Ray's girlfriend.

Sexual Development

Table 2 summarizes aspects of the rapists' sexual development, as well as various components of their current sexual adaptation. Of etiological significance is the fact, noted above, that 76% of the men reported either observing disturbing sexual acts or being sexually abused. This is alarmingly high when compared to percentages associated with the general population (Risin and Koss, 1991). Interestingly, while being interviewed, many of the rapists failed to define their sexual experience as abuse, initially indicating that they had not been sexually abused. However, when they were later asked at what age and with whom they had their first sexual encounter with another person, evidence of sexual abuse became evident.

Table 2   Serial Rapists, Sexual History and Current Sexual Behaviors

	N	%	Total/N
Childhood or Adolescent Sexual Trauma			
Witnessing sexual violence of others	8	25	32
Witnessing disturbing sexual activity on part of parents	17	44	39
Witnessing disturbing sexual activity on part of other family members or friends	9	25	36
Physical injury to sexual organs; venereal disease	5	14	36
Multiple sexual assault	11	31	35
Sex stress situations (e.g., punitive parental reaction to masturbation)	17	46	37
Adult Sexual Behavior			
Marked inhibition/aversion to sexual activity	4	10	40
Compulsive masturbation	21	54	39
Exhibitionism	12	29	41
Voyeurism (peeping)	27	68	40
Fetishism	16	41	39
Cross-dressing	9	23	39
Obscene phone calls	15	38	40
Prostitution (or pimp)	6	15	41
Sexual bondage	10	26	39
Collected detective magazines	11	28	39
Collected pornography	13	33	39

Cases No. 7 and No. 8

Fred, one of the rapists who initially denied being sexually abused, said that when he was seven, he went to a movie and a man sitting next to him attempted to fondle him. He moved to another part of the theater and the man followed him and offered him $2 to allow the activity. The boy agreed and continued to meet the man each weekend for a full year. The initial encounter bothered the boy enough to cause him to change seats, but as an adult, he rationalized it as a way of making money.

Another rapist said that when he was eight, his parents hired a 17-year-old woman to babysit him and she "taught me how to go down on women". For an 8 year old the experience had to be frightening, but as an adult he considered it a "score".

This inconsistency in reporting reflects certain cultural biases in defining the sexual abuse of young males by older females. The detrimental effect of this type of experience, however, has been discussed by Katan (1973), who suggests that these early sexual experiences lead to an overstimulation of the child's coping abilities and predispose him to interpret the acts as aggressive rather than sexual. Burgess et al. (1988) discuss these dynamics in terms of Freud's conceptualization of the repetition compulsion. They suggest that the abused child begins to fantasize and then re-enact the sexual aggression as the perpetrator rather than the victim in an attempt to "master" the earlier trauma.

Earlier studies suggest that many rapists practice a variety of sexual perversions. When the serial rapists were asked about their past or present sexual behavior, 27 (68%) reported that they began with window peeping while in childhood or adolescence (see Table 2). Most of the literature reports peeping as a "nuisance" sexual offense and generalizes that "peeping Toms" are not dangerous. It is not the authors' intent to state that all window peepers will become serial rapists, but to acquaint the reader with the fact that 68% of the subjects in this study began with such activities.

"Troy" began his peeping as an adolescent, an activity that unexpectedly escalated into rape and murder 3 years later.

Case No. 9

Troy, one of the interviewees, began window peeping at the age of 14. At 17, he spied on a 24-year-old woman and found her especially appealing. He began to focus his voyeuristic activities on her and eventually observed her making love to her boyfriend. This so enraged him that he made the decision to rape the woman. After she had gone to sleep one evening, he entered through an unlocked window and jumped on her. She awoke and began screaming. In a panic, he grabbed a handful of tissues from a bedside table, pushed them into her mouth, and accidentally suffocated her. Five days later, he was arrested for voyeurism in the same neighborhood. He was not questioned about the death because he was "just a peeper". Seven years later, he confessed to the unsolved crime, but was not believed until he gave information about the death scene that only the killer could have known.

Sixteen (41%) of the serial rapists reported fetishism and 15 (38%) reported having made obscene telephone calls. Thirteen (33%) collected pornography, 11 (28%) collected detective magazines, 10 (26%) were involved in sexual bondage, 9 (23%) had cross-dressed, and 6 (15%) had engaged in prostitution as either a prostitute or pimp.

The investigative value of such information is in the development of questions about suspects when interviewing former wives or girlfriends about the offender's sexual behavior. It will also prove useful when preparing search warrants for a suspect's residence, workplace, or automobile in that a significant proportion of the men collected pornography relevant to their diverse sexual interests.

Chronic Behavior Patterns

The rapists were questioned about certain chronic behavior patterns that might have characterized their behavior either as children or adolescents. A variety of delinquent behaviors were reported by more than one half of the rapists.

Stealing and shoplifting were reported by 27 (71%) out of 38 who responded. Many rapists advised that a great deal of their thefts occurred through break-ins of homes close to their own home. This early experience may account for why they were so adept at entering the homes of rape victims.

Temper tantrums/hyperactivity and alcohol abuse also had a high occurrence rate, with 63% of the sample reporting each behavior. Isolation/withdrawal occurred in 24 (62%) out of 39 of the cases, and 22 (55%) out of 40 respondents said that they were assaultive to adults. One rapist recalled trying to hit his female teacher over the head with a chair in the third grade. Chronic lying was reported by 20 (54%) out of 37 of the subjects.

These findings are in keeping with earlier studies. Rada (1978) found that when he asked 20 incarcerated rapists whether their parents considered them to be a disciplinary or behavioral problem, 65% responded in the affirmative, 75% admitted to stealing, 55% to temper tantrums, 50% to frequent fighting, and 40% to truancy and suspension from school.

Hellman and Blackman (1966) discuss the oft-cited hypothesis that enuresis, fire setting, and cruelty to animals are the triad of behavior patterns in childhood or adolescence which may be useful in predicting violent behavior in adulthood. In the current study, these behaviors were reported by 32, 24, and 19% of the respondents, respectively.

In terms of preadult institutionalization, 15% of the rapists reported living in an orphanage, 41% in a detention center, 8% in a foster home, 26% in some sort of mental health facility, and 4% in a boarding or military school. These findings suggest that a significant number of serial rapists were identified at an early age as being either delinquent or emotionally disturbed.

Victims of the Serial Rapists

Demographics

The serial rapists were asked a variety of questions about the 123 victims of their first, middle, and last sexual assaults (Table 3). The average age of the victim for the first, middle, and last attack was 22.8, 26.1, and 24.4 years, respectively. The victims of the serial rapist were predominantly white; of the 123 victims, 113 were white, 6 black, 1 Hispanic, 2 Asian, and 1 Native American. In this study, white rapists did not cross the racial line in their crimes against women, whereas the black offenders raped both white and black women. The youngest victim in this study was 5 years old and the oldest victim was 65.

While the overwhelming majority of victims were adult women, there were a significant minority of child (19%) and same-sex victims (2%). One example of same-sex rape occurred in a prison environment.

Case No. 10

Tony, a white male, was serving time for raping a woman, and upon entering prison, became the lover of an older white inmate. The older man ordered him to rape a young black male, and told him that if he failed to do this he would be given to other inmates sexually. On two separate occasions, Tony was used this way.

Table 3   Demographic Characteristics of Victims

	First rape		Middle rape		Last rape	
	N	%	N	%	N	%
Age						
0–10		—	—	—	5	12
11–17	7	17	6	15	4	10
18–25	15	37	15	38	13	32
26–33	14	34	14	35	11	27
34–41	4	10	4	10	7	17
41+	1	2	1	2	1	2
Race						
Caucasian	36	88	39	95	38	93
Black	3	7	2	5	1	2
Hispanic	—	—	—	—	1	2
Asian	1	2	—	—	1	2
Native American	1	2	—	—	—	—
Sex						
Female	40	98	41	100	40	98
Male	1	2	—	—	1	2

Children were the victims of the serial rapists in 22 (18%) instances. In some cases, they were the children or stepchildren of the offender; in other cases, neighbor children; and in other instances, total strangers.

As summarized in Table 4, the majority of victims were strangers to the offender. In only ten (8%) instances, the men reported raping an acquaintance, four (3%) a neighbor, and two (2%) either a friend or date. The rapists included in this study were selected because of their success in committing a large number of crimes over time. It is the authors' opinion that one of the primary reasons they were so successful is that they generally selected strangers as their victims. Combining the victims' fear with the fact that their attacker is a complete stranger is a strong impediment to providing necessary identification to the investigator.

Isolation of the Victim

The majority of victims (87 or 79%) were alone at the time of the assault. Of the 23 victims who were not, 4 (13%) were with their children, 2 (2%) with a female friend, 2 (2%) with a parent, two (2%) with a spouse, and 3 (3%) with some other person. There were co-victims in only seven cases: four females, two males, and one incident with co-victims of each sex.

The scene of the sexual assault was relatively consistent. In 59 assaults (50%), the assault occurred in the victim's home. In seven assaults (6%), the offense

Table 4 Victim Characteristics and Victim Selection

Reason for Selecting Victim	Yes (%)	NO (%)
Availability	98	2
Gender	95	5
Age	66	34
Location	66	34
Race	63	37
Physical characteristics	39	61
Other specific reasons	31	69
No special reason	25	75
Clothing	15	85
Vocation	7	93

Relationship to Victim	First rape		Middle rape		Last rape	
	N	%	N	%	N	%
Stranger	38	80	35	85	36	88
Acquaintance	3	7	5	12	2	5
Other	2	5	—	—	1	2
Date	1	2	—	—	—	—
Friend	1	2	—	—	—	—
Neighbor	1	2	1	2	2	5

Scene of Sexual Assault	First rape		Middle rape		Last rape	
	N	%	N	%	N	%
Victim's residence	21	52	20	53	18	45
Street/alleyway	4	10	1	3	2	5
Other	11	28	10	26	15	38
Parking lot	1	2	1	3	1	2
Subject's residence	2	5	3	8	1	2
Public facilities	1	2	—	—	1	2
Subject's workplace	—	—	1	3	—	—
Highway	—	—	2	5	2	5

occurred in a street or alleyway, while in seven (6%) instances, it occurred either in a parking lot or on a highway. Less often, the assaults occurred at the subject's home, public facility, or at the victim's place of work.

As noted, the victim's home was the scene of the assault in half of the rapes (50%). As mentioned earlier, 71% of the men had been involved in stealing as children and adolescents and many of them had done so by breaking into homes. Having this experience, they no doubt felt more comfortable in gaining access to homes. Many of the rapists selected their victims by peeping activities or following intended victims to their homes. Consequently, the offender learned the victim's habits in her home (i.e., visitors, phone calls, sleeping hours, hours away from home). In several instances, the rapist entered the victim's home while she was absent and familiarized himself with the residence.

Selection Criteria

A variety of reasons were cited by the rapists for selecting their victims, as indicated in Table 4. Forty (98%) of 41 men emphasized the "availability" of the victim, while 27 (66%) cited the importance of "location". Both these reasons are closely related and signify that the victim was chosen more for her vulnerability than any particular personal characteristic.

Information concerning what specific characteristics of the victims resulted in their being singled out for rape indicated that the victim's gender was the primary criterion cited by 39 (95%) of the men. Victims' ages were cited in 27 (66%) cases and race in 26 (63%) instances. Physical characteristics of the victim were reported as being significant by 16 (39%) of the rapists and clothing (or dress) by 6 (15%) of the respondents. Rather disconcertingly, 10 (25%) of the rapists advised that there was "no special reason" for the person being targeted for attack.

According to these data, the serial rapist apparently does not consciously engage in specific or symbolic consideration in selecting his victims. The various accounts suggest that the victims were not selected because they reminded the offender of a significant other in his life; rather, the victims' availability, gender, age, location, and race were cited as the determining factors.

The Criminal Behavior of the Serial Rapist

Premeditation

The majority of the sexual attacks (5 to 61%) committed by these men were premeditated across their first, middle, and last rapes, while fewer rapists reported their crimes as being impulsive (15 to 22%) or opportunistic (22 to 24%). Although no comparable data on serial rape are available, it is probable that the premeditation involved in these crimes is particularly characteristic of these serial rapists. It is also probable that this premeditation is reflective of their preferential interest in this type of crime and largely accounts for their ability to avoid detection.

Method of Approach

There are three different styles of approach rapists frequently use: the "con", the "blitz", and the "surprise" (Hazelwood, 1983). Each reflects a different means of selecting, approaching, and subduing a chosen victim.

Case No. 11

John, a man who raped more than 20 women, told the interviewers that he stopped on the highway late at night to assist a woman whose car had become disabled. After correcting the problem, he suggested that he drive the car to ensure that the problem would not recur. She agreed and he drove her to an isolated area and raped her. He then forced her from the vehicle and drove to where his own car was parked and continued on his trip.

As in the case presented above, the con approach involves subterfuge and is predicated on the rapist's ability to interact with women. With this technique, the rapist openly approaches the victim and requests or offers some type of assistance or direction. However, once the victim is within his control, the offender may suddenly become more aggressive.

The con approach was used in 8 (24%) of the first rapes, 12 (35%) of the middle rapes, and 14 (41%) of the last rapes. Various ploys used by the offenders included impersonating a police officer, providing transportation for hitchhiking victims, offering assistance, and picking up women in singles bars. Obviously, this style of initiating contact with victims requires an ability to interact with women.

In a blitz approach, the rapist uses an immediate and direct application of injurious force against his victim. The attacker may also use chemicals or gases but most frequently makes use of his ability to physically overpower a woman. Interestingly, despite its simplicity, this approach was used in 23% of the first rapes, 20% of the middle rapes, and 17% of the last rapes. Even though it is used less often than either the con or surprise approach, it results in more extensive physical injury to the victims.

Case No. 12

Phil, a 28-year-old male, approached a woman walking down a deserted street during the early morning hours. He struck her over the head with a steel bar, dragged her into a nearby park, and violently raped her. Whenever she began to regain consciousness, he would strike her in the face. Needless to say, she was physically and emotionally traumatized for an extended period of time following the incident.

The surprise approach, which involves the assailant waiting for the victim or approaching her after she is sleeping, presupposes that the rapist has targeted or preselected his victim through unobserved contact and knowledge of when the victim would be alone. Threats and/or the presence of a weapon are often associated with this type of approach; however, there is generally no physically injurious force applied.

Case No. 13

Sam, a 24-year-old male, would preselect his victims through "peeping Tom" activities. He would then watch his victim's home to establish her patterns of behavior. After deciding to rape the woman, he would wait until she had gone to sleep, enter the home, and place his hand over her mouth. He would advise the victim that he did not intend to harm her if she cooperated with him. He raped more than 20 women before he was apprehended.

The surprise approach was used by the serial rapists in 19 (54%) of the first rapes, 16 (46%) of the middle rapes, and 16 (44%) of the last rapes (percentages vary due to the number of rapes). This represents the most frequently used means of approach and is used most often by men who lack motivation or confidence in their ability to subdue the victim through physical violence or subterfuge.

Controlling the Victim

How rapists maintain control over a victim depends on their motivation for the sexual attack. Within this context, four control methods are frequently used in various combinations during a rape: (1) intimidating physical presence, (2) verbal threats, (3) display of a weapon, and (4) use of physical force.

The men in this study predominantly used a threatening physical presence (82 to 92%) and/or verbal threats (65 to 80%) to control their victims. Substantially less often they displayed a weapon (44 to 49%) or physically assaulted the victim (27 to 32%). When a weapon was displayed, it was most often a sharp instrument, such as a knife (27 to 42%).

One rapist explained that he chose a knife because he perceived it to be the most intimidating weapon to use against women in view of their fear of disfigurement. Firearms were less often used (14 to 20%). Surprisingly, all but a few of the rapists used binding located at the scene; one exception was a person who brought precut lengths of rope, adhesive tape, and handcuffs to the scene of his rapes.

Use of Force

The amount of force used during a rape provides valuable insight into the motivation of the rapist and must be analyzed by those investigating the offense or evaluating the offender. The majority of these men (75 to 84%) used minimal or no physical force across all three rapes (Hazelwood et al., 1989). Minimal force is defined as noninjurious force used more to intimidate than to punish.

Case No. 14

John began a career of 18 rapes at the age of 24. He estimated that he had illegally entered over 5000 homes to steal female undergarments. He advised that he had no desire to harm his victims and stated "… raping them is one thing. Beating on them is entirely something else. None of my victims were harmed and for a person to kill somebody after raping them, it just makes me mad".

Force resulting in bruises and lacerations or extensive physical trauma requiring hospitalization or resulting in death increased from 5% of the first rapes, to 8% of the middle rapes, and to 10% of the last rapes. Two victims (5%) were murdered during the middle rapes and an additional two (5%) were killed during the last rapes.

Case No. 15

Phil, an attractive 30-year-old male, described stabbing his mother to death when she awoke as he was attempting to remove her panties and bra. He had been drinking and smoking marijuana with her for a period of time before the attempted rape. She had fallen asleep and he began having fantasies of sex with her. She awoke, slapped him, and he responded by stabbing her twice.

Most of the rapists in this study did not increase the amount of force used across their first, middle, and last rapes (Hazelwood et al., 1989). However, 10 of the 41 rapists, termed "increasers", used progressively more force over successive rapes. The increasers raped a mean of 40 victims as opposed to 22 victims by the nonincreasers and committed a sexual assault every 19 days as opposed to the nonincreasers, who raped on the average every 55 days.

Victim Resistance

Victim resistance has been defined elsewhere in this book as any action or inaction on the part of the victim which precludes or delays the offender's attack. These behaviors have been described in the chapter titled "The Behavioral-Oriented Interview of Rape Victims".

The rapists reported that their victims verbally resisted them in 53% of the first assaults, 54% of the middle attacks, and 43% of the last rapes. Physical resistance occurred in only 19, 32, and 28% of the first, middle, and last rapes, respectively. The relatively low incidence of passive resistance (i.e., 28% in the first rape, 17% in the middle rape, and 9% in the last rape) most likely reflects the rapists' inability to discern this type of resistance.

In previous research, no relationship was found between verbal and/or physical resistance and the amount of physical injury sustained by the victim (Hazelwood et al., 1989). Interestingly, however, the degree of the rapists' pleasure and the duration of the rape did increase when the victim resisted.

In this study, the offenders reacted to resistance in the first, middle and last rapes by verbally threatening the victim (50 to 41%). Compromise or negotiation took place in 11 to 12% across the rapes, and physical force was used in 22% of the first rapes, 38% of the middle rapes, and 18% of the last rapes. The rapists also reported six incidents in which they left when the victim resisted; however, it is not clear at what point in the attack the resistance occurred.

Sexual Dynamics of the Rape

The sexual acts that the victim was forced to engage in remained relatively constant across all three rapes. The most common acts were vaginal intercourse (54 to 67%), oral sex (29 to 44%), kissing (8 to 13%), and fondling (10 to 18%). Anal intercourse (5 to 10%) and foreign object penetration (3 to 8%) were reported less often. In assessing changes in behavior over the first, middle, and last rapes, there appears to be a trend wherein the rapists' interest in oral sex increases while his interest in vaginal intercourse decreases.

The amount of pleasure that the rapist experienced during the three assaults was measured with the statement: "Think back to the penetration during the rape. Assuming '0' equals your worst sexual experience and '10' equals your absolute best sexual experience, rate the amount of pleasure you experienced". The majority of rapists reported surprisingly low levels of pleasure (3.7). However, the type of contact that resulted in higher scores differed widely (Hazelwood et al., 1989). One rapist reported appreciation for his victims' passivity and acquiescence, while another referred to the pleasure experienced in the rape murder of two young boys as being "off the scale".

Case No. 16

Paul had raped adult women and adolescent girls, and brought his criminal career to an end with the rape and murder of two 10-year-old boys. When asked to rate the sexual experiences, he said that he would rate the adult and adolescent females as "0" and the preadolescent girls as "3". He then stated, "When you're talking about sex with 10-year-old boys, your scale doesn't go high enough".

Verbal Interaction With Victims

Across the first, middle, and last rapes, the majority of serial rapists (78 to 85%) usually only conversed with the victims to threaten them. Much less frequently, their conversations were polite or friendly (30 to 34%), manipulative (23 to 37%), or personal in nature (23 to 37%). In a minority of instances, the rapist reported being inquisitive (15 to 20%), abusive/degrading (5 to 13%), or silent (8 to 13%). It appears that serial rapists use verbal threats to subdue the victim, and only after they believe they have gained control do they move on to various other modes of conversing or interacting.

Sexual Dysfunction

In a study of 170 rapists, it was determined that 34% experienced some type of sexual dysfunction during the rape (Groth and Burgess, 1977). The data on these serial rapists are strikingly similar. In the first rape, 38% of the subjects reported a sexual dysfunction, 39% in the middle rape, and 35% during the last assault. This type of information can prove helpful to the investigator in associating different offenses with a single offender; the nature of the dysfunction and the means used by the rapist to overcome the dysfunction are likely to remain constant over a number of rapes.

Evading Detection

Considering the rapists' aptitude for avoiding detection, it is surprising to note that very few of the serial rapists used specific behaviors designed to preclude identification. The majority (61 to 68%) did not report dressing in any special way for the offenses. Interestingly, disguises were reported in only 7 to 12% of the offenses, suggesting that other means of evading detection were used by these particular offenders.

Alcohol and Other Drugs

Rada (1978) reports that rape is commonly associated with the use of alcohol and drugs. The data on these rapists suggest a somewhat different relationship between the use of alcohol and/or drugs and serial sexual offending. Approximately one third of the rapists were drinking alcoholic beverages at the time of the first, middle, and last offenses, and 17 to 24% of the respondents reported using drugs. In a majority of these cases, these figures reflect the offender's typical consumption pattern and not an unusual increase in substance abuse.

Post Offense Behavior

The serial rapists were also asked about changes in their behavior following their assaults. The most frequent changes after each of these crimes included feeling remorseful and guilty (44 to 51%), following the case in the media (28%), and an increase in alcohol/drug consumption (20 to 27%). Investigators should also particularly note that 12 to 15% of the rapists reported revisiting the crime scene and 8-13% communicated with the victim after the crime.

Summary

The findings reported in this chapter were obtained from the extensive interviews of 41 men responsible for the rape of 837 victims. The interviews were conducted by FBI Agents assigned to the Behavioral Science Unit of the FBI Academy.

Many characteristics of the rapist population studied appear relatively "normal". Rather than being an isolated, poorly functioning person, the serial rapist more often than not comes from an average or advantaged home, and as an adult is a well-groomed, intelligent, employed person who is living with others in a family context. The greatest pathology is reflected in the serial rapists' developmental history. Few of the men described close relationships with either their mother or their father. A significant number of them had been institutionalized at some point in their adolescence, and an exceedingly high proportion reported sexual abuse as children or adolescents.

Interestingly, the majority of victims were strangers, and in almost one half of the cases the women were assaulted in their own homes. This, as well as the rapists' recognition of "availability" as an important factor in victim selection, highlights the potential significance of prevention programs. Most serial rapists are not carefully stalking a particular woman. Rather, their choice of victim depends on general proximity, the availability of the woman, and access to her home.

The majority of rapes committed by these men were premeditated and the "surprise" approach was used most often in initiating contact with the victims. The serial rapists relied primarily on a threatening physical presence to maintain control over their victims. The victims resisted their attacker in slightly over 50% of the offenses and the most common reaction to this resistance was verbally threatening behavior. Slightly over one third of the men suffered a sexual dysfunction during their attacks; their preferred sexual acts were vaginal rape and fellatio. The serial rapists tended not to be concerned with protecting their identity and approximately one third of them had consumed alcohol prior to the crime. The most common postoffense behaviors reported by the rapists were following the case in the media and increasing their alcohol and drug consumption.

The material presented in this chapter, though not generally applicable to all rapists, can be helpful in learning more about serial sexual offenders and their offense behavior.

References

Burgess, A. W., Hazelwood, R., Rokous, F., and Hartman, C., Serial rapists and their victims: reenactment and repetition, *Acad. Sci. Ann.*, 528, 277, 1988.

Groth, A., and Burgess, A., Sexual dysfunction during rape, *N. Engl. J. Med.*, 14, 764, 1977.

Hazelwood, R. R., The behavioral-oriented interview of rape victims: the key to profiling, *FBI Law Enforcement Bull.*, 58, 16, 1983.

Hazelwood, R. R. and Burgess, A., An introduction to the serial rapist: research by the FBI, *FBI Law Enforcement Bull.*, 58, 16, 1987a.

Hazelwood, R., Reboussin, R., and Warren, J., Serial rape: correlates of increased aggression and the relationship of offender pleasure to victim resistance, *J. Interpers. Violence*, p. 465, 1989.

Hellman, D. and Blackman, N., Enuresis, fire setting and cruelty to animals: a triad predictive of adult crime, *Am. J. Psychiatry*, 122, 1431, 1966.

Katan, A., Children who were raped, in *The Psychoanalytic Study of the Child*, Eissler, R. S., Ed., Yale University Press, New Haven, 1973, 208.

Rada, R., *Clinical Aspects of the Rapists*, Grune & Stratton, New York, 1978.

Rada, R., Psychological factors in rapist behavior, *Am. J. Psychiatry*, 132, 444, 1975; Rada, R., Ed., Psychological factors in rapist behavior in *Clinical Aspects of the Rapist*, Grune & Stratton, New York, 1978, 21.

Risin, L. and Koss, M., The sexual abuse of boys: frequency and descriptive characteristics of the childhood victimizations, in *Rape and Sexual Assault*, Burgess, A., Ed., Garland Press, New York, 1991.

The Criminal Sexual Sadist* 21

ROBERT R. HAZELWOOD
PARK ELLIOT DIETZ
JANET I. WARREN

Any investigator who has taken a statement from a tortured victim or who has worked the crime scene of a sexually sadistic homicide will never forget the experience. Human cruelty reveals itself in many kinds of offenses, but seldom more starkly than in the crimes of sexual sadists.

This chapter describes the more commonly encountered actions of sexual sadists and differentiates sexual sadism from other cruel acts. It also describes the common characteristics of sexually sadistic crimes and offers investigators suggestions to follow when confronted with the sexually sadistic offender's crimes.

What Is Sexual Sadism?

Sexual sadism is a persistent pattern of becoming sexually excited in response to another's suffering. Granted, sexual excitement can occur at odd times even in normal people; but to the sexually sadistic offender, it is the suffering of the victim that is sexually arousing.

The writings of two sexual sadists graphically convey their desires. One writes:

"... the most important radical aim is to make her suffer since there is no greater power over another person than that of inflicting pain on her to force her to undergo suffering without her being able to defend herself. The pleasure in the complete domination over another person is the very essence of the sadistic drive".

Of his sexually sadistic activities with a victim he killed, another offender writes:

"... she was writhering (sic) in pain and I loved it. I was now combining my sexual high of rape and my power high of fear to make a total sum that is now beyond explaining... I was alive for the sole purpose of causing pain and receiving sexual gratification... I was relishing the pain just as much as the sex... "

Each offender's account confirms that it is the suffering of the victim, not the infliction of physical or psychological pain, that is sexually arousing. In fact, one of these men resuscitated his victim from unconsciousness so that he could

* Reprinted with permission of the FBI Law Enforcement Bulletin.

0-8493-8152-1/95/$0.00+$.50
© 1995 by CRC Press, Inc.

continue to savor her suffering. Inflicting pain is a means to create suffering and to elicit the desired responses of obedience, submission, humiliation, fear, and terror.

Physical and Psychological Suffering

Specific findings uncovered during an investigation determine if the crime committed involves sexual sadism. The critical issues are whether the victim suffered, whether the suffering was intentionally caused, and whether the suffering sexually aroused the offender. This is why neither sexual nor cruel acts committed on an unconscious or dead victim are necessarily evidence of sexual sadism; such a victim cannot experience suffering. For this reason, postmortem injuries alone do not indicate sexual sadism.

Rapists cause their victims to suffer, but only sexual sadists intentionally inflict that suffering, whether physical or psychological, to enhance their own arousal. Neither the severity of an offender's cruelty nor the extent of a victim's suffering is evidence of sexual sadism. Acts of extreme cruelty or those that cause great suffering are often performed for nonsexual purposes, even during sexual assaults.

Sexually Sadistic Behavior

The behavior of sexual sadists, like that of other sexual deviants, extends along a wide spectrum. Sexual sadists can be law-abiding citizens who fantasize but do not act, or who fulfill these fantasies with freely consenting partners. Only when sexual sadists commit crimes do their fantasies become relevant to law enforcement.

Sadistic Fantasy

All sexual acts and sexual crimes begin with fantasy. However, in contrast with normal sexual fantasies, those of the sexual sadist center on domination, control, humiliation, pain, injury, and violence, or a combination of these themes, as a means to elicit suffering. As the fantasies of the sexual sadist vary, so does the degree of violence.

The fantasies discerned from offenders' personal records are complex, elaborate, and involve detailed scenarios that include specific methods of capture and control, location, scripts to be followed by the victim, sequence of sexual acts, and desired victim responses. Sexual sadists dwell frequently on these fantasies, which often involve multiple victims and sometimes include partners.

Case No. 1

One offender who is believed to have kidnapped, tortured, and murdered more than 20 women and young girls wrote extensively about his sexually sadistic fantasies involving women. The writings included descriptions of his victim's capture, torment, and death by hanging. At the time of his arrest, photographs were found depicting the subject in female dress, participating in autoerotic asphyxia. The offender had apparently acted out his fantasies on both himself and others.

Sadism Toward Symbols

Some people act out their sadistic desires against inanimate objects, most often dolls, pictures, and clothing, but occasionally corpses. As in the case of fantasy, the suffering in such activity is imagined.

Case No. 2

A female doll was found hanging outside the emergency room of a hospital. Around its neck was a hangman's noose, and its hands were bound behind its back. Needles penetrated one eye and one ear. Burn marks were present on the doll, and cotton protruded from its mouth. Drawn on the chest of the doll were what appeared to be sutures. An incision had been made between the legs, creating an orifice to which hair had been glued and into which a pencil had been inserted. Nothing indicated that a crime had occurred.

Although it is commonly believed that sexual sadists are cruel toward animals, it has not been determined that such cruelty is related to sexual sadism. Violent men were often cruel to animals during childhood, but without sexual excitement. Cruel acts toward animals may reflect nonsexual aggressive and sadistic motives, or may be sacrifices demanded by religious rituals or delusional beliefs. Someone who is sexually excited by an animal's suffering is probably both a sexual sadist and a zoophile (one attracted to animals).

Consenting or Paid Partners

Sexual sadism may also be acted out with freely consenting or paid partners, e.g., prostitutes who specialize in role-playing the "submissive" for sexually sadistic clients. The nature of the acts varies from simulations of discomfort to actions that result in severe injury. A consenting partner turns into a victim when her withdrawal of consent goes unheeded or when an act results in unexpected injury or death. This is when such acts come to the attention of law enforcement.

Compliant Victims

Some sexual sadists cultivate compliant victims (Hazelwood et al., 1993), i.e., those who enter into a voluntary relationship but are manipulated into sadomasochistic activities for an extended time. These victims can be the wives or girlfriends who underwent extreme emotional, physical, and sexual abuse over months or years of a relationship that began as an ordinary courtship. In these instances, the offenders shaped the behavior of the women into gradual acceptance of progressively deviant sexual acts, and then, through social isolation and repeated abuse, battered their self-images until the women believed they deserved the punishments meted out by their "lovers".

A woman in her 30s told authorities that she had been coerced into an emotionally, physically, and sexually abusive relationship over an 18-month period. At
first, she considered the offender to be the most loving and caring man she had
ever known, and she fell deeply in love. Having occasionally used cocaine in the
past, she was receptive to his suggestion that they use cocaine to enhance their
sexual relations. Eventually, she became addicted. After 6 months together, he
began to abuse her sexually. This abuse included forced anal sex, whipping,
painful sexual bondage, anal rape by other males, and the insertion of large
objects into her rectum. This abusive behavior continued for a full year before she
made her initial complaint to the police.

These cases pose special problems to investigators because it appears as
though the complainant "consented" to the abuse. However, the transformation
of the vulnerable partner into a compliant victim resembles the process by which
other abusive men intimidate and control battered women into remaining with
their abusers.

Behavior Patterns Confused With Sexual Sadism

Many crimes involve the intentional infliction of physical and psychological suffering; sexual sadism is only one of several motives for such crimes. To avoid
misinterpretation, investigators should be aware of those behavior patterns that
appear to be sexually sadistic, but which, in fact, arise from different motives and
contexts.

Sadistic Personality Disorder

Persons with this condition usually exhibit cruel, demeaning, and aggressive
behavior in both social and work situations, most often toward subordinates. They
tend to establish dominance in interpersonal relationships and convey a lack of
respect or empathy for others. Such individuals are often fascinated by violence,
take pleasure in demeaning, humiliating, and frightening others, and may enjoy
inflicting physical or psychological abuse. In this condition, the purpose of these
behaviors is not that of becoming aroused.

A woman left her husband because of his verbal abuse, control over her relations
with family members, intimidating behavior, and violent outbursts when drinking. Vengeful that she left him, he lured her back to the apartment under the
pretext of dividing their possessions. He then tried to tie her to the bed, beside
which he had arranged a variety of torture instruments. In the ensuing struggle,
he told her of his plans to kill her as he stabbed her repeatedly. She eventually
persuaded him that she wanted to reconcile and convinced him to summon
medical assistance, whereupon he was arrested.

The husband did not have a history of sexual offenses or deviations, nor did he show evidence of sexual sadism during the psychiatric examination. He denied any sexual arousal in response to suffering or any sexually sadistic fantasies. Although it is possible that the husband was a sexual sadist who only showed this tendency when he attacked his wife, the absence of evidence noting a persistent pattern of sexual arousal in response to suffering precluded this diagnosis.

Cruelty During Crime

While many crimes contain elements of cruelty, the acts are not necessarily sexually sadistic in nature.

Case No. 5

Two men who escaped from a state prison captured a young couple and took them to an isolated area. After repeatedly raping the woman, they severely beat the couple and locked them in the trunk of their car. They then set the car on fire and left the couple to burn to death.

Although these men intentionally inflicted physical and psychological suffering on their victims, there was no indication they did so for sexual excitement. They beat the couple after the rape and left as the victims were screaming and begging for mercy. Sexual sadists would have been sexually stimulated by the victims' torment and would have remained at the scene until the suffering ended.

Pathological Group Behavior

Cruelty often arises in offenses committed as a group, even when the persons have no history of cruelty.

Case No. 6

A group of adolescents attacked a mother of six as she walked through her neighborhood. They dragged her into a shed where they beat her and repeatedly inserted a long steel rod into her rectum, causing her death. Some of her attackers were friends of her children.

Most likely, the participants in this attack tried to prove themselves to the others by intensifying the acts of cruelty.

Sanctioned Cruelty

History is replete with reigns of terror during which powerful institutions sanctioned atrocious behaviors. Consider the rape and plunder of defeated populations during the Crusades of the Middle Ages, or the execution of women in the Salem witch hunts in colonial America. One of the most notorious times of cruelty occurred in the 20th century, when millions of people fell victim to the Nazis.

Case No. 7

Commandant Koch, who headed the concentration camp at Buchenwald, punished a man who tried to escape by confining him in a wooden box so small he could only crouch. He then ordered that small nails be driven through its walls so that he could not move without being pierced. This man was kept on public display without food for 2 days and 3 nights until his screams ceased to sound human (Manvell and Fraenkel, 1967).

In all likelihood, sexual sadists volunteered to perform such deeds, but the widespread deployment of such tactics was politically and racially motivated.

Revenge-Motivated Cruelty

Cruelty is often evident during acts that are inspired by an obsessional desire for revenge, either real or imagined.

Case No. 8

A physician married a show girl and came to believe that she was being unfaithful, even though there was no evidence for this. Eventually, his obsession overcame his logic, and he decided to ensure that no man would ever take her away from him. After lashing her to a table, he poured sulfuric acid over her body and face. She survived for 84 days in agony before succumbing to her injuries.

The offender in this case wanted to punish his wife and make sure that she would not be desirable to any man. His act was not designed to gratify him sexually.

Interrogative Cruelty

Torture during interrogation may involve sexual areas of the body, which is sometimes misinterpreted as being sexually sadistic in nature.

Case No. 9

A government agent was captured in another country. During his months in captivity, he was continually subjected to physical torture, including beatings with clubs and electrical shocks to all parts of his body, including his genitals.

The victim was tortured in this manner to obtain information concerning his government's activities in that country, not to enhance sexual arousal.

Postmortem Mutilation

The intentional mutilation of a victim after death is often mistakenly attributed to sexual sadism. However, in a majority of these cases, the offender kills the victim quickly and does not try to prolong suffering, in total contrast to the actions of the sexual sadist.

Case No. 10

A father bludgeoned his adult daughter to death. Afterward, he attempted to dispose of the body. On the day of his arrest, he bought a food processor. Investigators found portions of her remains in the bathtub, the kitchen sink, in pots boiling on the stove, and in the refrigerator.

The man killed his daughter either in self-defense or because of his frustration over her disruptive and hostile behavior caused by her chronic mental illness. His actions were not intended to give him sexual satisfaction in seeing his daughter suffer.

Study Conducted

The authors studied 30 sexually sadistic criminals, 22 of whom were responsible for at least 187 murders (Dietz et al., 1990). Most of these cases had been submitted to the FBI's National Center for the Analysis of Violent Crime (NCAVC). Sources of information for the study included police reports, crime scene photographs, victim statements, statements by family members, confessions, psychiatric reports, trial transcripts, presentence reports, and prison records. The authors also reviewed evidence created by the offenders themselves, e.g., diaries, photographs, sketches, audio tapes, videos, calendars, and letters. These materials, which recorded their fantasies and represented memorabilia of their crimes, provided windows into the minds of sexually sadistic offenders.

In addition, 5 of the 30 offenders were interviewed by the authors. When interviewed, these men revealed less about their sexual desires than they had in their writings and recordings of the offenses. This is consistent with the authors' experience when interviewing subjects during ongoing investigations, that is, offenders speak much more readily about their violent acts than about their sexual acts or fantasies.

Each of the 30 sexual sadists studied intentionally tortured their victims. Their methods of physical torture included the use of such instruments as hammers, pliers, and electric cattle prods, and such actions as biting, whipping, burning, insertion of foreign objects into the rectum or vagina, bondage, amputation, asphyxiation to the point of unconsciousness, and insertion of glass rods in the male urethra, to name a few.

Some offenders used a particular means of torture repeatedly. Such actions could constitute an offender's signature, showing that this is the work of a single offender. However, the absence of a common feature among crimes does not eliminate the possibility of a single serial offender, for he may be experimenting with various techniques in search of the perfect scenario, or may be attempting to mislead investigators.

The 30 sexual sadists studied also inflicted psychological suffering on their victims. Binding, blindfolding, gagging, and holding a victim captive all produce psychological suffering, even if not physically painful. Other psychological tactics used included threats or other forms of verbal abuse; forcing the victim to beg, plead, or describe sexual acts; telling the victim in precise detail what was intended;

having the victim choose between slavery or death; and offering the victim a choice of means by which to die.

Offender Characteristics

All 30 of the sexual sadists in the study were men, and only one was non-white. Fewer than one half were educated beyond high school. One half used alcohol or other drugs, and one third had served in the Armed Forces. Forty-three percent were married at the time of their offense.

Sexual deviations are often associated with other sexual abnormalities, and this study confirmed this for sexual sadism. Fifty percent of the men participated in homosexual activity as adults, 20% engaged in cross-dressing, and 20% committed other sexual offenses such as peeping, obscene phone calls, and indecent exposure.

Case No. 11

As a teenager, one sexual sadist "peeped" throughout his neighborhood, masturbating as he watched women undress or have sex. At home, he masturbated repeatedly to fantasies in which he incorporated what he had seen while peeping. As a young adult, he made obscene telephone calls, which led to his first arrest when he agreed to meet a victim who had informed the police.

He later exposed himself to a series of victims, which, he eventually explained, was for the purpose of eliciting their "shock and fear". He followed women home from shopping malls, determined how much cover was available for peeping and entering the home, and eventually raped a series of women. In his early rapes, he depended on weapons of opportunity, but later carried with him a rape kit, which consisted of adhesive tape, handcuffs, precut lengths of rope, and a .45 caliber handgun. He became progressively more violent in his sexual assaults, torturing his victims by beating, burning, and pulling their breasts. His violence escalated to the point that he so severely pummeled one victim that she lost both breasts. He forcibly raped more than 50 women and was contemplating murder when he was finally apprehended.

Investigators should not be misled by the fact that the sexual sadist may have been involved in what are commonly referred to as "nuisance" sexual offenses. A history of such activity is common, but not universal, among sex offenders of all types. It is a myth that people who engage in "nuisance" offenses do not have a propensity for violence (Hazelwood and Warren, 1989).

Crime Characteristics

Careful planning epitomizes the crimes of the sexual sadist, who devotes considerable time and effort to the offense. Many demonstrate cunning and methodical planning. The capture of the victim, the selection and preparation of equipment, and the methodical elicitation of suffering often reflect meticulous attention to detail.

The overwhelming majority of offenders studied by the authors used a pretext or ruse to first make contact with the victims. The sexual sadist would offer or request help, pretend to be a police officer, respond to a classified advertisement, meet a realtor at an isolated property, or otherwise gain the victim's confidence.

Almost invariably, the victims were taken to a preselected location that offered privacy and safety for the sadist and little opportunity of escape or rescue for the victim. Such locations included the offender's home, isolated forests, and even elaborately built facilities designed for captivity.

Case No. 12

A white male entered a respected modeling agency and advised that he was filming a documentary on drug abuse among preadolescents. He made arrangements to hire two young girls from the agency, and two elderly matrons accompanied them as chaperons. He drove to his trailer and, at gunpoint, bound the women and placed the girls in a plywood cell he had built in the trailer. The cell contained beds and additional mattresses for soundproofing. He killed the women, placing their bodies in garbage bags, and then terrorized the girls for more than 2 days before they were rescued.

Twenty-three (77%) of the offenders used sexual bondage on their victims, often tying them with elaborate and excessive materials, using neat and symmetrical bindings, and restraining them in a variety of positions. Eighteen (60%) held their victims in captivity for more than 24 hours.

The most common sexual activity was anal rape (22 offenders), followed in frequency by forced fellatio, vaginal rape, and foreign object penetration. Two thirds of the men subjected their victims to at least three of these four acts.

Sixty percent of the offenders beat their victims. Twenty-two of the men murdered a total of 187 victims; 17 of them killed three or more people. The manner in which they killed varied.

Case No. 13

Two men, who worked as a team, used a variety of methods to kill a series of victims. One victim was strangled during sex. Another was injected in the neck with a caustic substance, electrocuted, and gassed in an oven. A third victim was shot.

Twenty-nine of the 30 men selected white victims only. Eighty-three percent of the victims were strangers to the offender. While the majority of the men selected female victims, one fourth attacked males exclusively. Sixteen percent of the men assaulted child victims only, and 26% attacked both children and adults.

Evidence of Crime

More than a half of the offenders in the study kept records of their offenses, including calendars, maps, diaries, drawings, letters, manuscripts, photographs, audio tapes, video tapes, and media accounts of their crimes. For the most part, these secret and prized possessions were hidden in their homes, offices, or vehicles, kept in rental storage space, or stored in buried containers.

Forty percent of the men took and kept personal items from their victims. These items included driver's licenses, jewelry, clothing, and photographs; they served as mementos of the offense, and some of the offenders referred to them as "trophies" of their conquests. However, none of the offenders retained parts of their victim's bodies, though some kept the entire corpse temporarily or permanently.

Investigating Crimes of the Sexual Sadist

The law enforcement community's legitimate concern rests with the criminal sexual sadist, who can be a noteworthy adversary. The sexual sadist is cunning and accomplished at deception. He rationalizes his actions, feels no remorse or guilt, and is not moved by compassion. He considers himself superior to society, in general, and law enforcement, in particular; and, while he envies the power and authority associated with the police, he does not respect them.

Sources

An invaluable source of information about suspects in sexual offenses is their former spouses and/or girlfriends. As noted previously, sexual sadists sometimes force sexual partners to become compliant victims (Hazelwood et al., 1993). However, because of the embarrassing nature of the sexual acts involved, these people are often reluctant to divulge information.

Search Warrants

Because offenders retain incriminating evidence and crime paraphernalia, these items should be listed in search warrant applications. This would include the records and mementos described previously, as well as photographic equipment, tape recorders, reverse telephone directories, and weapons or other instruments used to elicit suffering. Pornography, detective and mercenary magazines, bondage paraphernalia, women's undergarments, and sexual devices are other materials commonly collected by sexual sadists.

Interviewing the Sexual Sadist

Sexual sadists are masters of manipulation; therefore, the investigator must be well prepared for the interview. The investigator must know the suspect intimately and be aware of his strengths and weaknesses. Premature interviews of primary suspects often fail (Chapter 12).

Despite their seeming sophistication, sexual sadists are likely to consent to interview, even after being advised of their rights. These offenders often have an exaggerated self-image and consider themselves intellectually superior to the police. They believe they are in no danger of divulging detrimental information about themselves. More importantly, they expect to get more information from the officer than they give in the interview. From the questions asked, they hope to determine how much the investigator knows and the current status of the investigation.

The interviewer should be of detective status or above, preferably older than the suspect, and superior to him in physical stature, personality, and intelligence. The interviewer must appear confident, relaxed, and at least as calm as the suspect. Any personal feelings about the crime or the suspect must be suppressed. The interviewer should not try to become "friends" with the suspect, as this will cause him to lose respect for the interviewer and give him an opportunity to manipulate the conversation. Instead, the interview should be conducted formally and professionally.

Because these offenders enjoy attention, the interviewer should be prepared for a lengthy and exhausting interview. Questions should be thought out in advance and structured so that the offender cannot evade a line of questioning with a simple "no" answer. For example, rather than asking the suspect if he likes to torture women, it is preferable to ask him his favorite instruments for torturing women. Posing questions this way reflects the interviewer's knowledge, does not give additional information to the suspect, and may facilitate incriminating disclosures by the subject.

Above all, the suspect must not be allowed to provoke the interviewer's anger. In all likelihood, he will try to shock or antagonize the interviewer, and if the interviewer yields to human emotion, the suspect will score a significant victory.

Summary

Sexually sadistic offenders commit well-planned and carefully concealed crimes. Their crimes are repetitive, serious, and shocking, and they take special steps to prevent detection. The harm that these men wreak is so devastating and their techniques so sophisticated that those who attempt to apprehend and convict them must be armed with uncommon insight, extensive knowledge, and sophisticated investigative resources.

References

Dietz, P. E., Hazelwood, R. R., and Warren, J. I., The sexually sadistic criminal and his offenses, *Bull. Am. Acad. Psychiatry Law*, p. 163, 1990.

Hazelwood, R. R. and Warren, J. I., The serial rapist: his characteristics and victims, *FBI Law Enforcement Bull.*, p. 18, February 1989.

Hazelwood, R. R., Warren, J. I., and Dietz, P. E., Compliant victims of sexual sadists, *Aust. Fam. Physician*, 22(4), 1993, p. 11.

Manvell, R. and Fraenkel, H., *The Incomparable Crime: Mass Extermination in the Twentieth Century — The Legacy of Guilt*, G. P. Putnam's Sons, New York, 1967.

INDEX

Index

A

Abduction rape (CCM 319), 200–201
ACD (acid citrate dextrose), 104–105
Acid citrate dextrose (ACD), 104–105
Active resistance, 145
Adaptation continuum and false rape
    allegations, 232–234
Adhesive lifts, 79–80
  contraindicated for hair, 81
  tape selection, 79–80
Admissibility of rape trauma syndrome
    evidence, 302–303
Affect, isolation of, 120–121, 244–245
Age
  and probable military history, 179–180
  of rapist, 178
Age anger rape (CCM 314.02), 199
  racial (CCM 314.03), 199–200
AIDS, see Sexually transmitted diseases
Aiken, Margaret M., 219–240
Alcohol analysis of blood, 105
Allegation defined, 220
American Psychiatric Association *Diagnostic
    and Statistical Manual*, see DSM
American Psychology-Law Society *Speciality
    Guidelines for Forensic Psychologists*, 302
Anal sex
  ex-convict as possible offender, 149, 178
  motivational significance, 173
  oral sex demanded following, 149
  punishment aspect of, 149
Anal swabbing, 63, 65
Analysts, criminal investigative, 119–123, see
    also Rape investigator(s)
Analytical logic, 121
Anger
  at rapist, 5
  at system, 6
  victim's displaced, 6
Anger-excitation rapists, 164–165
Anger rape (CCM 314), 197–198
Anger-retaliatory rapists, 163–164
Animals, cruelty to and sexual sadism, 363

Anticoagulants, 104–105
  contraindicated for DNA analysis, 105
Appearance and grooming of rapist, 180
Approaches, see also Attack style and purpose
  investigators' to crime scene, 69
  rapist's, 171–172, 268
    blitz, 142–143, 353–355
    con, 142, 165
    surprise, 143, 171, 353–355
  serial rapist's, 352–355
  sexual sadist's, 369
Arrest history
  anal sex as suggesting ex-convict, 149, 178
  of serial rapists, 342–343
  of sexual sadists, 368
The Art of Cross-Examination (Wellman), 290–
    292
Aspirate, vaginal, 64, 65
Assessment, indirect personality, 204–217, see
    also Indirect personality assessment;
    Profiling attack style and purpose
  anger-excitation, 164–165
  anger-retaliatory, 163–164
  case studies, 175–176
  case study, 167–170
  gang rape, 166–167
  opportunistic, 166
  power-assertive, 162–163
  power-reassurance, 161–162
Attention
  need for and false rape allegations, 229–230
  sexual sadism as means to, 371
Attitudes toward rape
  importance of awareness, 3–4
  intuitive reactions to victims, 4–7
  and isolation of affect, 120–121, 244–245
  police, 13–25
  subjective reactions based on myths, 7–12,
    221–222, 265
Attitudinal change of rapist, 150–151, 174–175
Audiotaping by offender/deviant, 132, 133–134
Ault, Richard L. Jr., 205–218
Autoeroticism, 132
Avoidance on part of investigator, 5

Q

S